Diabolo

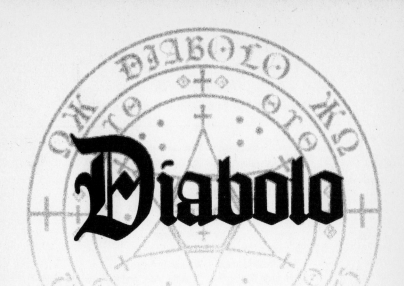

Diabolo Vol. 3
Created by Kei Kusunoki & Kauro Ohashi

Translation - Beni Axia Hirayama
English Adaptation - Jackie Medel
Associate Editor - Aaron Sparrow
Retouch and Lettering - SSI Production Support Team
Cover Design - Christian Lownds

Editor - Tim Beedle
Digital Imaging Manager - Chris Buford
Pre-Press Manager - Antonio DePietro
Production Managers - Jennifer Miller and Mutsumi Miyazaki
Art Director - Matt Alford
Managing Editor - Jill Freshney
VP of Production - Ron Klamert
Editor-in-Chief - Mike Kiley
President and C.O.O. - John Parker
Publisher and C.E.O. - Stuart Levy

A  Manga

TOKYOPOP Inc.
5900 Wilshire Blvd. Suite 2000
Los Angeles, CA 90036

E-mail: info@TOKYOPOP.com
Come visit us online at www.TOKYOPOP.com

ISBN: 1-59532-594-8

First TOKYOPOP printing: February 2005
10 9 8 7 6 5 4 3 2 1
Printed in the USA

Diabolo

Vol. 3

Created by
Kei Kusunoki & Kauro Ohashi

HAMBURG // LONDON // LOS ANGELES // TOKYO

Diabolo 3

CONTENTS

THE CHARACTERS...

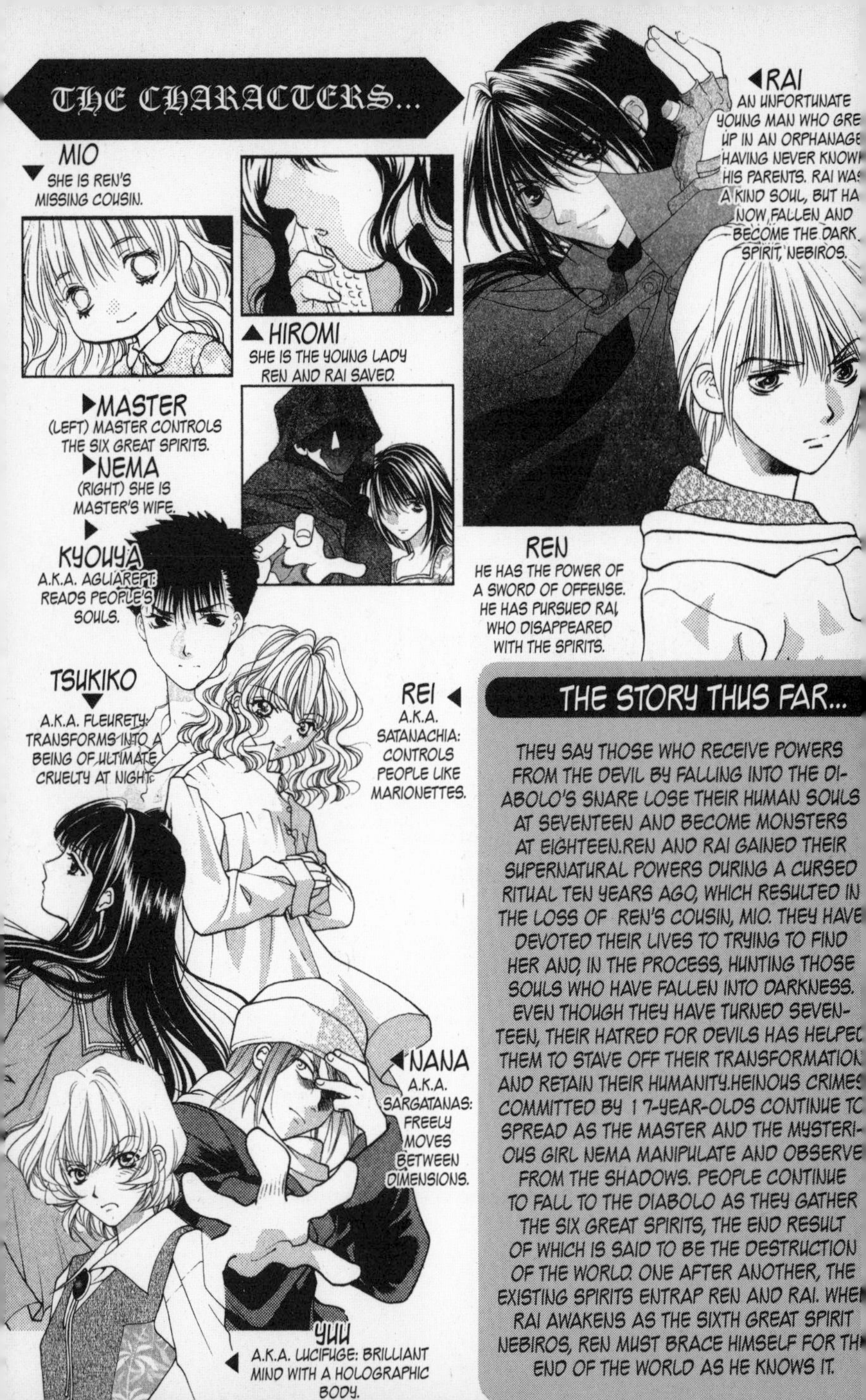

RAI
AN UNFORTUNATE YOUNG MAN WHO GRE UP IN AN ORPHANAGE HAVING NEVER KNOWI HIS PARENTS. RAI WAS A KIND SOUL, BUT HA NOW FALLEN AND BECOME THE DARK SPIRIT, NEBIROS.
MIO
SHE IS REN'S MISSING COUSIN.
HIROMI
SHE IS THE YOUNG LADY REN AND RAI SAVED.
MASTER
(LEFT) MASTER CONTROLS THE SIX GREAT SPIRITS.
NEMA
(RIGHT) SHE IS MASTER'S WIFE.
REN
HE HAS THE POWER OF A SWORD OF OFFENSE. HE HAS PURSUED RAI, WHO DISAPPEARED WITH THE SPIRITS.
KYOUYA
A.K.A. AGUIAREPT: READS PEOPLE'S SOULS.
TSUKIKO
A.K.A. FLEURETY: TRANSFORMS INTO A BEING OF ULTIMATE CRUELTY AT NIGHT.
REI
A.K.A. SATANACHIA: CONTROLS PEOPLE LIKE MARIONETTES.
NANA
A.K.A. SARGATANAS: FREELY MOVES BETWEEN DIMENSIONS.
YUU
A.K.A. LUCIFUGE: BRILLIANT MIND WITH A HOLOGRAPHIC BODY.

THE STORY THUS FAR...

THEY SAY THOSE WHO RECEIVE POWERS FROM THE DEVIL BY FALLING INTO THE DIABOLO'S SNARE LOSE THEIR HUMAN SOULS AT SEVENTEEN AND BECOME MONSTERS AT EIGHTEEN.REN AND RAI GAINED THEIR SUPERNATURAL POWERS DURING A CURSED RITUAL TEN YEARS AGO, WHICH RESULTED IN THE LOSS OF REN'S COUSIN, MIO. THEY HAVE DEVOTED THEIR LIVES TO TRYING TO FIND HER AND, IN THE PROCESS, HUNTING THOSE SOULS WHO HAVE FALLEN INTO DARKNESS. EVEN THOUGH THEY HAVE TURNED SEVENTEEN, THEIR HATRED FOR DEVILS HAS HELPED THEM TO STAVE OFF THEIR TRANSFORMATION AND RETAIN THEIR HUMANITY.HEINOUS CRIMES COMMITTED BY 17-YEAR-OLDS CONTINUE TO SPREAD AS THE MASTER AND THE MYSTERIOUS GIRL NEMA MANIPULATE AND OBSERVE FROM THE SHADOWS. PEOPLE CONTINUE TO FALL TO THE DIABOLO AS THEY GATHER THE SIX GREAT SPIRITS, THE END RESULT OF WHICH IS SAID TO BE THE DESTRUCTION OF THE WORLD. ONE AFTER ANOTHER, THE EXISTING SPIRITS ENTRAP REN AND RAI. WHEN RAI AWAKENS AS THE SIXTH GREAT SPIRIT NEBIROS, REN MUST BRACE HIMSELF FOR THE END OF THE WORLD AS HE KNOWS IT.

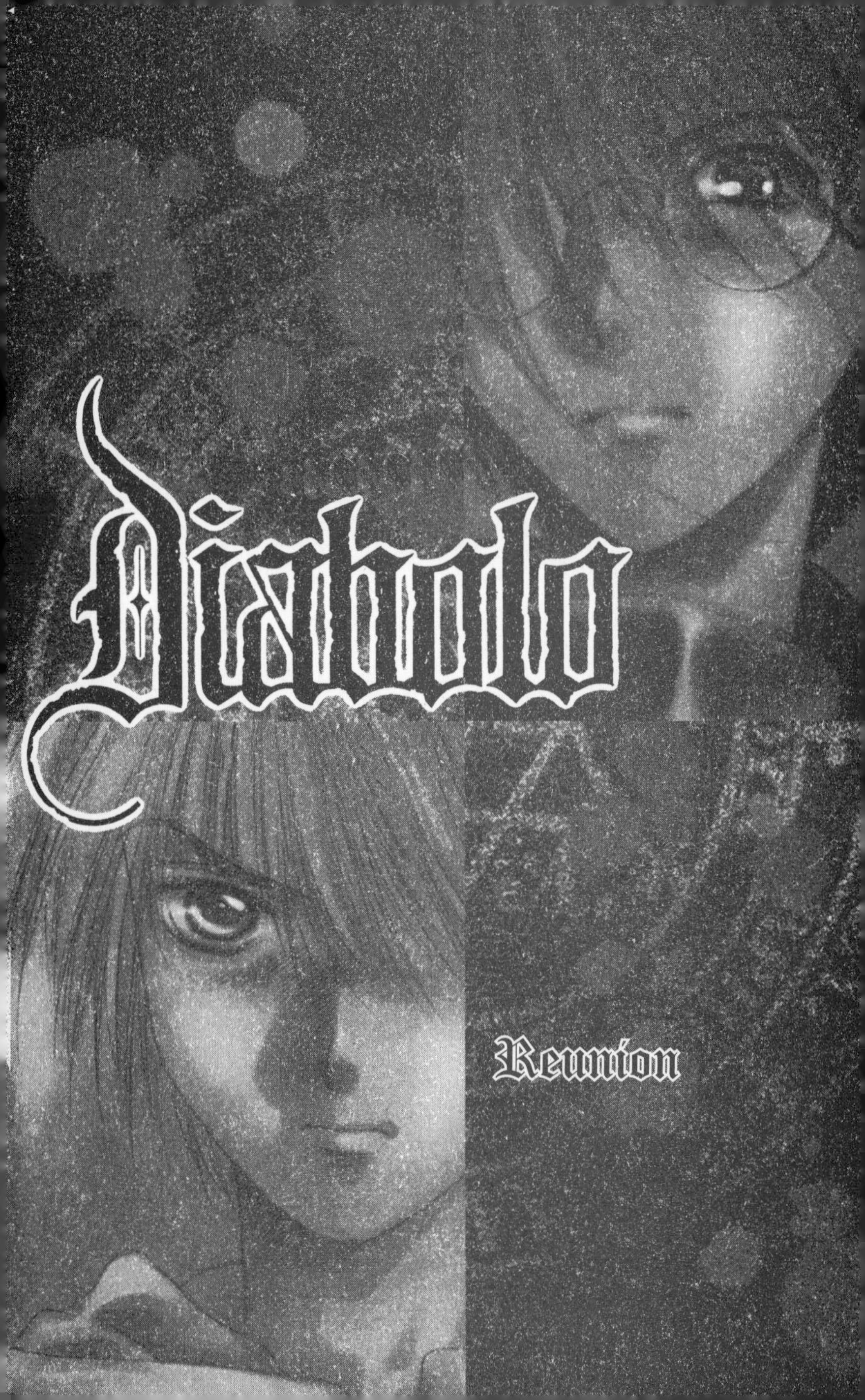
Diabolo
Reunion

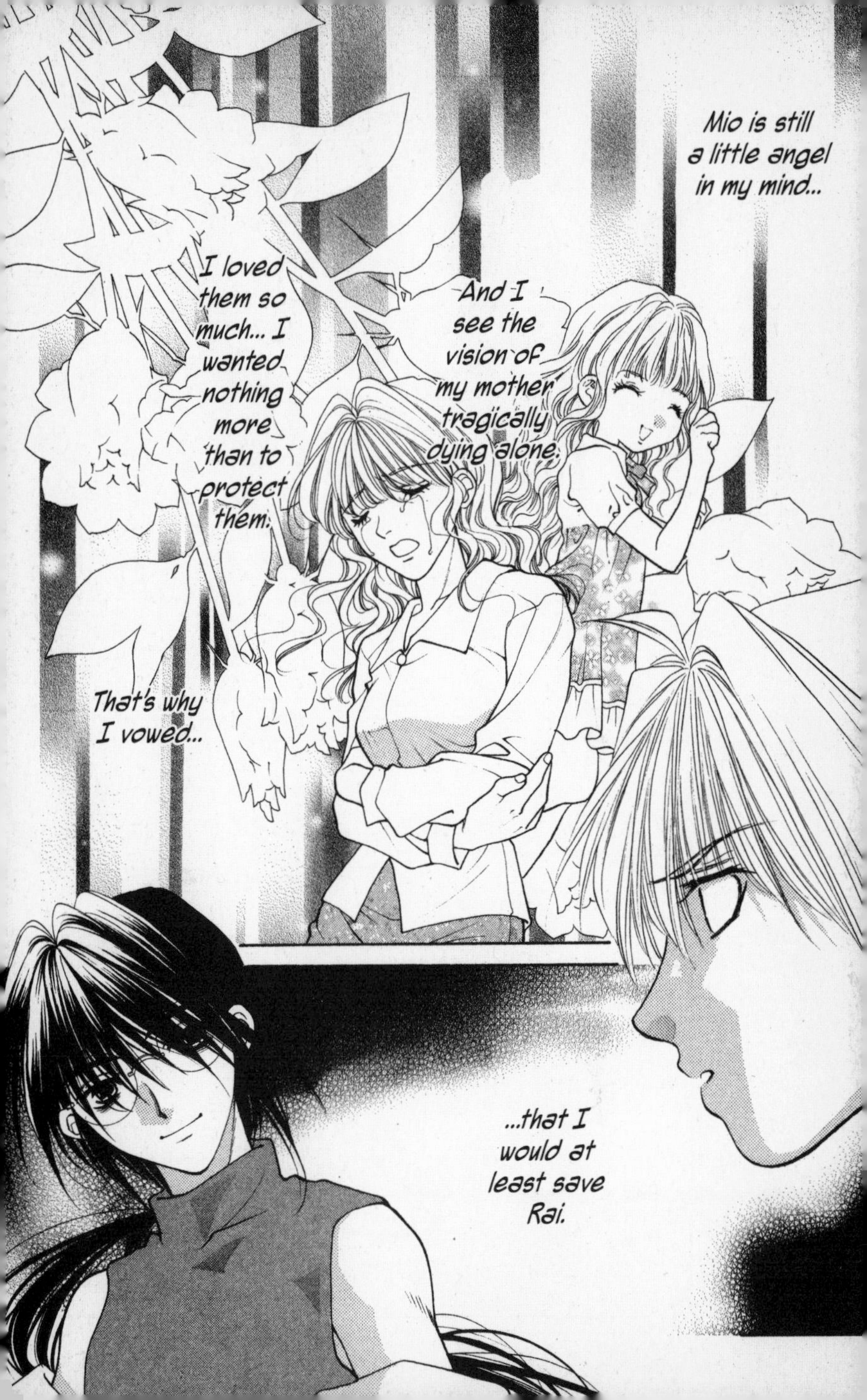
Mio is still a little angel in my mind...
And I see the vision of my mother tragically dying alone.
I loved them so much... I wanted nothing more than to protect them.
That's why I vowed...
...that I would at least save Rai.

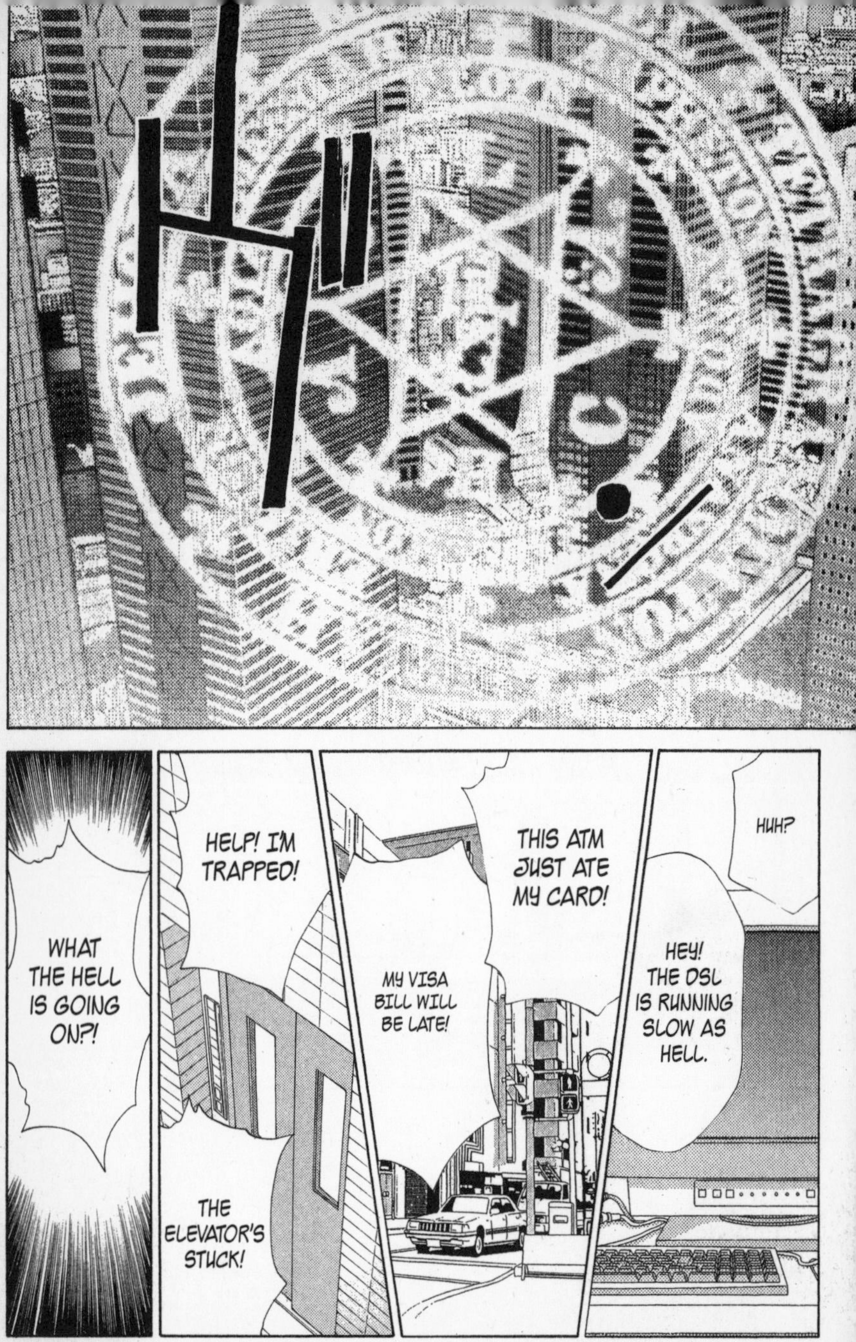
HUH?
HEY! THE DSL IS RUNNING SLOW AS HELL.
THIS ATM JUST ATE MY CARD!
MY VISA BILL WILL BE LATE!
HELP! I'M TRAPPED!
THE ELEVATOR'S STUCK!
WHAT THE HELL IS GOING ON?!

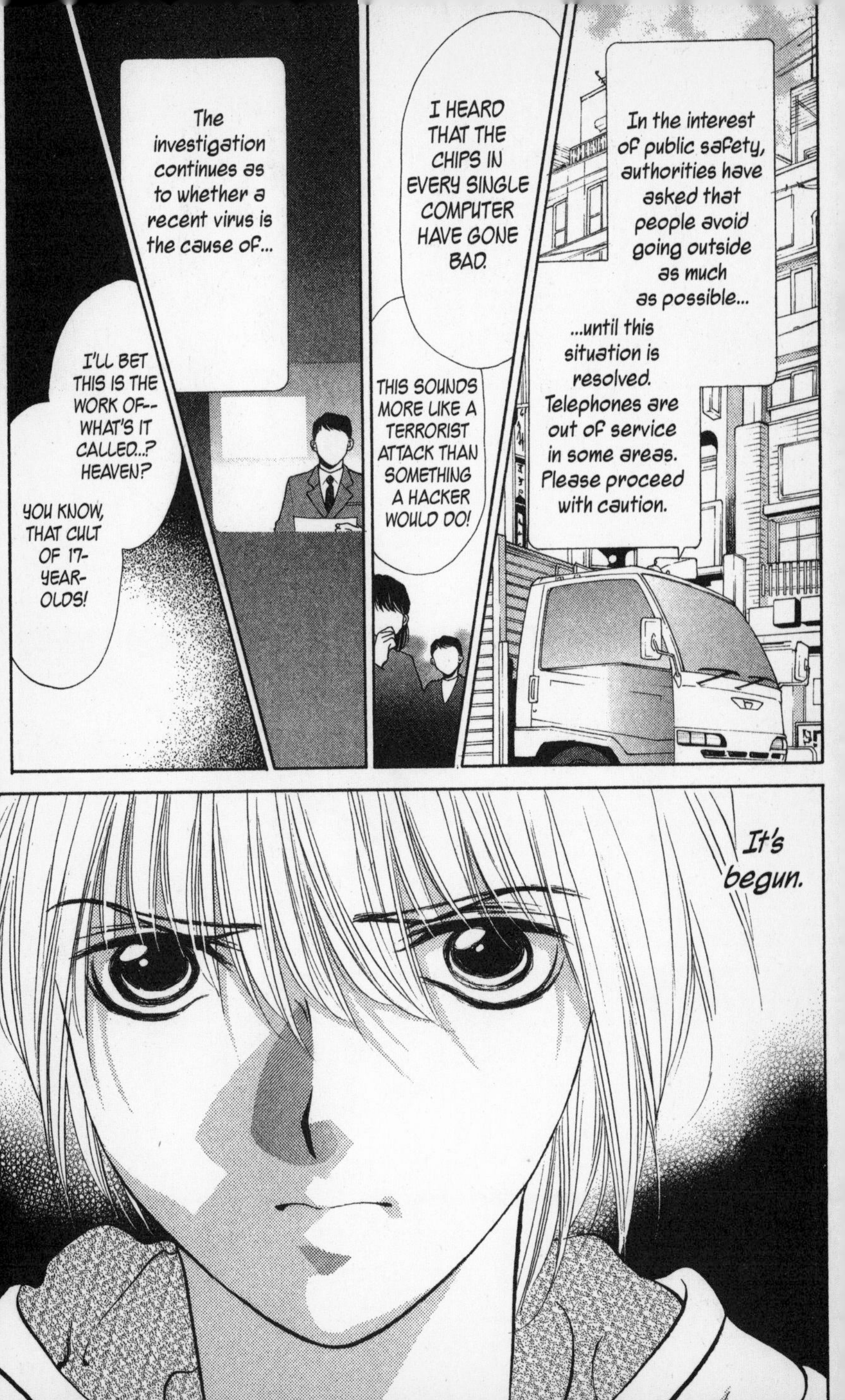
In the interest of public safety, authorities have asked that people avoid going outside as much as possible...
...until this situation is resolved. Telephones are out of service in some areas. Please proceed with caution.
I HEARD THAT THE CHIPS IN EVERY SINGLE COMPUTER HAVE GONE BAD.
THIS SOUNDS MORE LIKE A TERRORIST ATTACK THAN SOMETHING A HACKER WOULD DO!
The investigation continues as to whether a recent virus is the cause of...
I'LL BET THIS IS THE WORK OF-- WHAT'S IT CALLED..? HEAVEN?
YOU KNOW, THAT CULT OF 17-YEAR-OLDS!
It's begun.

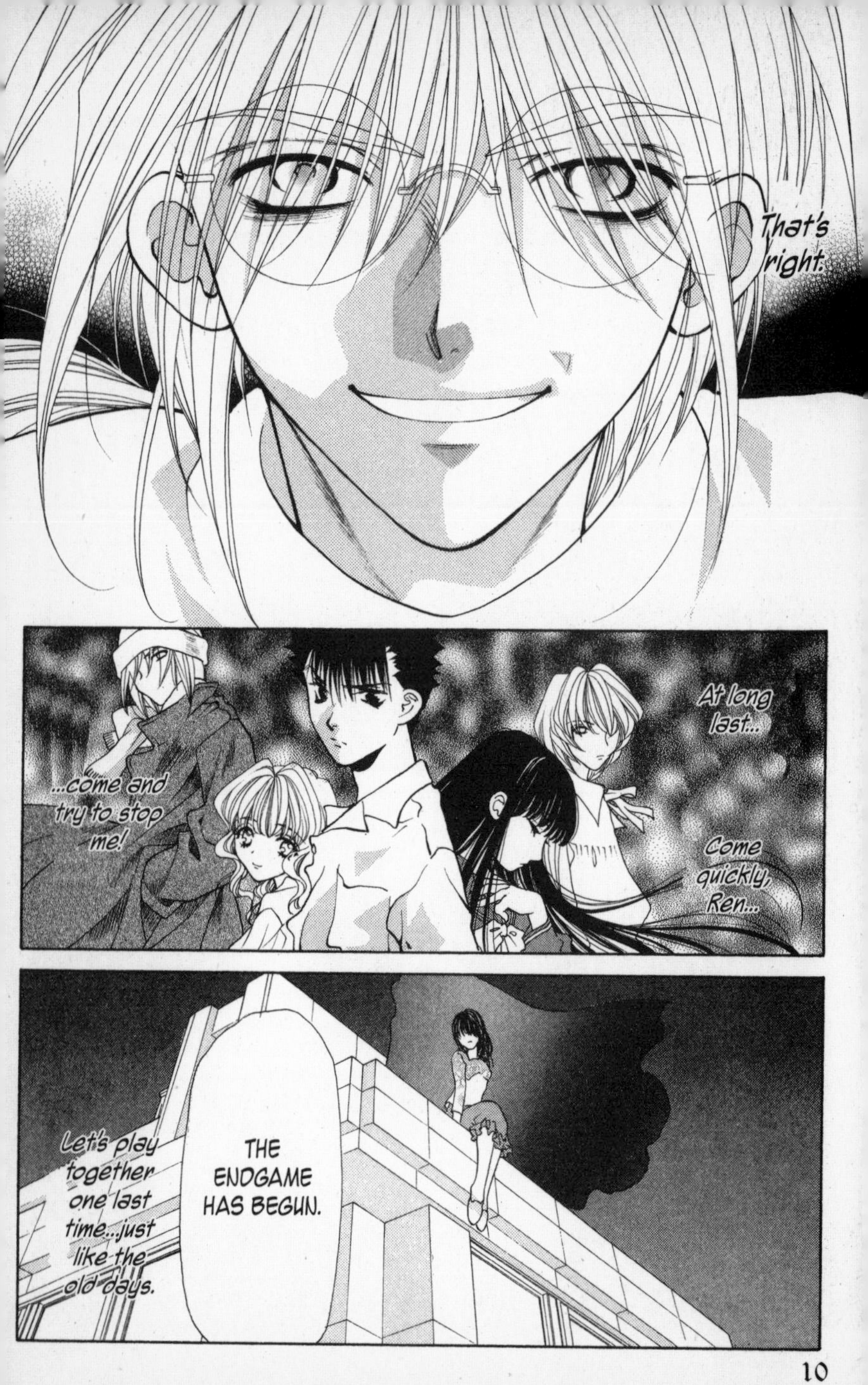
That's right.
At long last...
...come and try to stop me!
Come quickly, Ren...
THE ENDGAME HAS BEGUN.
Let's play together one last time...just like the old days.

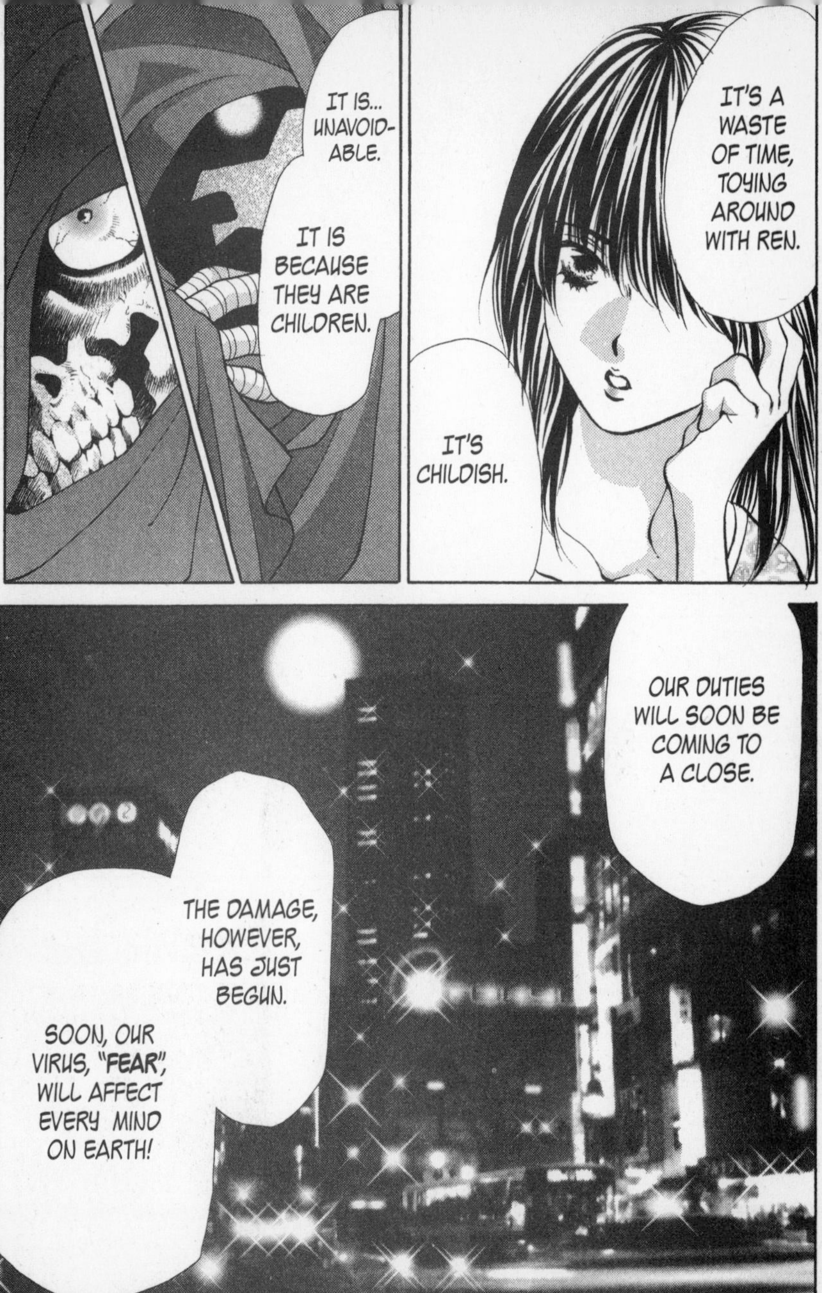
IT'S A WASTE OF TIME, TOYING AROUND WITH REN.
IT'S CHILDISH.
IT IS... UNAVOID-ABLE.
IT IS BECAUSE THEY ARE CHILDREN.
OUR DUTIES WILL SOON BE COMING TO A CLOSE.
THE DAMAGE, HOWEVER, HAS JUST BEGUN.
SOON, OUR VIRUS, "**FEAR**", WILL AFFECT EVERY MIND ON EARTH!

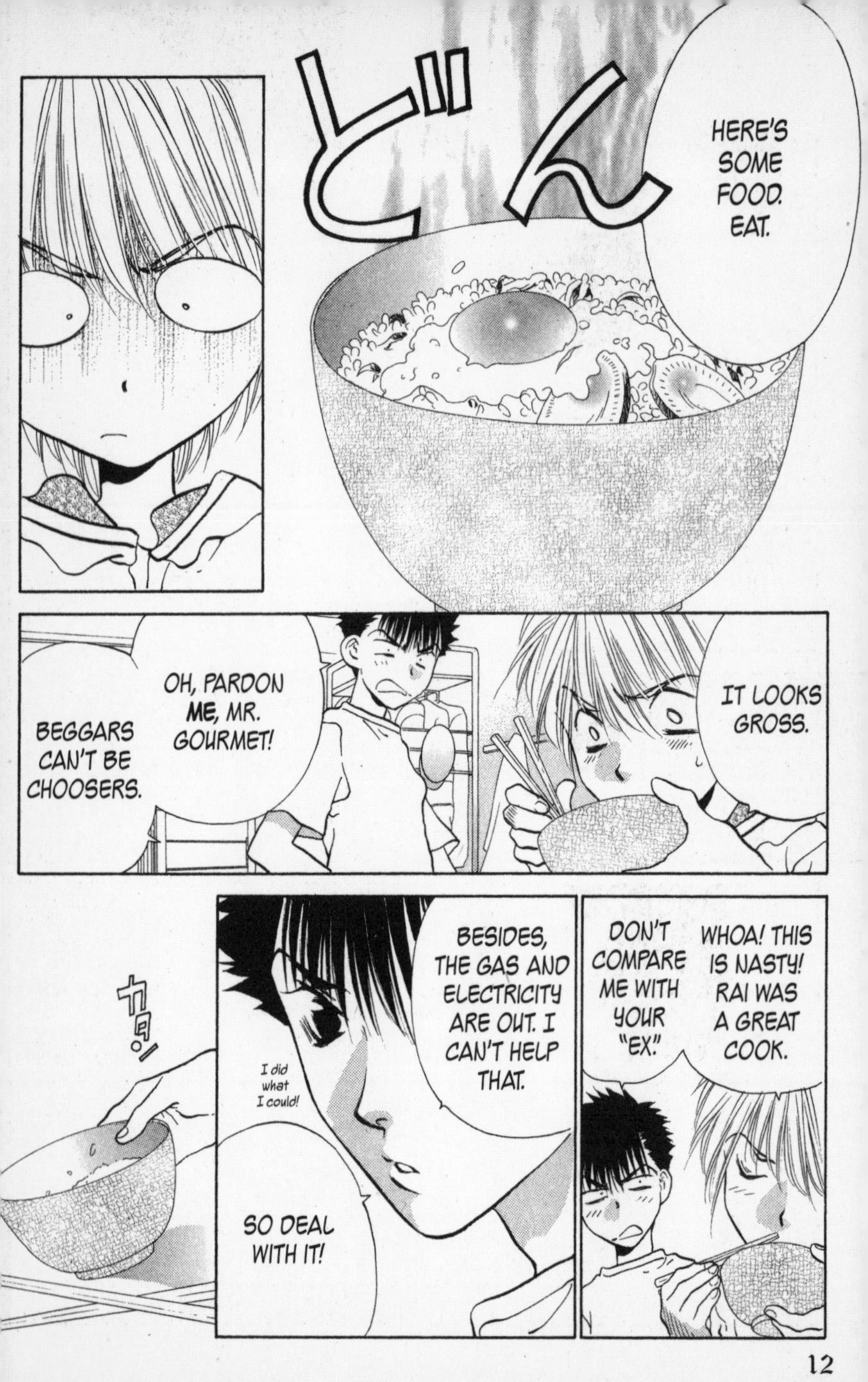

どん
HERE'S SOME FOOD. EAT.
IT LOOKS GROSS.
OH, PARDON ME, MR. GOURMET!
BEGGARS CAN'T BE CHOOSERS.
WHOA! THIS IS NASTY! RAI WAS A GREAT COOK.
DON'T COMPARE ME WITH YOUR "EX."
BESIDES, THE GAS AND ELECTRICITY ARE OUT. I CAN'T HELP THAT.
I did what I could!
SO DEAL WITH IT!
カタ!

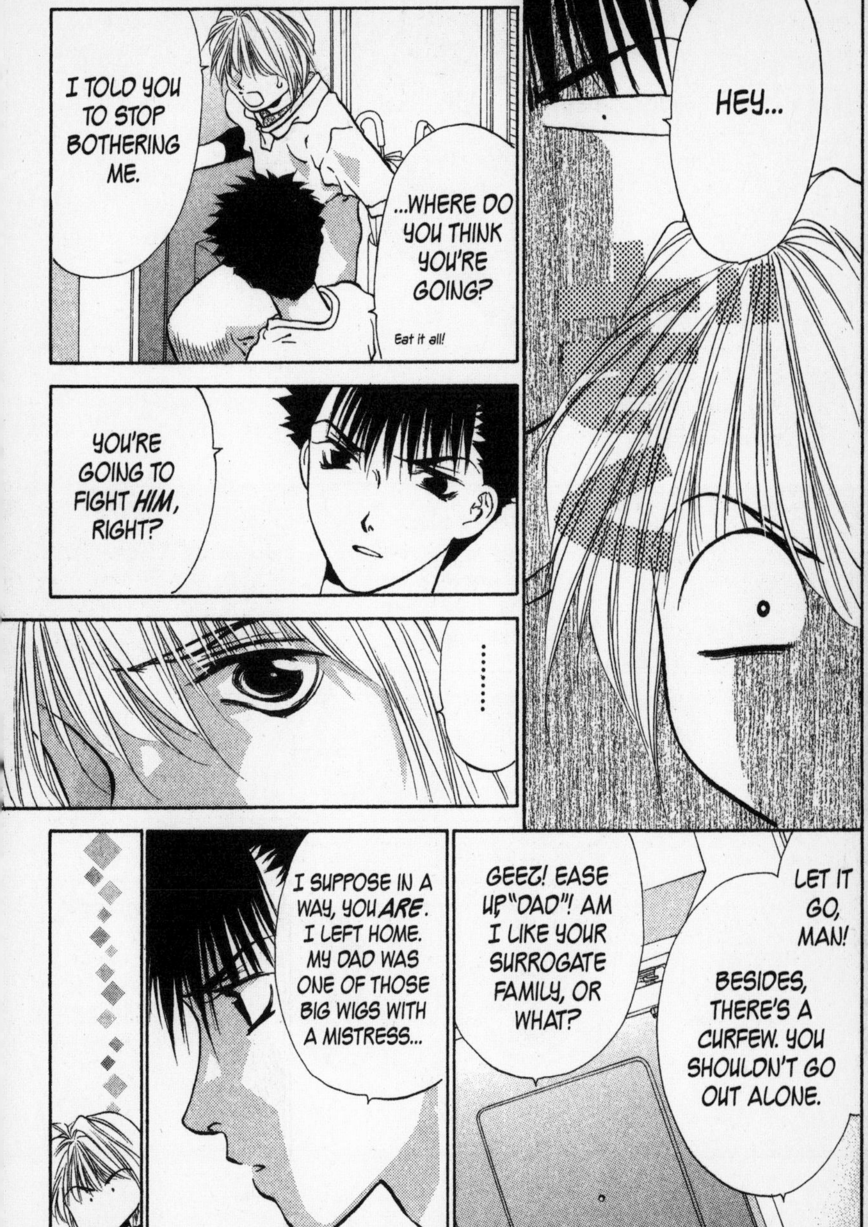
HEY...
...WHERE DO YOU THINK YOU'RE GOING?
I TOLD YOU TO STOP BOTHERING ME.
Eat it all!
YOU'RE GOING TO FIGHT *HIM*, RIGHT?
......
LET IT GO, MAN!
BESIDES, THERE'S A CURFEW. YOU SHOULDN'T GO OUT ALONE.
GEEZ! EASE UP, "DAD"! AM I LIKE YOUR SURROGATE FAMILY, OR WHAT?
I SUPPOSE IN A WAY, YOU *ARE*. I LEFT HOME. MY DAD WAS ONE OF THOSE BIG WIGS WITH A MISTRESS...

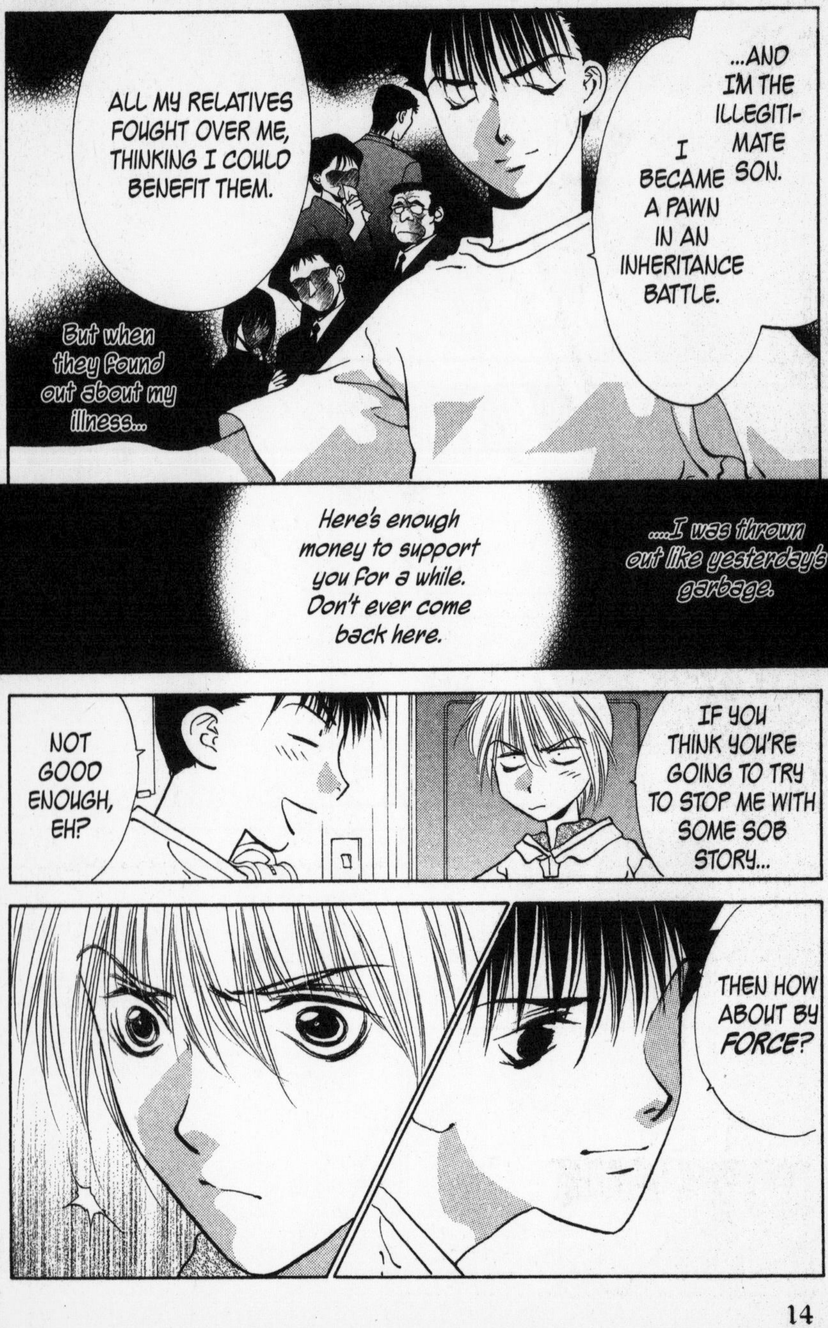
...AND I'M THE ILLEGITI-MATE SON.
I BECAME A PAWN IN AN INHERITANCE BATTLE.
ALL MY RELATIVES FOUGHT OVER ME, THINKING I COULD BENEFIT THEM.
But when they found out about my illness...
...I was thrown out like yesterday's garbage.
Here's enough money to support you for a while. Don't ever come back here.
IF YOU THINK YOU'RE GOING TO TRY TO STOP ME WITH SOME SOB STORY...
NOT GOOD ENOUGH, EH?
THEN HOW ABOUT BY *FORCE*?

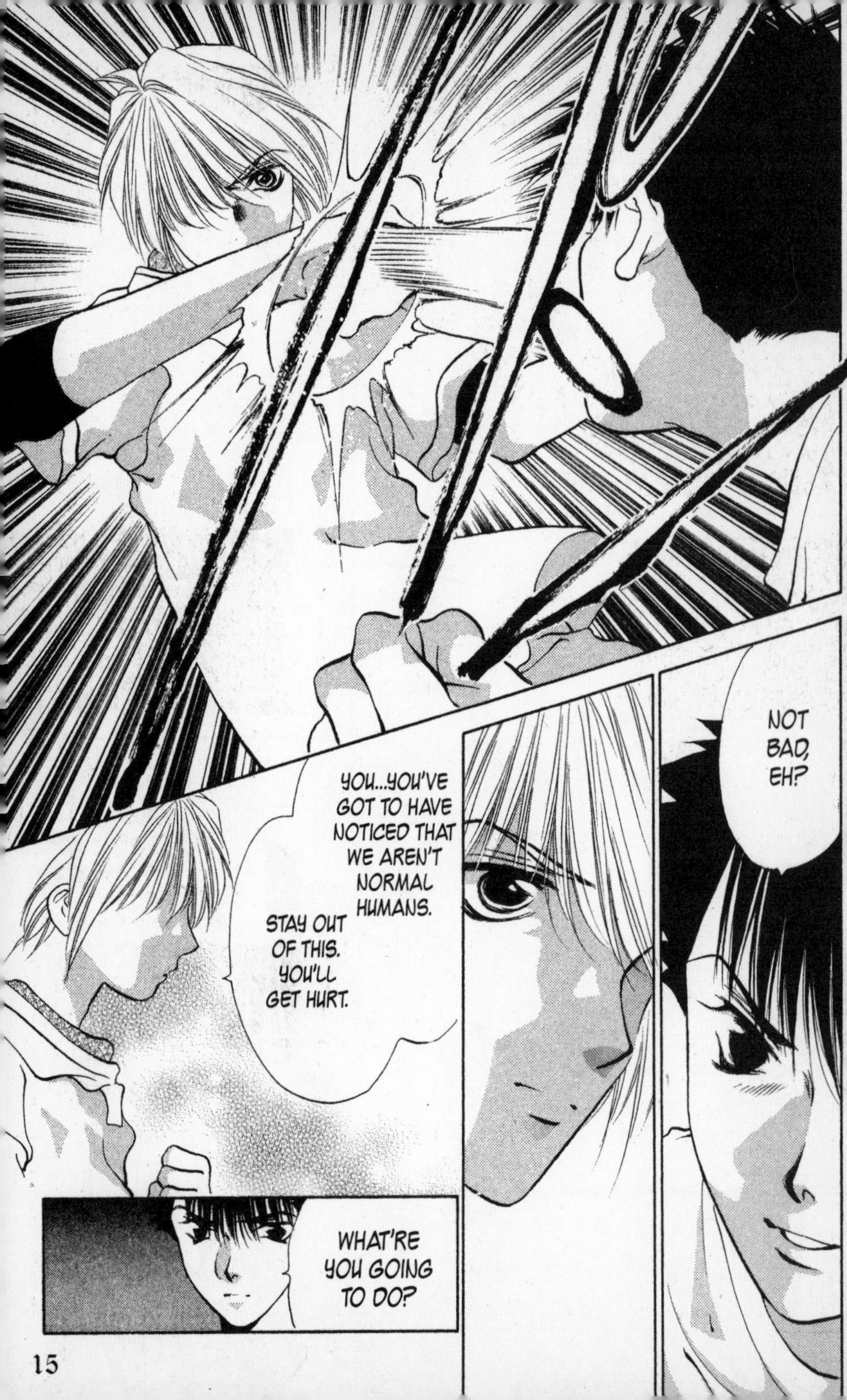
NOT BAD, EH?
YOU...YOU'VE GOT TO HAVE NOTICED THAT WE AREN'T NORMAL HUMANS.
STAY OUT OF THIS. YOU'LL GET HURT.
WHAT'RE YOU GOING TO DO?

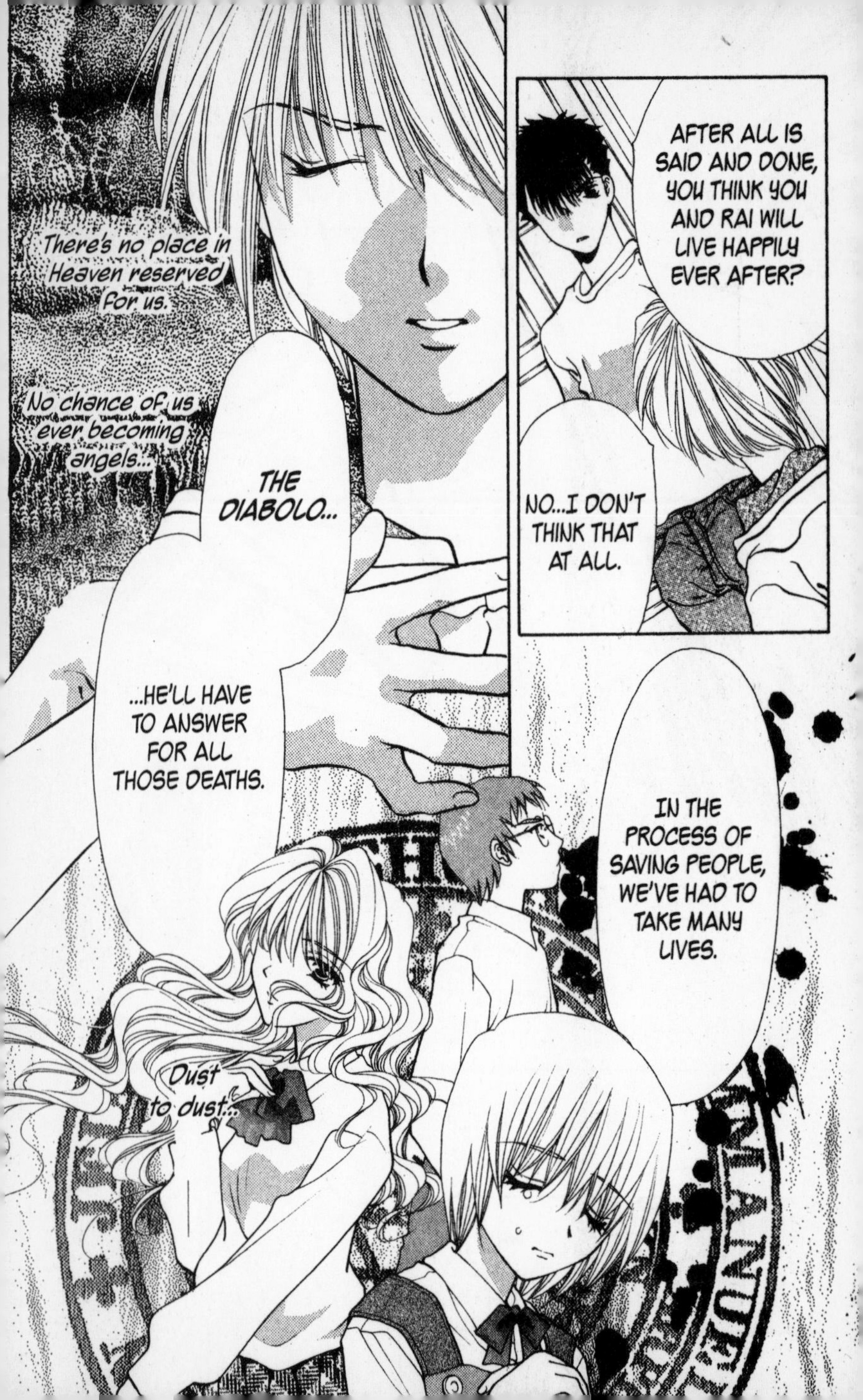
AFTER ALL IS SAID AND DONE, YOU THINK YOU AND RAI WILL LIVE HAPPILY EVER AFTER?
NO...I DON'T THINK THAT AT ALL.
IN THE PROCESS OF SAVING PEOPLE, WE'VE HAD TO TAKE MANY LIVES.
THE DIABOLO...
...HE'LL HAVE TO ANSWER FOR ALL THOSE DEATHS.
There's no place in Heaven reserved for us.
No chance of us ever becoming angels...
Dust to dust...

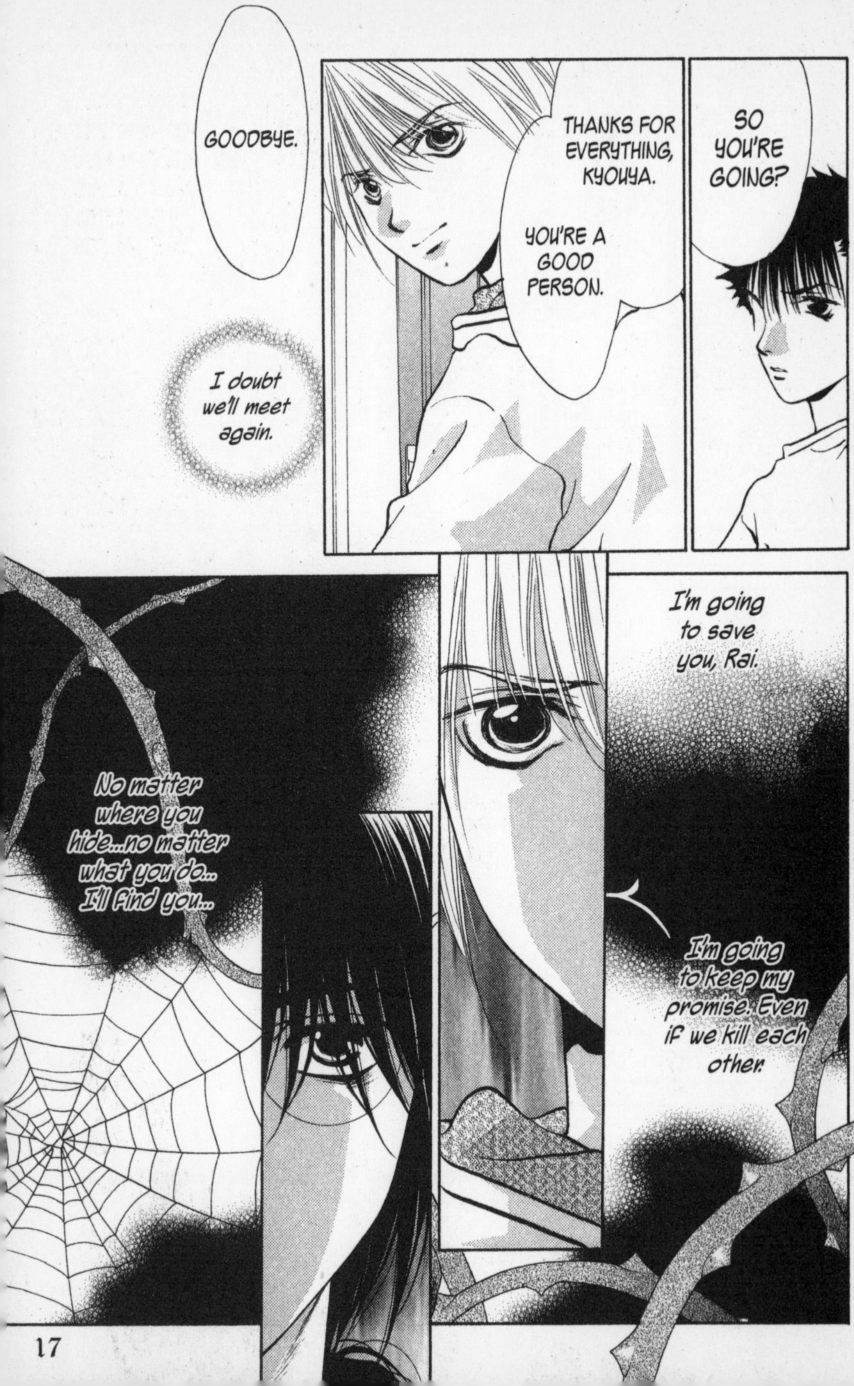
SO YOU'RE GOING?
THANKS FOR EVERYTHING, KYOUYA.
YOU'RE A GOOD PERSON.
GOODBYE.
I doubt we'll meet again.
I'm going to save you, Rai.
I'm going to keep my promise. Even if we kill each other.
No matter where you hide...no matter what you do.. I'll find you...

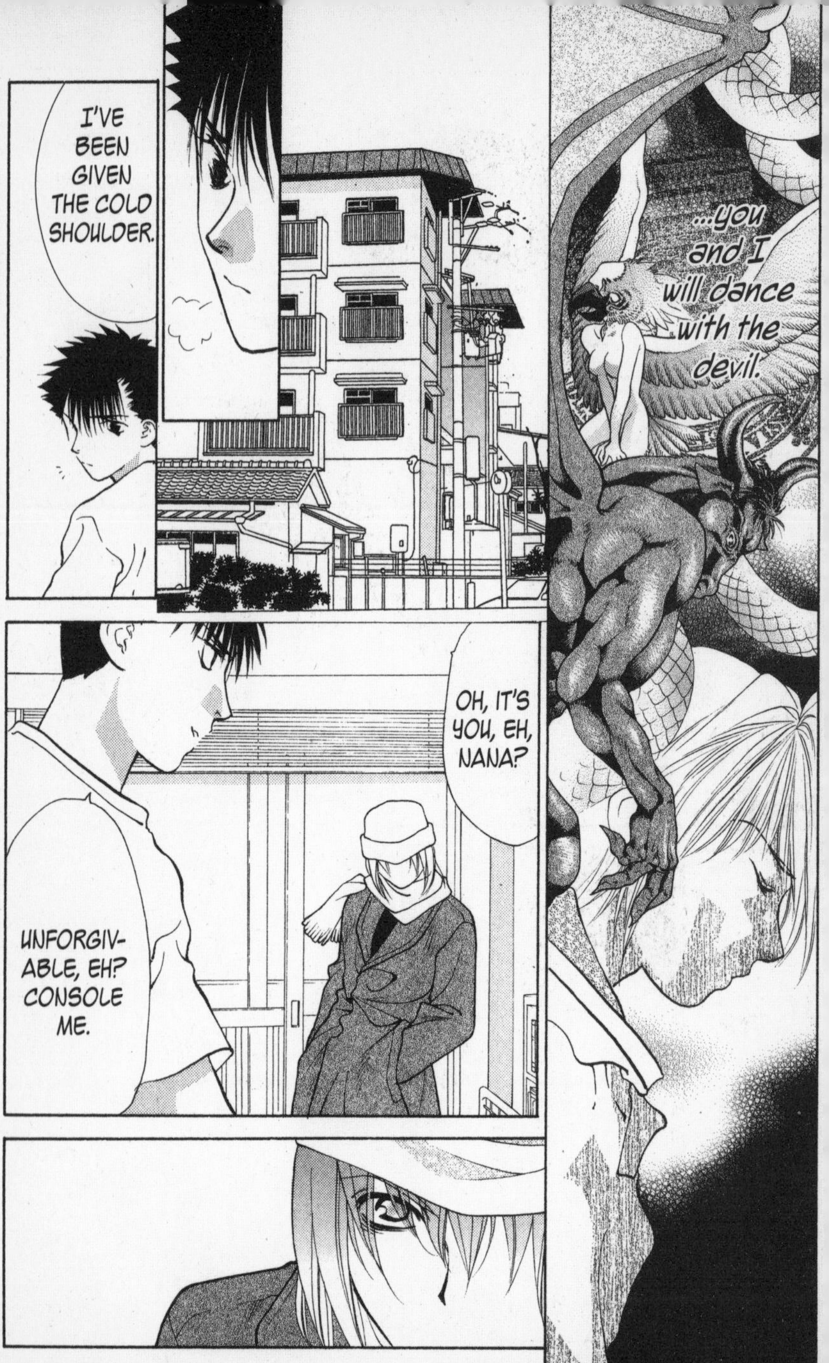
...you and I will dance with the devil.
I'VE BEEN GIVEN THE COLD SHOULDER.
OH, IT'S YOU, EH, NANA?
UNFORGIV-ABLE, EH? CONSOLE ME.

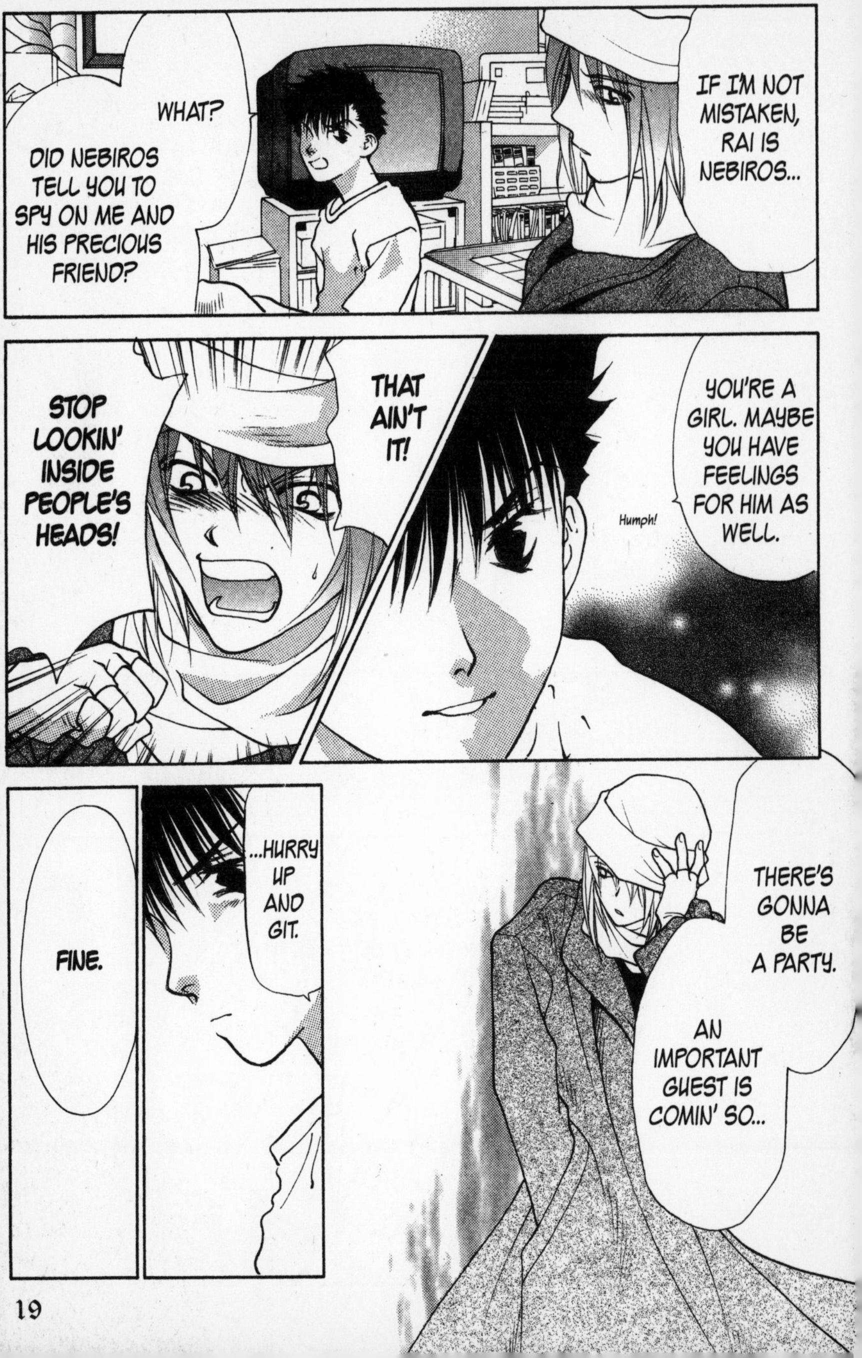
IF I'M NOT MISTAKEN, RAI IS NEBIROS...
WHAT?
DID NEBIROS TELL YOU TO SPY ON ME AND HIS PRECIOUS FRIEND?
YOU'RE A GIRL. MAYBE YOU HAVE FEELINGS FOR HIM AS WELL.
Humph!
THAT AIN'T IT!
STOP LOOKIN' INSIDE PEOPLE'S HEADS!
THERE'S GONNA BE A PARTY.
AN IMPORTANT GUEST IS COMIN' SO...
...HURRY UP AND GIT.
FINE.

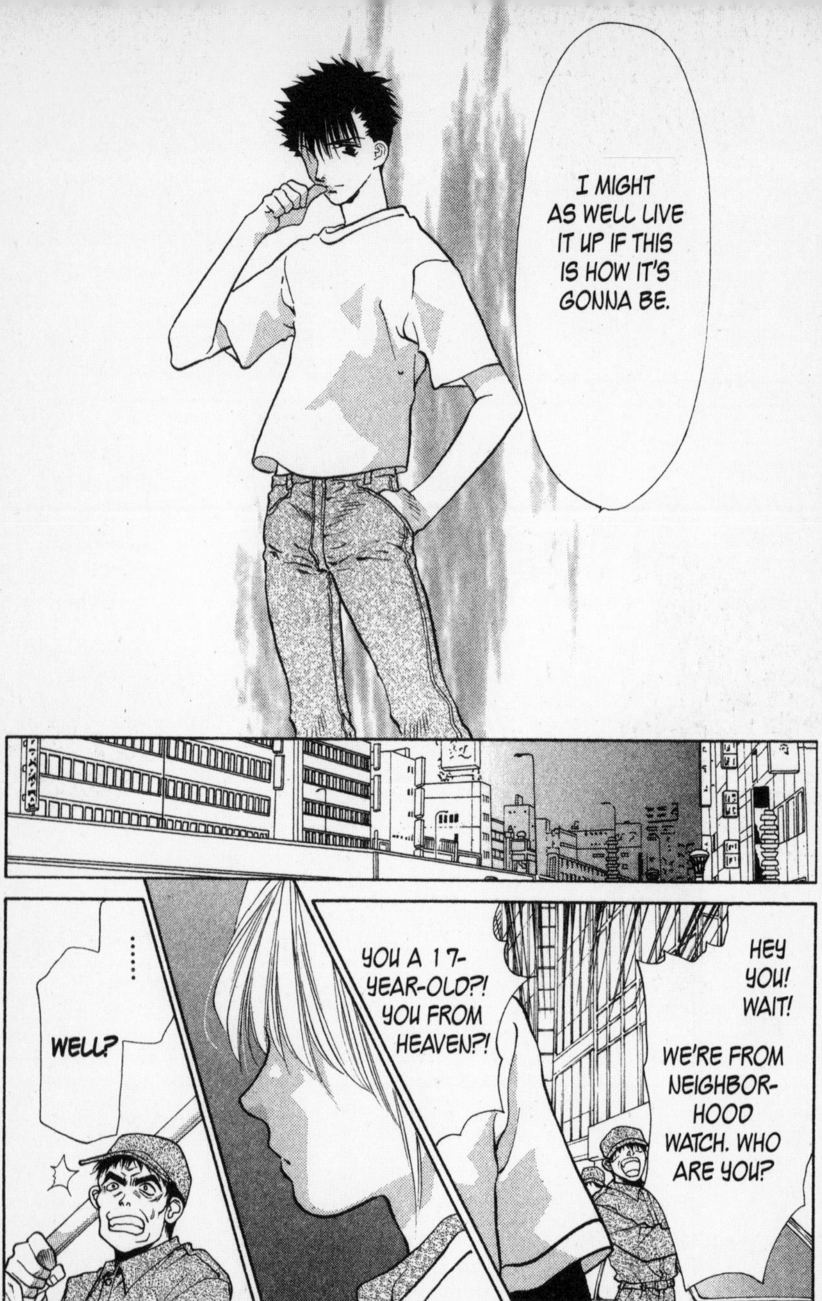
I MIGHT AS WELL LIVE IT UP IF THIS IS HOW IT'S GONNA BE.
HEY YOU! WAIT!
WE'RE FROM NEIGHBOR-HOOD WATCH. WHO ARE YOU?
YOU A 17-YEAR-OLD?! YOU FROM HEAVEN?!
......
WELL?

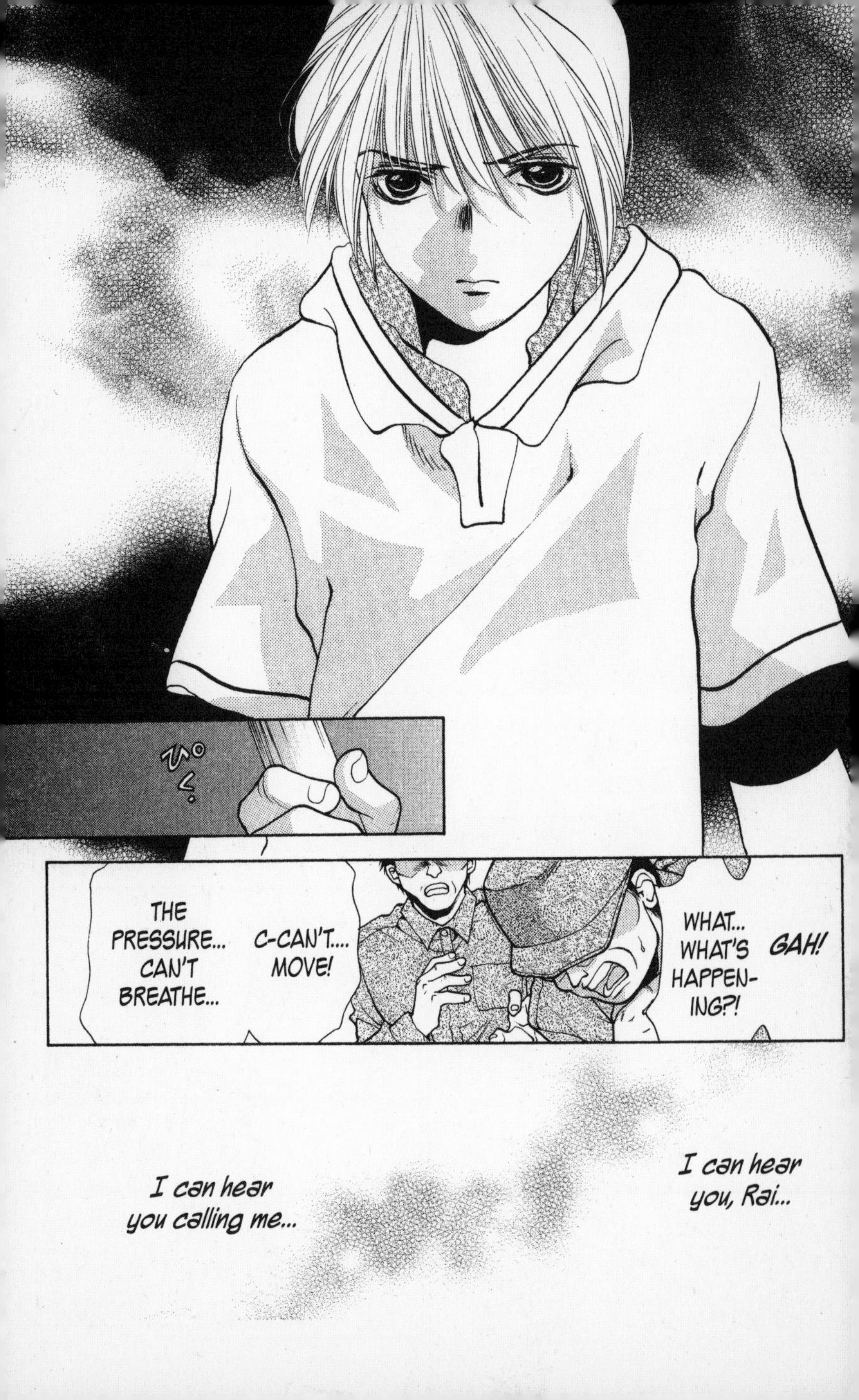
GAH!
WHAT... WHAT'S HAPPENING?!
C-CAN'T.... MOVE!
THE PRESSURE... CAN'T BREATHE...
I can hear you, Rai...
I can hear you calling me...

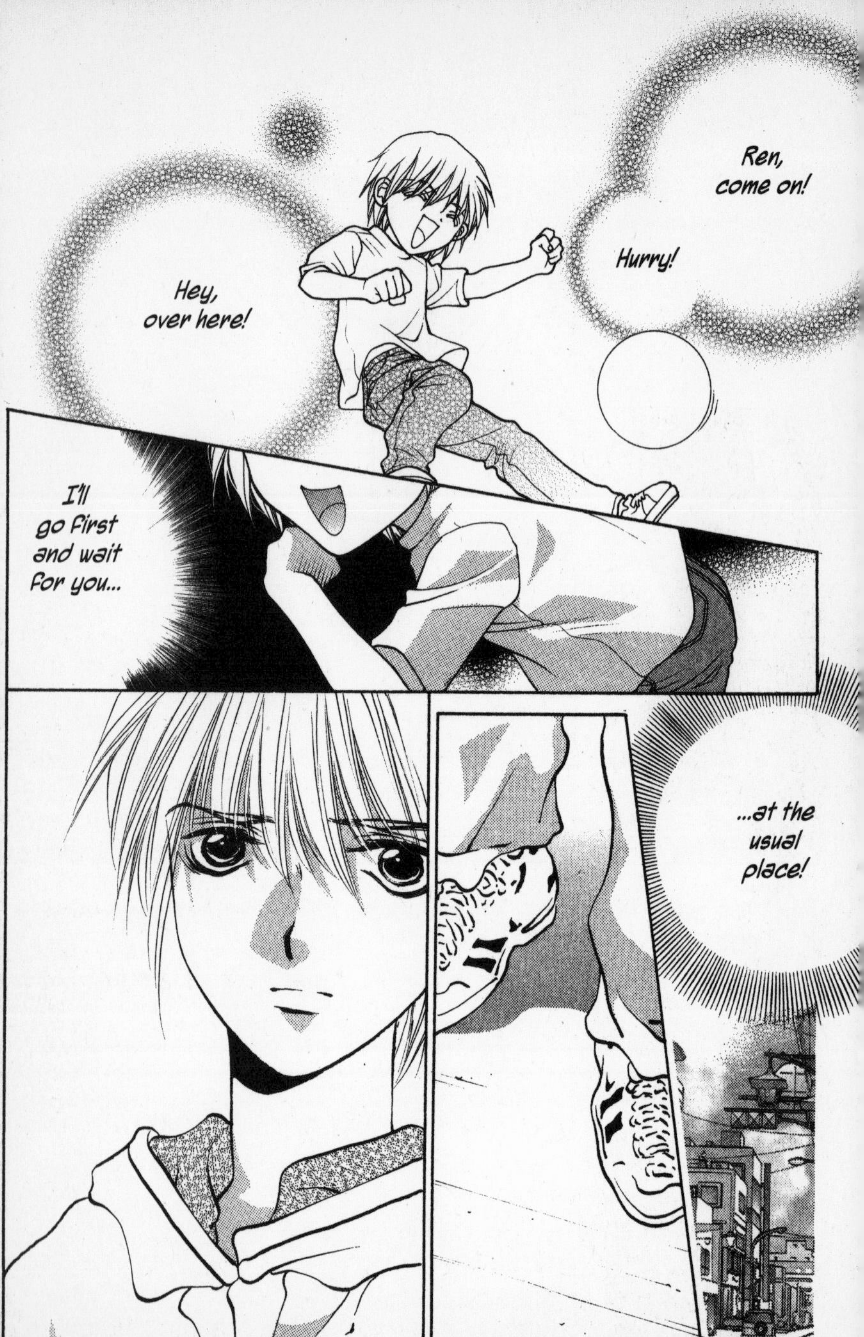
Ren, come on!
Hurry!
Hey, over here!
I'll go first and wait for you...
...at the usual place!

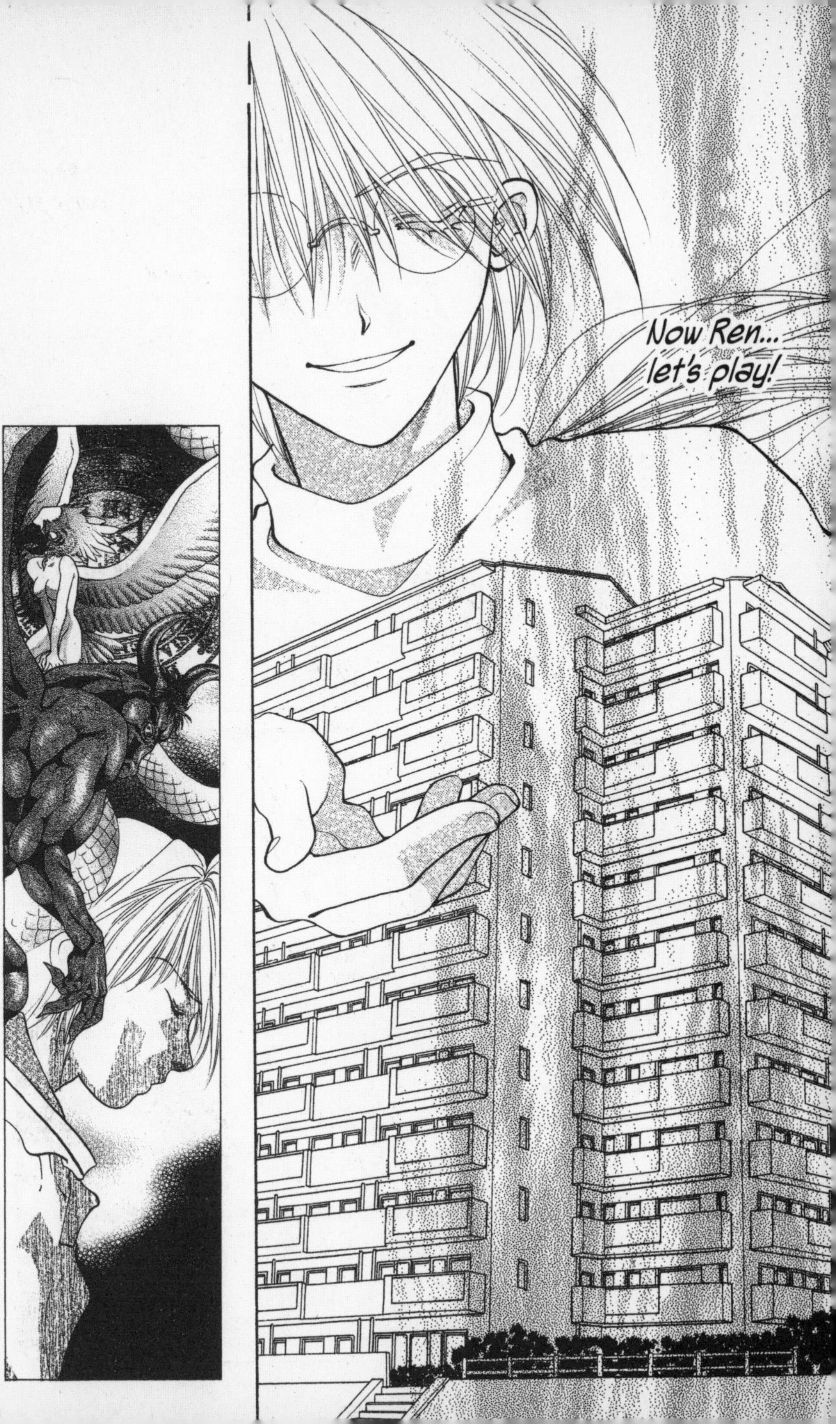
Now Ren...
let's play!

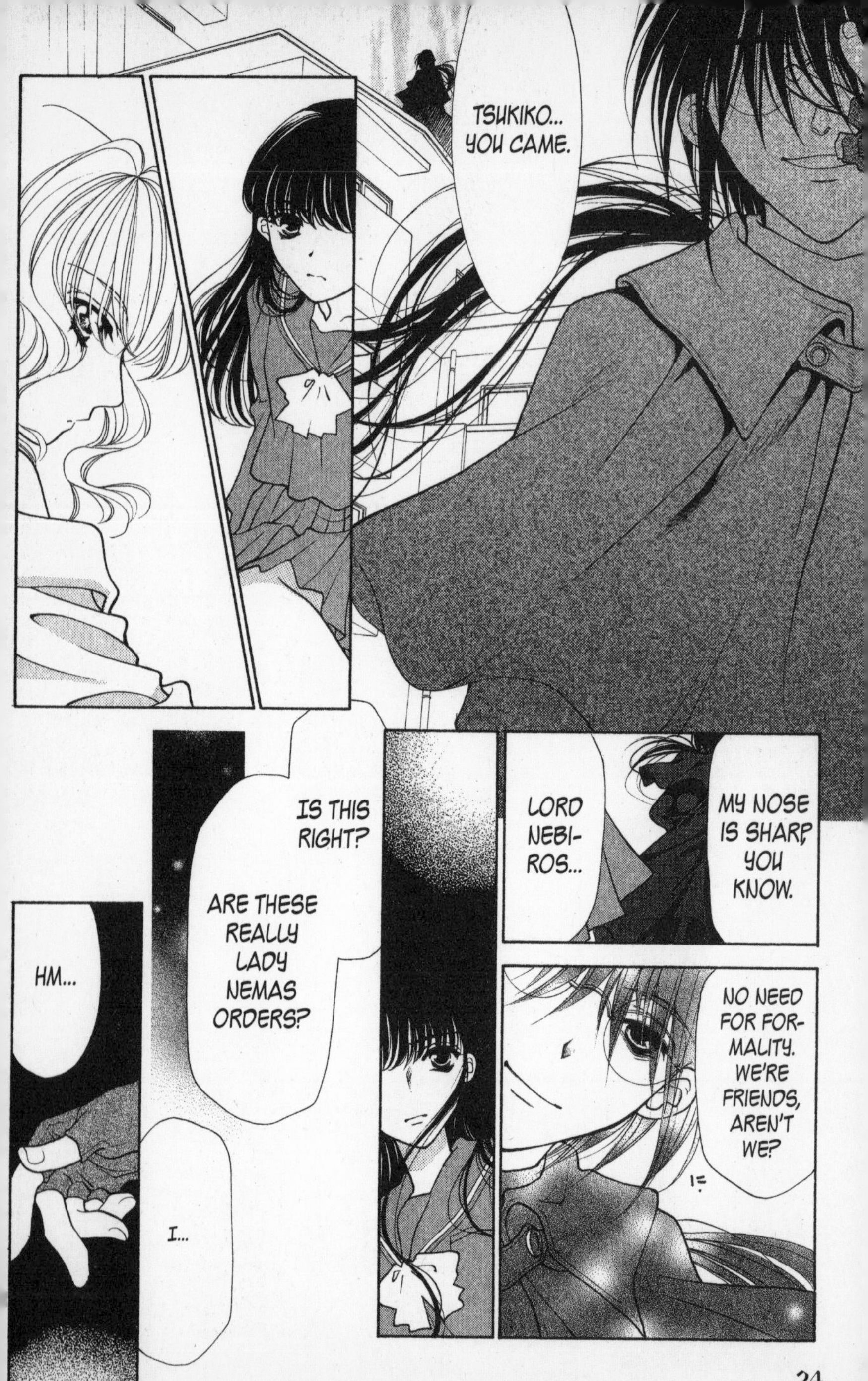
TSUKIKO... YOU CAME.
MY NOSE IS SHARP, YOU KNOW.
LORD NEBIROS...
NO NEED FOR FORMALITY. WE'RE FRIENDS, AREN'T WE?
!=
IS THIS RIGHT?
ARE THESE REALLY LADY NEMAS ORDERS?
HM...
I...

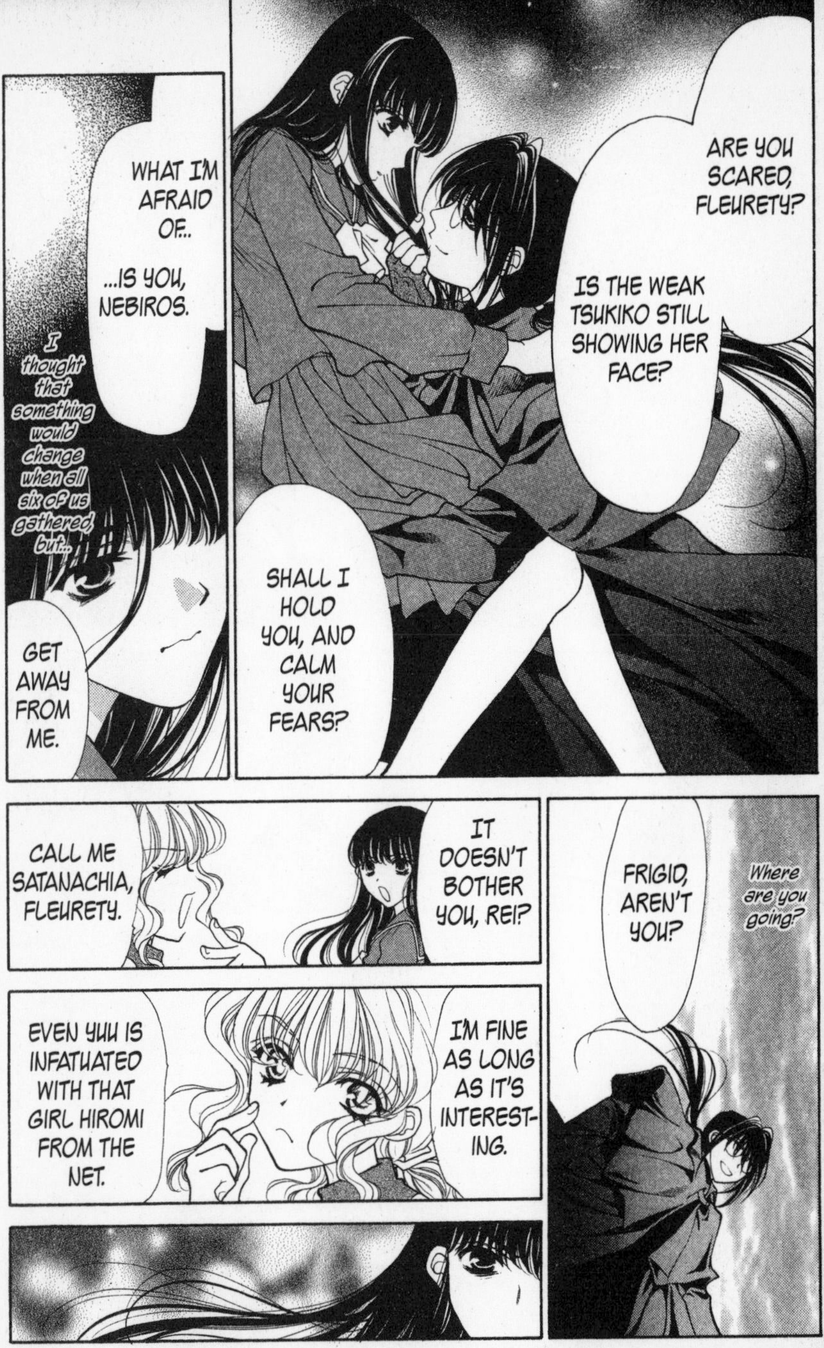
ARE YOU SCARED, FLEURETY?
IS THE WEAK TSUKIKO STILL SHOWING HER FACE?
SHALL I HOLD YOU, AND CALM YOUR FEARS?
WHAT I'M AFRAID OF...
...IS YOU, NEBIROS.
I thought that something would change when all six of us gathered, but...
GET AWAY FROM ME.
Where are you going?
FRIGID, AREN'T YOU?
IT DOESN'T BOTHER YOU, REI?
CALL ME SATANACHIA, FLEURETY.
I'M FINE AS LONG AS IT'S INTERESTING.
EVEN YUU IS INFATUATED WITH THAT GIRL HIROMI FROM THE NET.

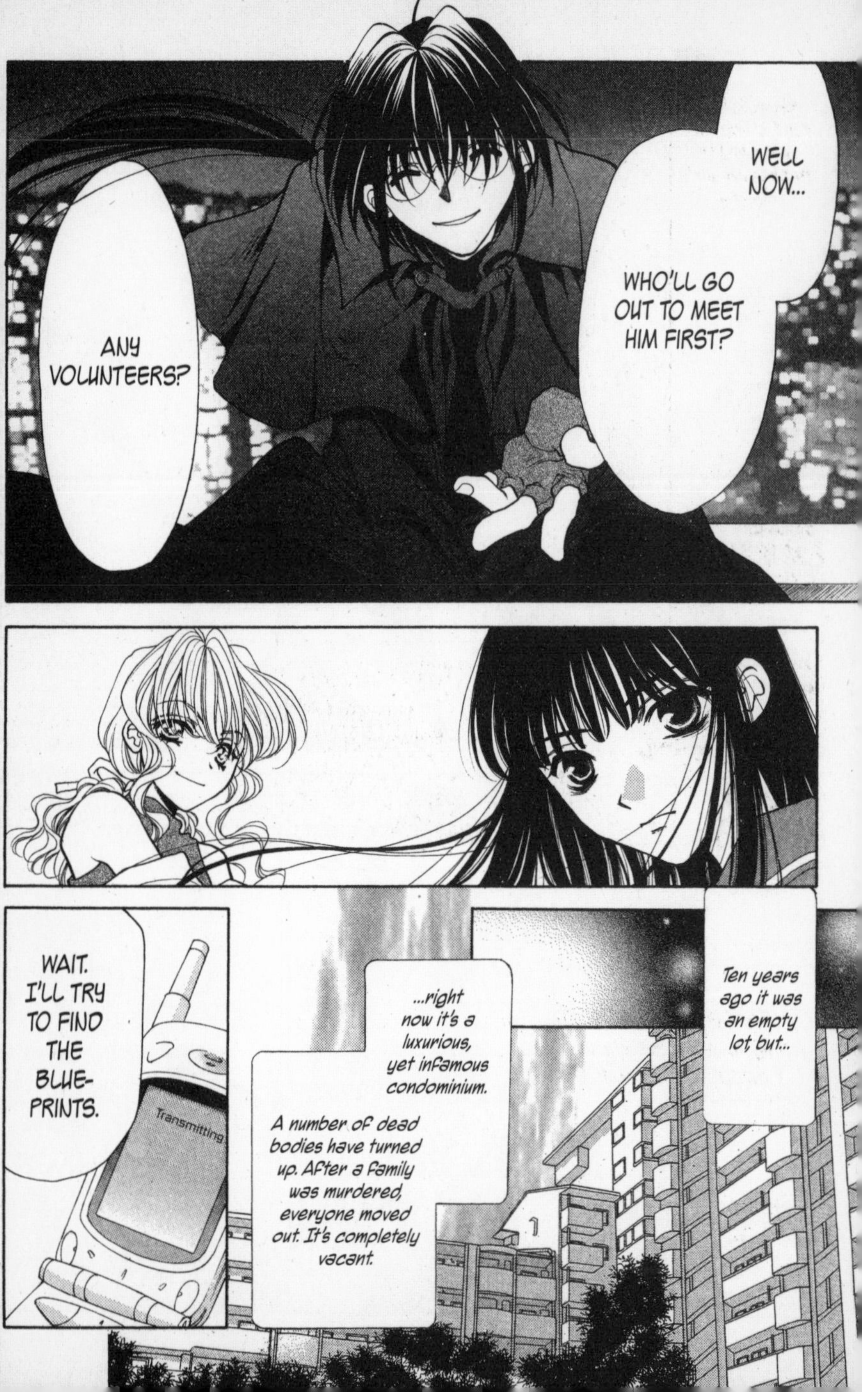
WELL NOW...
WHO'LL GO OUT TO MEET HIM FIRST?
ANY VOLUNTEERS?
Ten years ago it was an empty lot, but...
...right now it's a luxurious, yet infamous condominium.
A number of dead bodies have turned up. After a family was murdered, everyone moved out. It's completely vacant.
WAIT. I'LL TRY TO FIND THE BLUE-PRINTS.
Transmitting

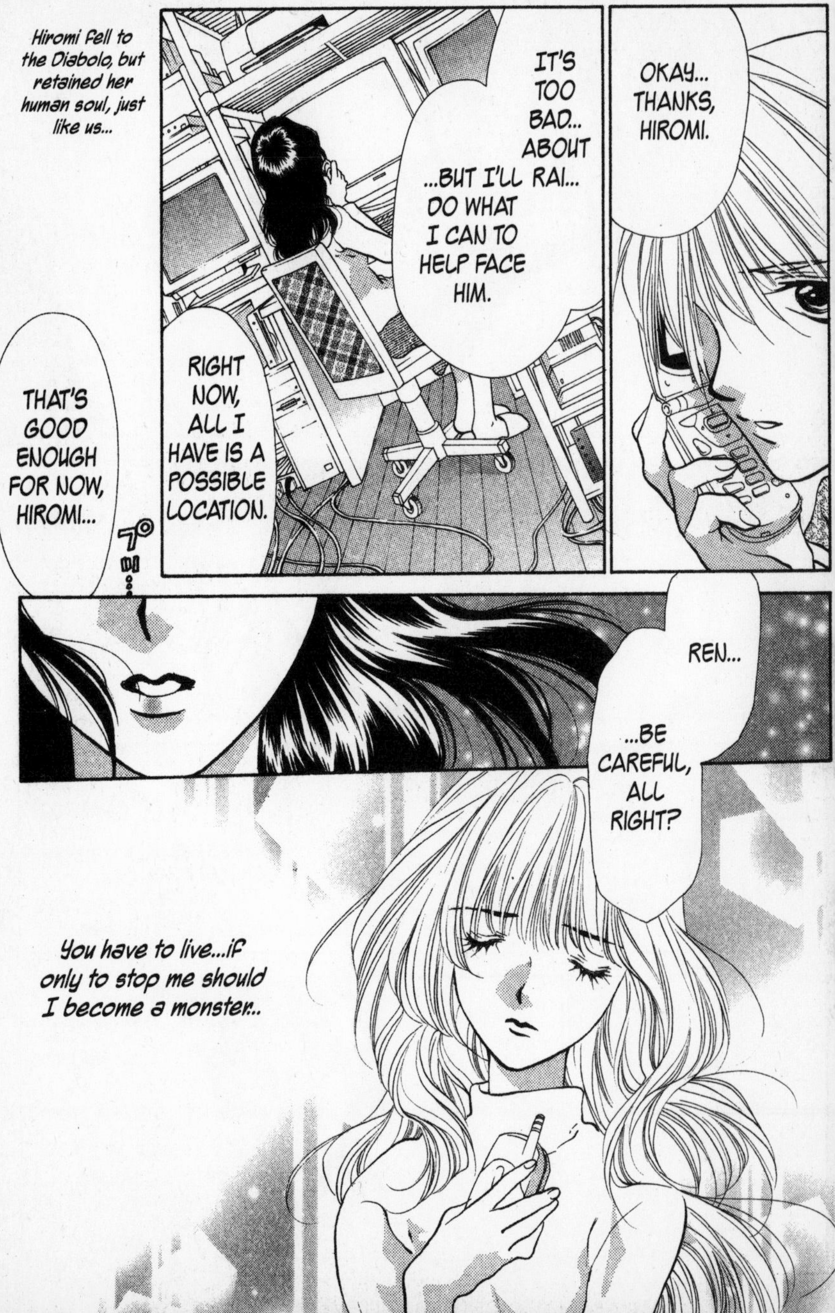
OKAY... THANKS, HIROMI.
IT'S TOO BAD... ABOUT RAI...
...BUT I'LL DO WHAT I CAN TO HELP FACE HIM.
RIGHT NOW, ALL I HAVE IS A POSSIBLE LOCATION.
Hiromi fell to the Diabolo, but retained her human soul, just like us...
THAT'S GOOD ENOUGH FOR NOW, HIROMI...
REN...
...BE CAREFUL, ALL RIGHT?
You have to live...if only to stop me should I become a monster..

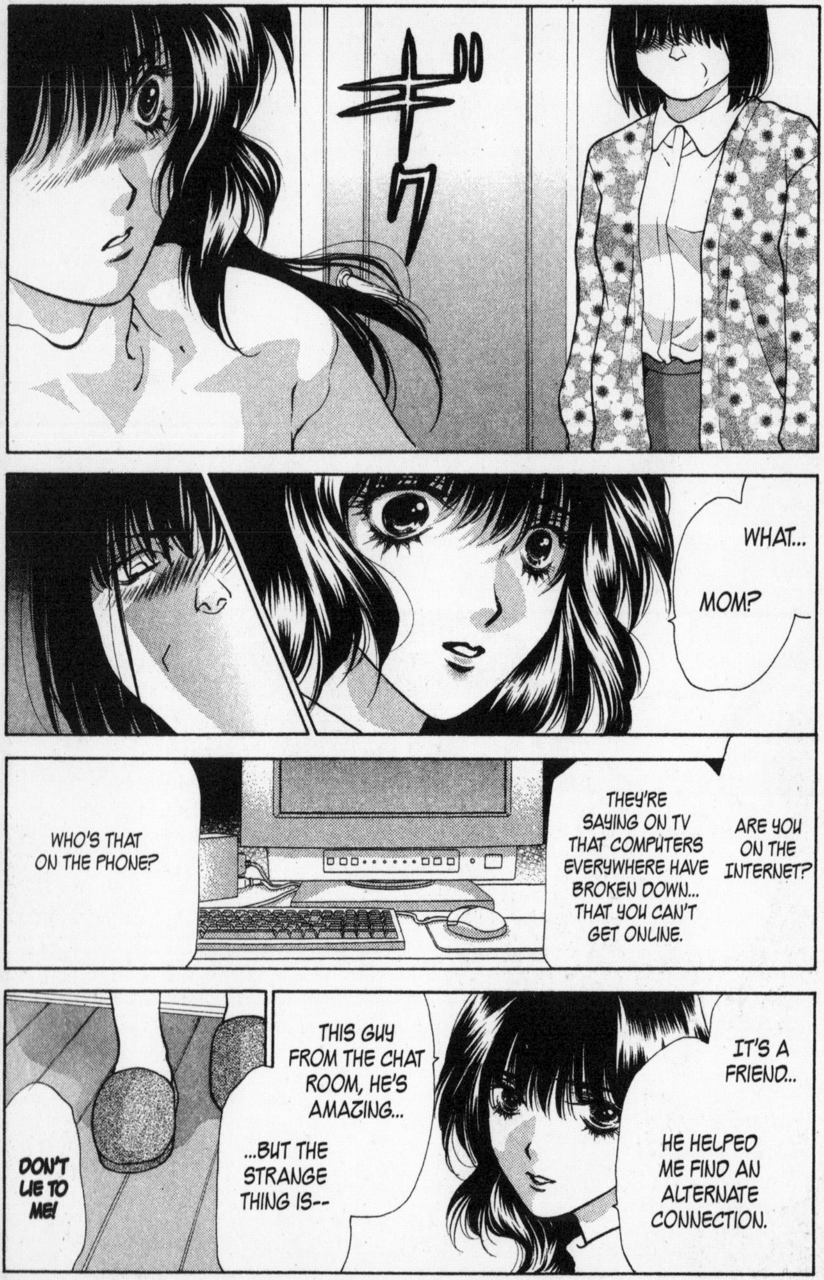

ギク
WHAT...
MOM?
ARE YOU ON THE INTERNET?
THEY'RE SAYING ON TV THAT COMPUTERS EVERYWHERE HAVE BROKEN DOWN... THAT YOU CAN'T GET ONLINE.
WHO'S THAT ON THE PHONE?
IT'S A FRIEND...
HE HELPED ME FIND AN ALTERNATE CONNECTION.
THIS GUY FROM THE CHAT ROOM, HE'S AMAZING...
...BUT THE STRANGE THING IS--
DON'T LIE TO ME!

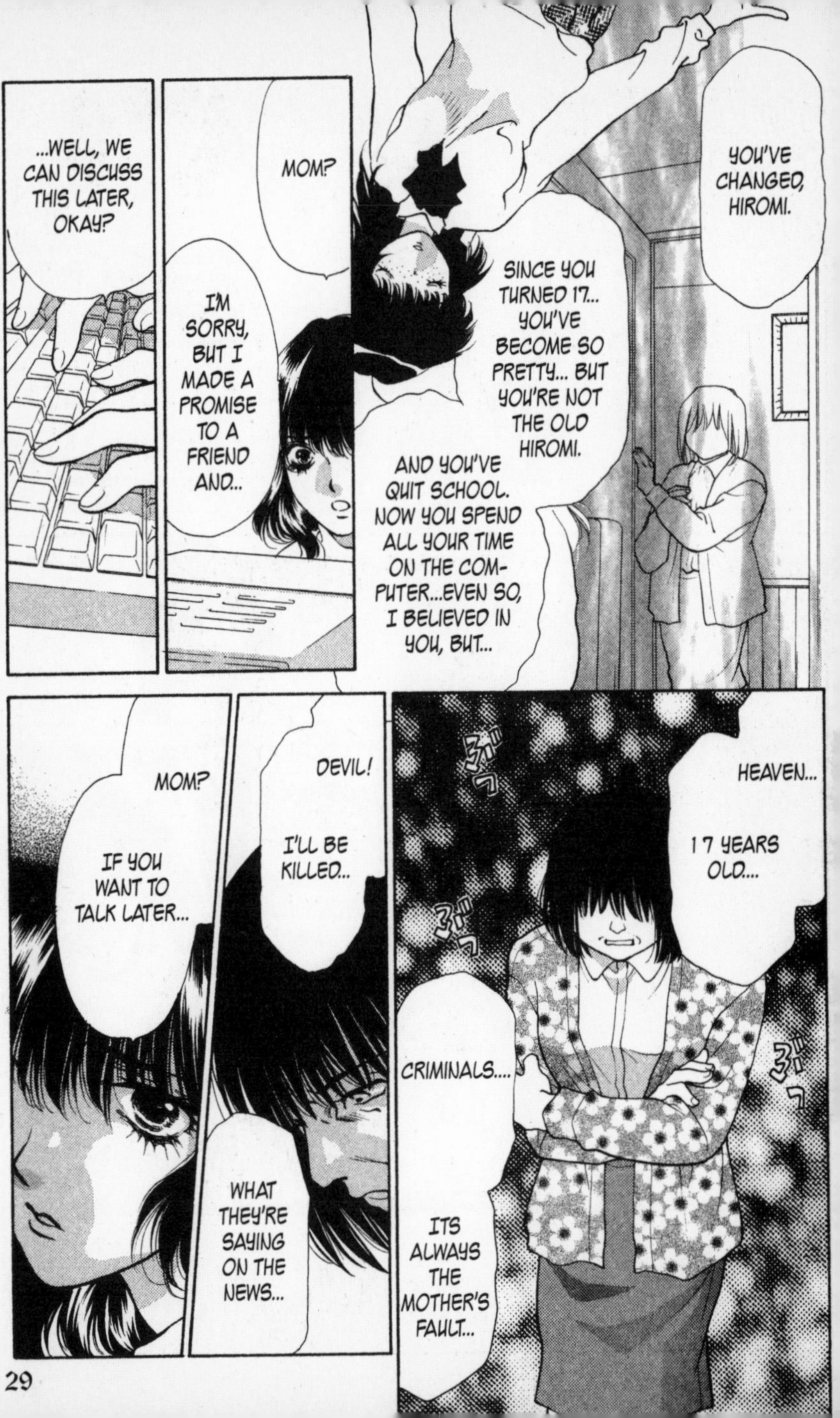
YOU'VE CHANGED, HIROMI.
SINCE YOU TURNED 17... YOU'VE BECOME SO PRETTY... BUT YOU'RE NOT THE OLD HIROMI.
AND YOU'VE QUIT SCHOOL. NOW YOU SPEND ALL YOUR TIME ON THE COM-PUTER...EVEN SO, I BELIEVED IN YOU, BUT...
MOM?
I'M SORRY, BUT I MADE A PROMISE TO A FRIEND AND...
...WELL, WE CAN DISCUSS THIS LATER, OKAY?
HEAVEN...
17 YEARS OLD....
CRIMINALS....
ITS ALWAYS THE MOTHER'S FAULT...
DEVIL!
I'LL BE KILLED...
WHAT THEY'RE SAYING ON THE NEWS...
MOM?
IF YOU WANT TO TALK LATER...

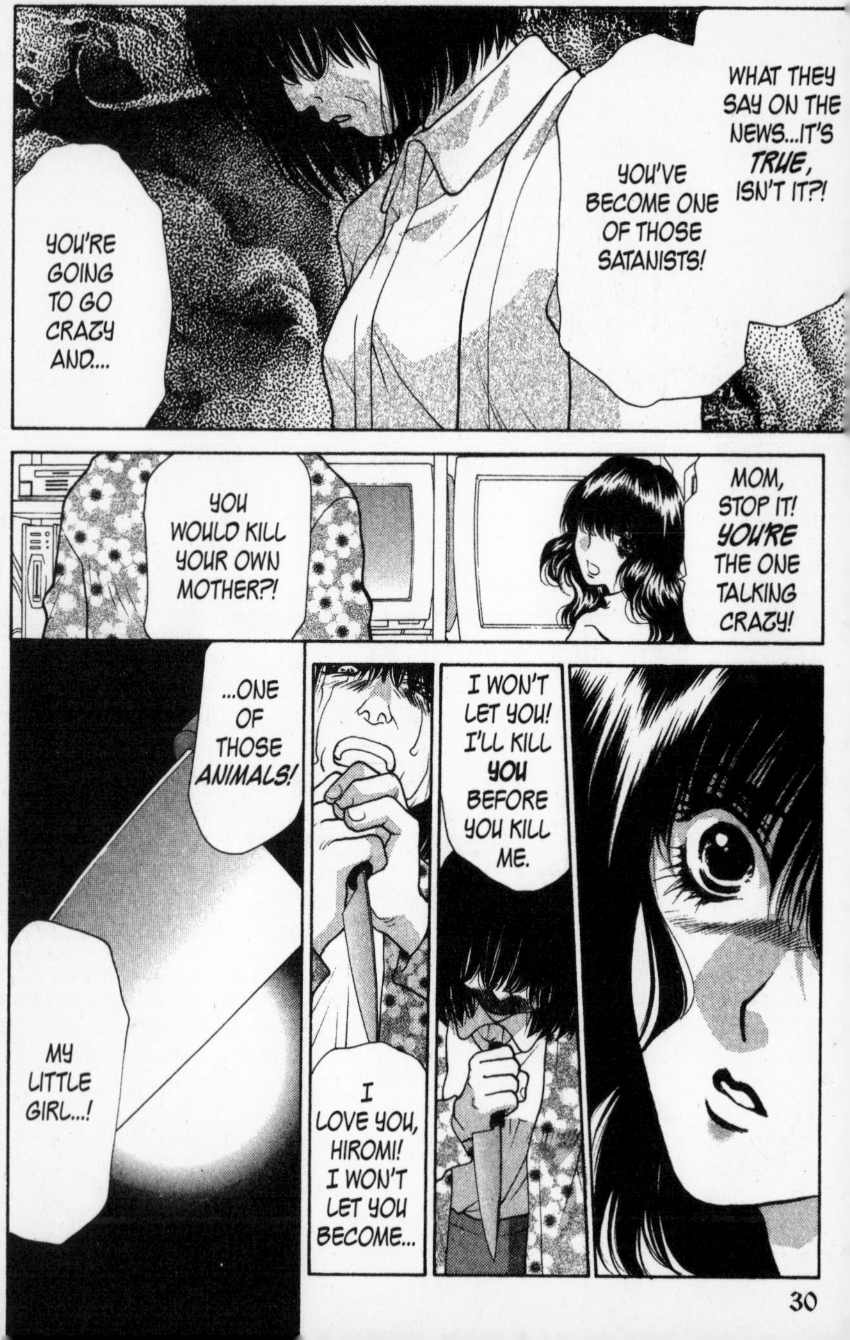
WHAT THEY SAY ON THE NEWS...IT'S TRUE, ISN'T IT?!
YOU'VE BECOME ONE OF THOSE SATANISTS!
YOU'RE GOING TO GO CRAZY AND...
MOM, STOP IT! YOU'RE THE ONE TALKING CRAZY!
YOU WOULD KILL YOUR OWN MOTHER?!
I WON'T LET YOU! I'LL KILL YOU BEFORE YOU KILL ME.
I LOVE YOU, HIROMI! I WON'T LET YOU BECOME...
...ONE OF THOSE ANIMALS!
MY LITTLE GIRL...!

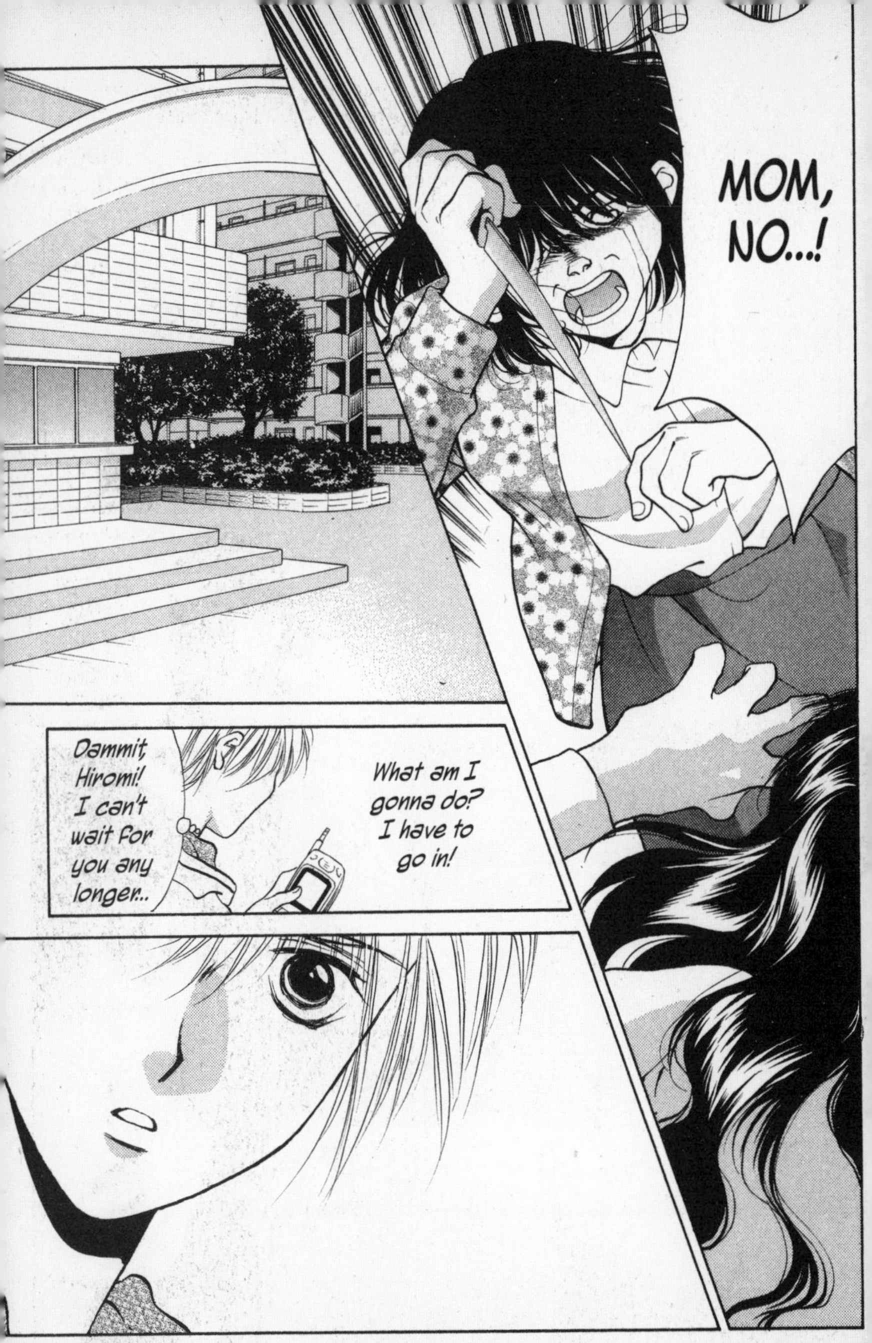
MOM, NO...!
Dammit, Hiromi! I can't wait for you any longer...
What am I gonna do? I have to go in!

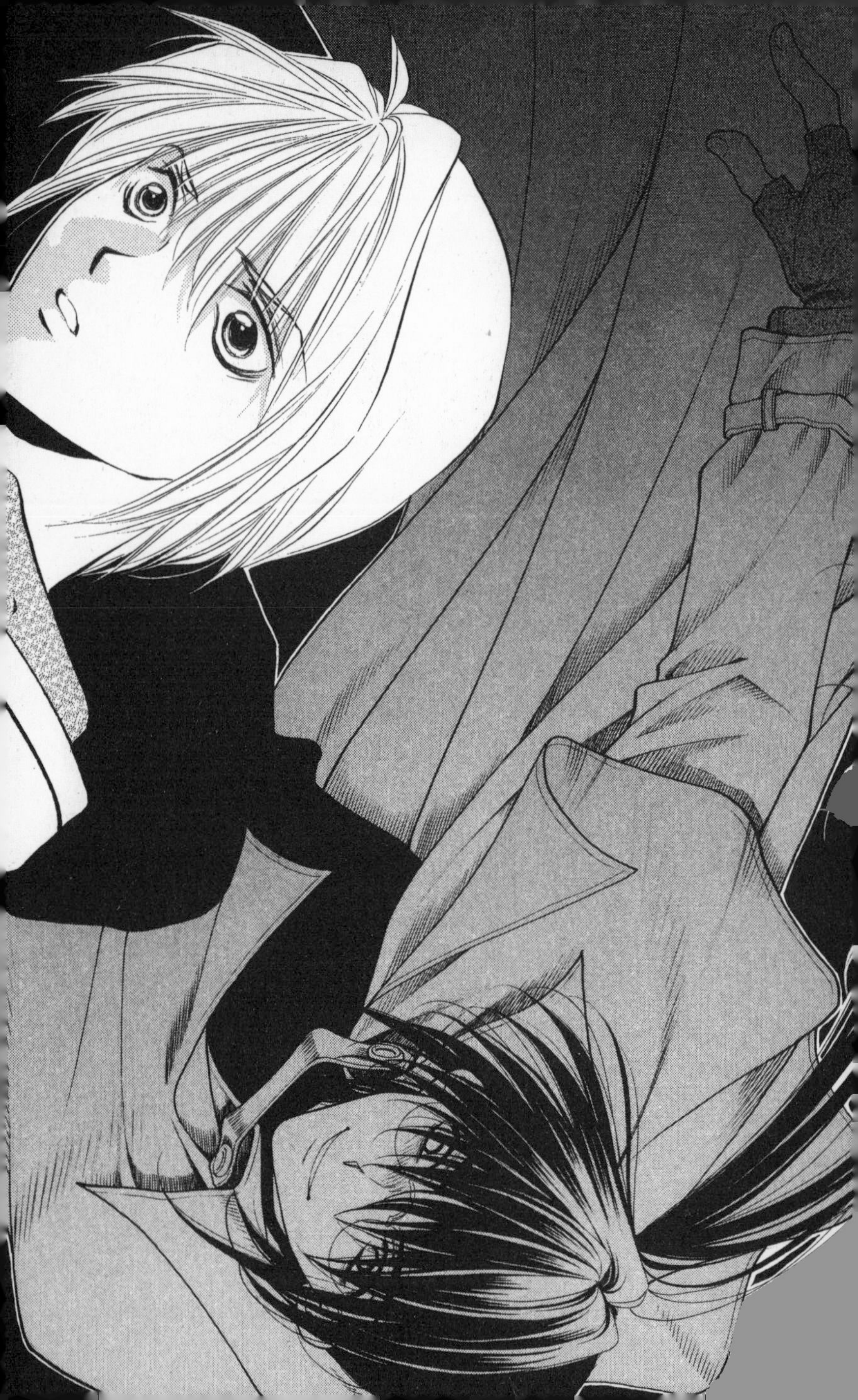

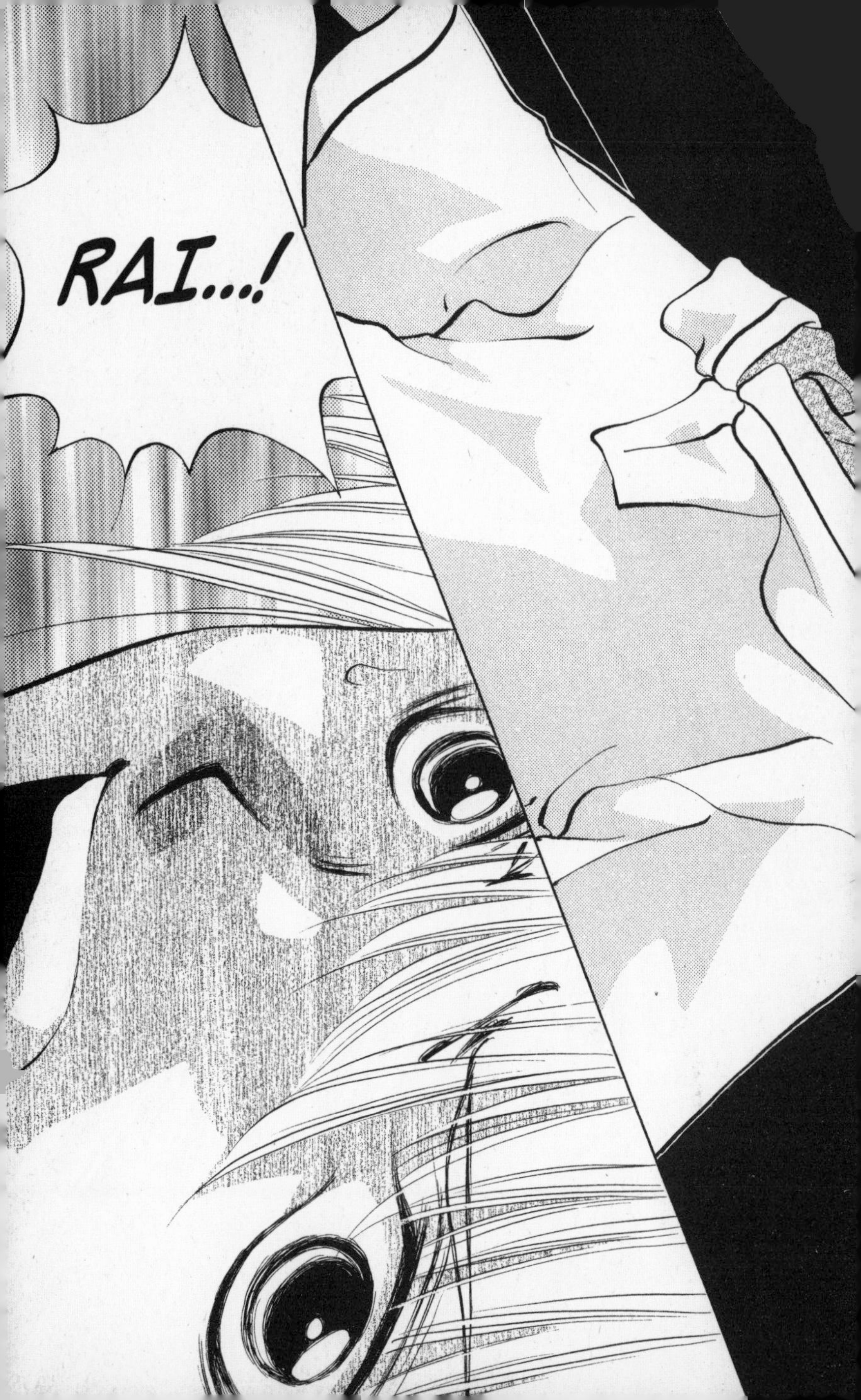
RAI...!

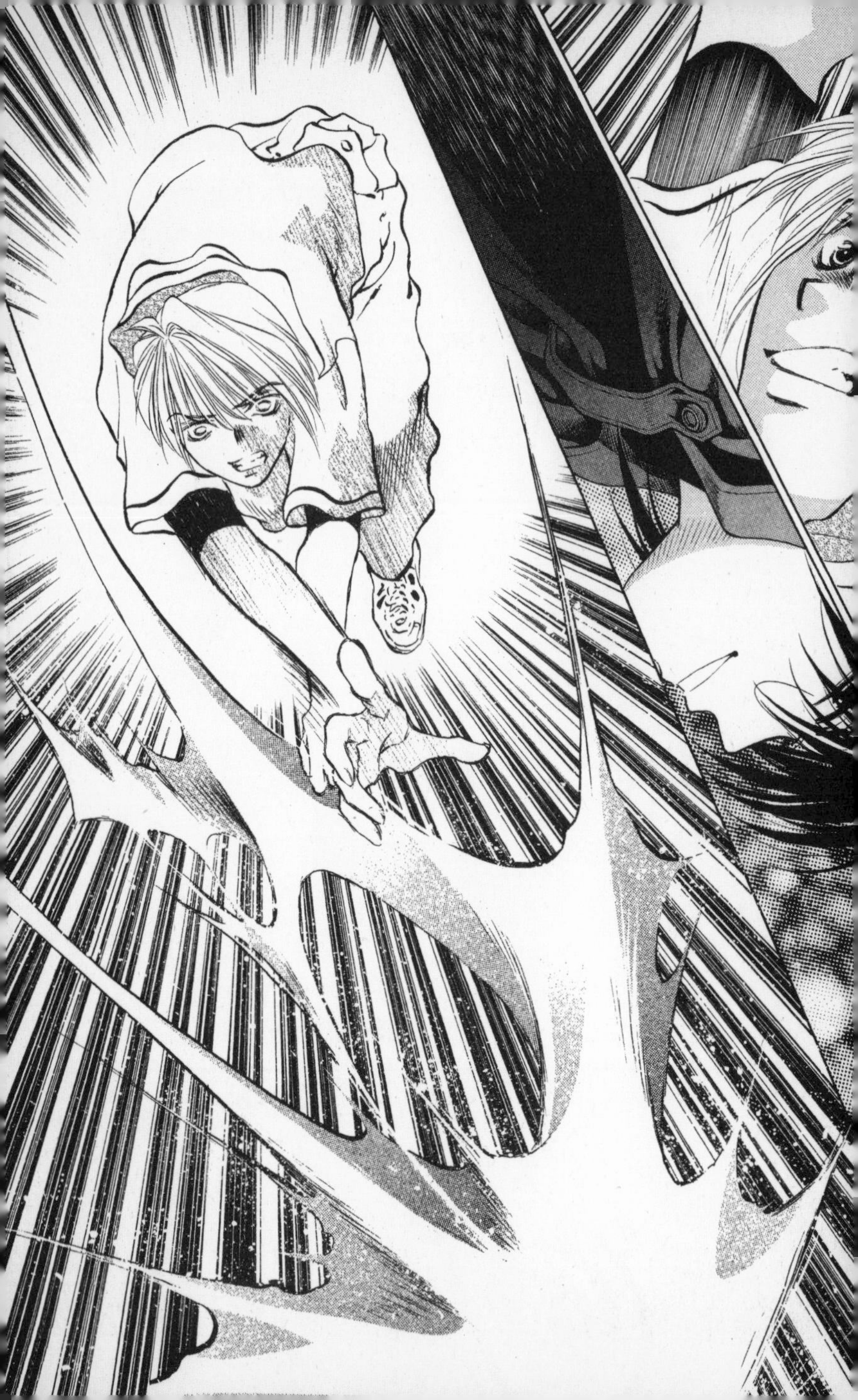

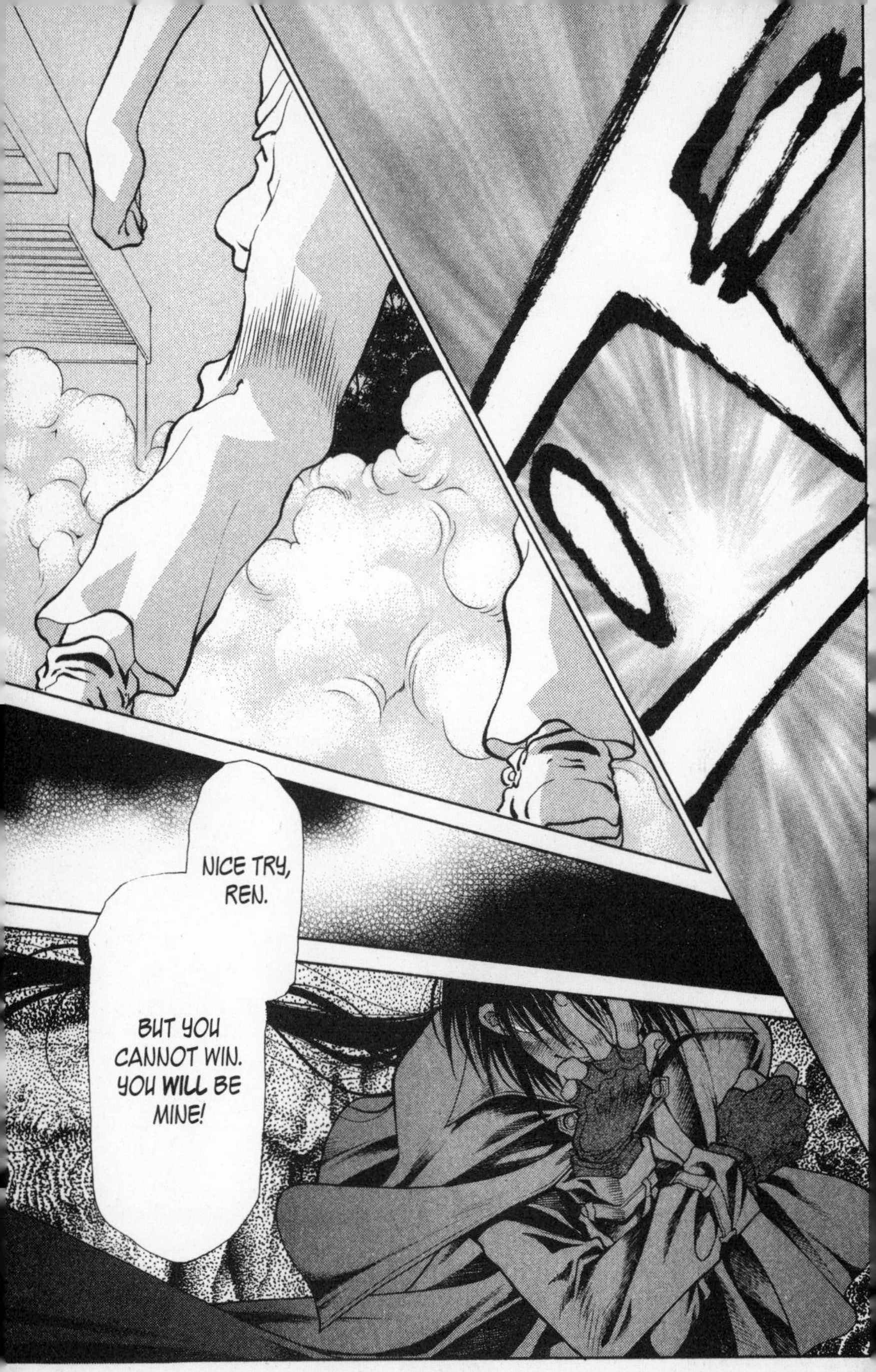
NICE TRY, REN.
BUT YOU CANNOT WIN. YOU WILL BE MINE!

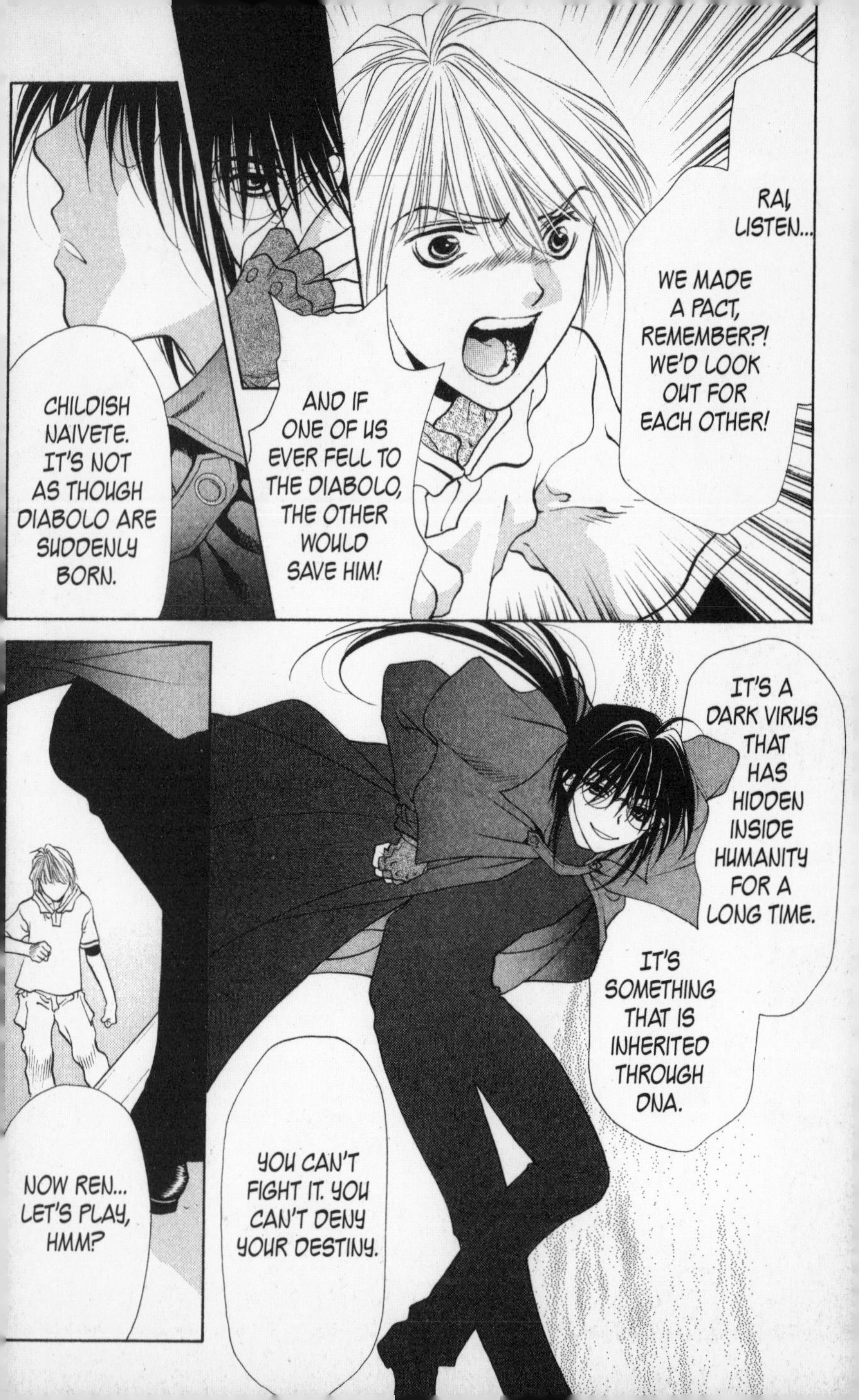
RAI, LISTEN...
WE MADE A PACT, REMEMBER?! WE'D LOOK OUT FOR EACH OTHER!
AND IF ONE OF US EVER FELL TO THE DIABOLO, THE OTHER WOULD SAVE HIM!
CHILDISH NAIVETE. IT'S NOT AS THOUGH DIABOLO ARE SUDDENLY BORN.
IT'S A DARK VIRUS THAT HAS HIDDEN INSIDE HUMANITY FOR A LONG TIME.
IT'S SOMETHING THAT IS INHERITED THROUGH DNA.
YOU CAN'T FIGHT IT. YOU CAN'T DENY YOUR DESTINY.
NOW REN... LET'S PLAY, HMM?

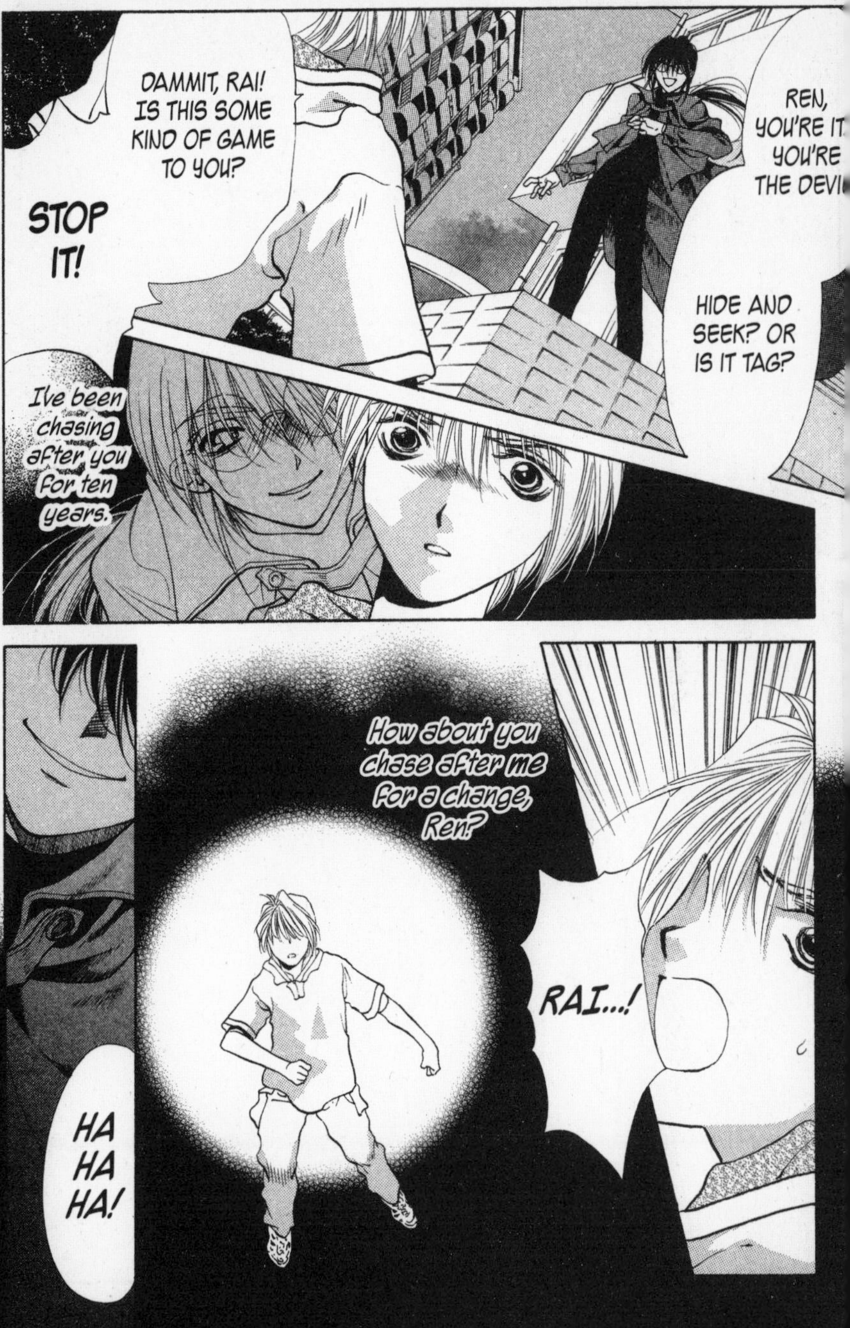
REN, YOU'RE IT. YOU'RE THE DEVI
HIDE AND SEEK? OR IS IT TAG?
DAMMIT, RAI! IS THIS SOME KIND OF GAME TO YOU?
STOP IT!
I've been chasing after you for ten years.
RAI...!
How about you chase after me for a change, Ren?
HA HA HA!

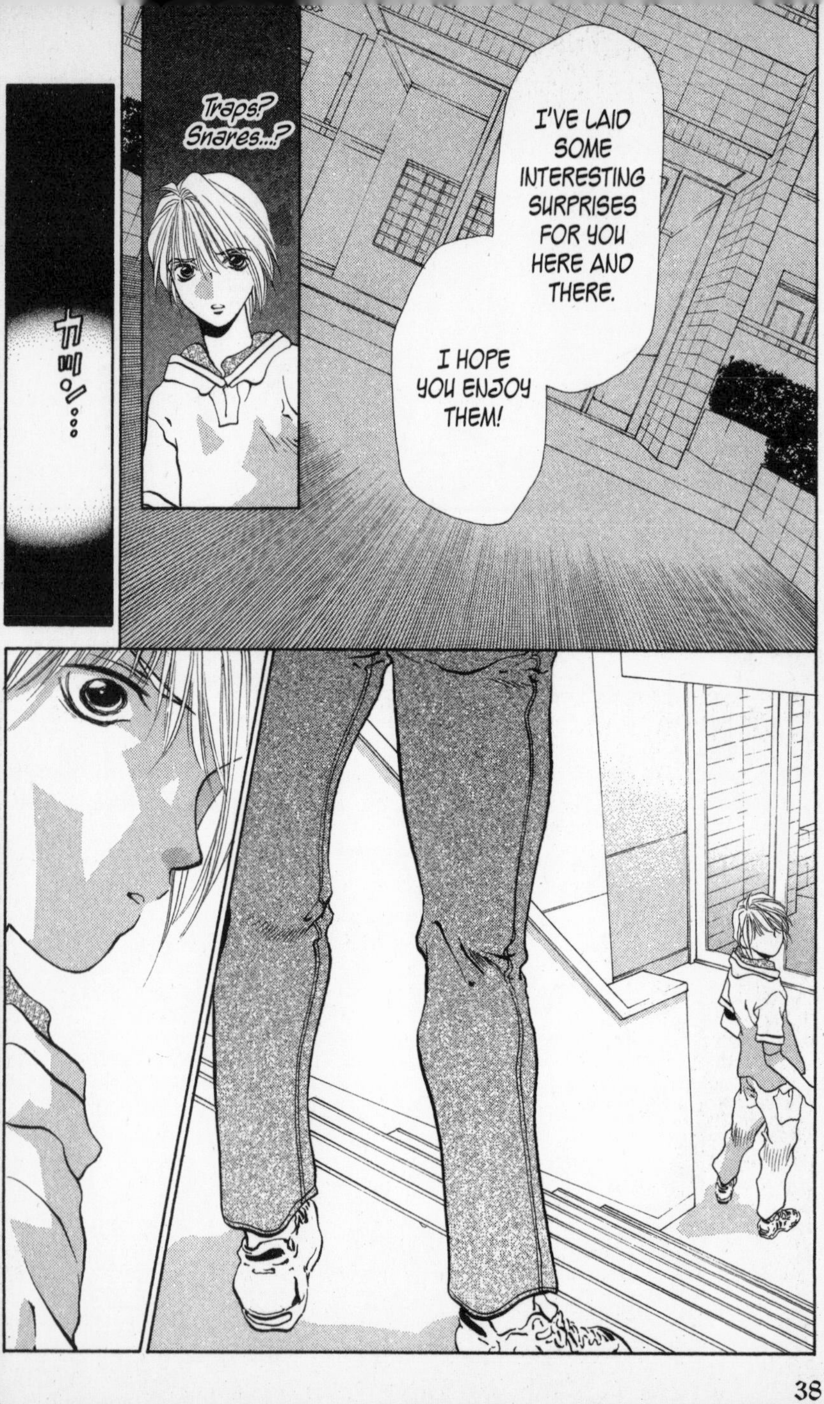
I'VE LAID SOME INTERESTING SURPRISES FOR YOU HERE AND THERE.
I HOPE YOU ENJOY THEM!
Traps? Snares...?

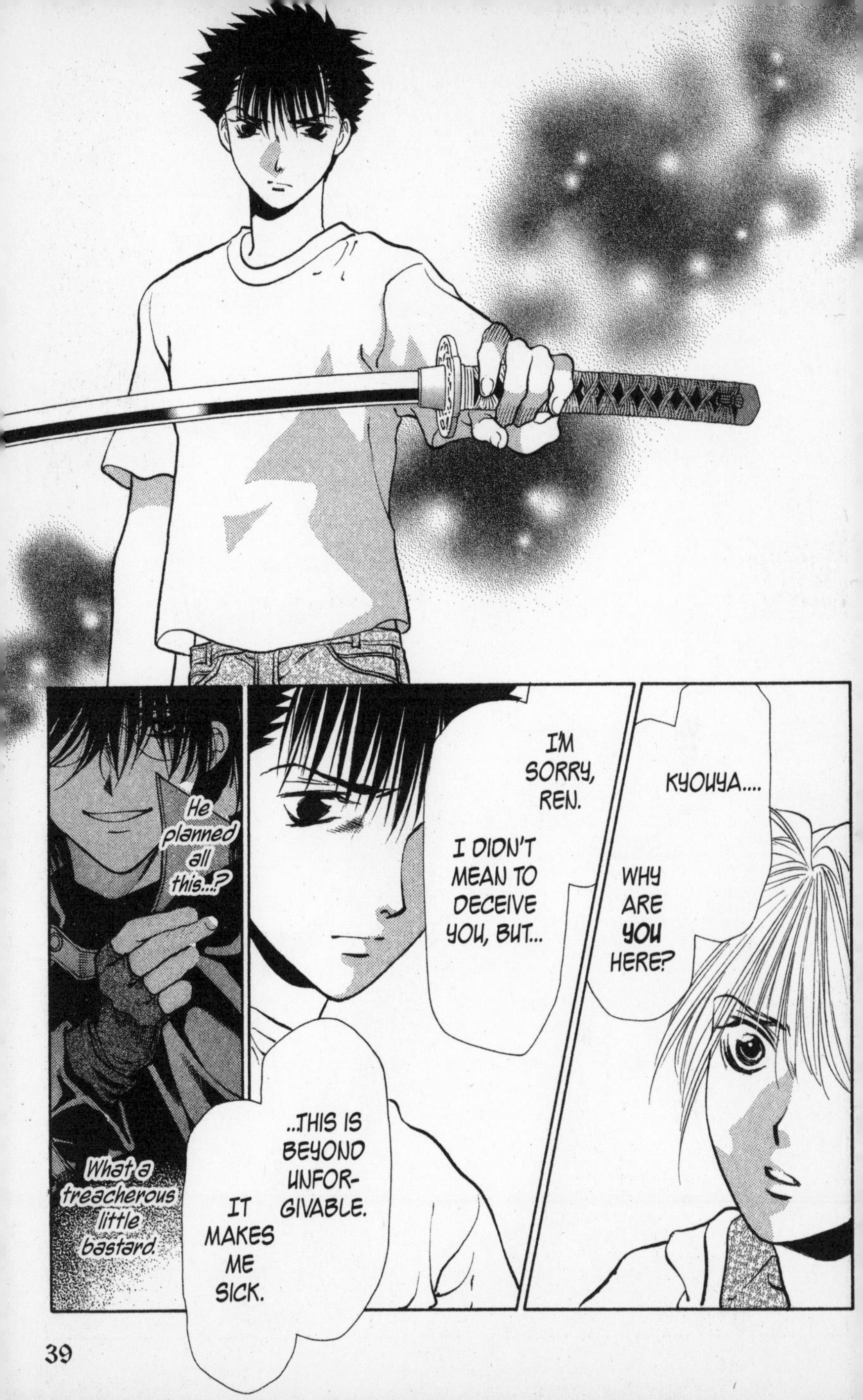
KYOUYA....
WHY ARE YOU HERE?
I'M SORRY, REN.
I DIDN'T MEAN TO DECEIVE YOU, BUT...
...THIS IS BEYOND UNFORGIVABLE.
IT MAKES ME SICK.
He planned all this...?
What a treacherous little bastard.

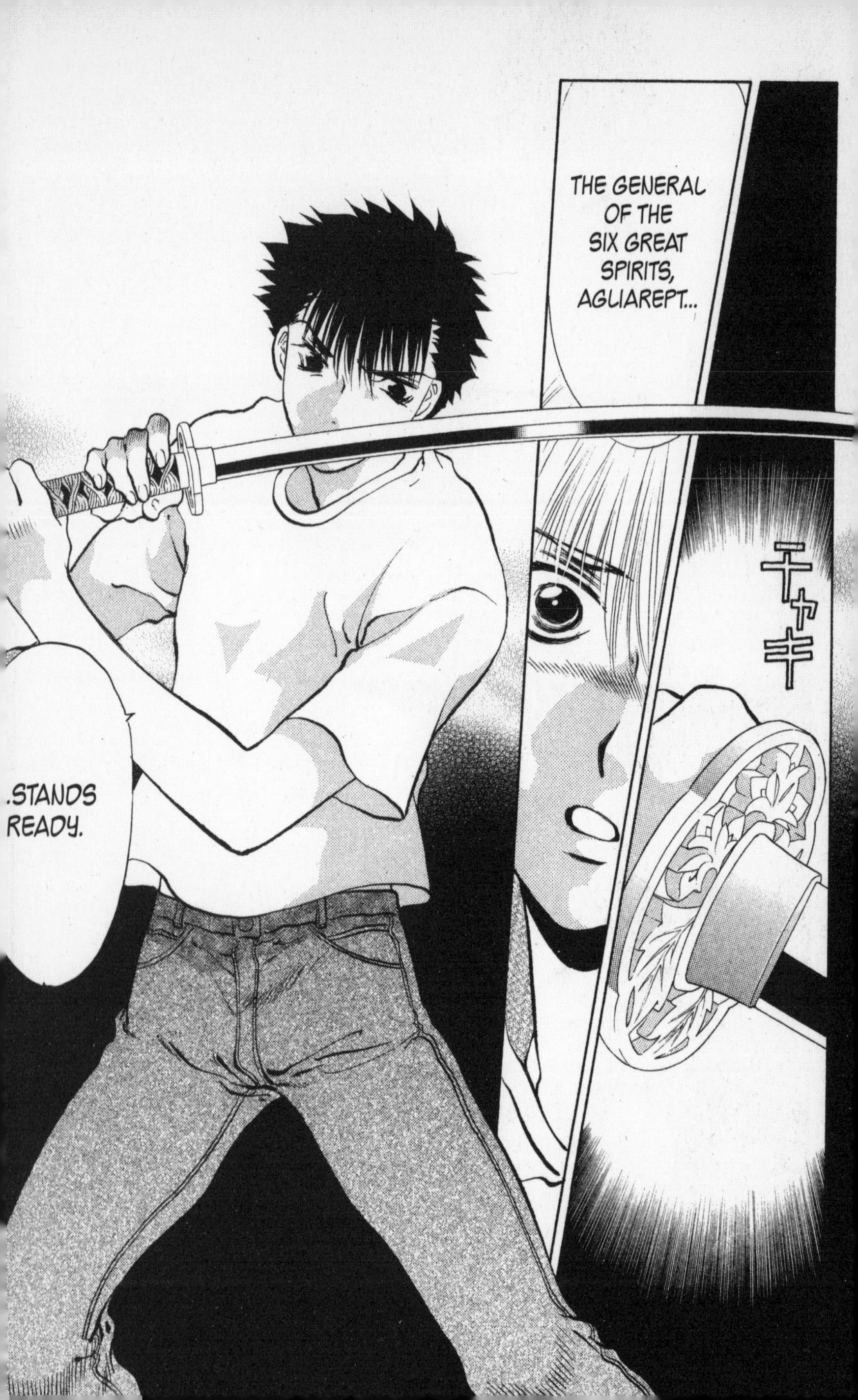
THE GENERAL OF THE SIX GREAT SPIRITS, AGUIAREPT...
チャキ
.STANDS READY.

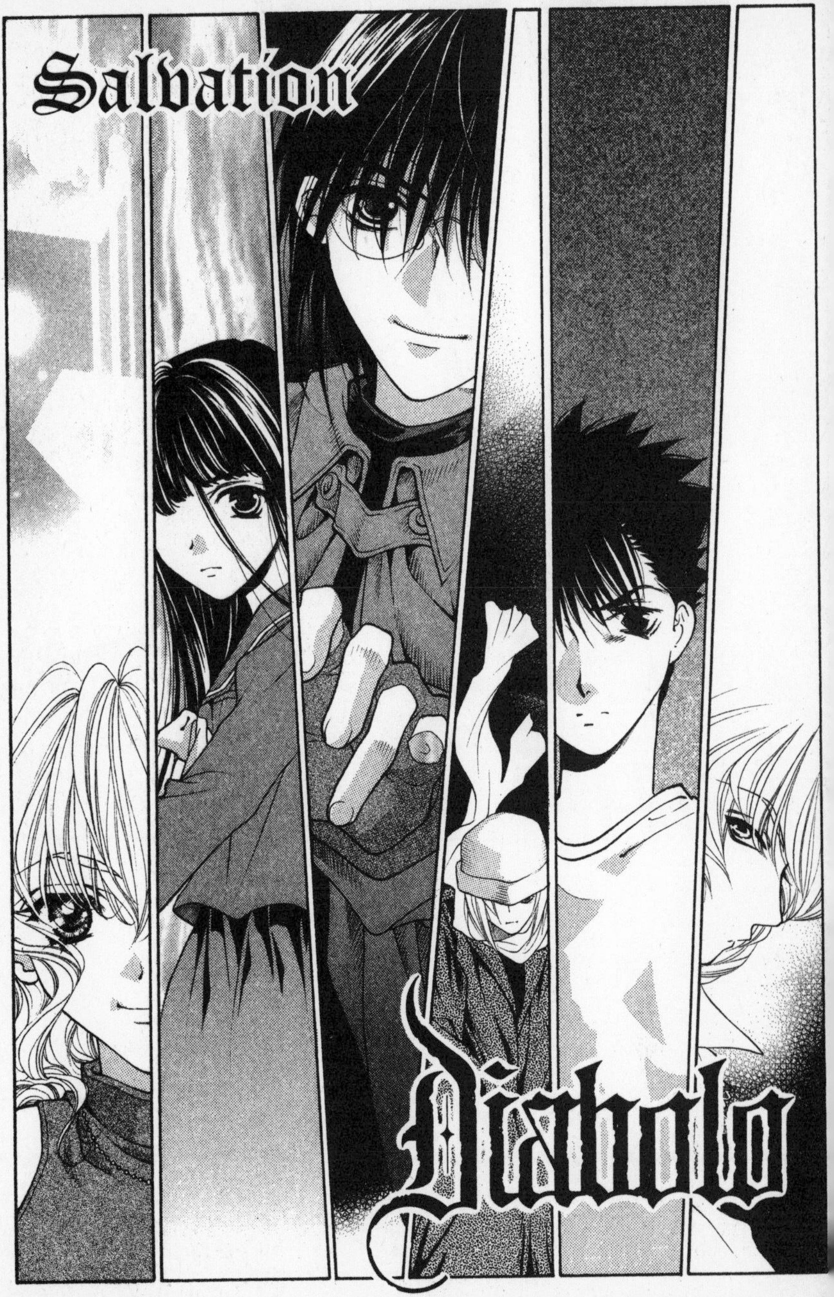
Salvation
Diabolo

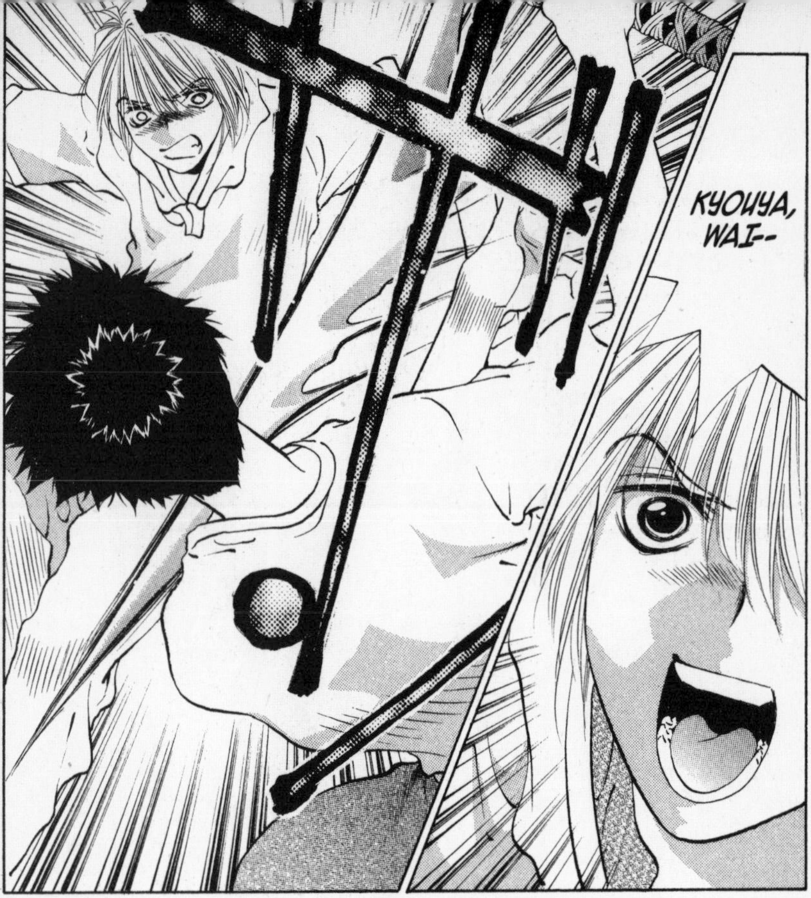
KYOUYA, WAI--

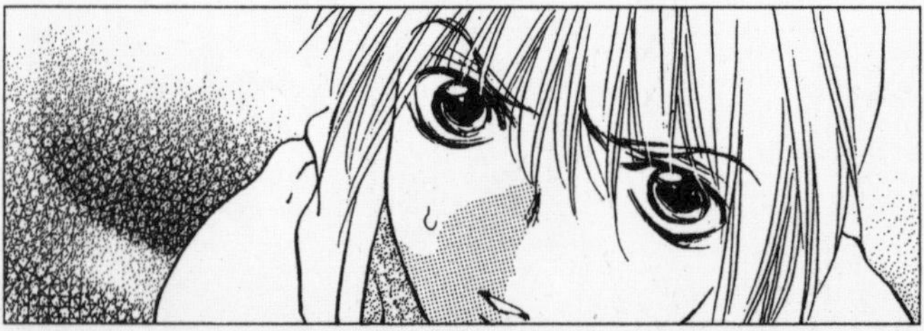

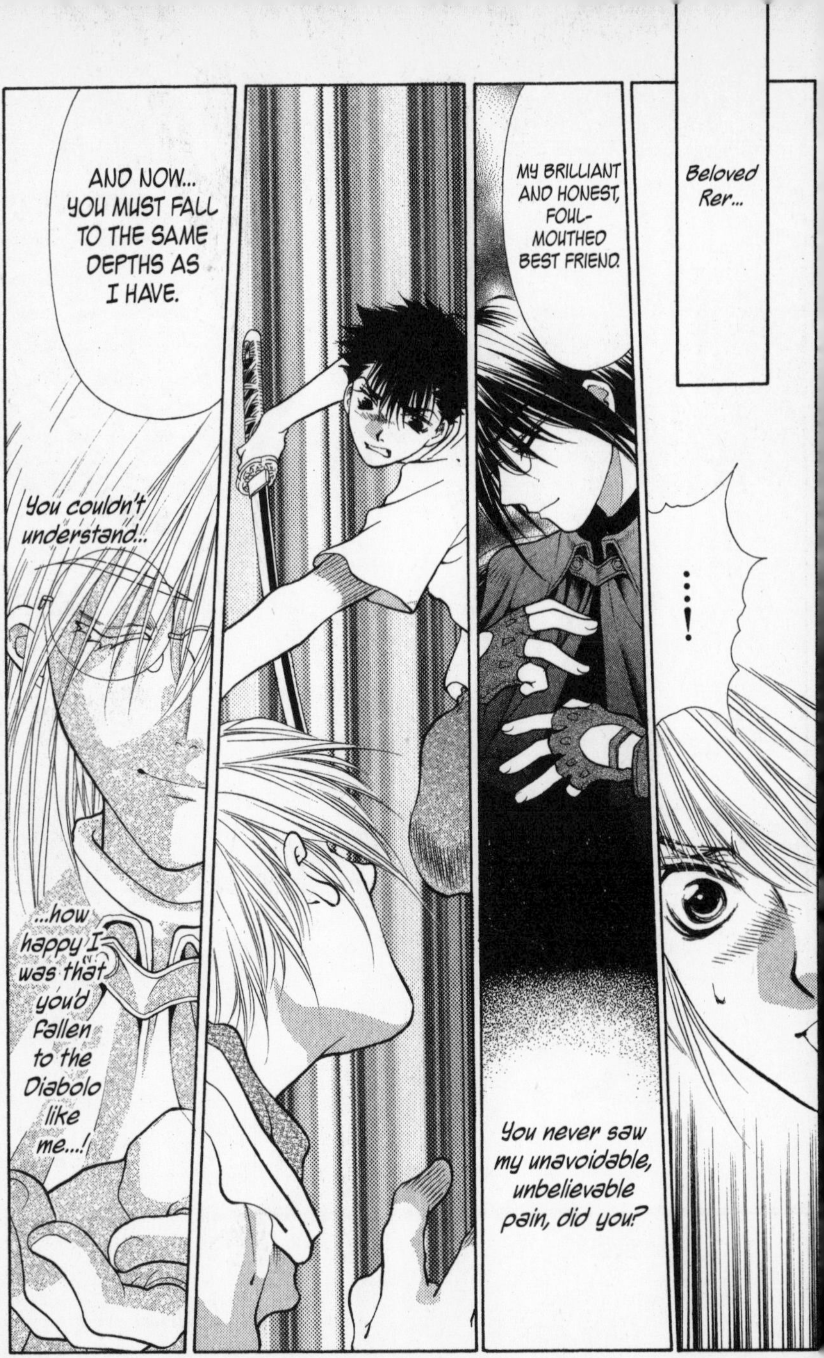
Beloved Rer...
...!
MY BRILLIANT AND HONEST, FOUL-MOUTHED BEST FRIEND.
You never saw my unavoidable, unbelievable pain, did you?
AND NOW... YOU MUST FALL TO THE SAME DEPTHS AS I HAVE.
You couldn't understand...
...how happy I was that you'd fallen to the Diabolo like me...!

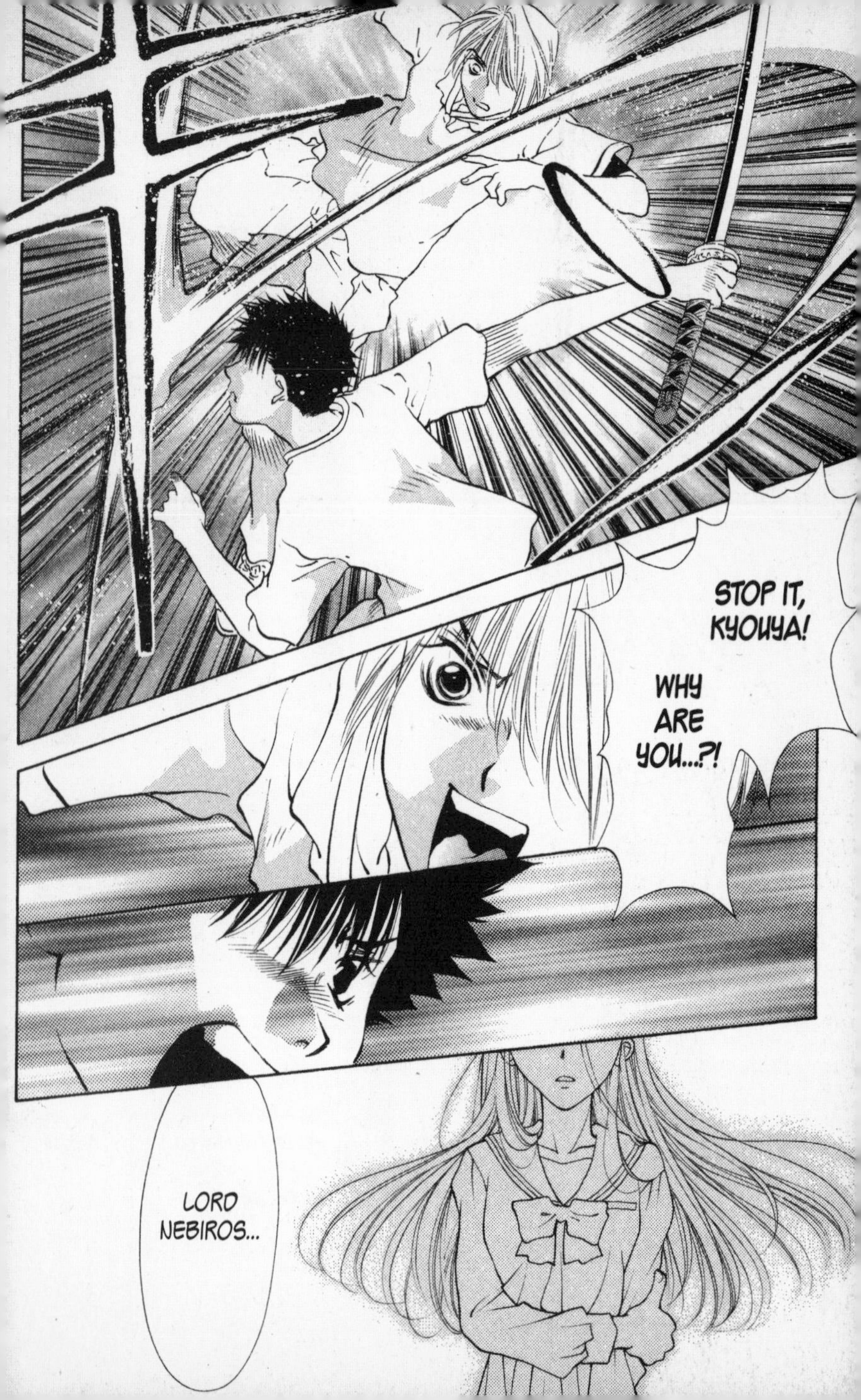
STOP IT, KYOUYA!
WHY ARE YOU...?!
LORD NEBIROS...

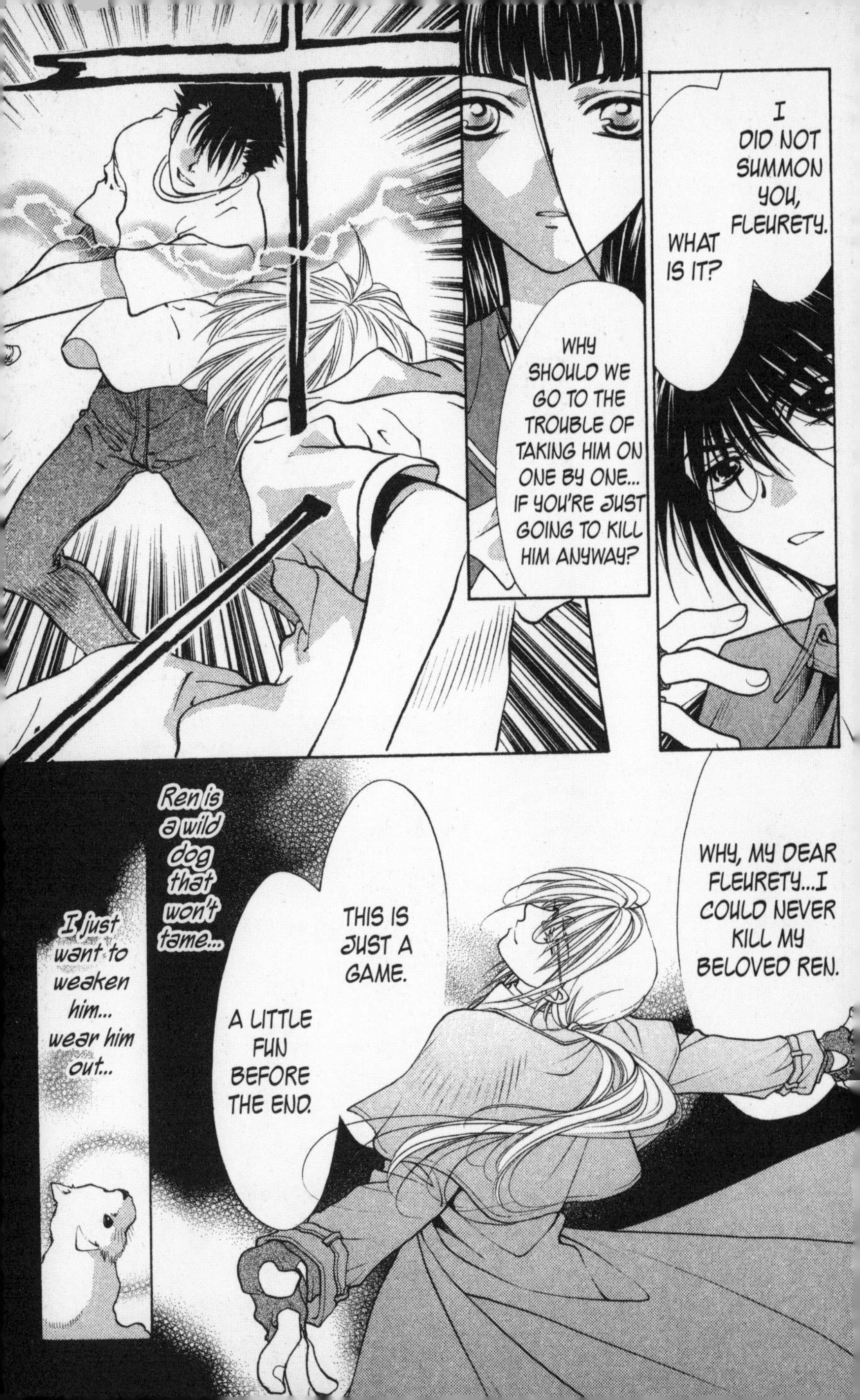
I DID NOT SUMMON YOU, FLEURETY.
WHAT IS IT?
WHY SHOULD WE GO TO THE TROUBLE OF TAKING HIM ON ONE BY ONE... IF YOU'RE JUST GOING TO KILL HIM ANYWAY?
WHY, MY DEAR FLEURETY...I COULD NEVER KILL MY BELOVED REN.
THIS IS JUST A GAME.
A LITTLE FUN BEFORE THE END.
Ren is a wild dog that won't tame...
I just want to weaken him... wear him out...

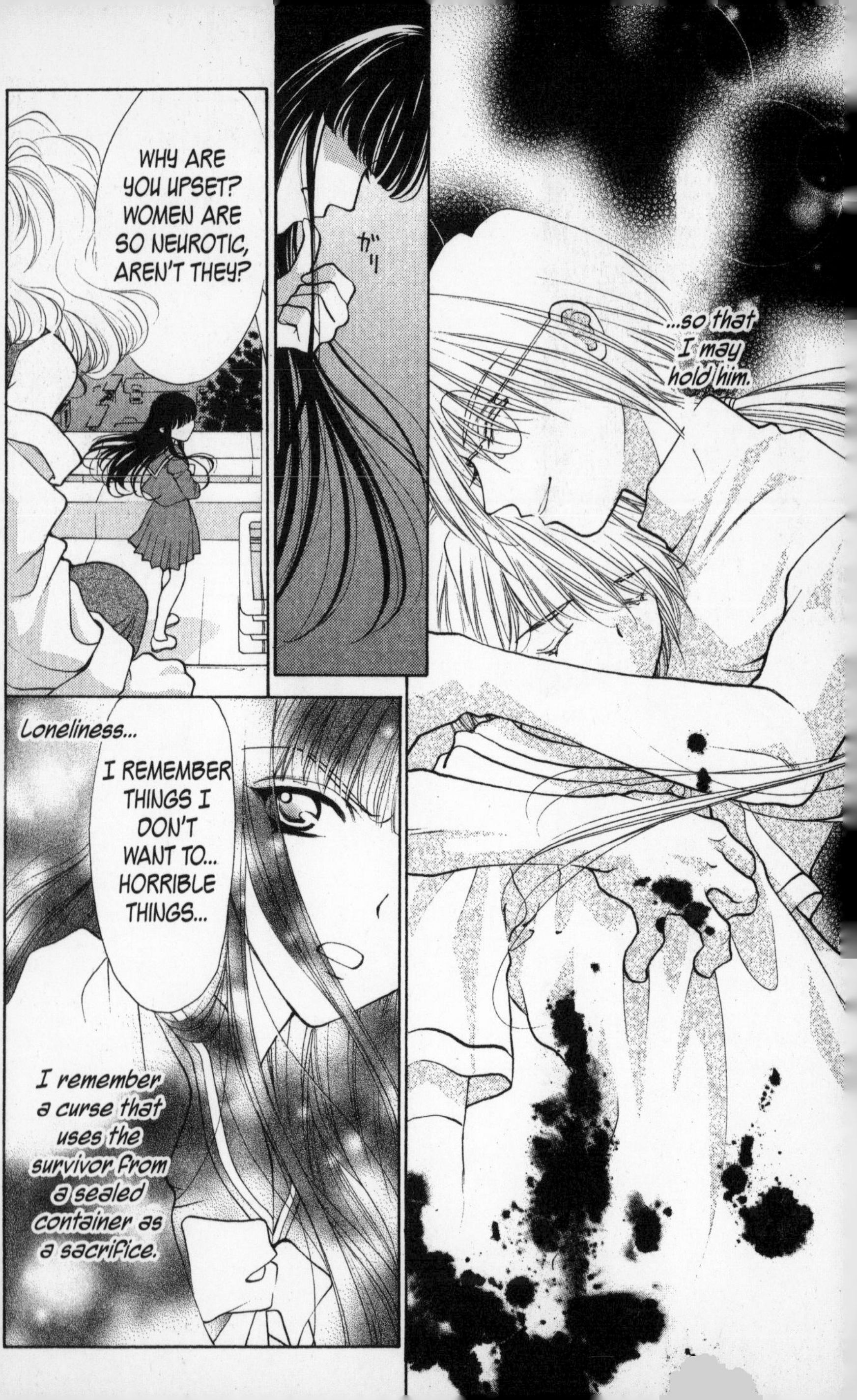
...so that I may hold him.
ガリ
WHY ARE YOU UPSET? WOMEN ARE SO NEUROTIC, AREN'T THEY?
Loneliness...
I REMEMBER THINGS I DON'T WANT TO... HORRIBLE THINGS...
I remember a curse that uses the survivor from a sealed container as a sacrifice.

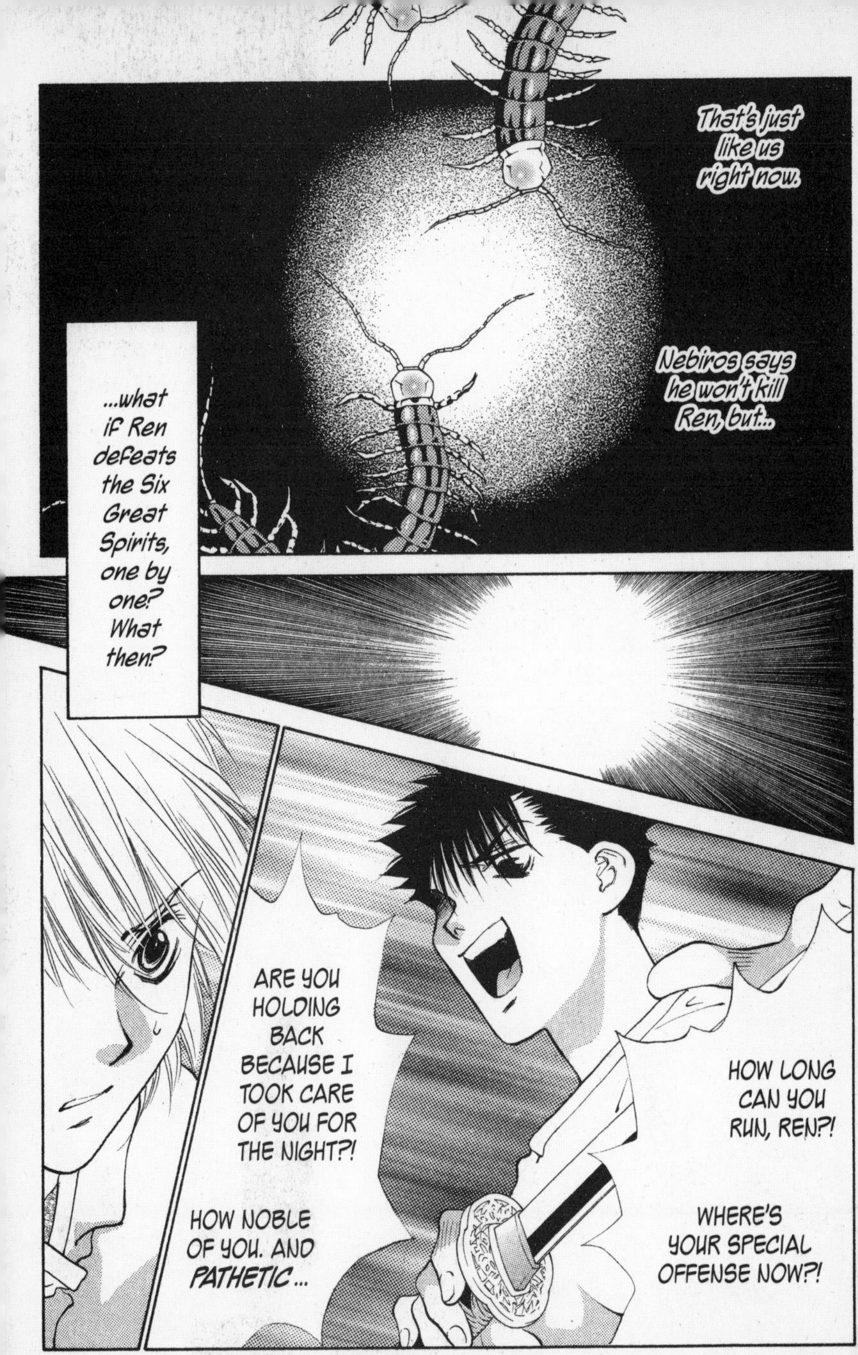
That's just like us right now.
Nebiros says he won't kill Ren, but...
...what if Ren defeats the Six Great Spirits, one by one? What then?
HOW LONG CAN YOU RUN, REN?!
WHERE'S YOUR SPECIAL OFFENSE NOW?!
ARE YOU HOLDING BACK BECAUSE I TOOK CARE OF YOU FOR THE NIGHT?!
HOW NOBLE OF YOU. AND *PATHETIC*...

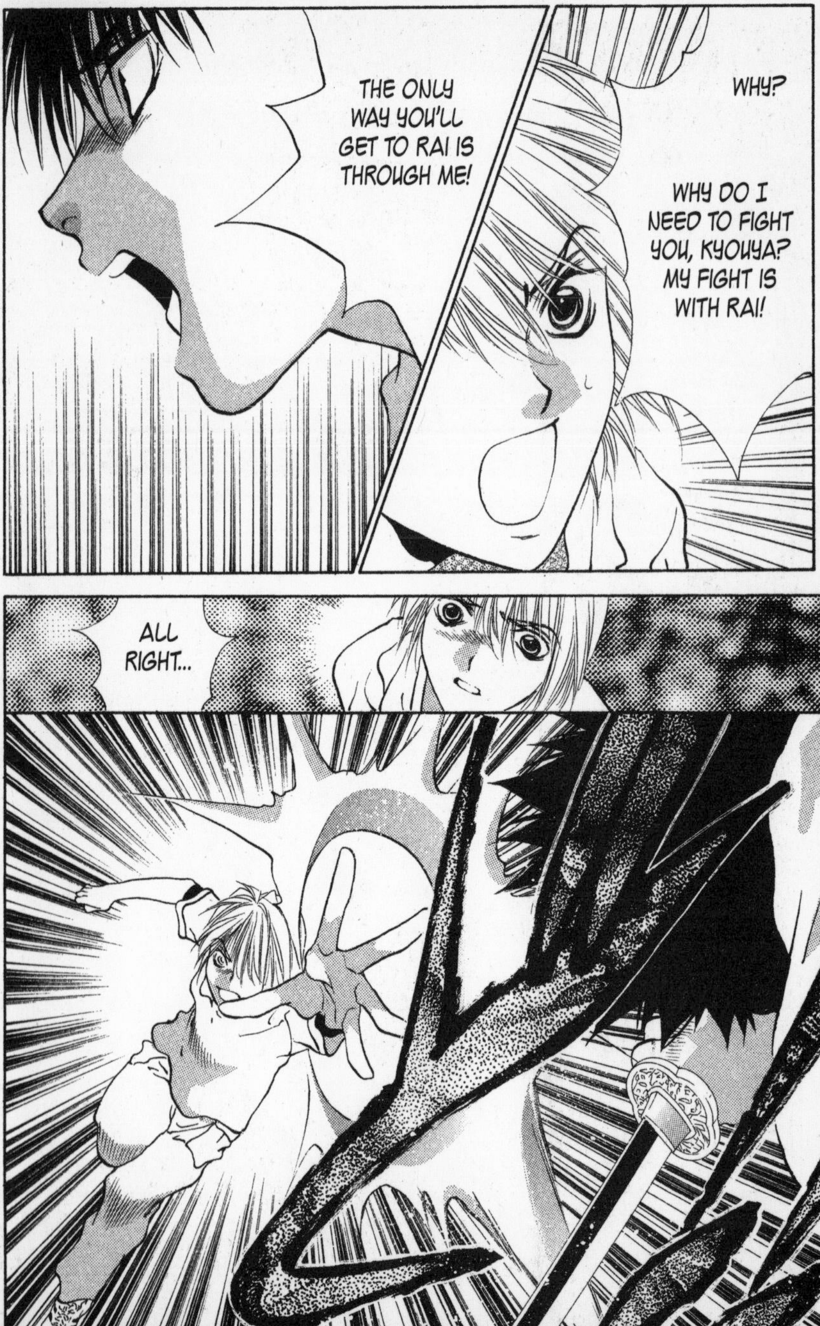
WHY?
WHY DO I NEED TO FIGHT YOU, KYOUYA? MY FIGHT IS WITH RAI!
THE ONLY WAY YOU'LL GET TO RAI IS THROUGH ME!
ALL RIGHT...

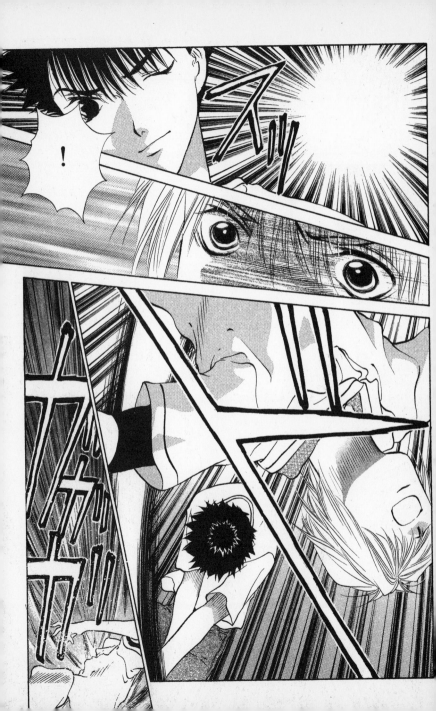

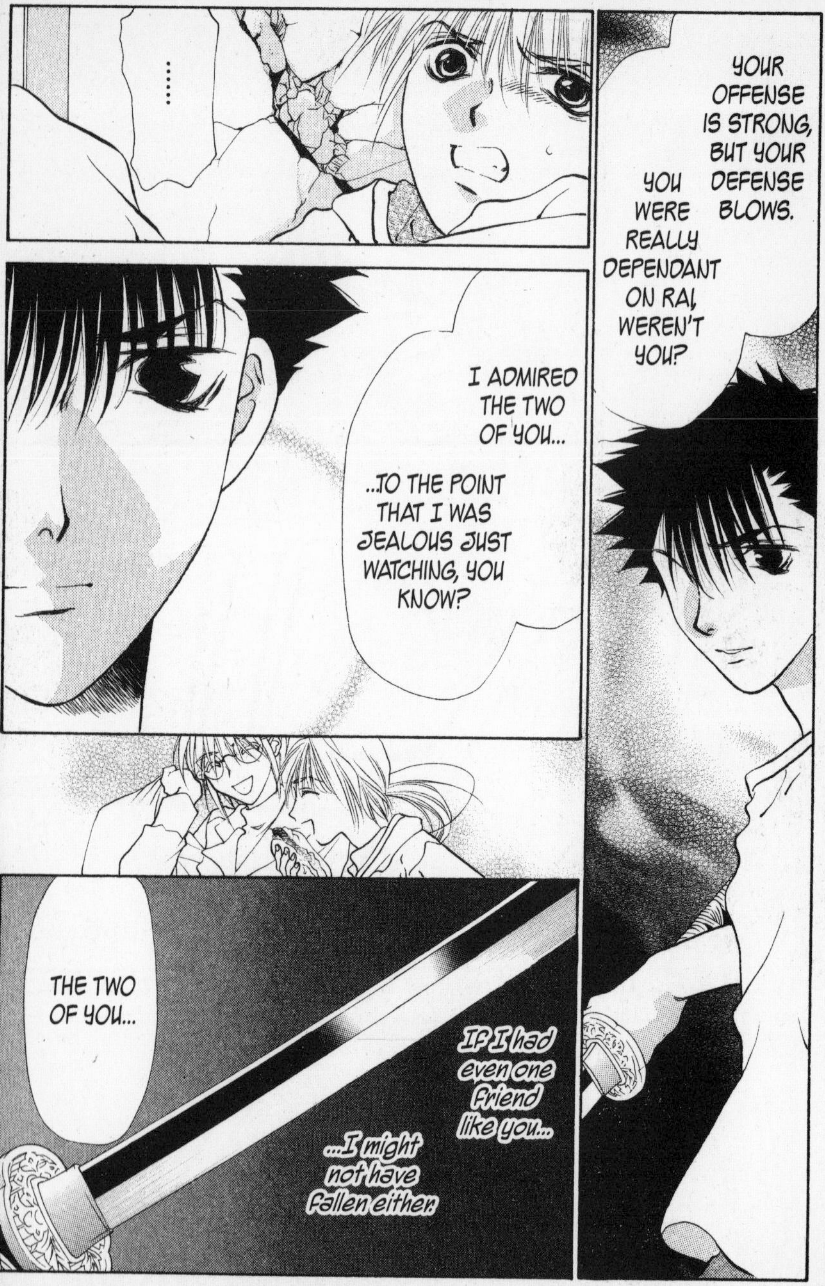
YOUR OFFENSE IS STRONG, BUT YOUR DEFENSE BLOWS.
YOU WERE REALLY DEPENDANT ON RAI, WEREN'T YOU?
......
I ADMIRED THE TWO OF YOU...
...TO THE POINT THAT I WAS JEALOUS JUST WATCHING, YOU KNOW?
THE TWO OF YOU...
If I had even one friend like you...
...I might not have fallen either.

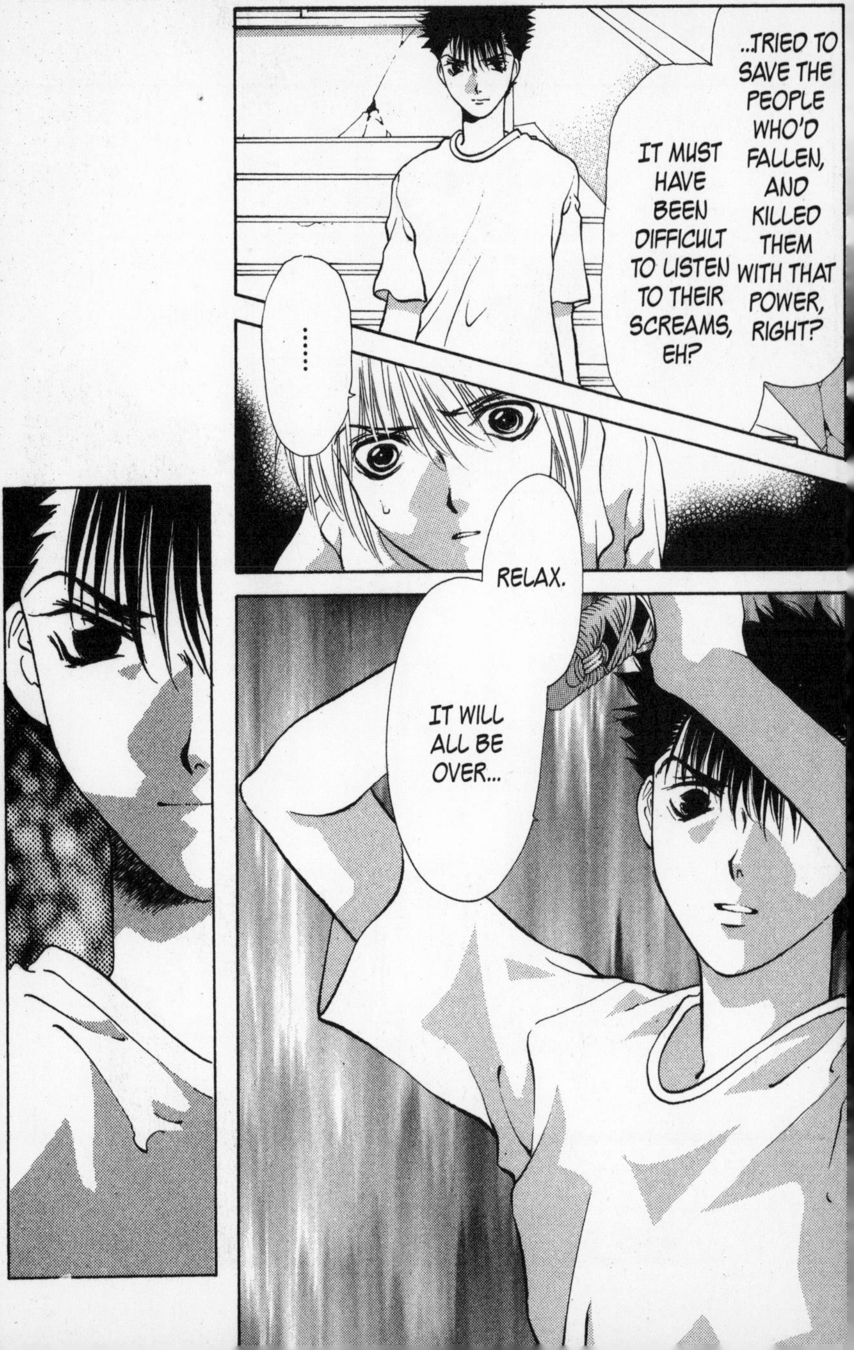
...TRIED TO SAVE THE PEOPLE WHO'D FALLEN, AND KILLED THEM WITH THAT POWER, RIGHT?
IT MUST HAVE BEEN DIFFICULT TO LISTEN TO THEIR SCREAMS, EH?
......
RELAX.
IT WILL ALL BE OVER...

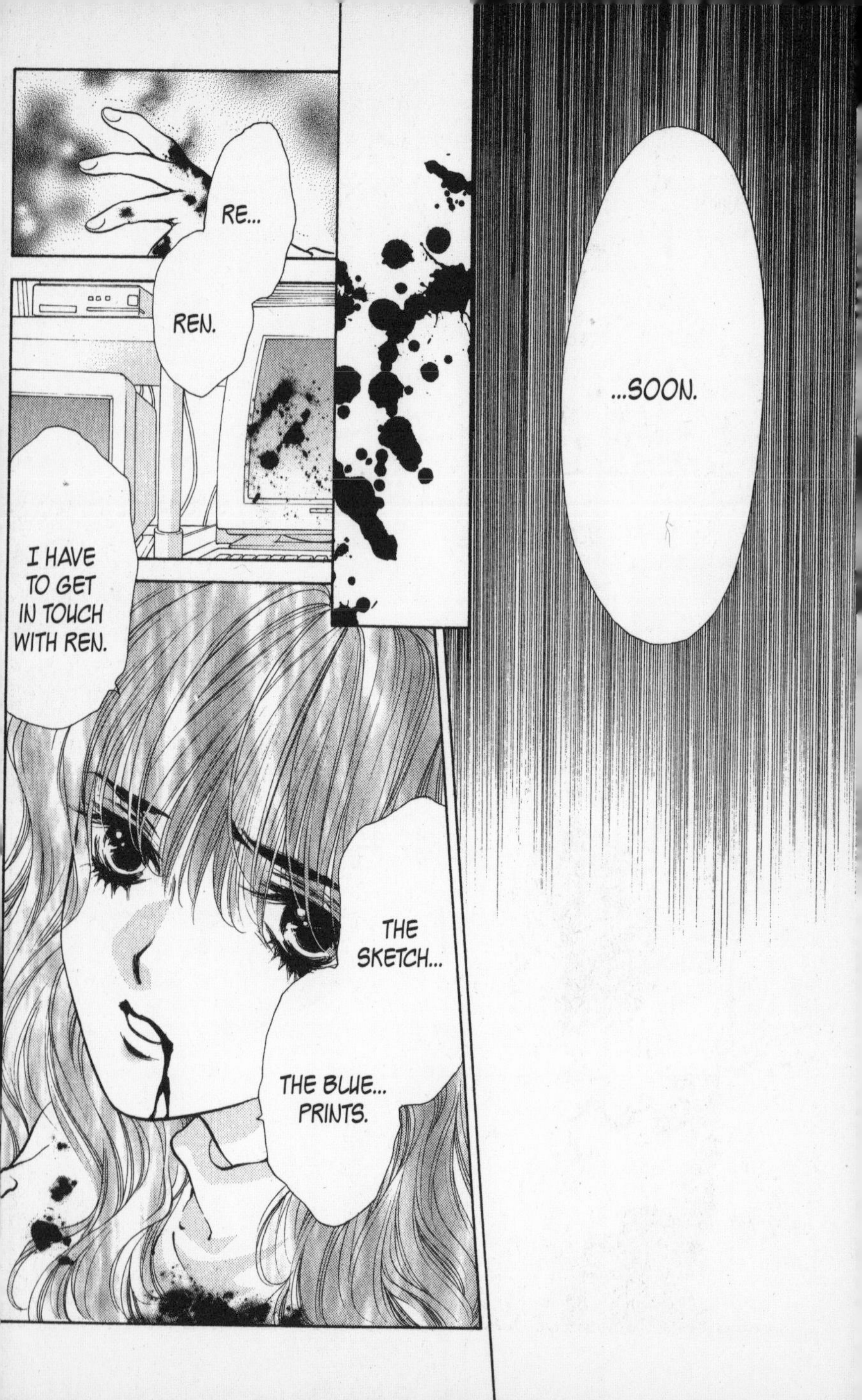
...SOON.
RE...
REN.
I HAVE TO GET IN TOUCH WITH REN.
THE SKETCH...
THE BLUE... PRINTS.

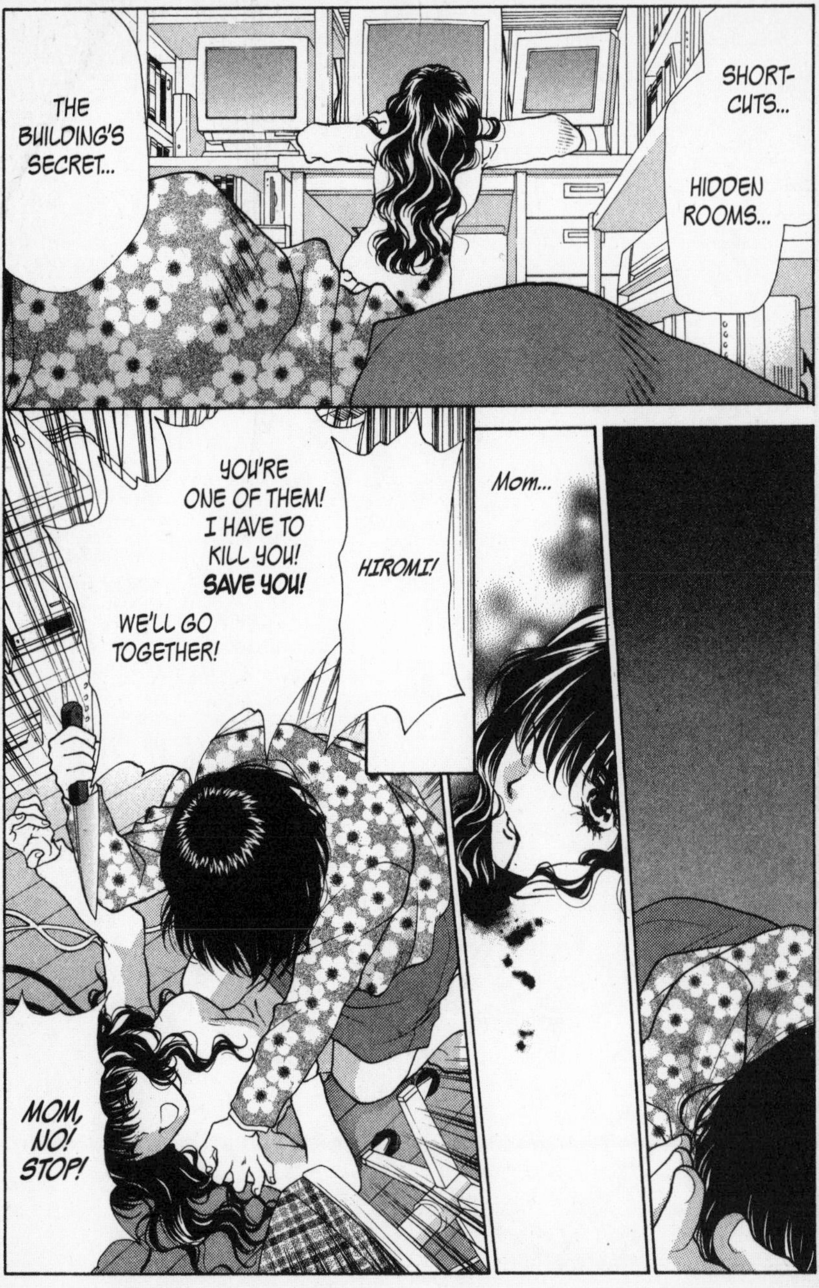
SHORT-CUTS...
HIDDEN ROOMS...
THE BUILDING'S SECRET...
Mom...
HIROMI!
YOU'RE ONE OF THEM! I HAVE TO KILL YOU! SAVE YOU!
WE'LL GO TOGETHER!
MOM, NO! STOP!

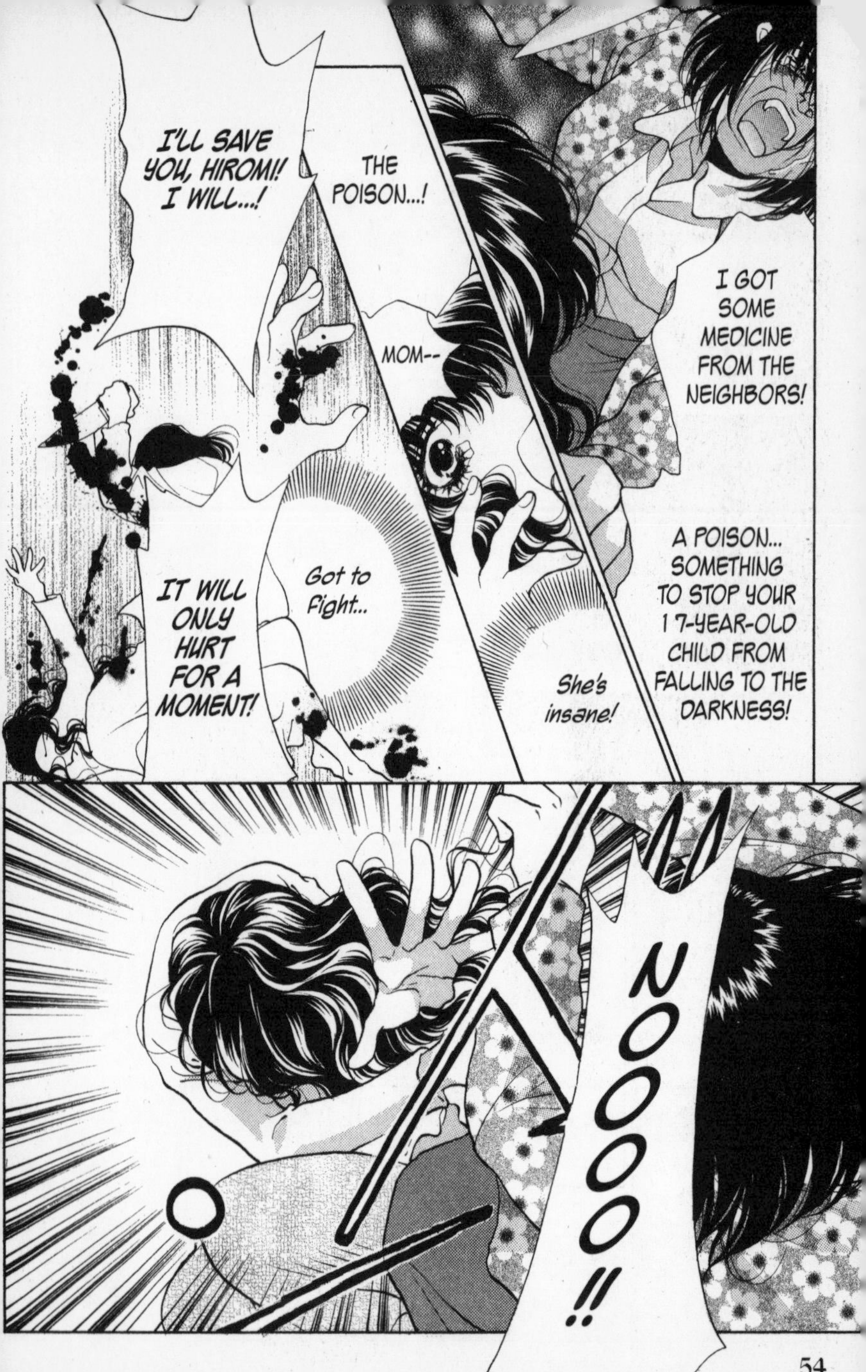
I GOT SOME MEDICINE FROM THE NEIGHBORS!
A POISON... SOMETHING TO STOP YOUR 17-YEAR-OLD CHILD FROM FALLING TO THE DARKNESS!
THE POISON...!
MOM--
She's insane!
Got to fight...
I'LL SAVE YOU, HIROMI! I WILL...!
IT WILL ONLY HURT FOR A MOMENT!
NOOOOO!!

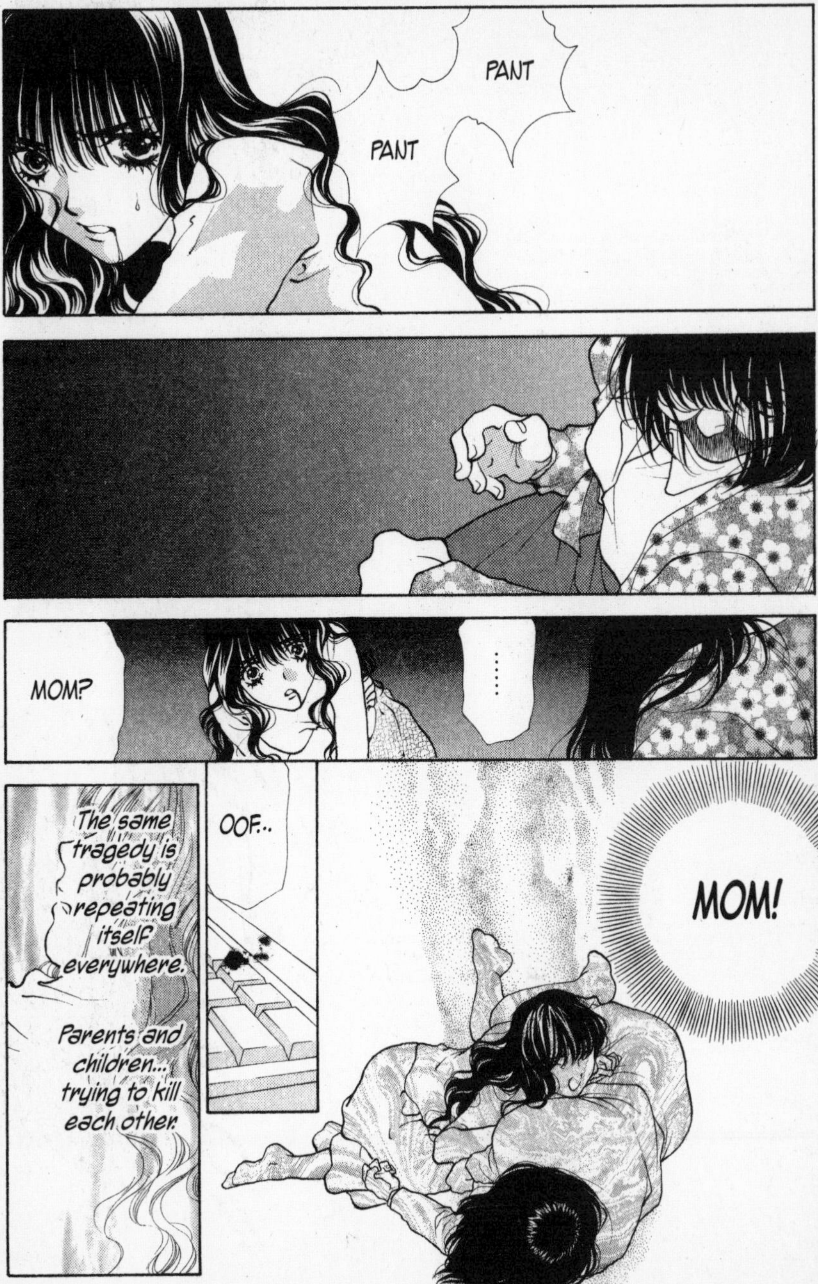
PANT
PANT
......
MOM?
MOM!
OOF...
The same tragedy is probably repeating itself everywhere.
Parents and children... trying to kill each other.

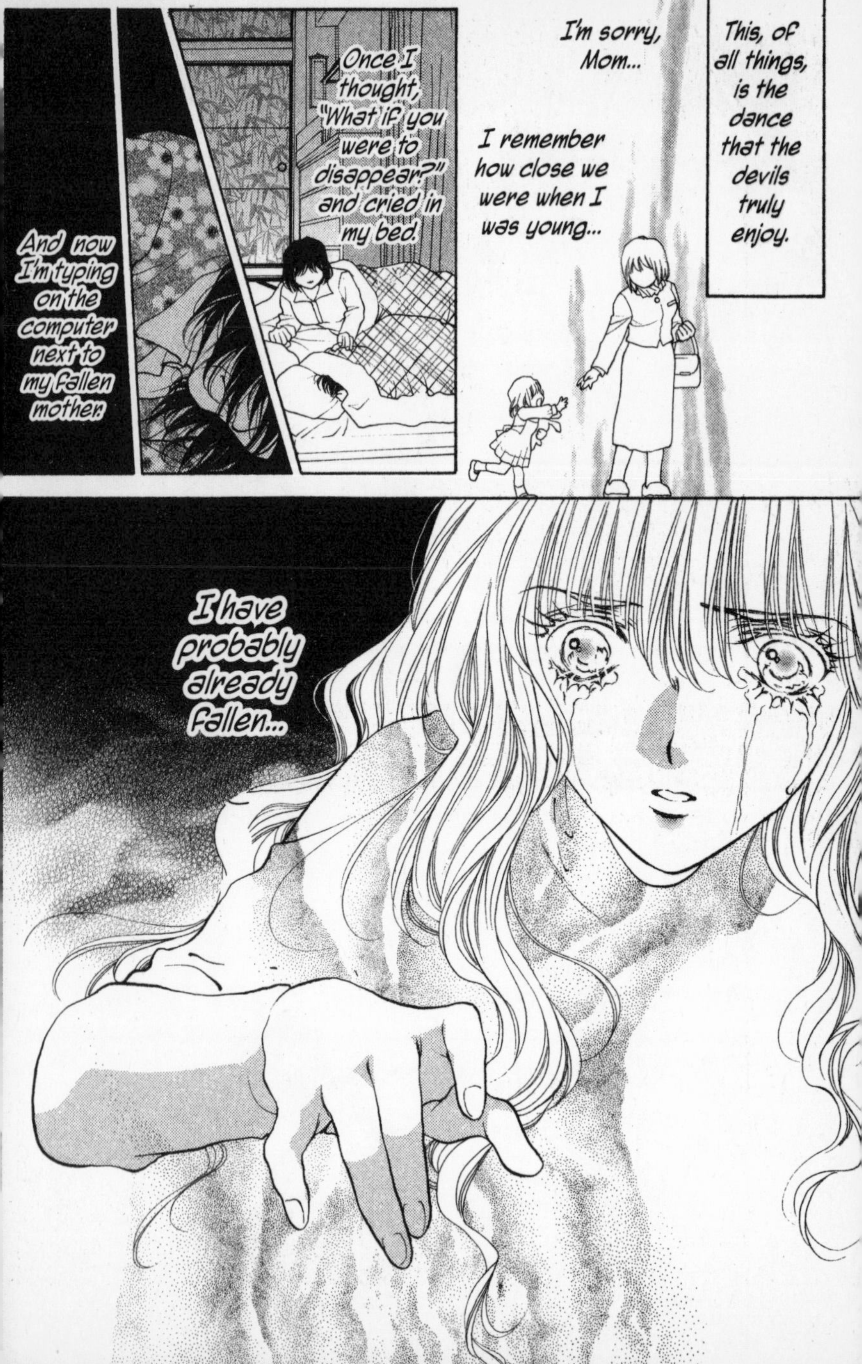
This, of all things, is the dance that the devils truly enjoy.
I'm sorry, Mom...
I remember how close we were when I was young...
Once I thought, "What if you were to disappear?" and cried in my bed.
And now I'm typing on the computer next to my fallen mother.
I have probably already fallen...

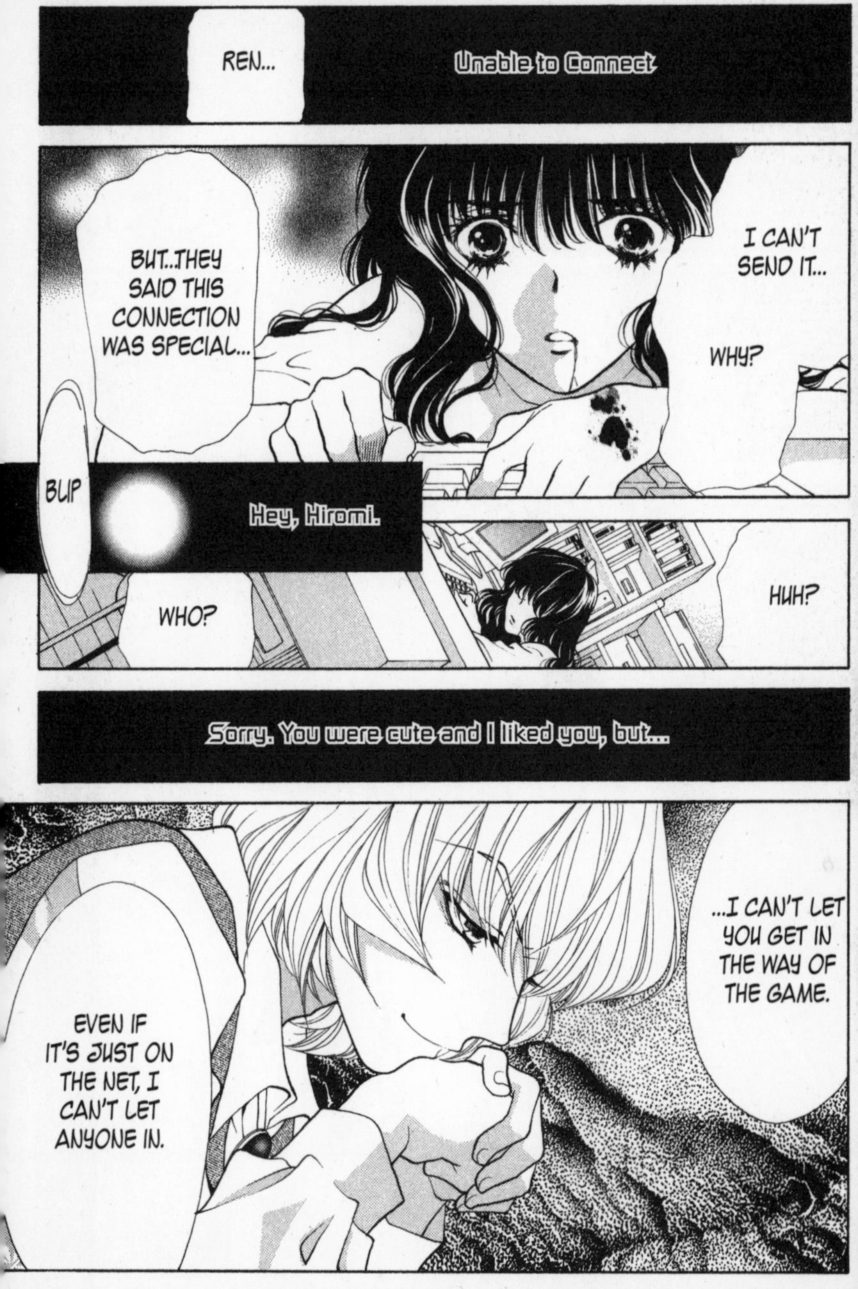
Unable to Connect
REN...
I CAN'T SEND IT...
WHY?
BUT...THEY SAID THIS CONNECTION WAS SPECIAL...
HUH?
Hey, Hiromi.
BLIP
WHO?
Sorry. You were cute and I liked you, but...
...I CAN'T LET YOU GET IN THE WAY OF THE GAME.
EVEN IF IT'S JUST ON THE NET, I CAN'T LET ANYONE IN.

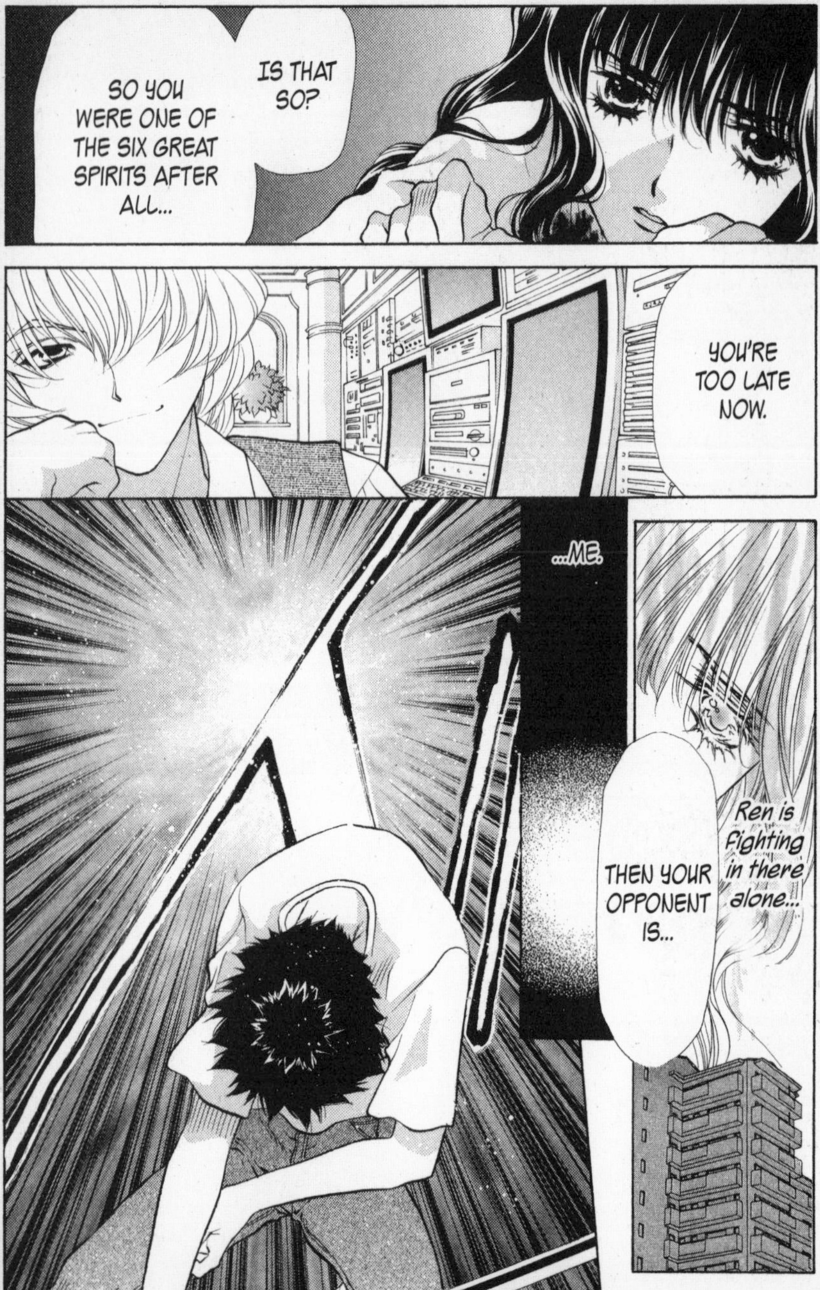
IS THAT SO?
SO YOU WERE ONE OF THE SIX GREAT SPIRITS AFTER ALL...
YOU'RE TOO LATE NOW.
Ren is fighting in there alone...
THEN YOUR OPPONENT IS...
...ME.

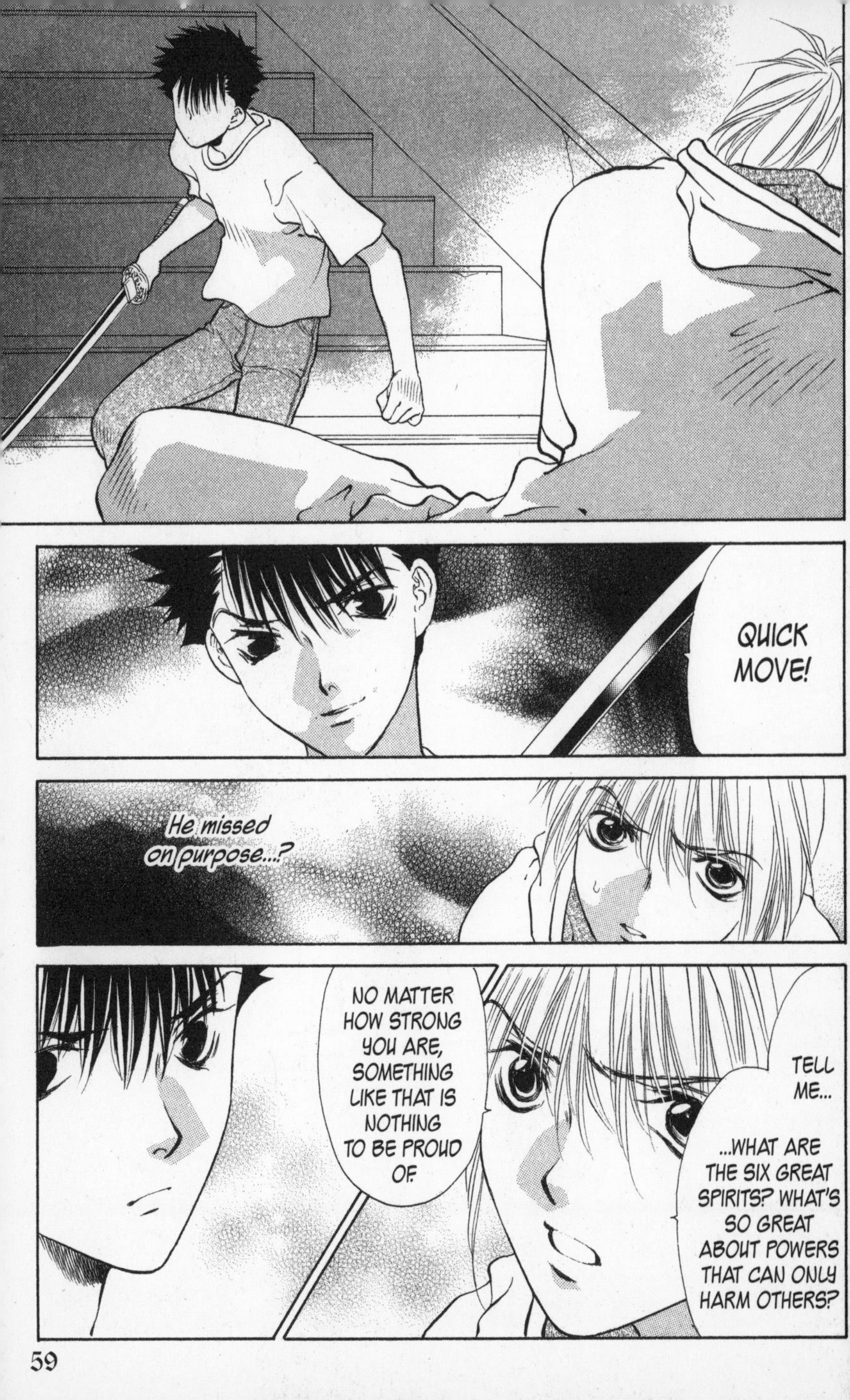
QUICK MOVE!
He missed on purpose...?
TELL ME...
...WHAT ARE THE SIX GREAT SPIRITS? WHAT'S SO GREAT ABOUT POWERS THAT CAN ONLY HARM OTHERS?
NO MATTER HOW STRONG YOU ARE, SOMETHING LIKE THAT IS NOTHING TO BE PROUD OF.

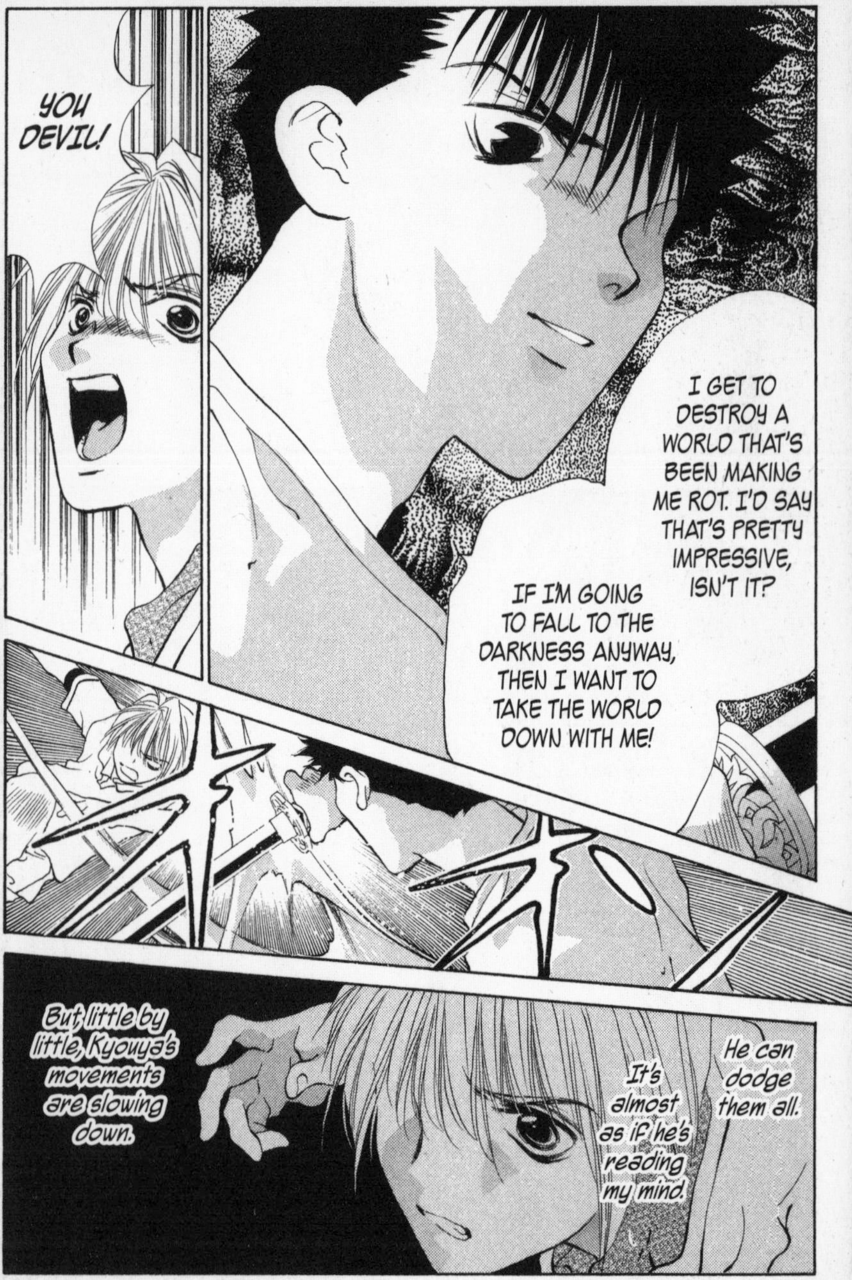
I GET TO DESTROY A WORLD THAT'S BEEN MAKING ME ROT. I'D SAY THAT'S PRETTY IMPRESSIVE, ISN'T IT?
IF I'M GOING TO FALL TO THE DARKNESS ANYWAY, THEN I WANT TO TAKE THE WORLD DOWN WITH ME!
YOU DEVIL!
He can dodge them all.
It's almost as if he's reading my mind.
But little by little, Kyouya's movements are slowing down.

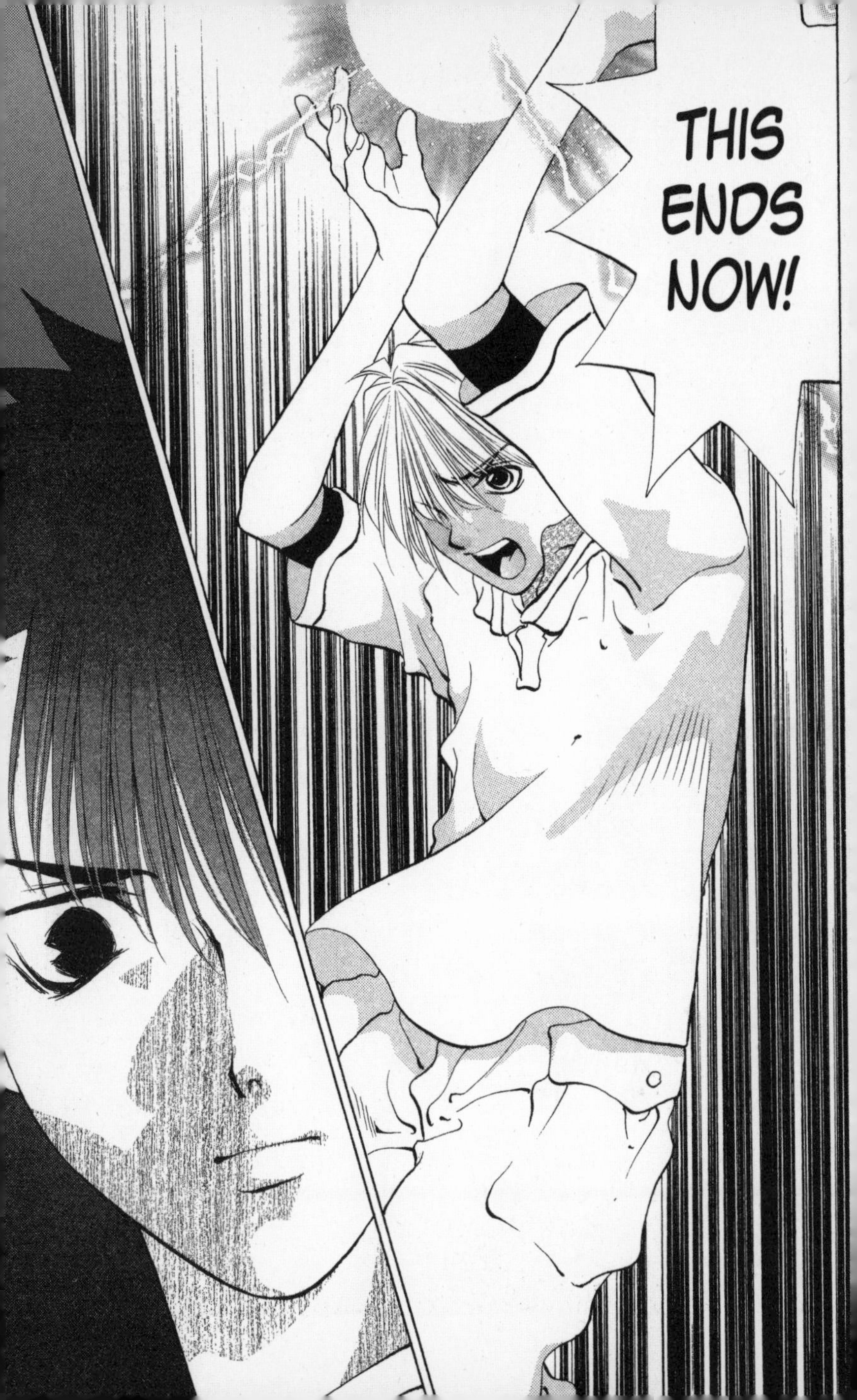
THIS ENDS NOW!

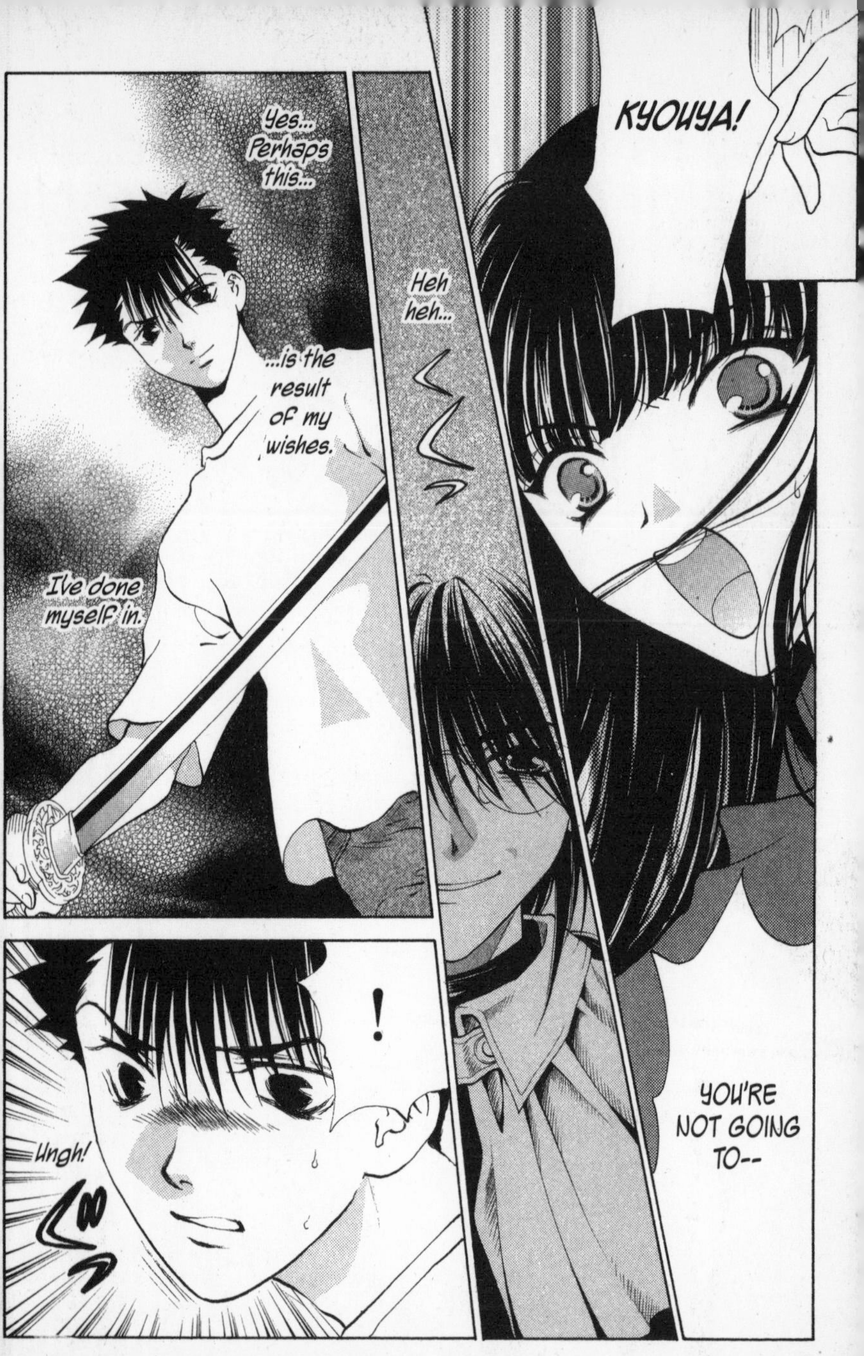
KYOUYA!
YOU'RE NOT GOING TO--
Heh heh...
Yes... Perhaps this...
...is the result of my wishes.
I've done myself in.
!
Ungh!

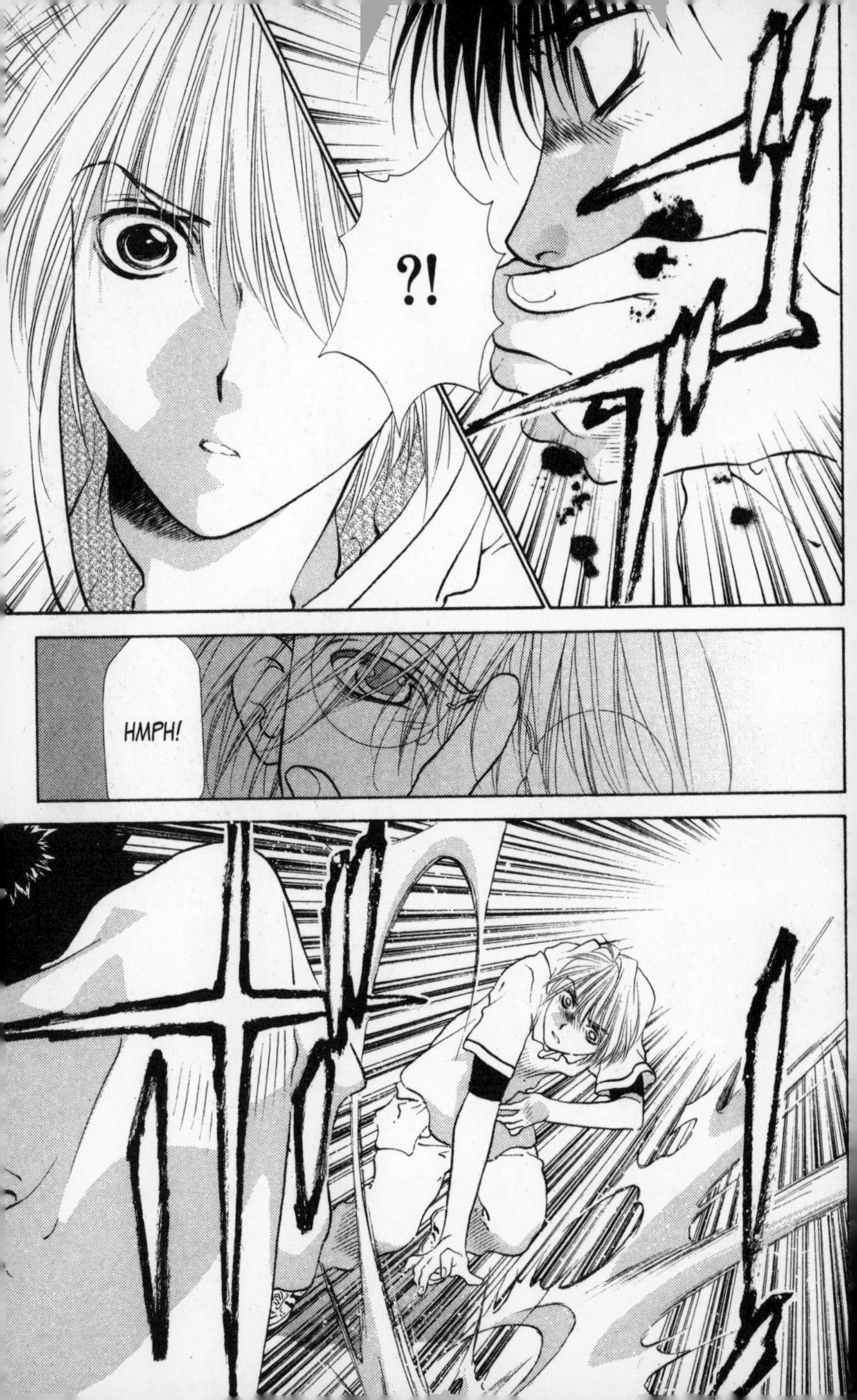
?!
HMPH!

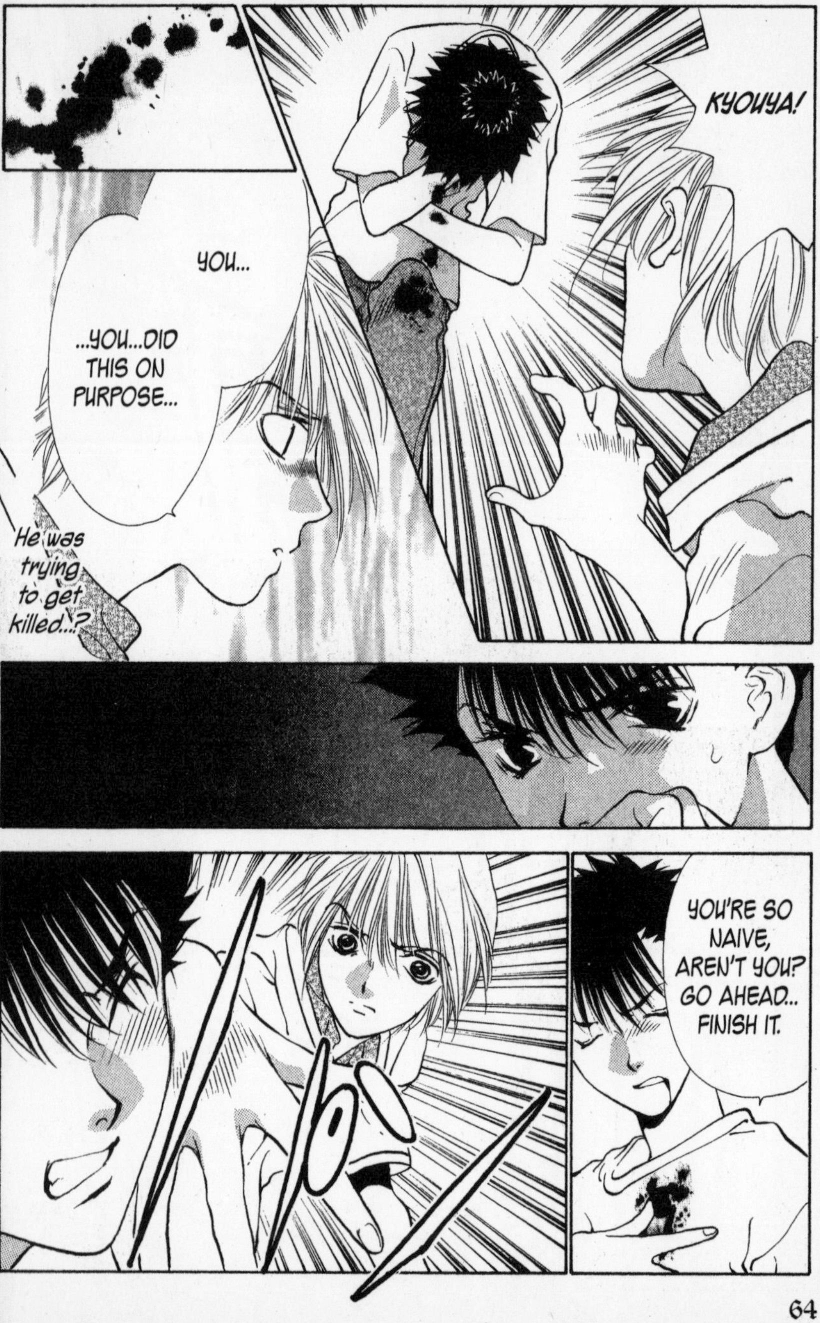
KYOUYA!
YOU...
...YOU...DID THIS ON PURPOSE...
He was trying to get killed...?
YOU'RE SO NAIVE, AREN'T YOU? GO AHEAD... FINISH IT.

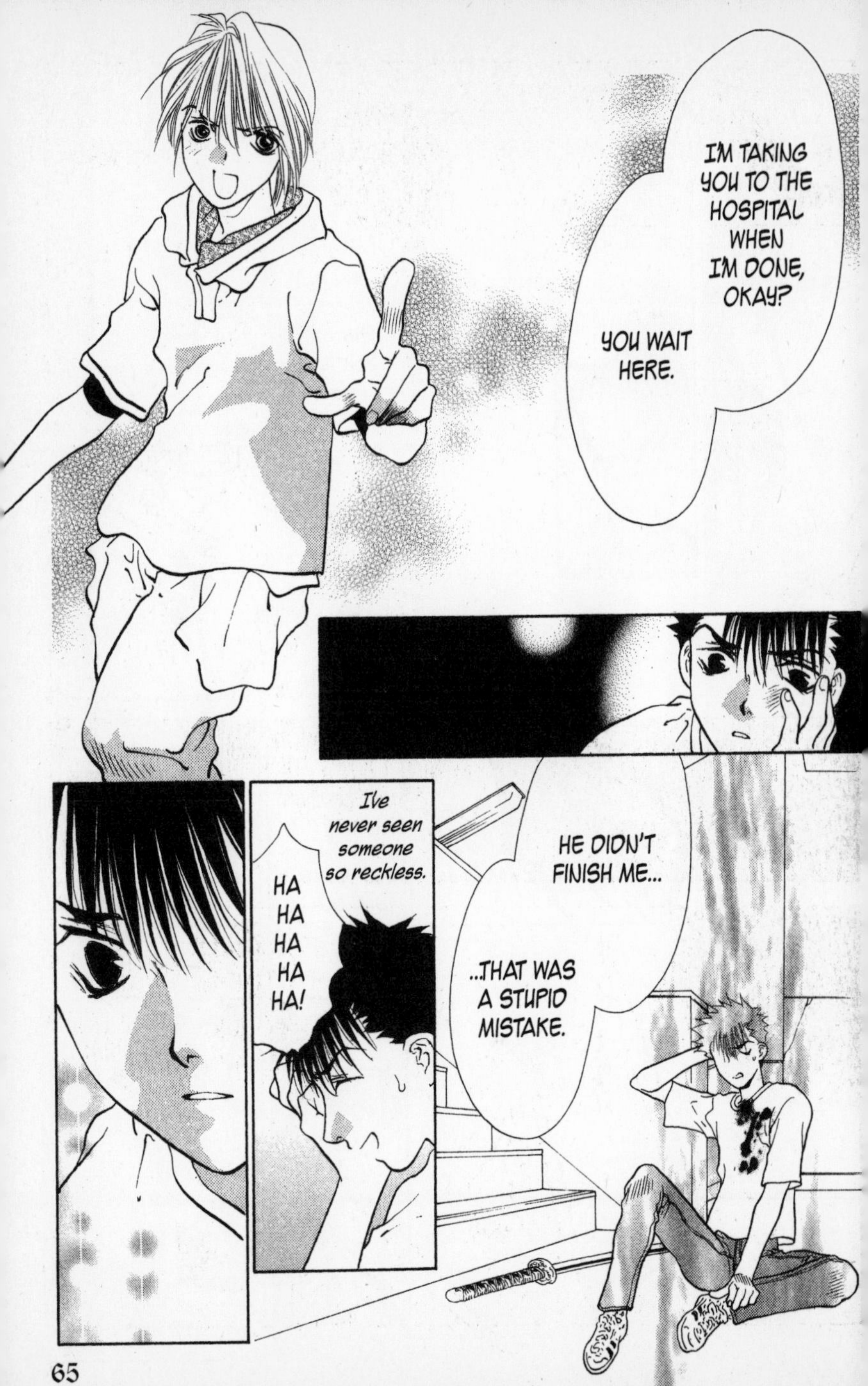
I'M TAKING YOU TO THE HOSPITAL WHEN I'M DONE, OKAY?
YOU WAIT HERE.
HE DIDN'T FINISH ME...
...THAT WAS A STUPID MISTAKE.
I've never seen someone so reckless.
HA HA HA HA HA!

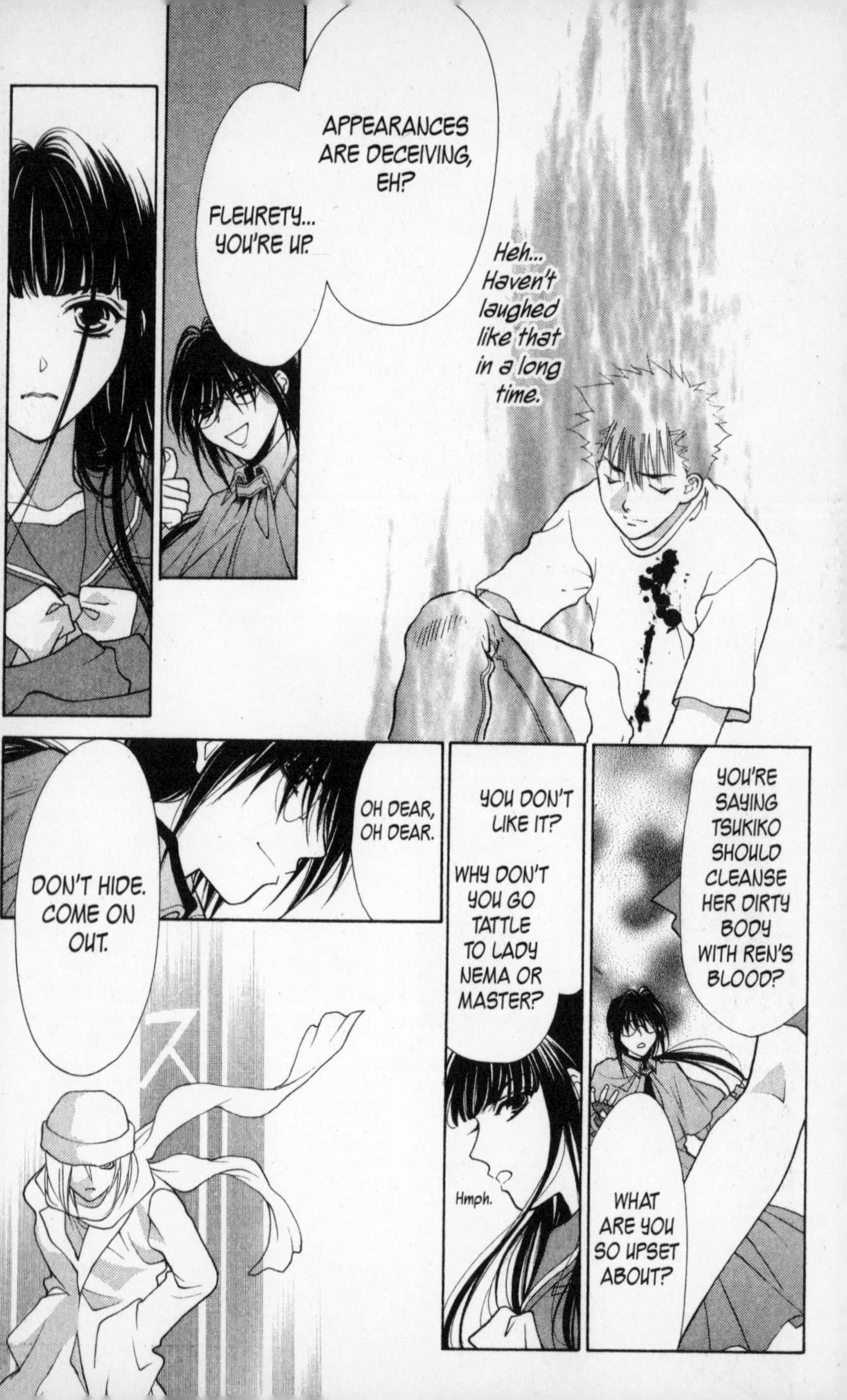
Heh... Haven't laughed like that in a long time.
APPEARANCES ARE DECEIVING, EH?
FLEURETY... YOU'RE UP.
YOU'RE SAYING TSUKIKO SHOULD CLEANSE HER DIRTY BODY WITH REN'S BLOOD?
WHAT ARE YOU SO UPSET ABOUT?
YOU DON'T LIKE IT?
WHY DON'T YOU GO TATTLE TO LADY NEMA OR MASTER?
Hmph.
OH DEAR, OH DEAR.
DON'T HIDE. COME ON OUT.

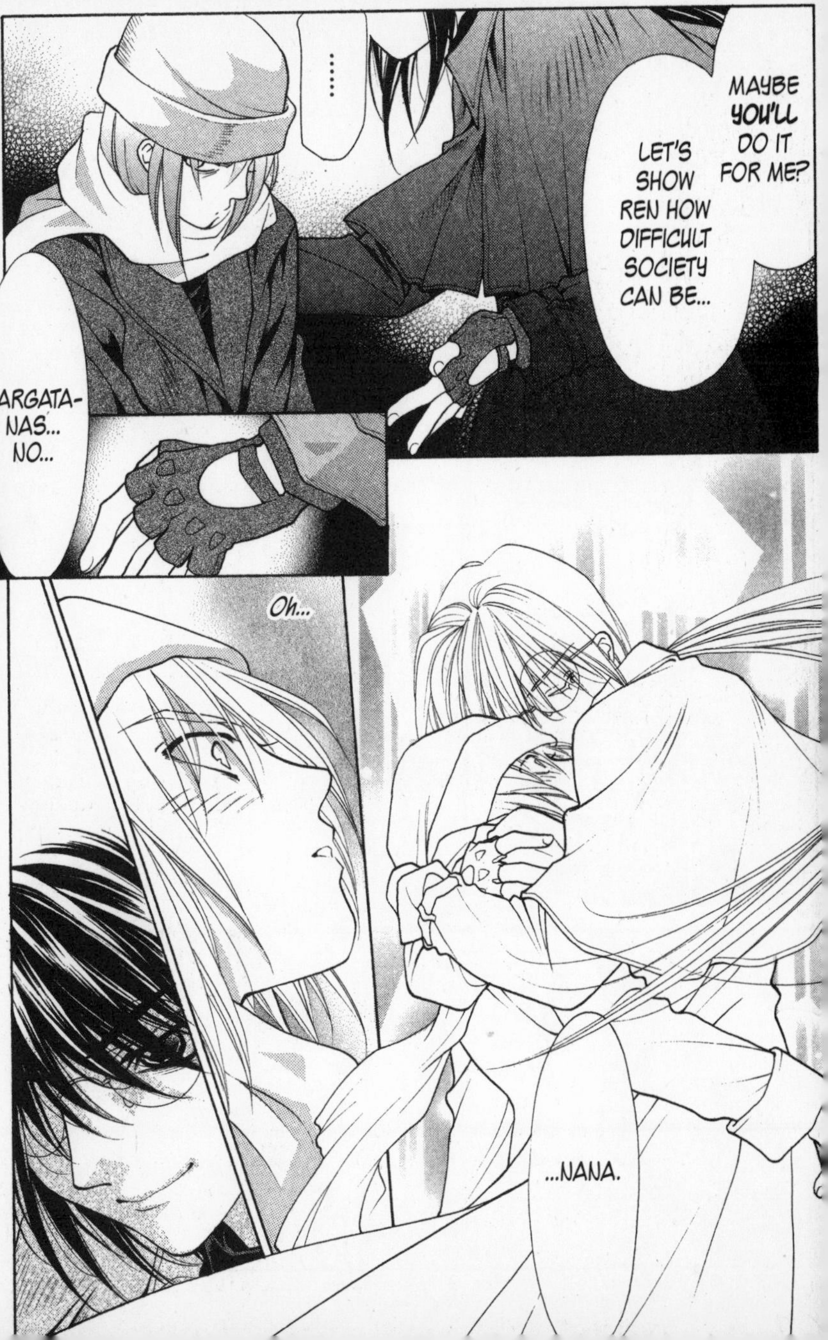
MAYBE YOU'LL DO IT FOR ME?
LET'S SHOW REN HOW DIFFICULT SOCIETY CAN BE...
......
SARGATANAS... NO...
...NANA.
Oh...

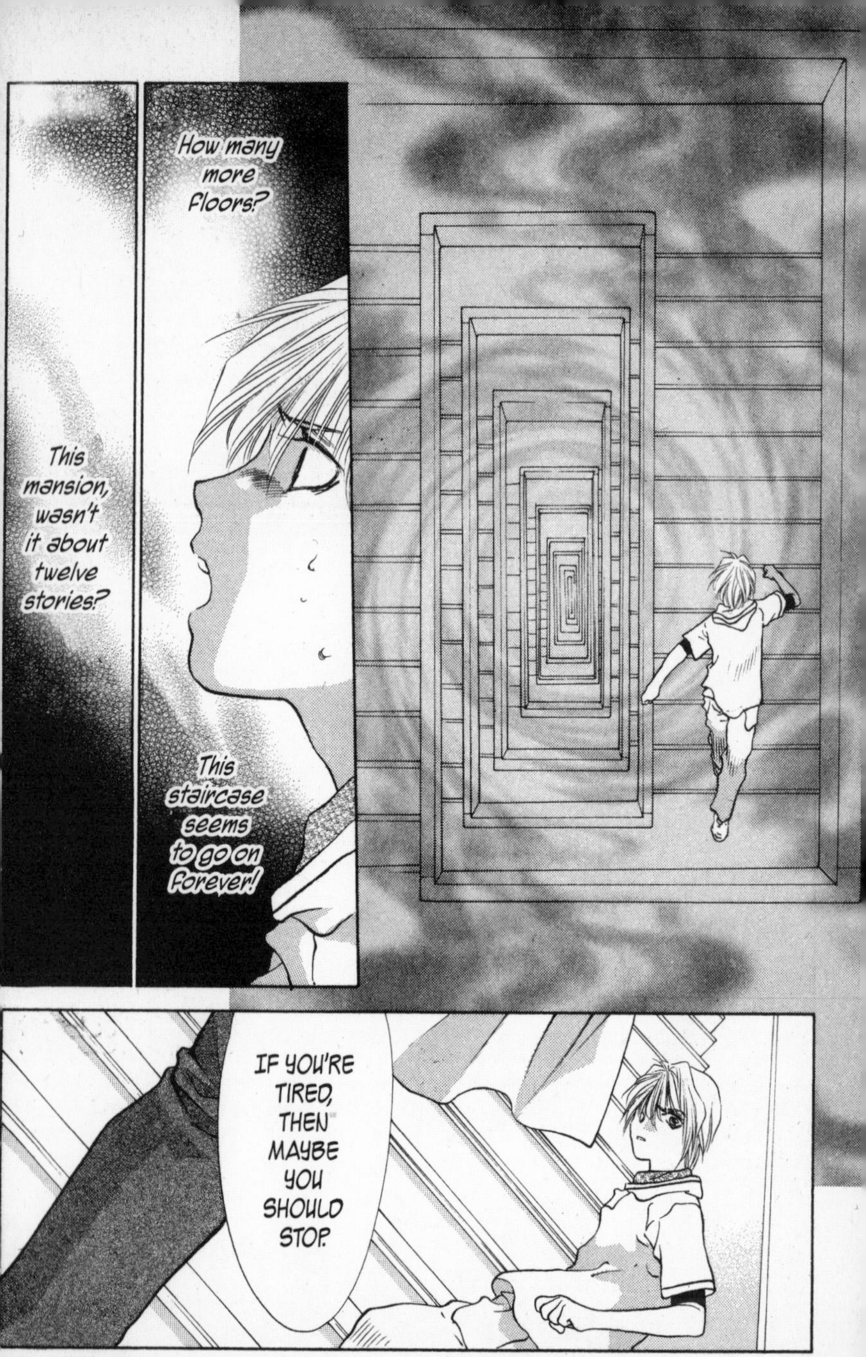
How many more floors?
This mansion, wasn't it about twelve stories?
This staircase seems to go on forever!
IF YOU'RE TIRED, THEN MAYBE YOU SHOULD STOP.

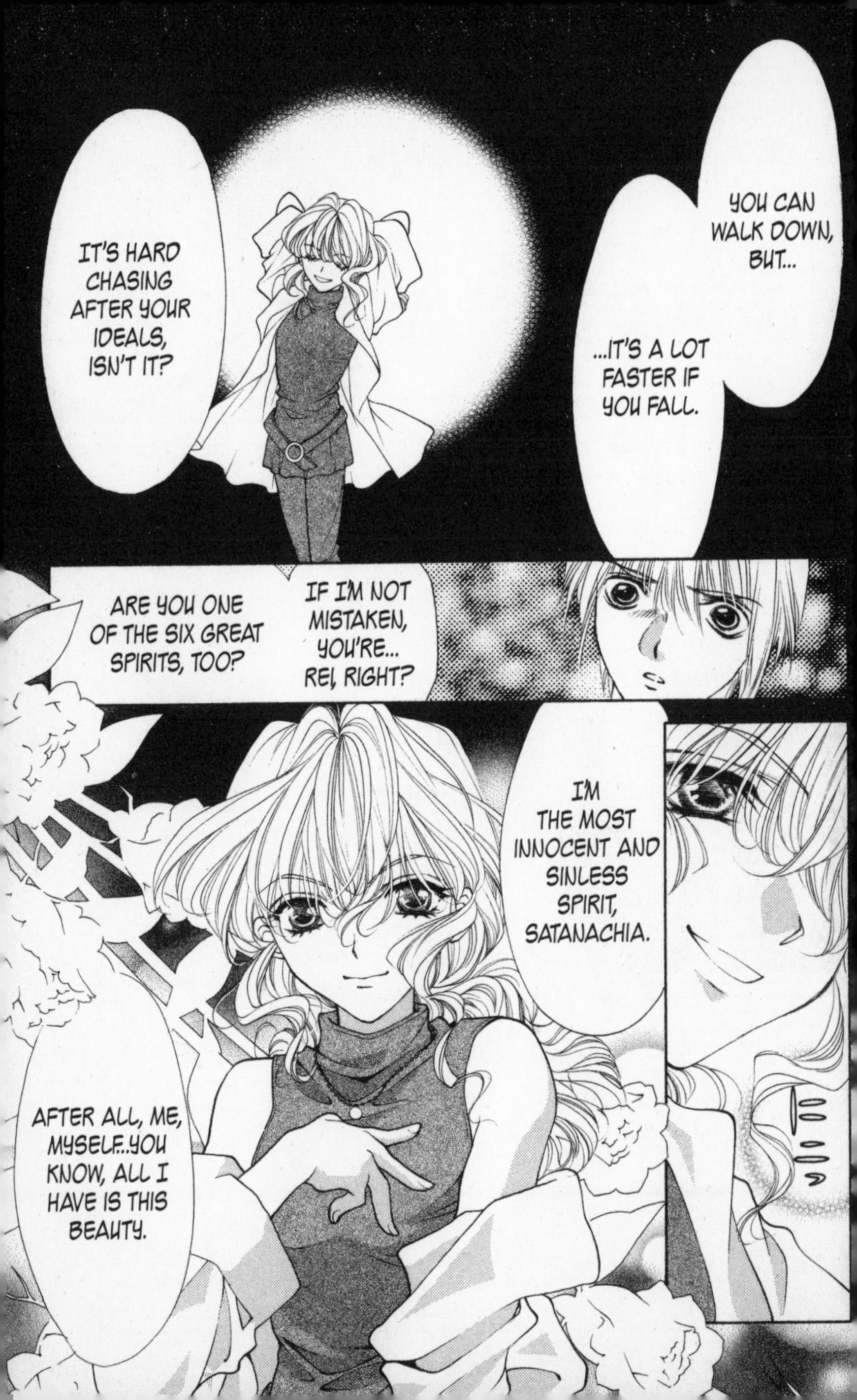
YOU CAN WALK DOWN, BUT...
...IT'S A LOT FASTER IF YOU FALL.
IT'S HARD CHASING AFTER YOUR IDEALS, ISN'T IT?
IF I'M NOT MISTAKEN, YOU'RE... REI, RIGHT?
ARE YOU ONE OF THE SIX GREAT SPIRITS, TOO?
I'M THE MOST INNOCENT AND SINLESS SPIRIT, SATANACHIA.
AFTER ALL, ME, MYSELF...YOU KNOW, ALL I HAVE IS THIS BEAUTY.

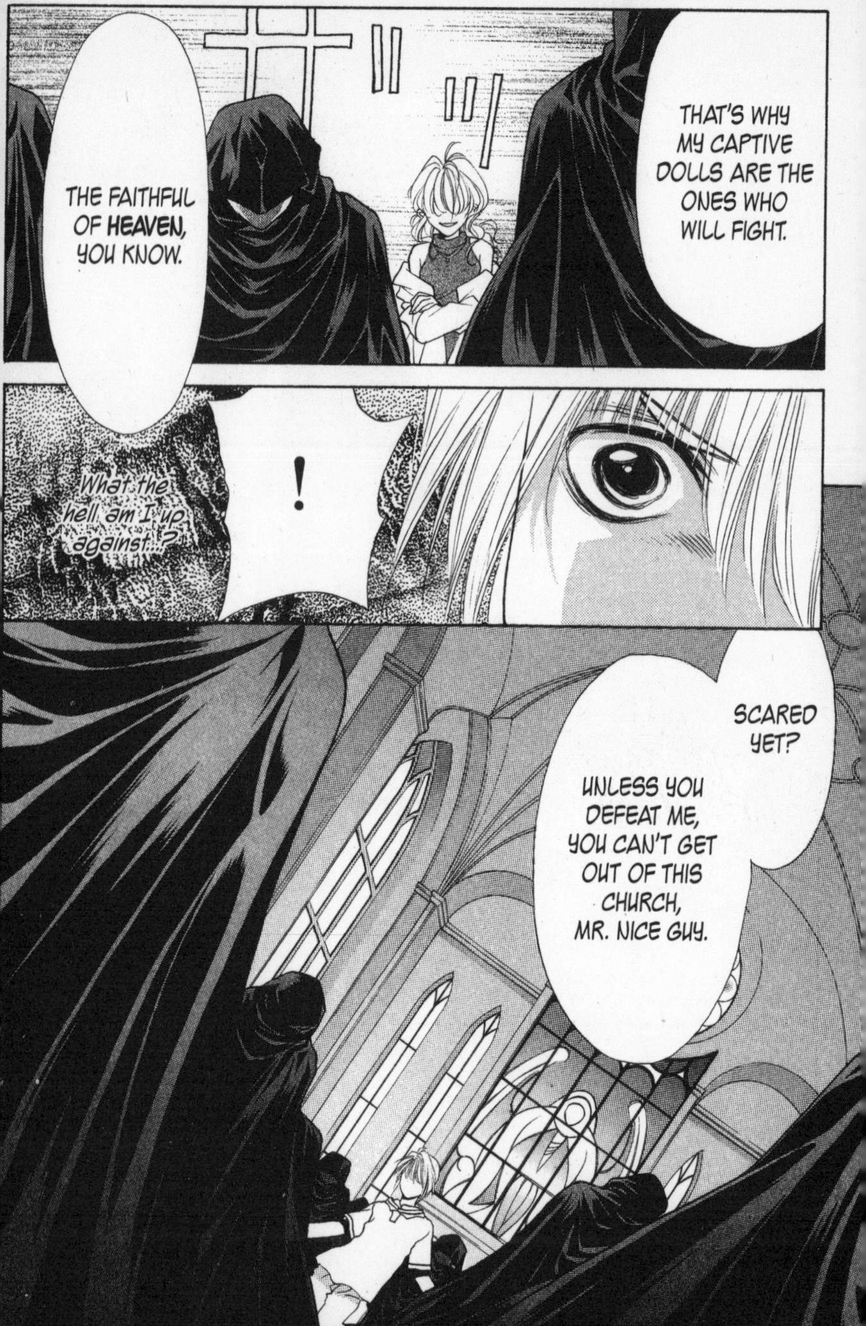
THAT'S WHY MY CAPTIVE DOLLS ARE THE ONES WHO WILL FIGHT.
THE FAITHFUL OF **HEAVEN,** YOU KNOW.
!
What the hell am I up against...?
SCARED YET?
UNLESS YOU DEFEAT ME, YOU CAN'T GET OUT OF THIS CHURCH, MR. NICE GUY.

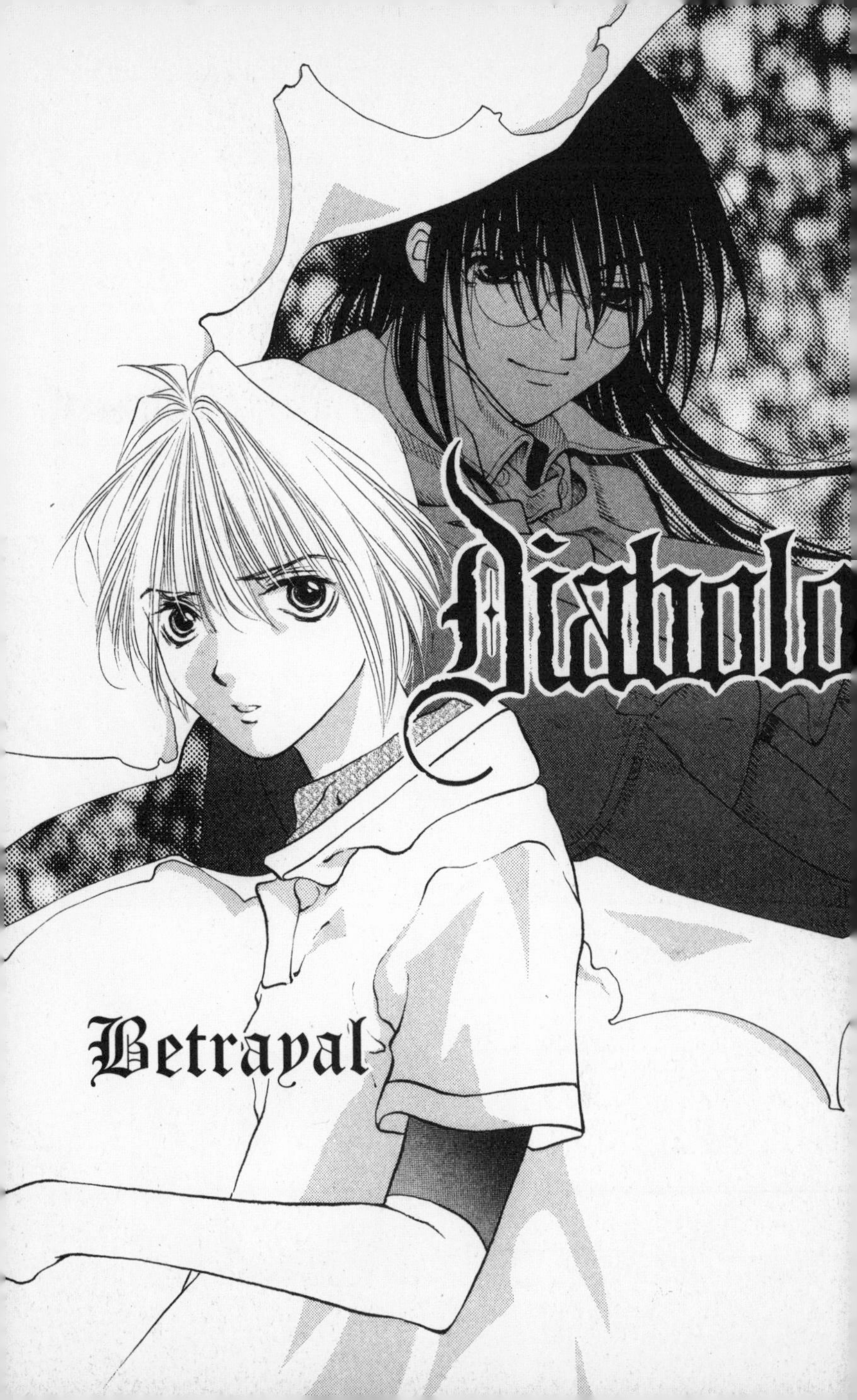
Diabolo
Betrayal

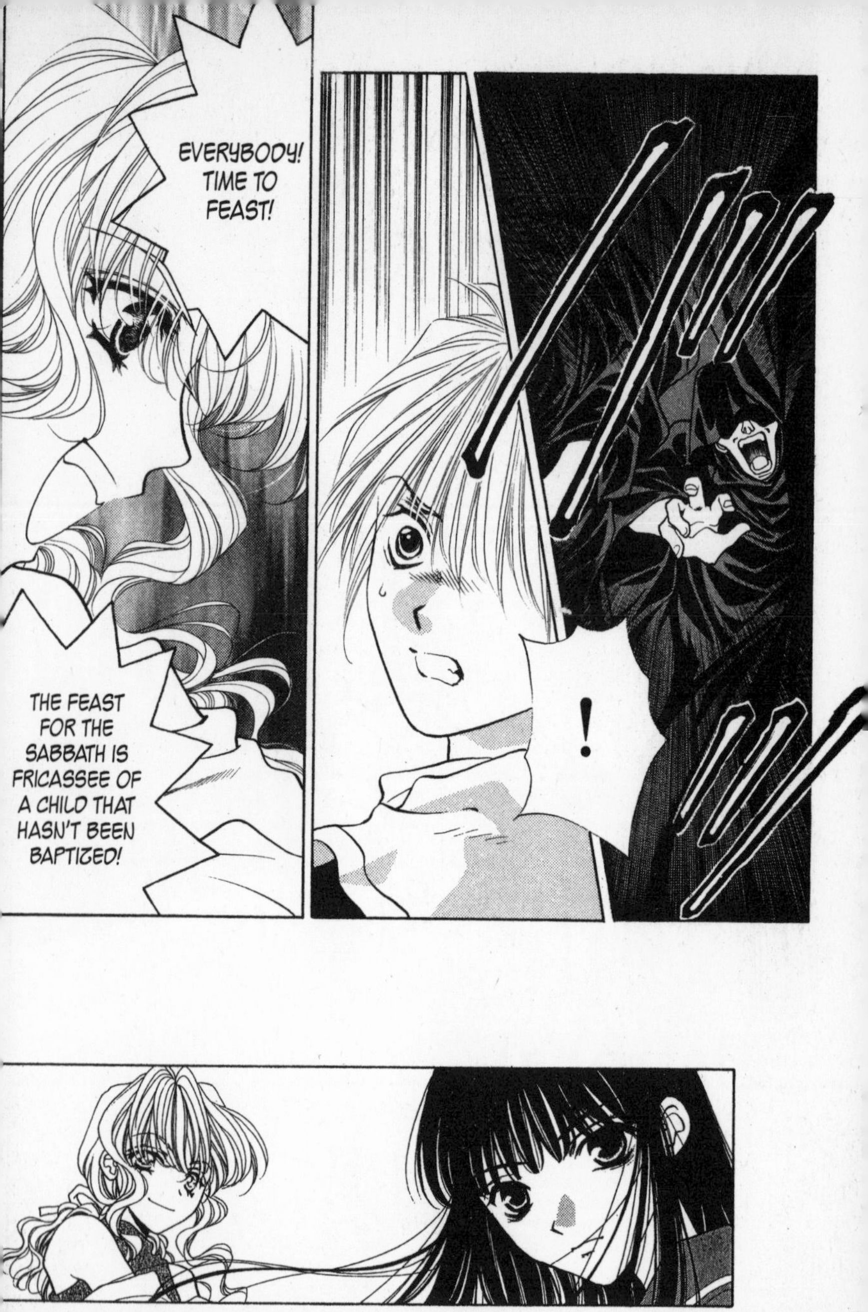
!
EVERYBODY! TIME TO FEAST!
THE FEAST FOR THE SABBATH IS FRICASSEE OF A CHILD THAT HASN'T BEEN BAPTIZED!

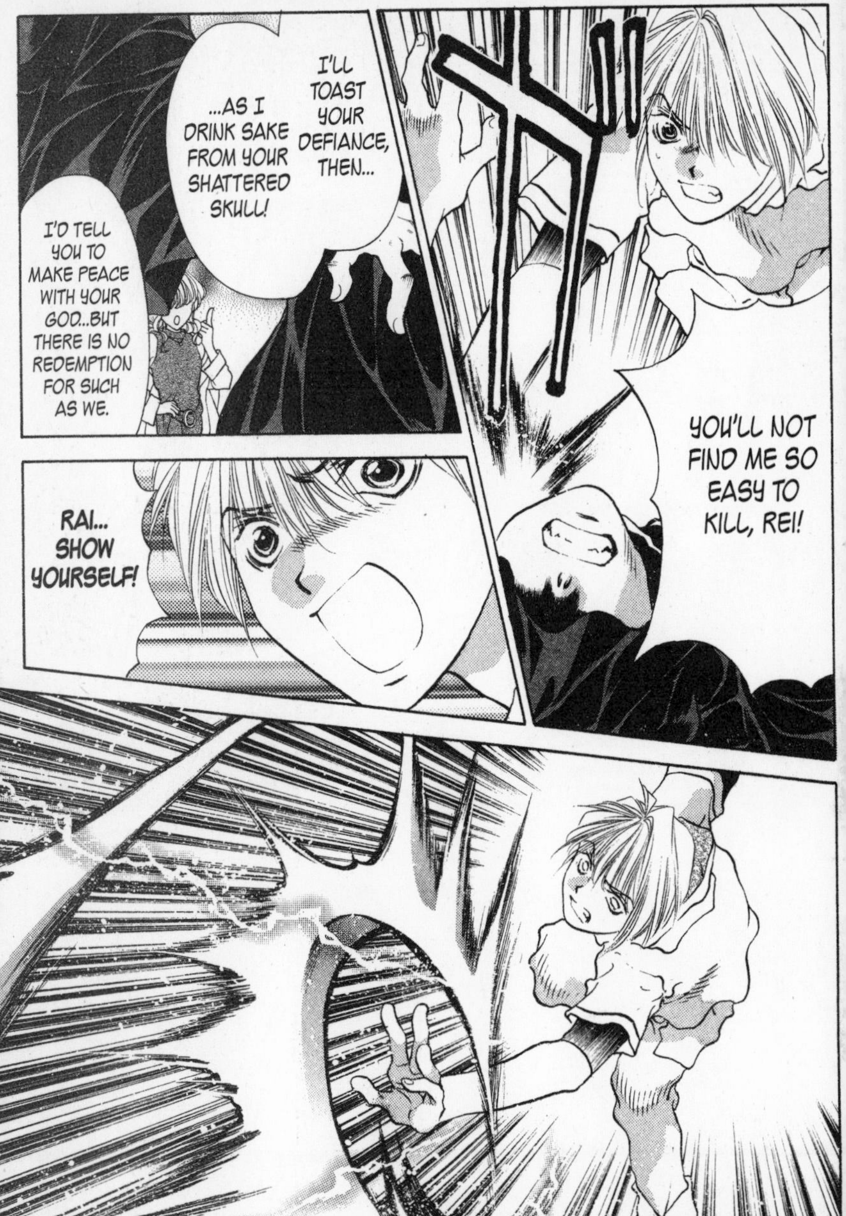
YOU'LL NOT FIND ME SO EASY TO KILL, REI!
I'LL TOAST YOUR DEFIANCE, THEN...
...AS I DRINK SAKE FROM YOUR SHATTERED SKULL!
I'D TELL YOU TO MAKE PEACE WITH YOUR GOD...BUT THERE IS NO REDEMPTION FOR SUCH AS WE.
RAI... SHOW YOURSELF!

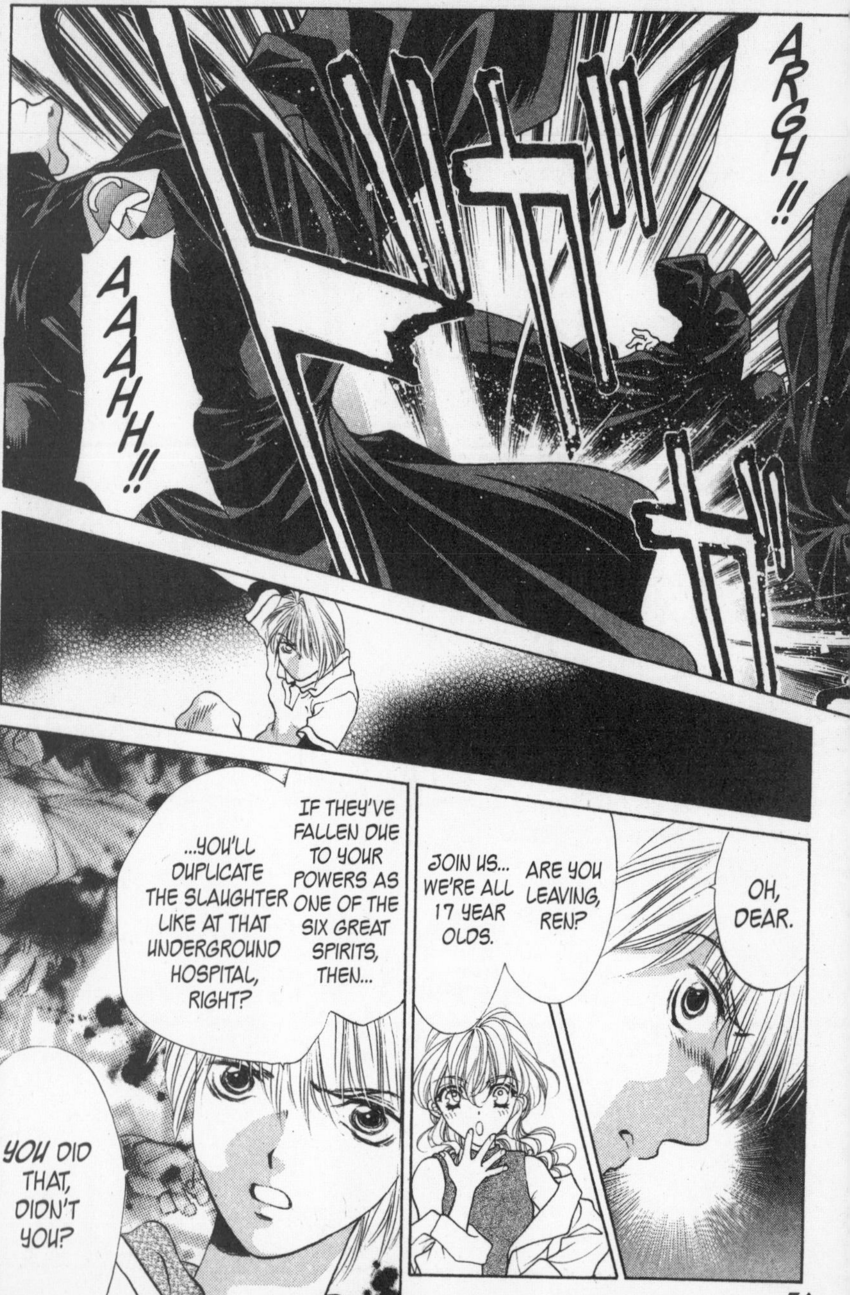
ARGH!!
AAAHH!!
OH, DEAR.
ARE YOU LEAVING, REN?
JOIN US... WE'RE ALL 17 YEAR OLDS.
IF THEY'VE FALLEN DUE TO YOUR POWERS AS ONE OF THE SIX GREAT SPIRITS, THEN...
...YOU'LL DUPLICATE THE SLAUGHTER LIKE AT THAT UNDERGROUND HOSPITAL, RIGHT?
YOU DID THAT, DIDN'T YOU?

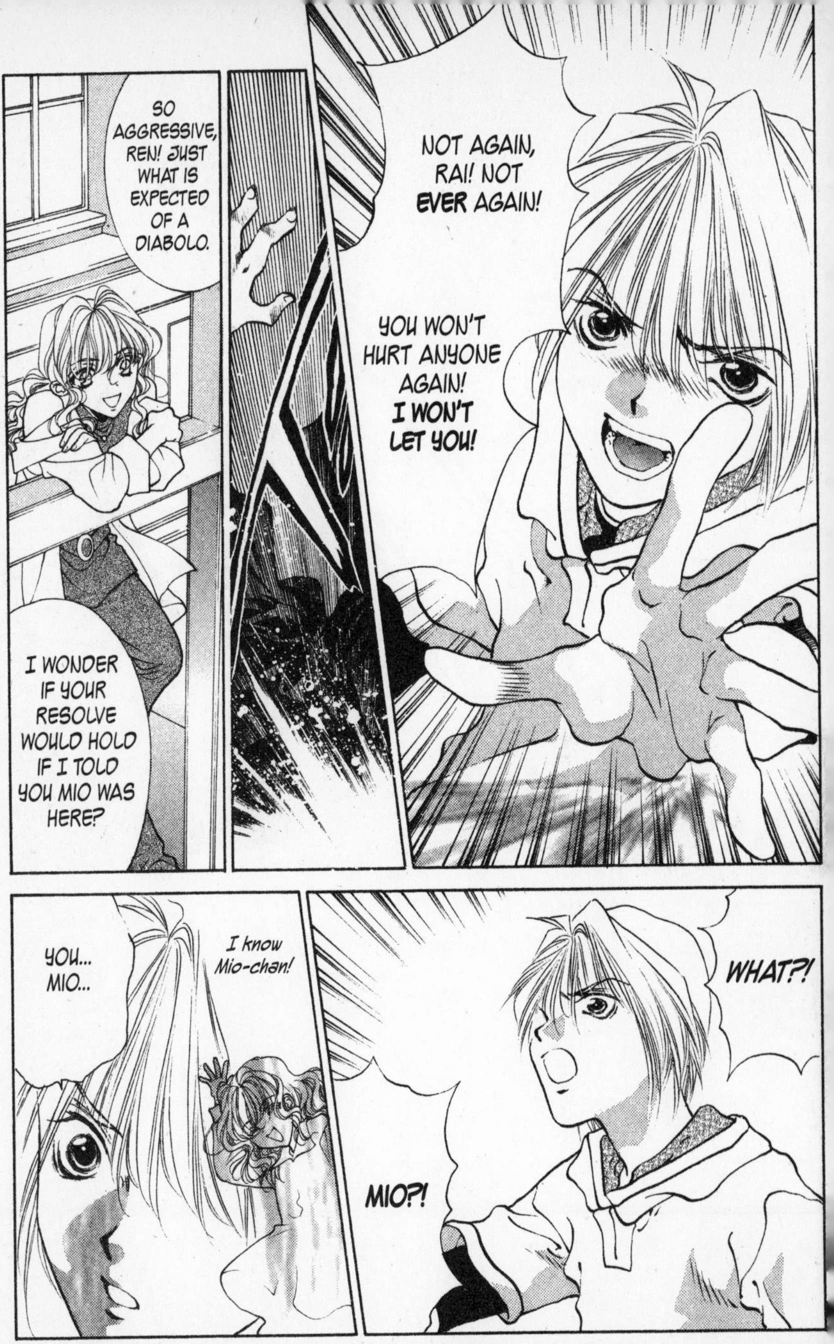
NOT AGAIN, RAI! NOT **EVER** AGAIN!
YOU WON'T HURT ANYONE AGAIN! **I WON'T LET YOU!**
SO AGGRESSIVE, REN! JUST WHAT IS EXPECTED OF A DIABOLO.
I WONDER IF YOUR RESOLVE WOULD HOLD IF I TOLD YOU MIO WAS HERE?
WHAT?!
MIO?!
I know Mio-chan!
YOU... MIO...

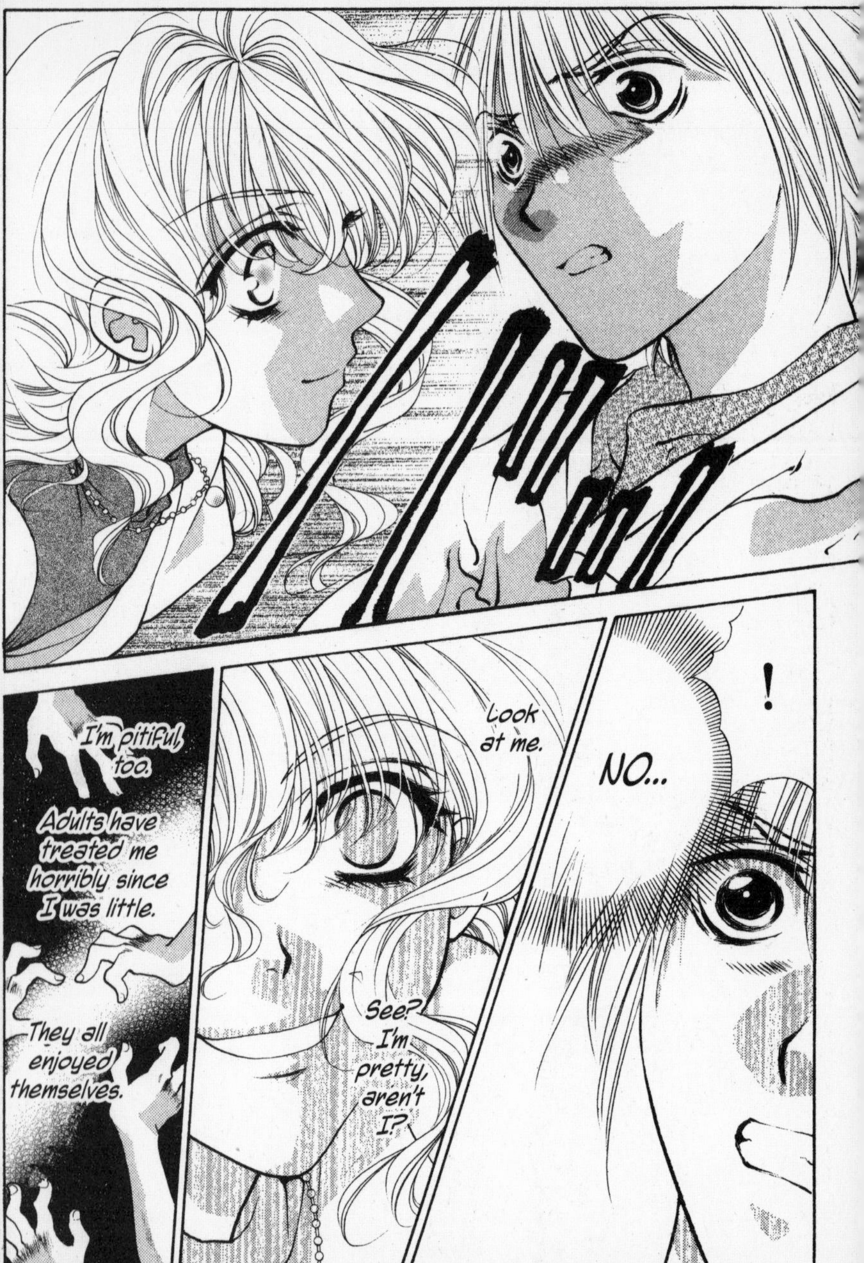
!
NO...
Look at me.
See? I'm pretty, aren't I?
I'm pitiful, too.
Adults have treated me horribly since I was little.
They all enjoyed themselves.

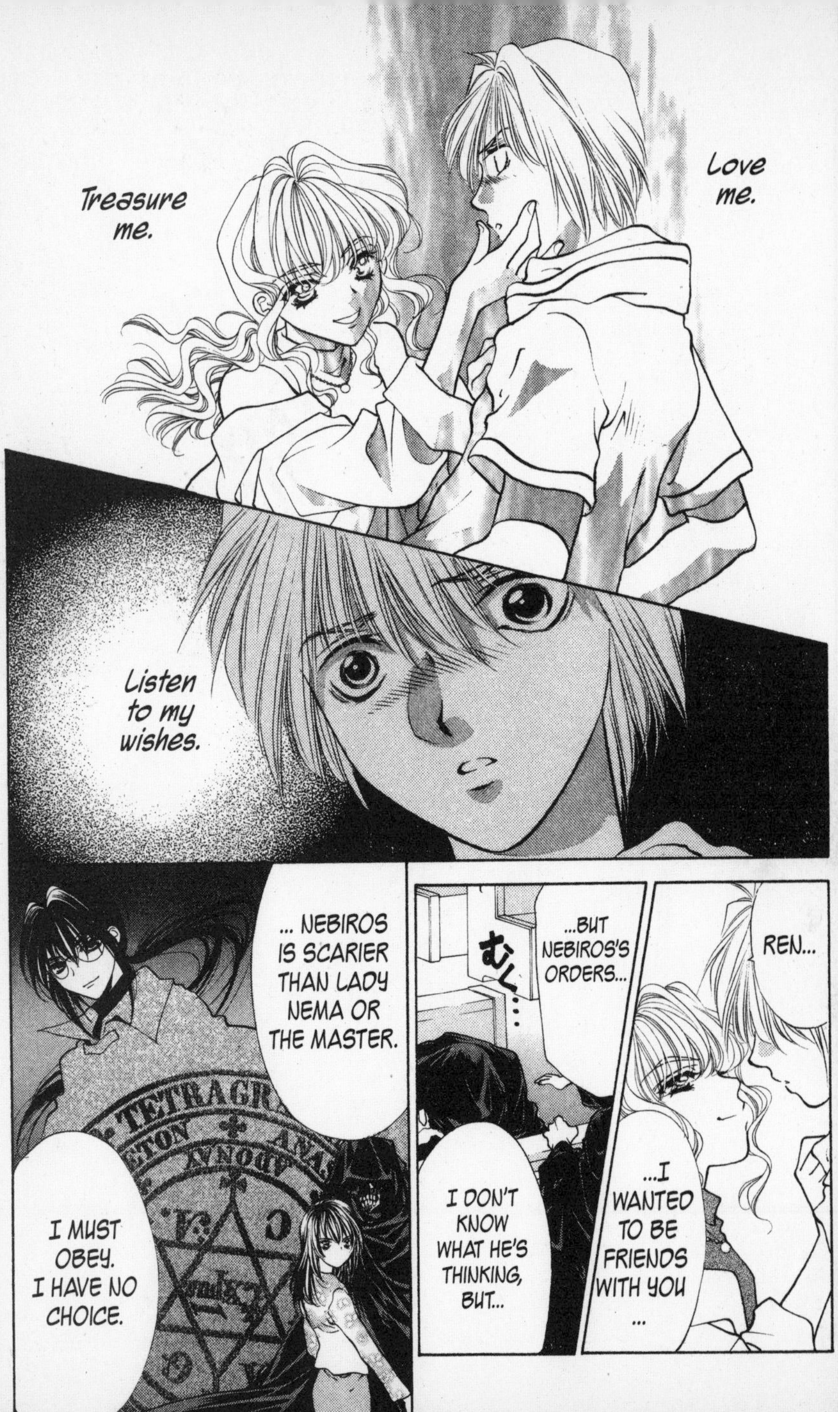
Love me.
Treasure me.
Listen to my wishes.
REN...
...I WANTED TO BE FRIENDS WITH YOU ...
...BUT NEBIROS'S ORDERS...
むく...
I DON'T KNOW WHAT HE'S THINKING, BUT...
... NEBIROS IS SCARIER THAN LADY NEMA OR THE MASTER.
I MUST OBEY. I HAVE NO CHOICE.

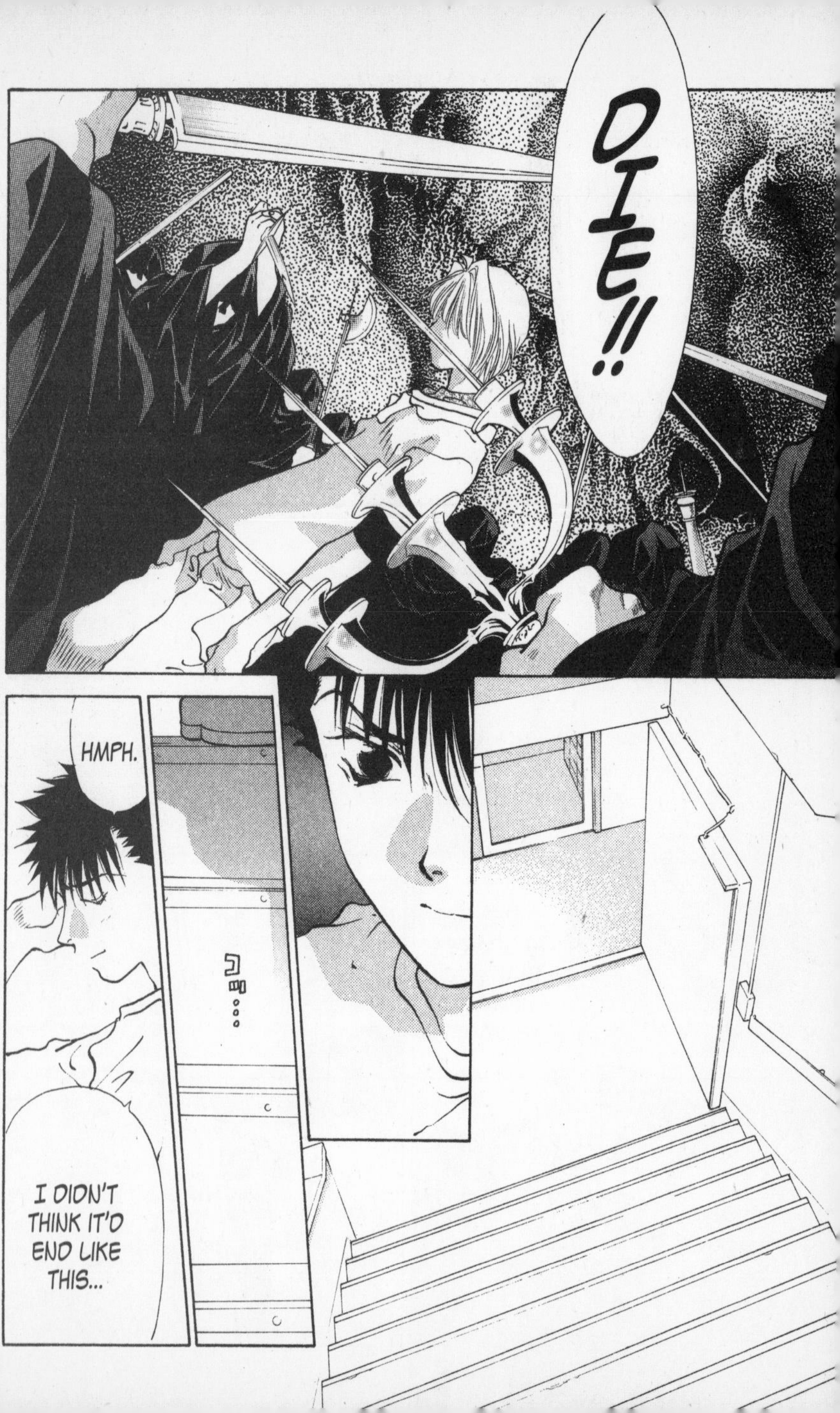
DIE!!
コッ…
HMPH.
I DIDN'T THINK IT'D END LIKE THIS...

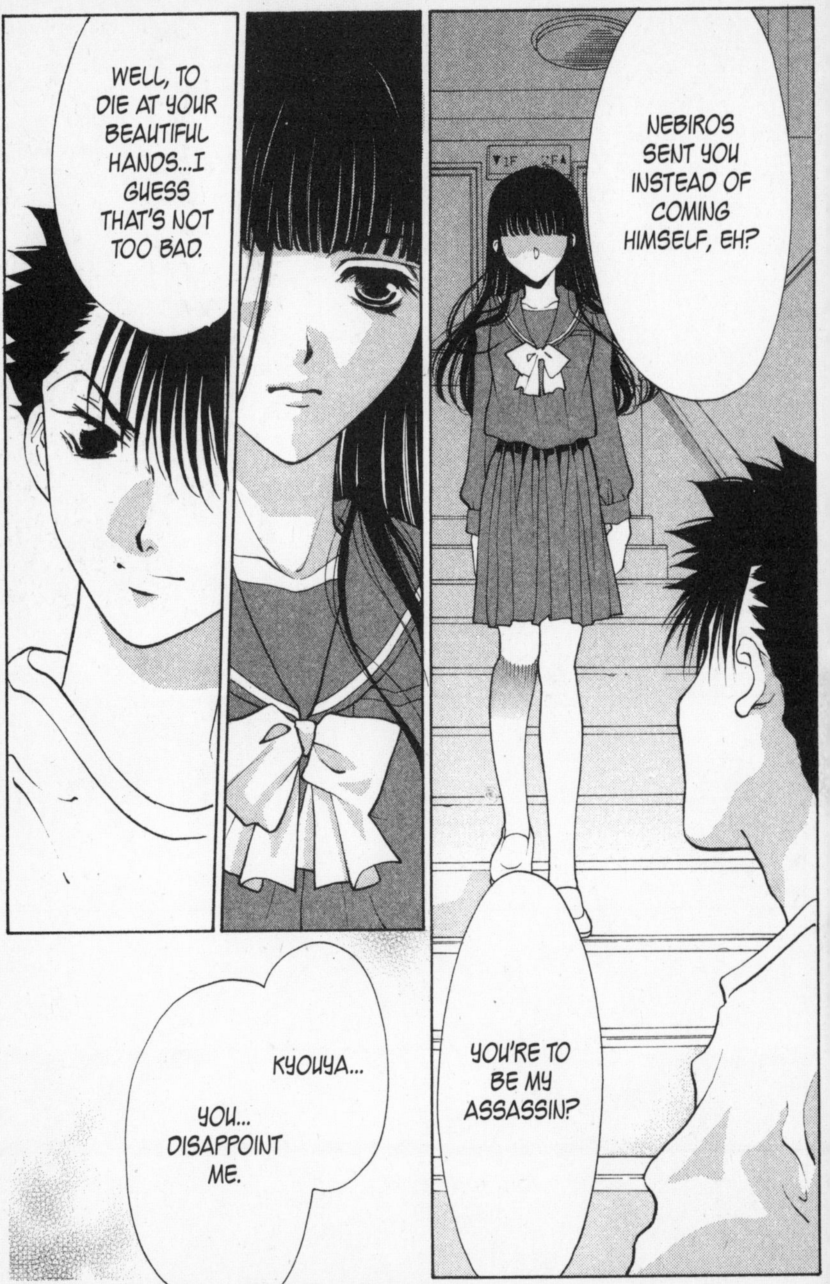
NEBIROS SENT YOU INSTEAD OF COMING HIMSELF, EH?
YOU'RE TO BE MY ASSASSIN?
WELL, TO DIE AT YOUR BEAUTIFUL HANDS...I GUESS THAT'S NOT TOO BAD.
KYOUYA...
YOU... DISAPPOINT ME.

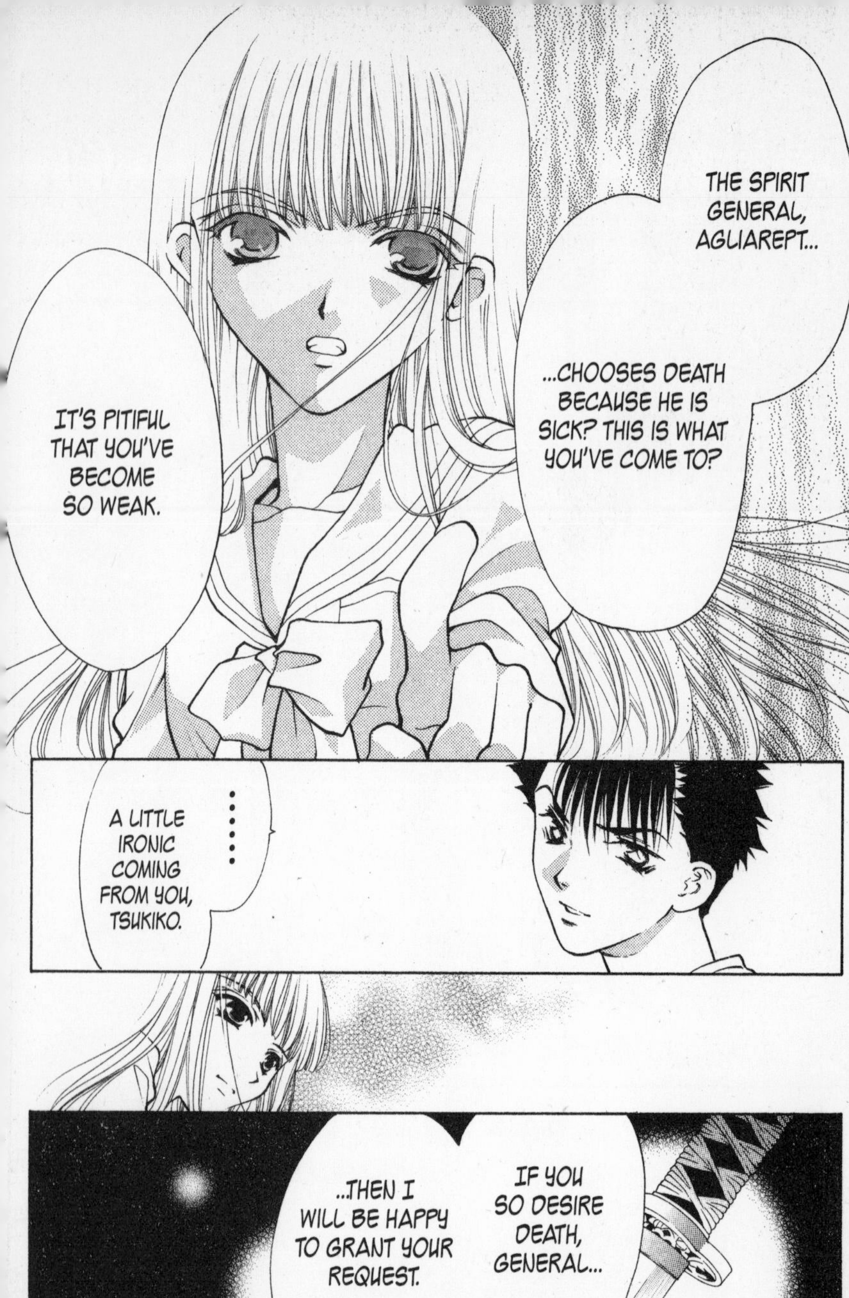
THE SPIRIT GENERAL, AGLIAREPT...
...CHOOSES DEATH BECAUSE HE IS SICK? THIS IS WHAT YOU'VE COME TO?
IT'S PITIFUL THAT YOU'VE BECOME SO WEAK.
......
A LITTLE IRONIC COMING FROM YOU, TSUKIKO.
IF YOU SO DESIRE DEATH, GENERAL...
...THEN I WILL BE HAPPY TO GRANT YOUR REQUEST.

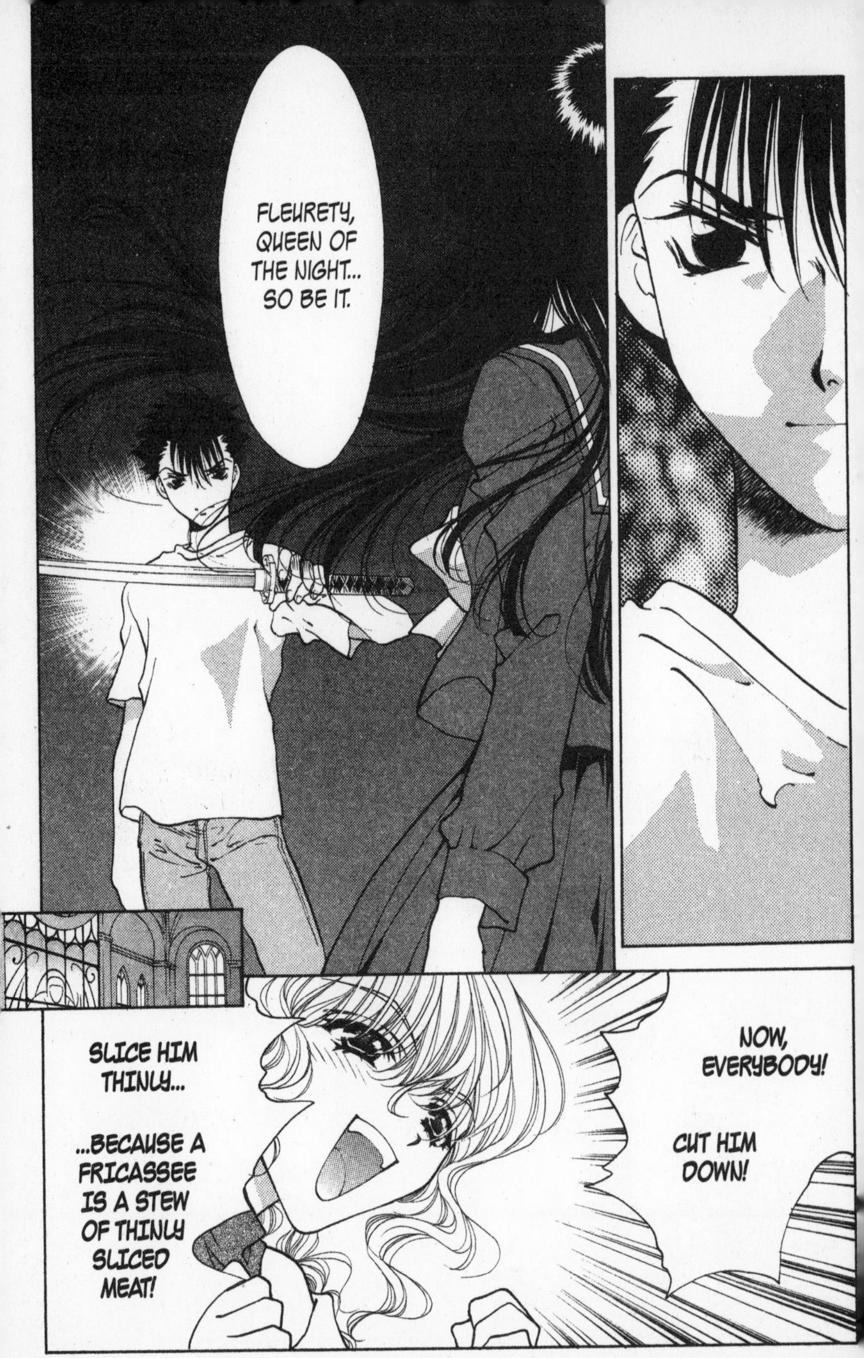
FLEURETY, QUEEN OF THE NIGHT... SO BE IT.
NOW, EVERYBODY!
CUT HIM DOWN!
SLICE HIM THINLY...
...BECAUSE A FRICASSEE IS A STEW OF THINLY SLICED MEAT!

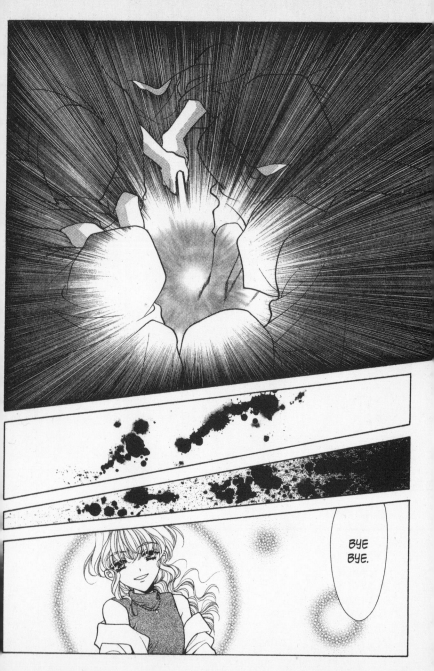

BYE
BYE.

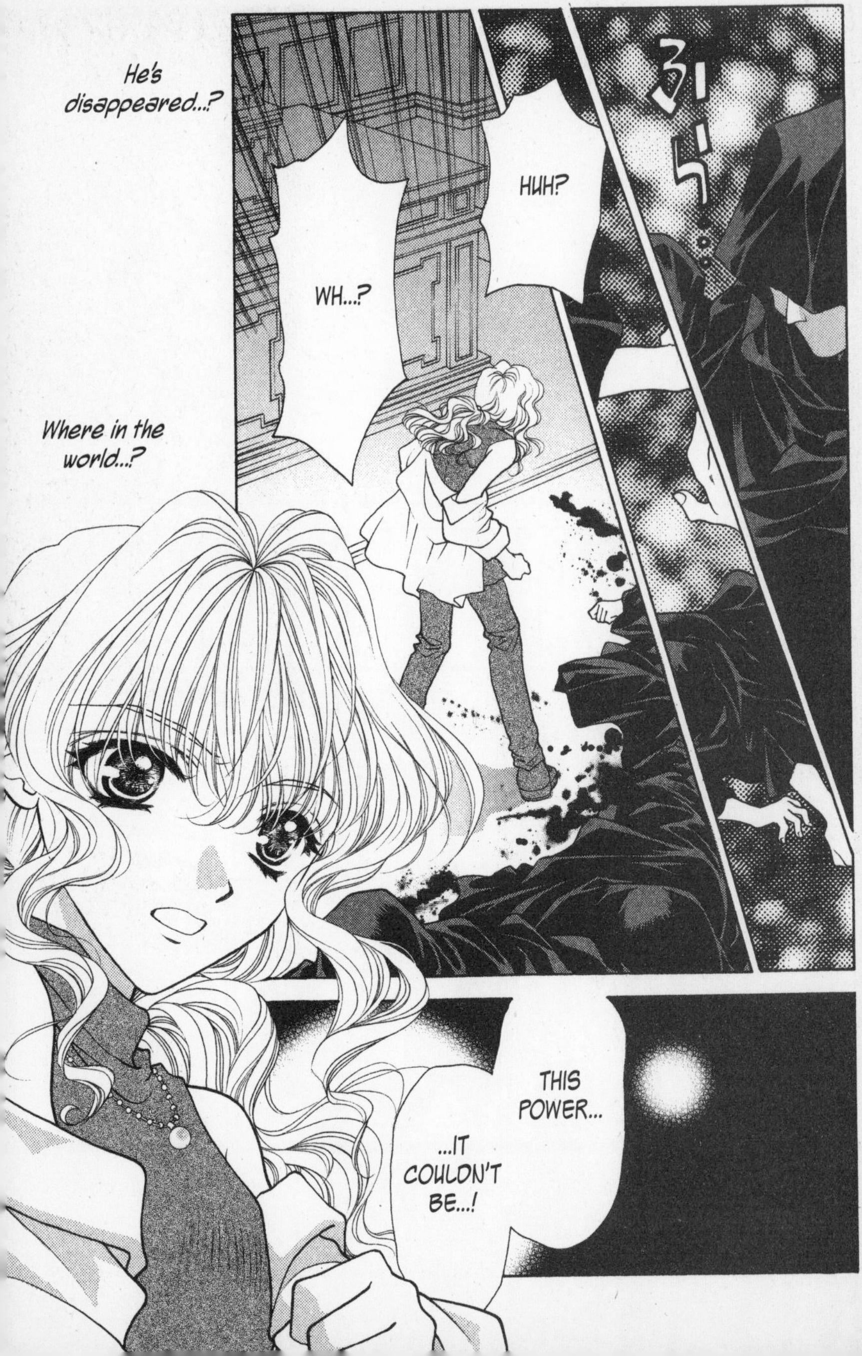
HUH?
WH...?
He's disappeared...?
Where in the world...?
THIS POWER...
...IT COULDN'T BE...!

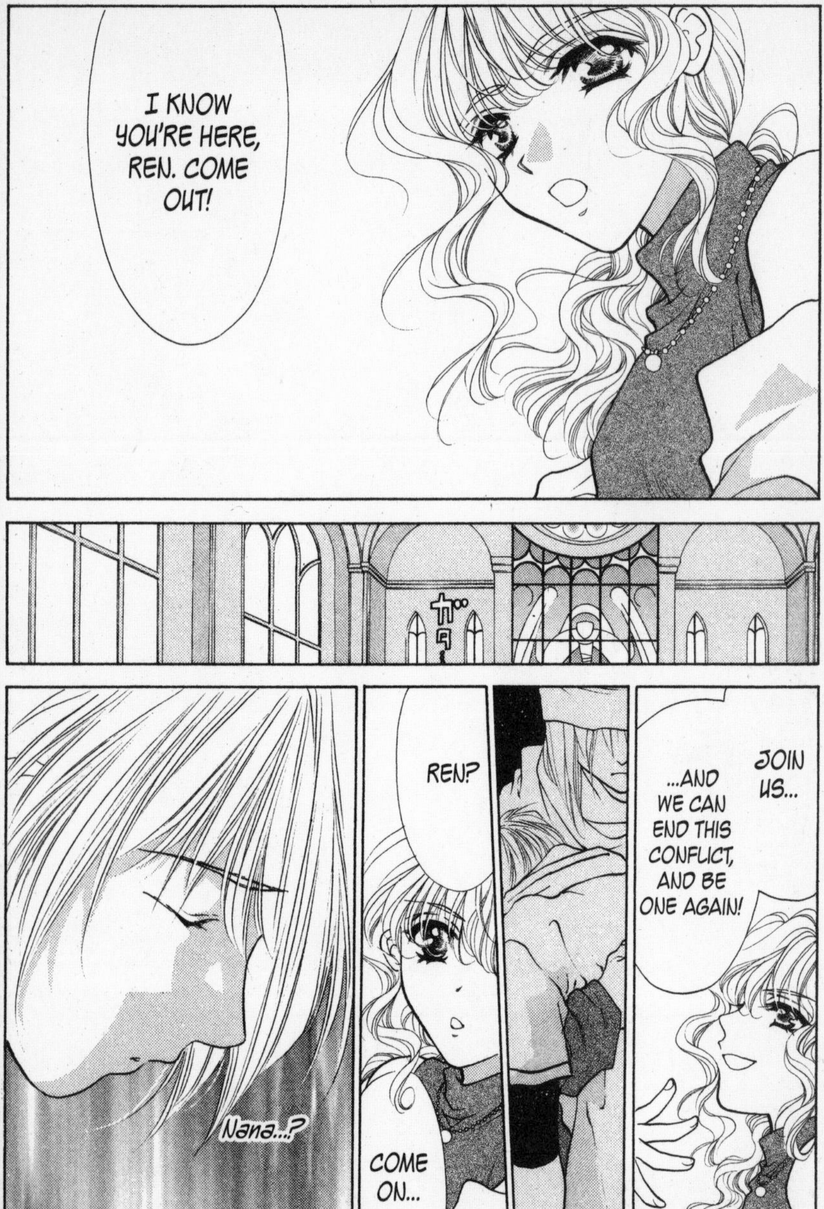
I KNOW YOU'RE HERE, REN. COME OUT!
ガタ
JOIN US...
...AND WE CAN END THIS CONFLICT, AND BE ONE AGAIN!
REN?
COME ON...
Nana...?

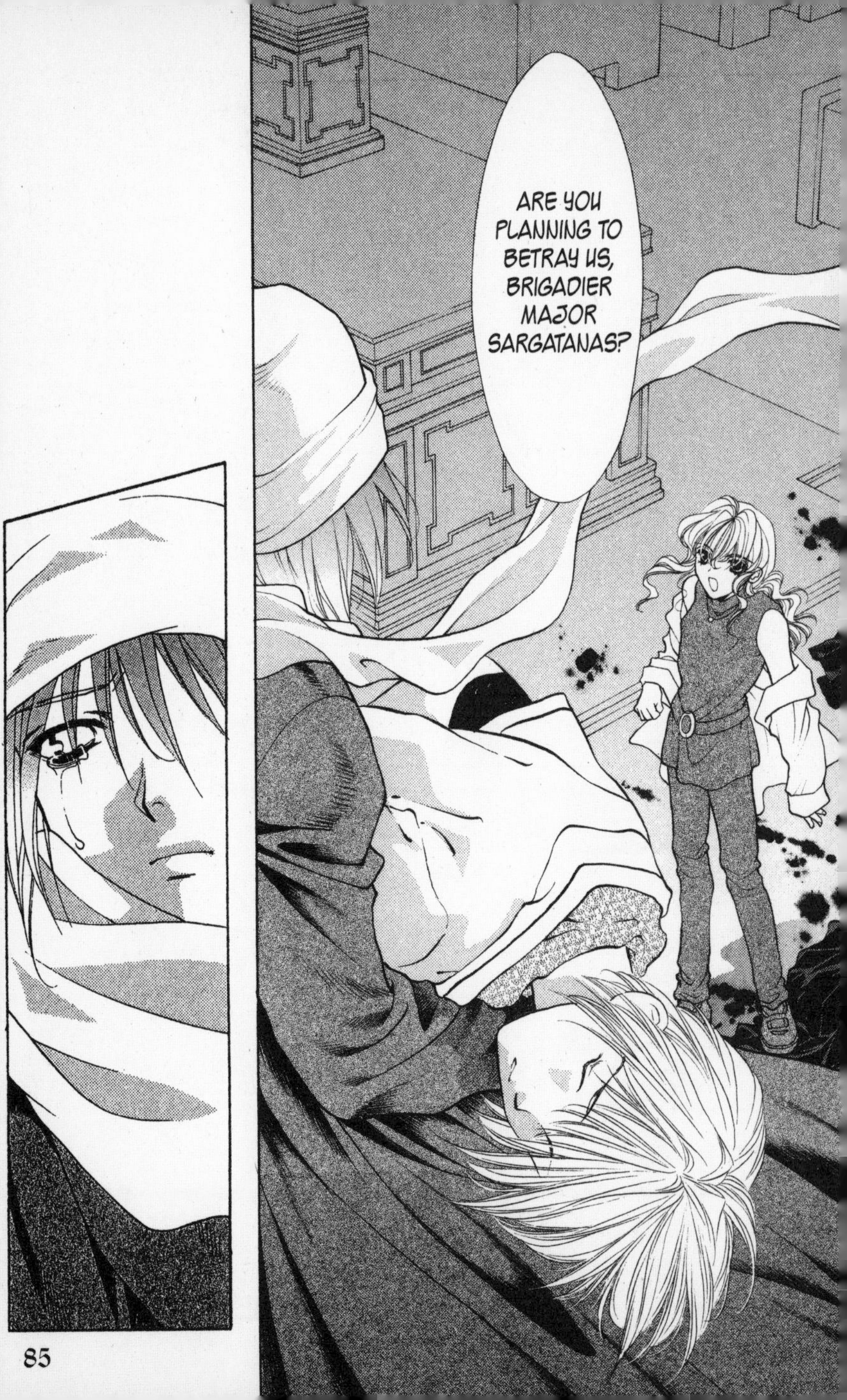
ARE YOU PLANNING TO BETRAY US, BRIGADIER MAJOR SARGATANAS?

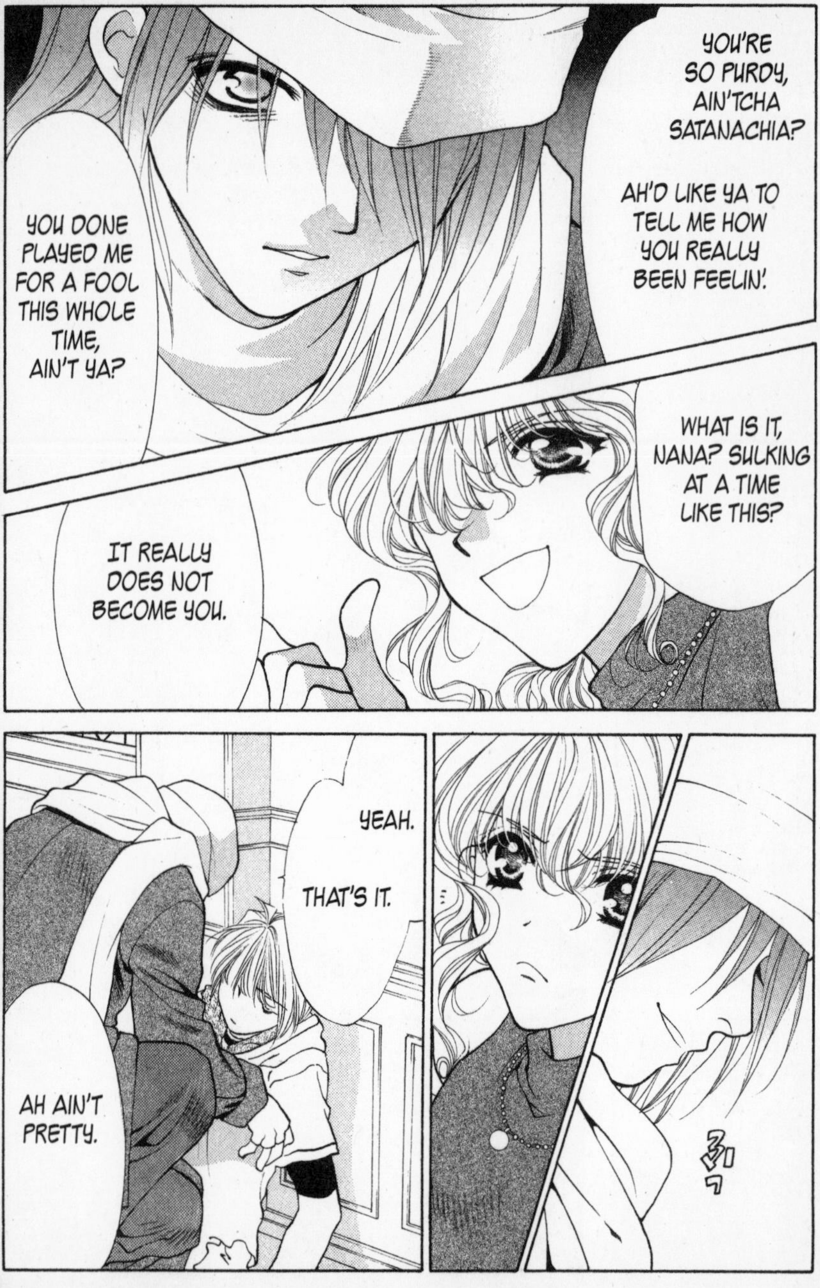
YOU'RE SO PURDY, AIN'TCHA SATANACHIA?
AH'D LIKE YA TO TELL ME HOW YOU REALLY BEEN FEELIN'.
YOU DONE PLAYED ME FOR A FOOL THIS WHOLE TIME, AIN'T YA?
WHAT IS IT, NANA? SULKING AT A TIME LIKE THIS?
IT REALLY DOES NOT BECOME YOU.
YEAH.
THAT'S IT.
AH AIN'T PRETTY.

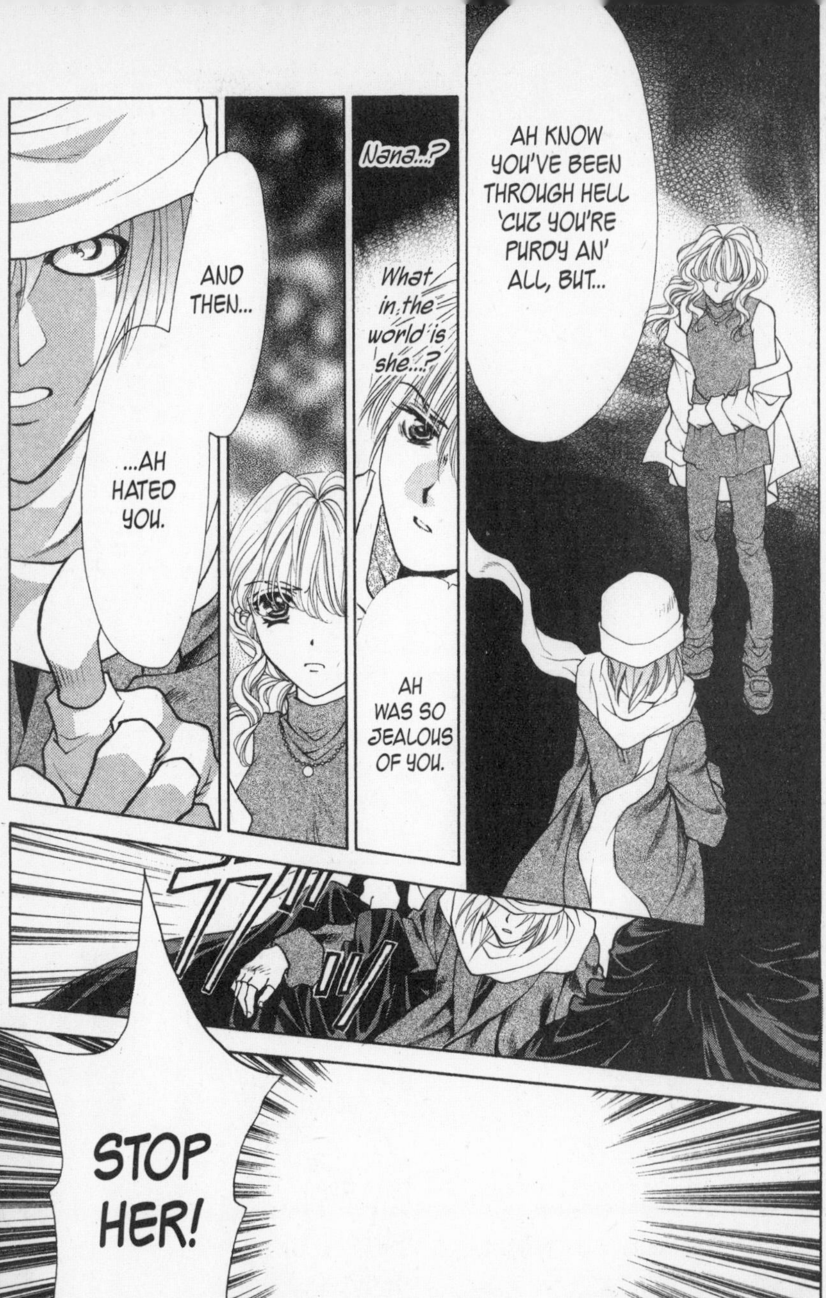
AH KNOW YOU'VE BEEN THROUGH HELL 'CUZ YOU'RE PURDY AN' ALL, BUT...
Nana...?
What in the world is she...?
AH WAS SO JEALOUS OF YOU.
AND THEN...
...AH HATED YOU.
STOP HER!

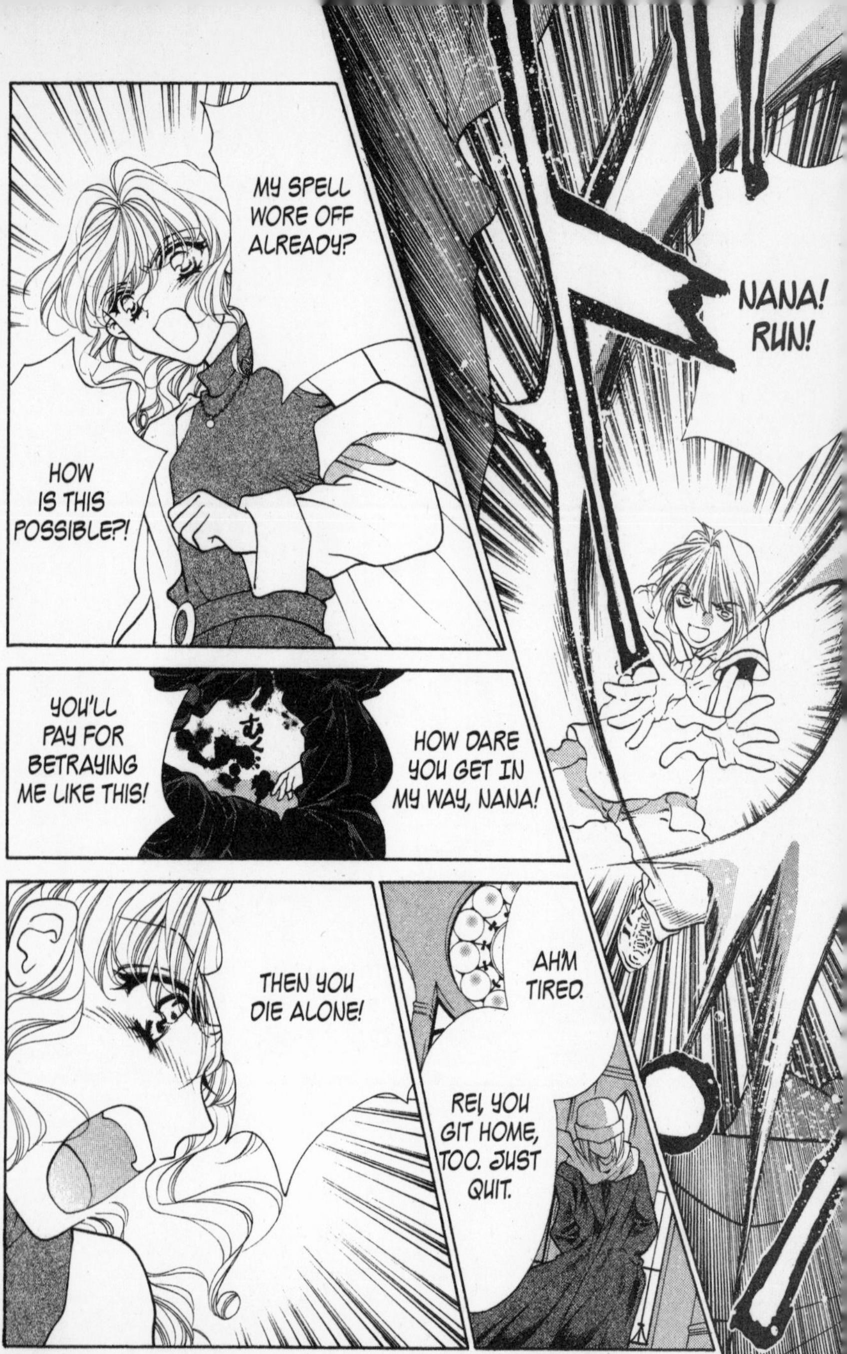
NANA! RUN!
MY SPELL WORE OFF ALREADY?
HOW IS THIS POSSIBLE?!
HOW DARE YOU GET IN MY WAY, NANA!
YOU'LL PAY FOR BETRAYING ME LIKE THIS!
AH'M TIRED.
REI, YOU GIT HOME, TOO. JUST QUIT.
THEN YOU DIE ALONE!

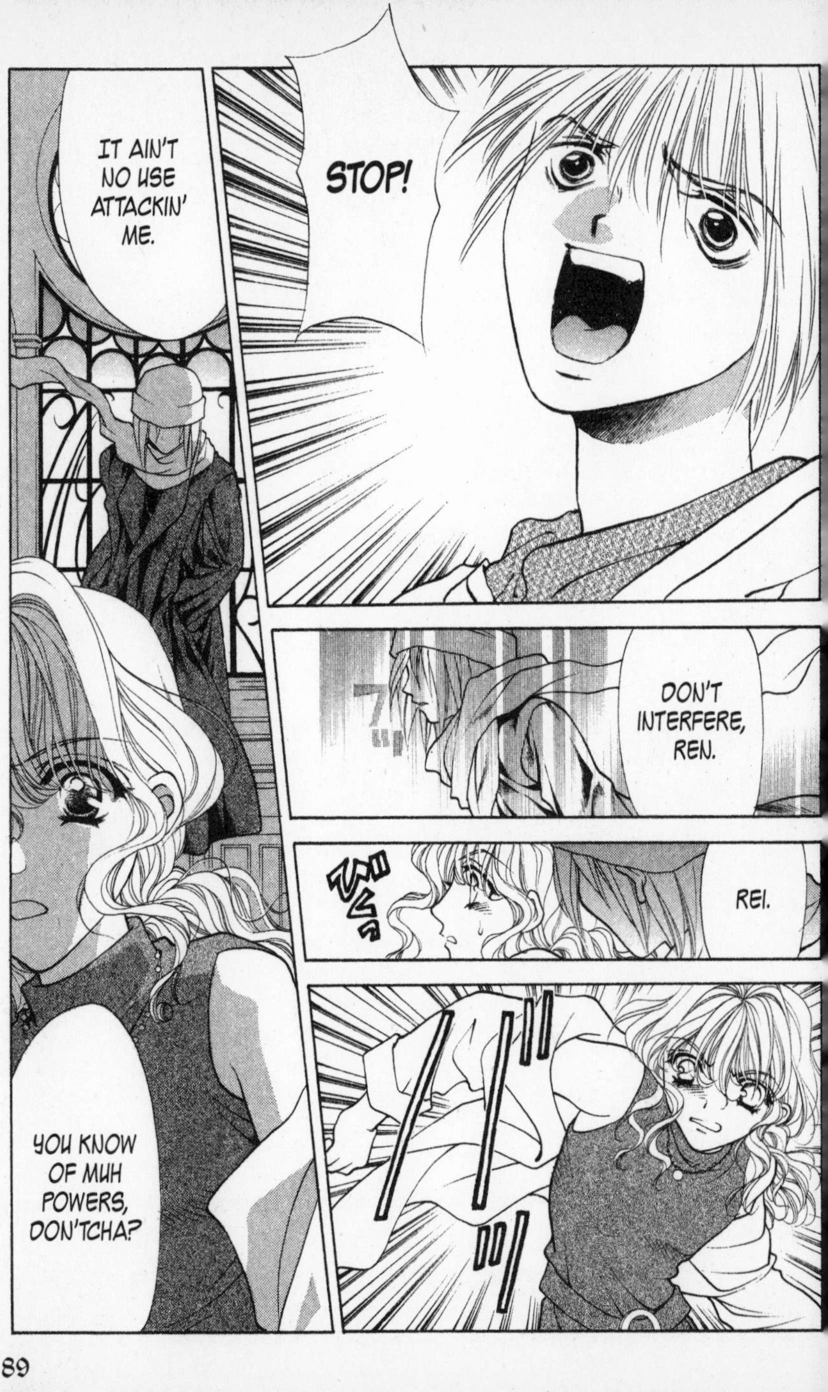
STOP!
DON'T INTERFERE, REN.
REI.
IT AIN'T NO USE ATTACKIN' ME.
YOU KNOW OF MUH POWERS, DON'TCHA?

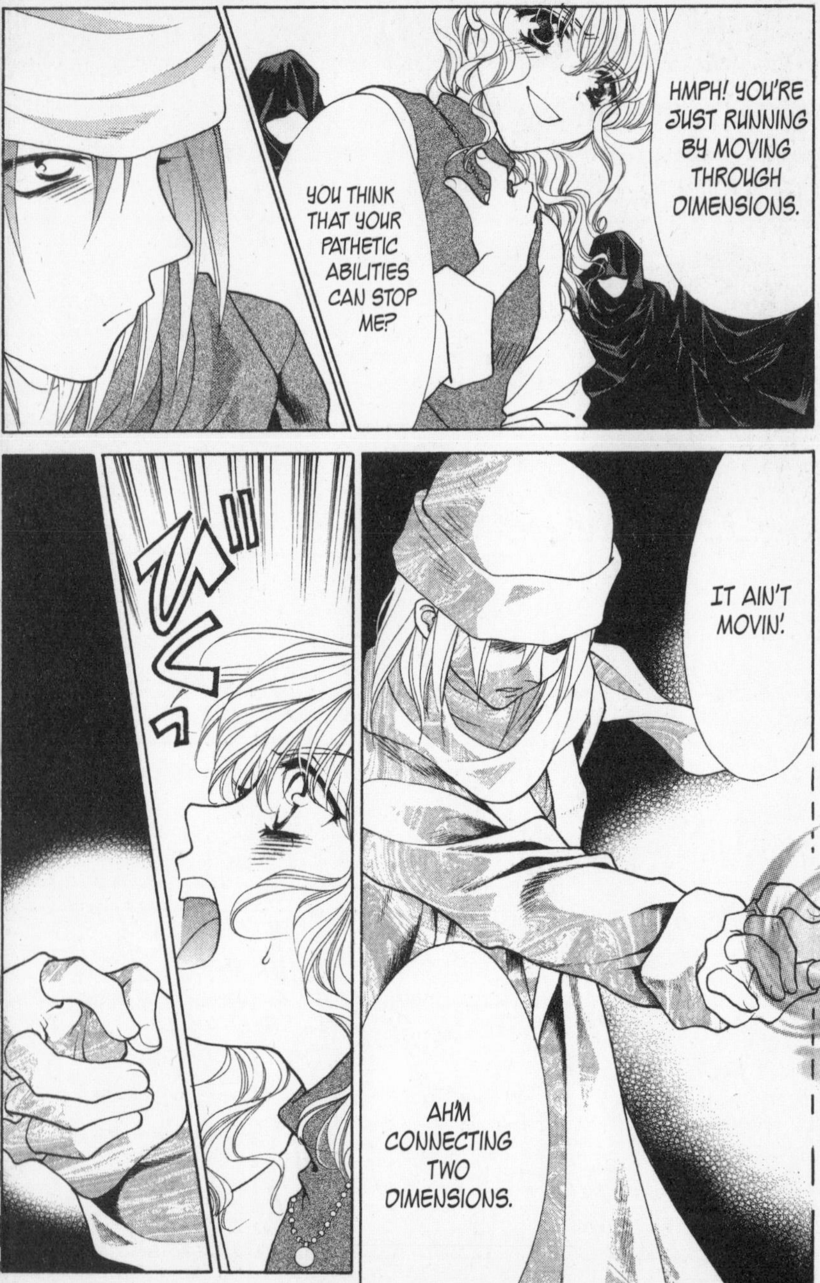
HMPH! YOU'RE JUST RUNNING BY MOVING THROUGH DIMENSIONS.
YOU THINK THAT YOUR PATHETIC ABILITIES CAN STOP ME?
IT AIN'T MOVIN'.
AH'M CONNECTING TWO DIMENSIONS.

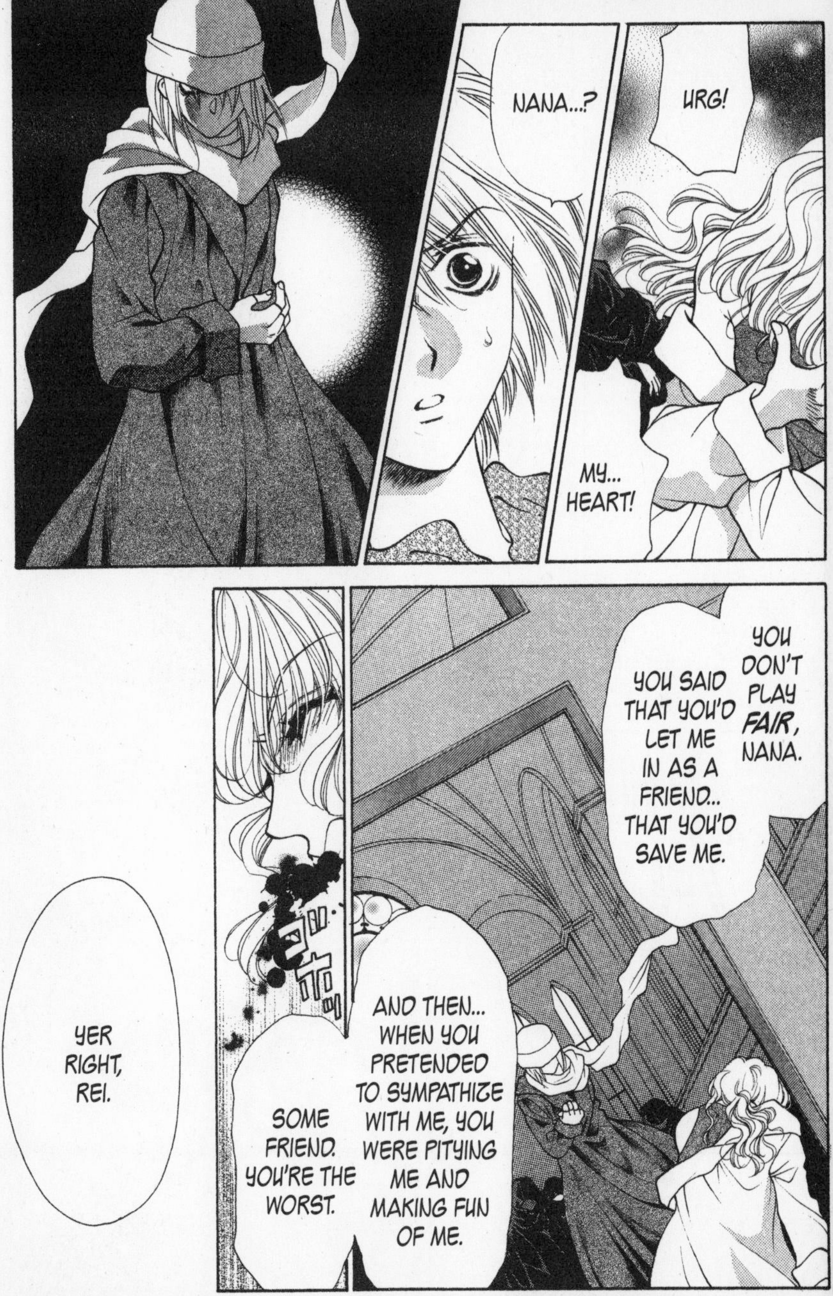
URG!
MY... HEART!
NANA...?
YOU DON'T PLAY *FAIR*, NANA.
YOU SAID THAT YOU'D LET ME IN AS A FRIEND... THAT YOU'D SAVE ME.
AND THEN... WHEN YOU PRETENDED TO SYMPATHIZE WITH ME, YOU WERE PITYING ME AND MAKING FUN OF ME.
SOME FRIEND. YOU'RE THE WORST.
YER RIGHT, REI.

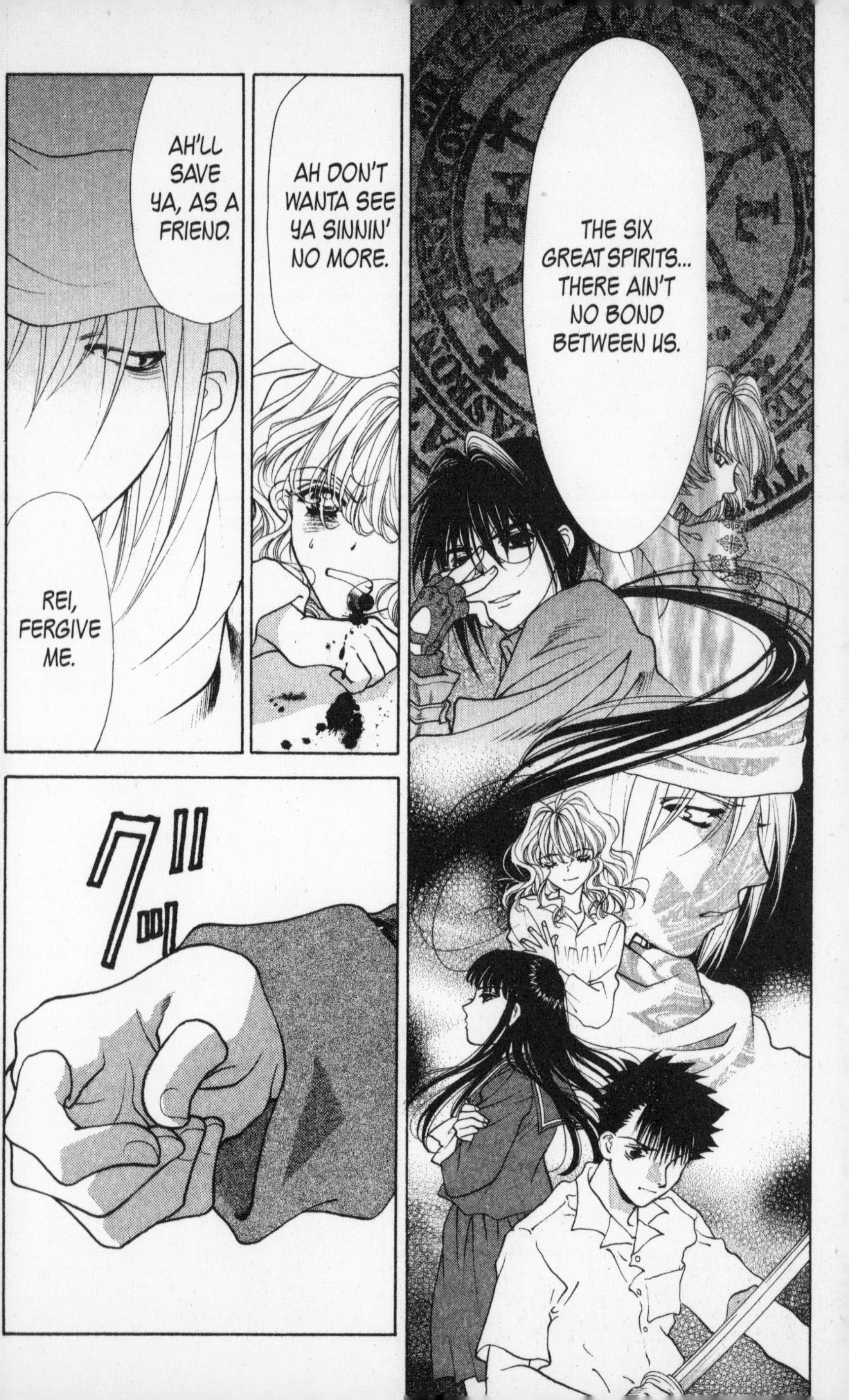
THE SIX GREAT SPIRITS... THERE AIN'T NO BOND BETWEEN US.
AH DON'T WANTA SEE YA SINNIN' NO MORE.
AH'LL SAVE YA, AS A FRIEND.
REI, FERGIVE ME.
グッ

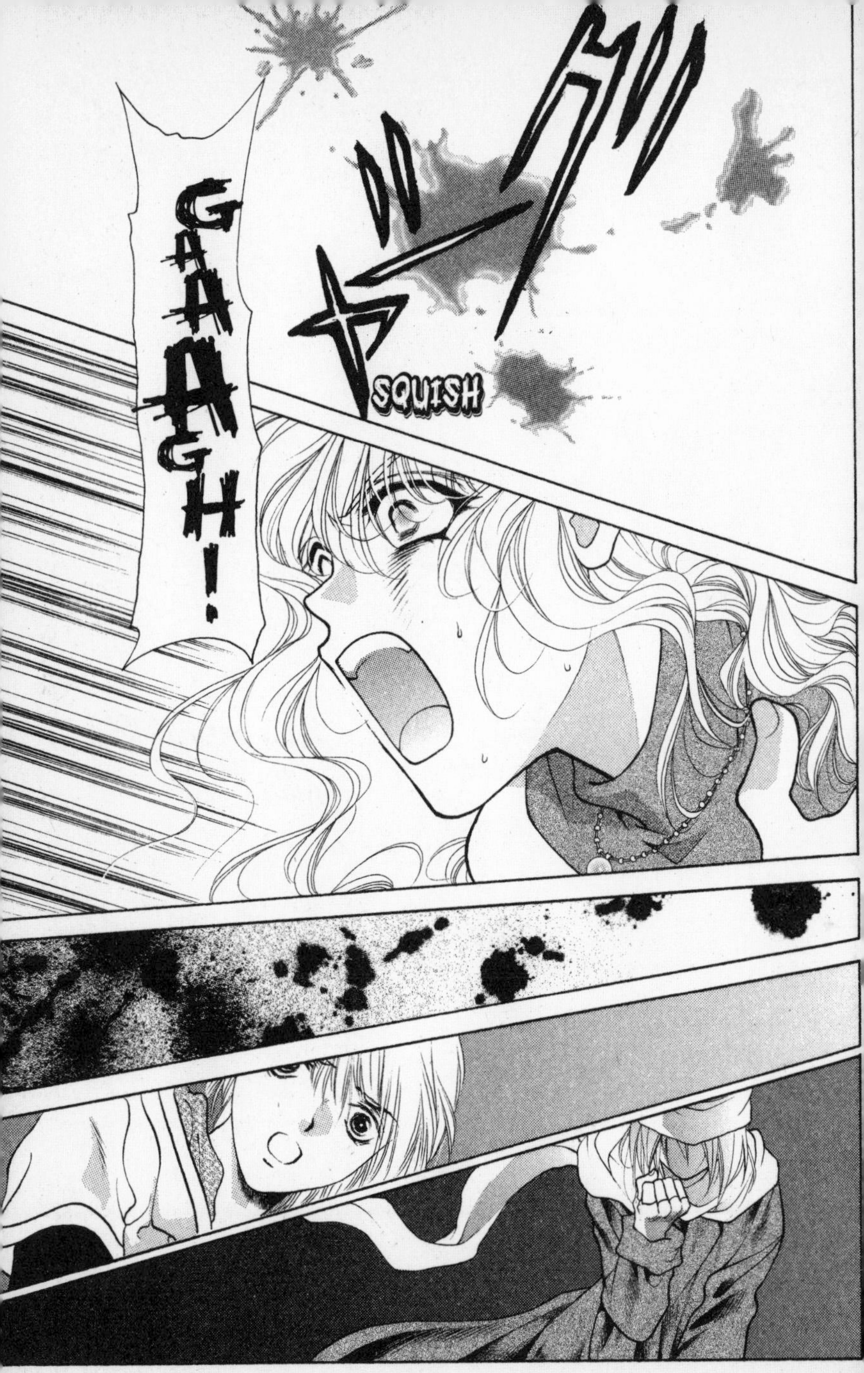
SQUISH
GAAAGH!

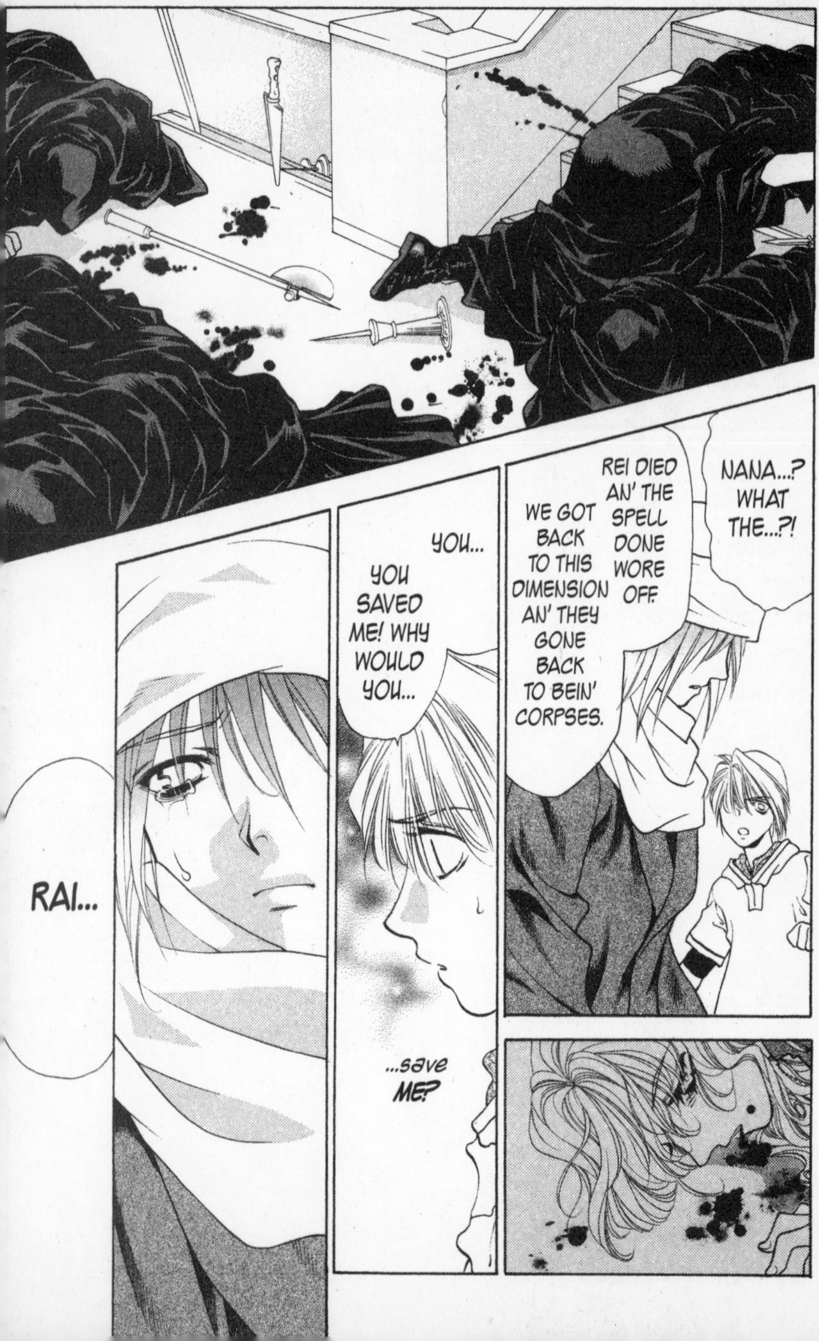
NANA...? WHAT THE...?!
REI DIED AN' THE SPELL DONE WORE OFF.
WE GOT BACK TO THIS DIMENSION AN' THEY GONE BACK TO BEIN' CORPSES.
YOU...
YOU SAVED ME! WHY WOULD YOU...
...save ME?
RAI...

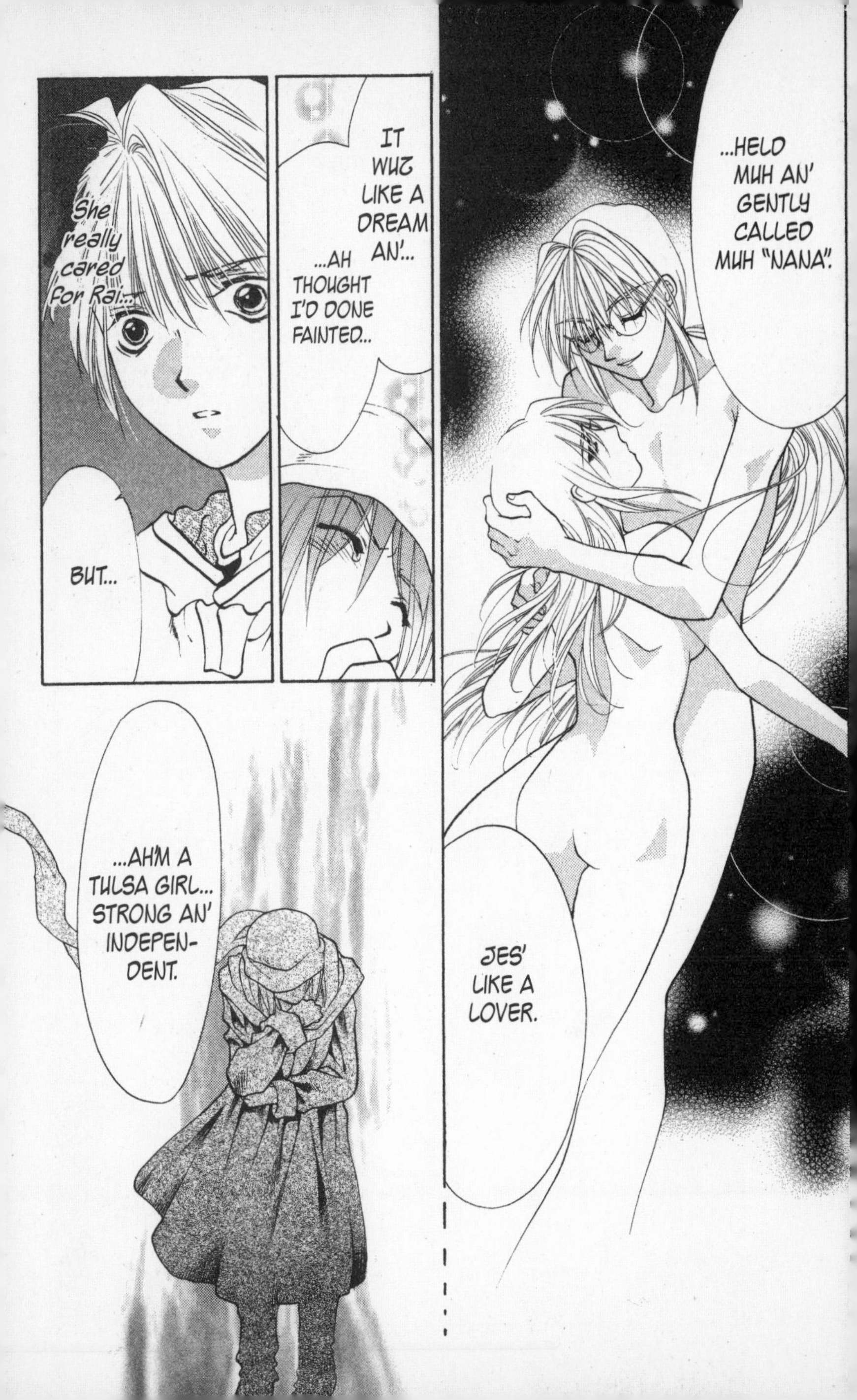

...HELD MUH AN' GENTLY CALLED MUH "NANA".
JES' LIKE A LOVER.
IT WUZ LIKE A DREAM AN'...
...AH THOUGHT I'D DONE FAINTED...
She really cared for Rai...
BUT...
...AH'M A TULSA GIRL... STRONG AN' INDEPEN-DENT.

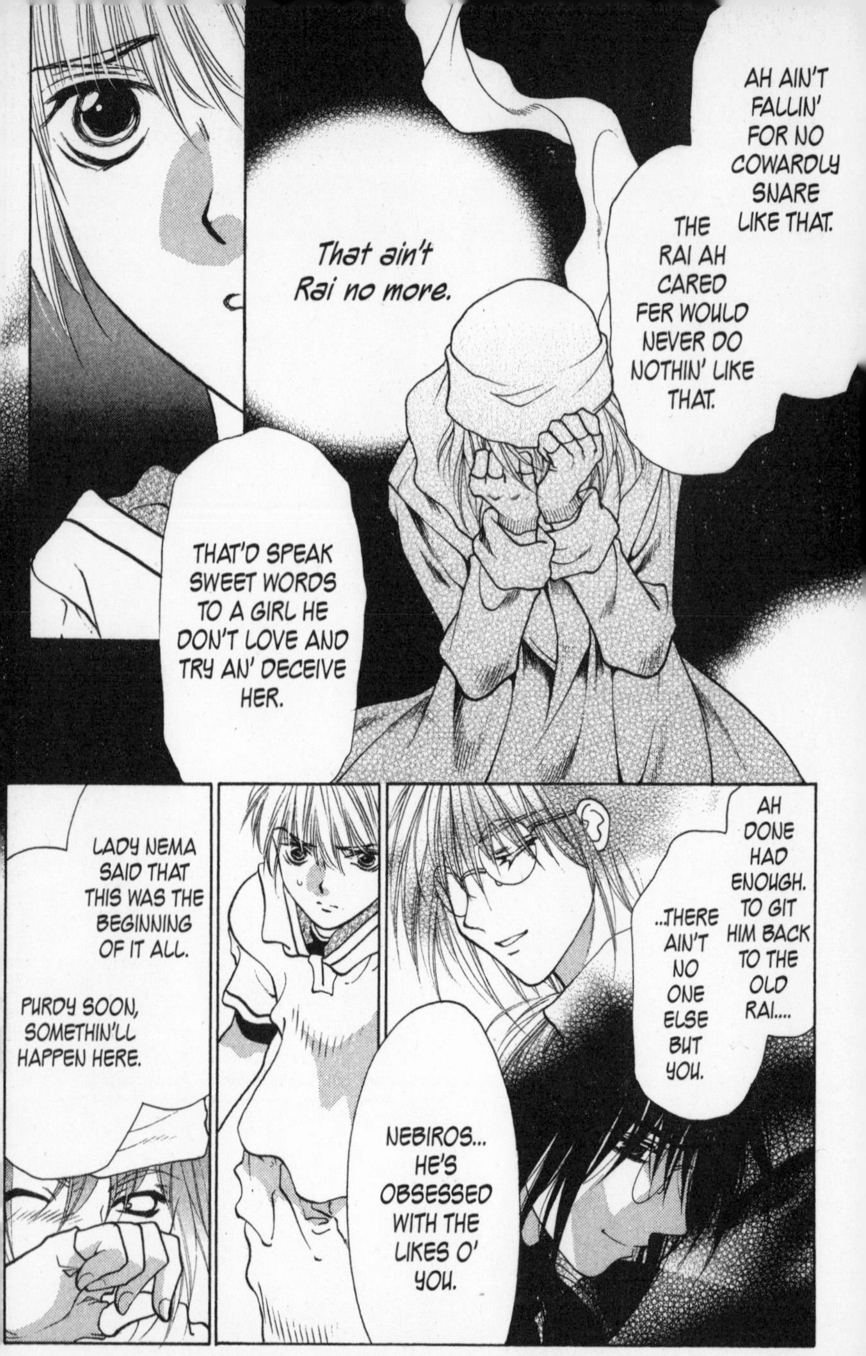
AH AIN'T FALLIN' FOR NO COWARDLY SNARE LIKE THAT.
THE RAI AH CARED FER WOULD NEVER DO NOTHIN' LIKE THAT.
That ain't Rai no more.
THAT'D SPEAK SWEET WORDS TO A GIRL HE DON'T LOVE AND TRY AN' DECEIVE HER.
AH DONE HAD ENOUGH. TO GIT HIM BACK TO THE OLD RAI....
...THERE AIN'T NO ONE ELSE BUT YOU.
NEBIROS... HE'S OBSESSED WITH THE LIKES O' YOU.
LADY NEMA SAID THAT THIS WAS THE BEGINNING OF IT ALL.
PURDY SOON, SOMETHIN'LL HAPPEN HERE.

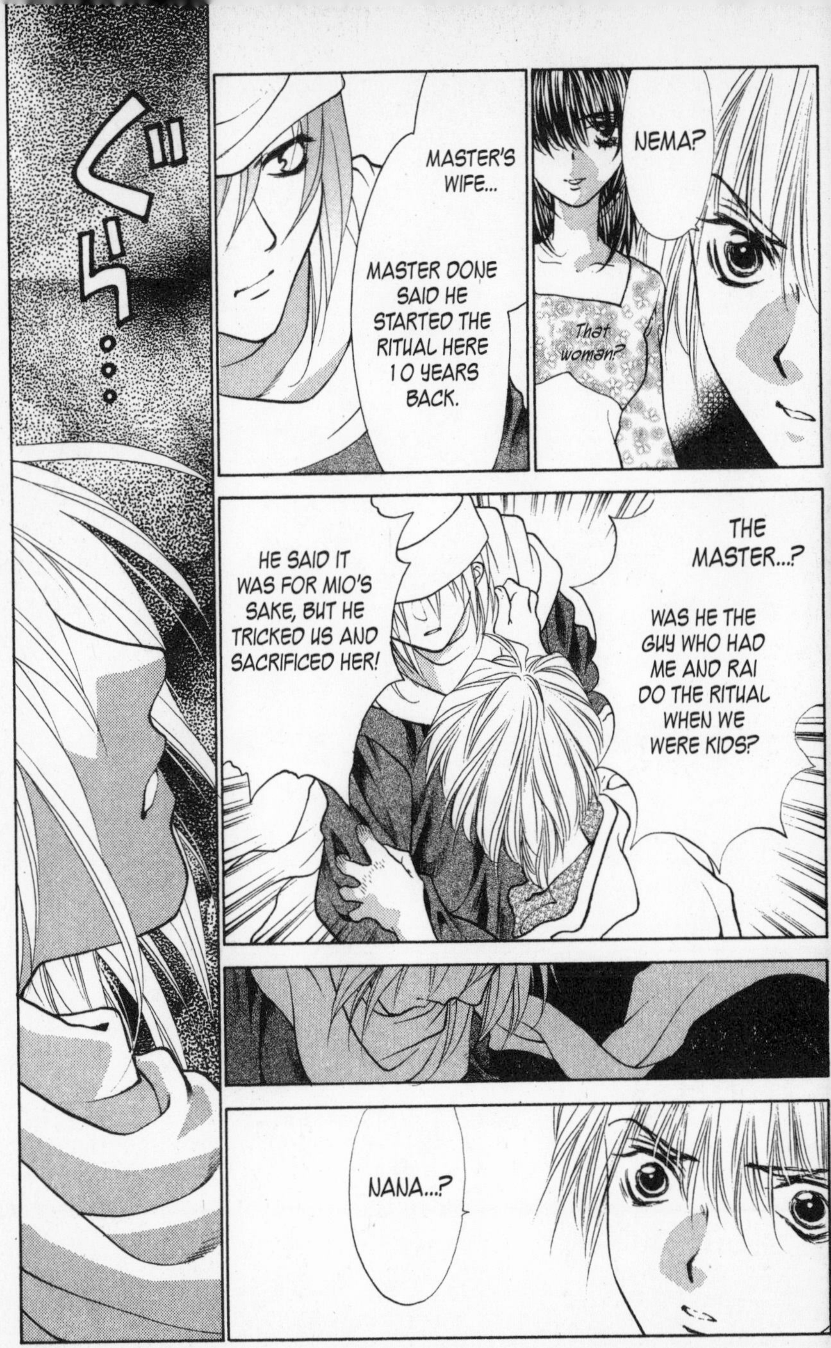
NEMA?
That woman?
MASTER'S WIFE...
MASTER DONE SAID HE STARTED THE RITUAL HERE 10 YEARS BACK.
THE MASTER...?
WAS HE THE GUY WHO HAD ME AND RAI DO THE RITUAL WHEN WE WERE KIDS?
HE SAID IT WAS FOR MIO'S SAKE, BUT HE TRICKED US AND SACRIFICED HER!
NANA...?
ぐら゛…

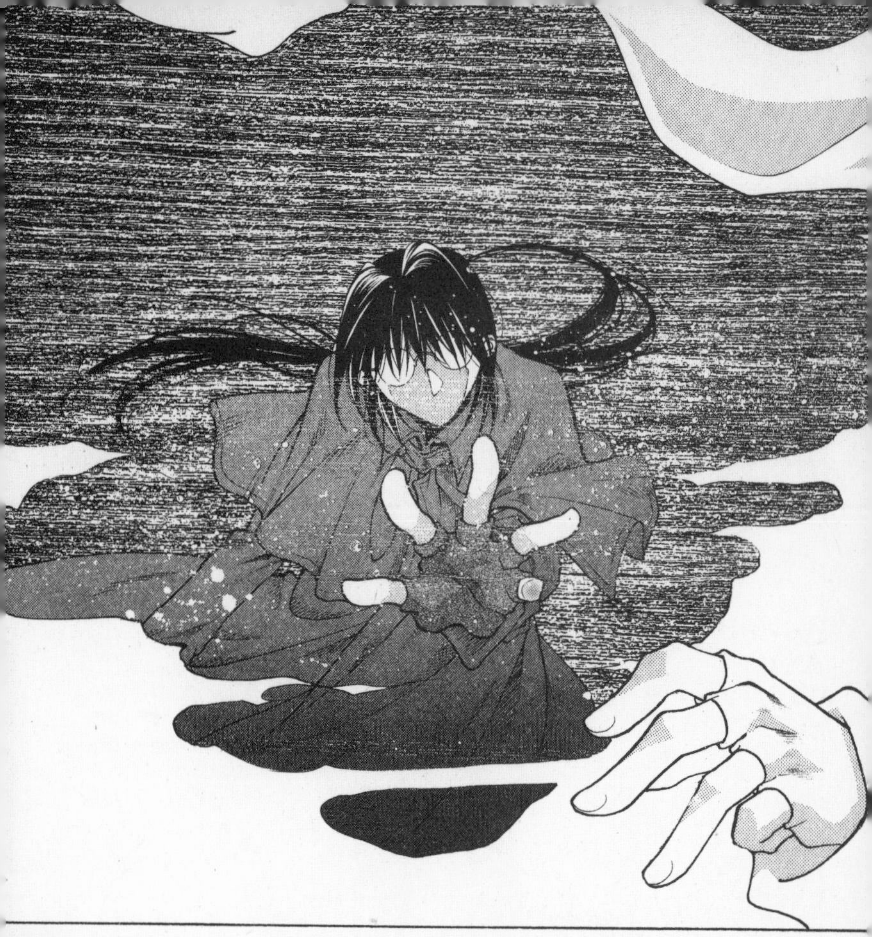
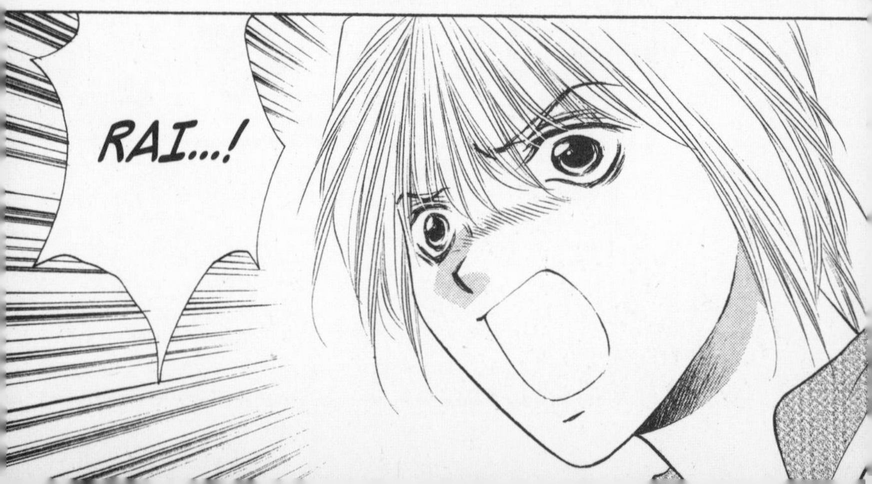
RAI...!

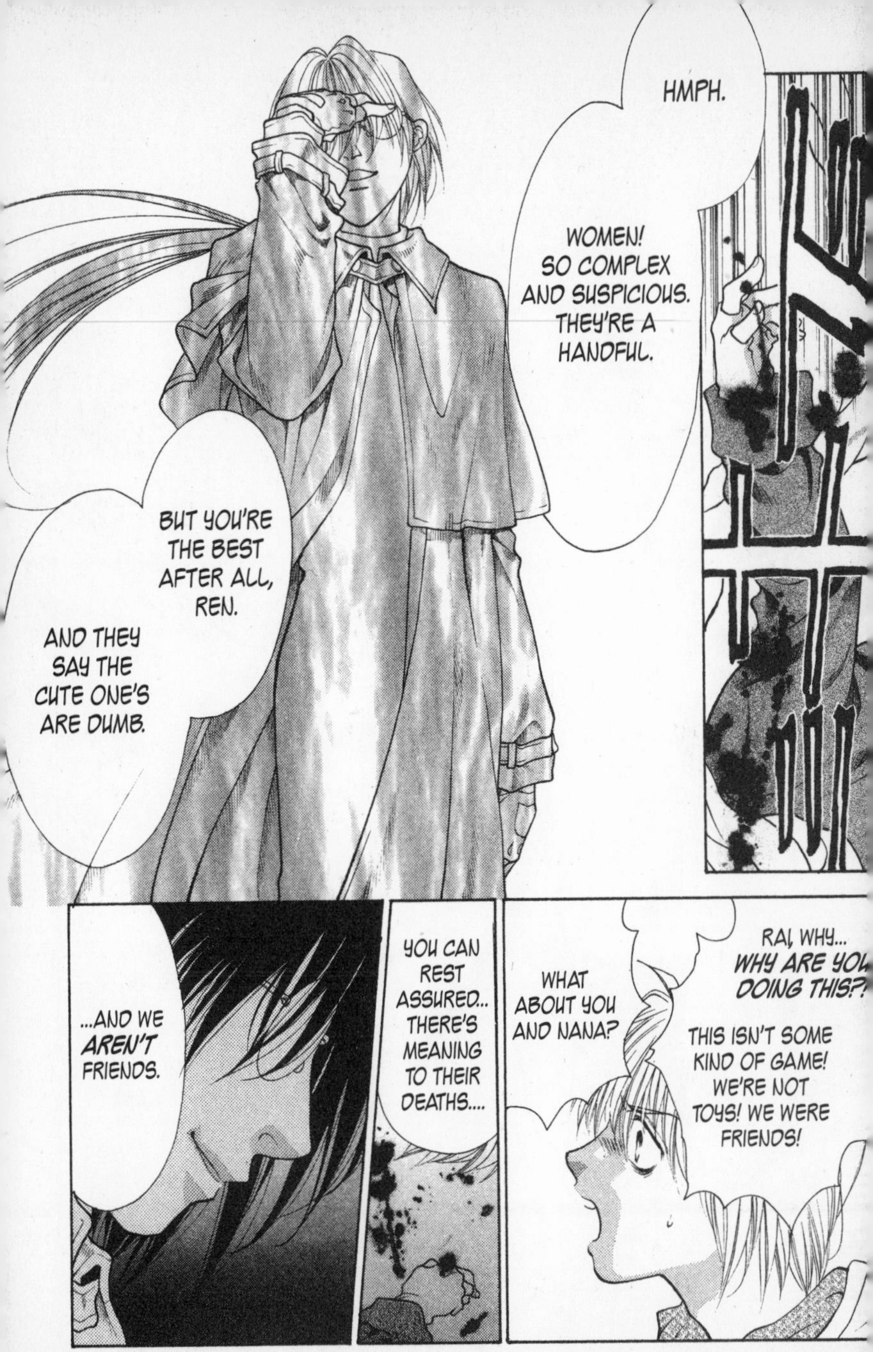
HMPH.
WOMEN! SO COMPLEX AND SUSPICIOUS. THEY'RE A HANDFUL.
BUT YOU'RE THE BEST AFTER ALL, REN.
AND THEY SAY THE CUTE ONE'S ARE DUMB.
RAI, WHY... *WHY ARE YOU DOING THIS?!*
THIS ISN'T SOME KIND OF GAME! WE'RE NOT TOYS! WE WERE FRIENDS!
WHAT ABOUT YOU AND NANA?
YOU CAN REST ASSURED... THERE'S MEANING TO THEIR DEATHS....
...AND WE *AREN'T* FRIENDS.

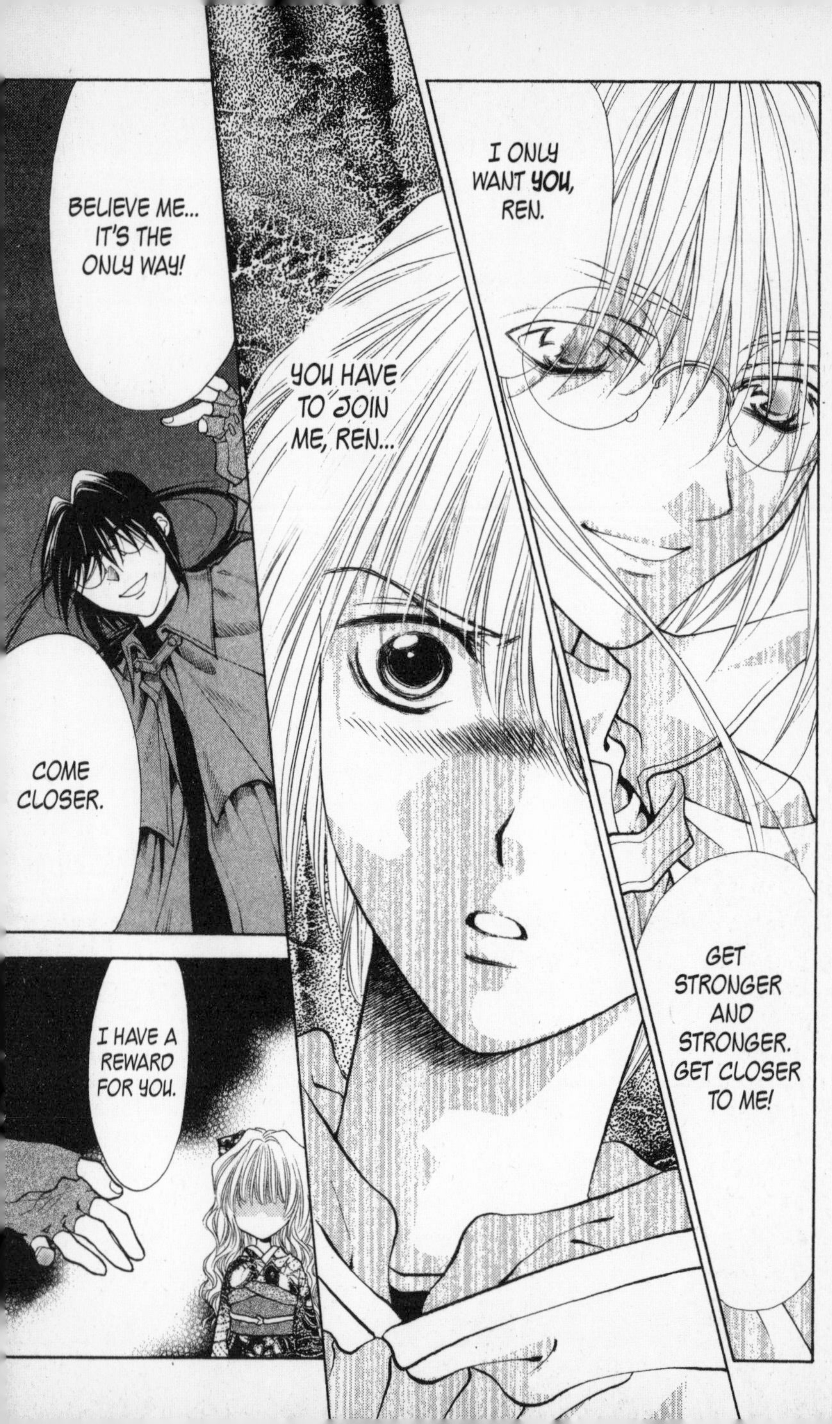
I ONLY WANT **YOU**, REN.
GET STRONGER AND STRONGER. GET CLOSER TO ME!
YOU HAVE TO JOIN ME, REN...
BELIEVE ME... IT'S THE ONLY WAY!
COME CLOSER.
I HAVE A REWARD FOR YOU.

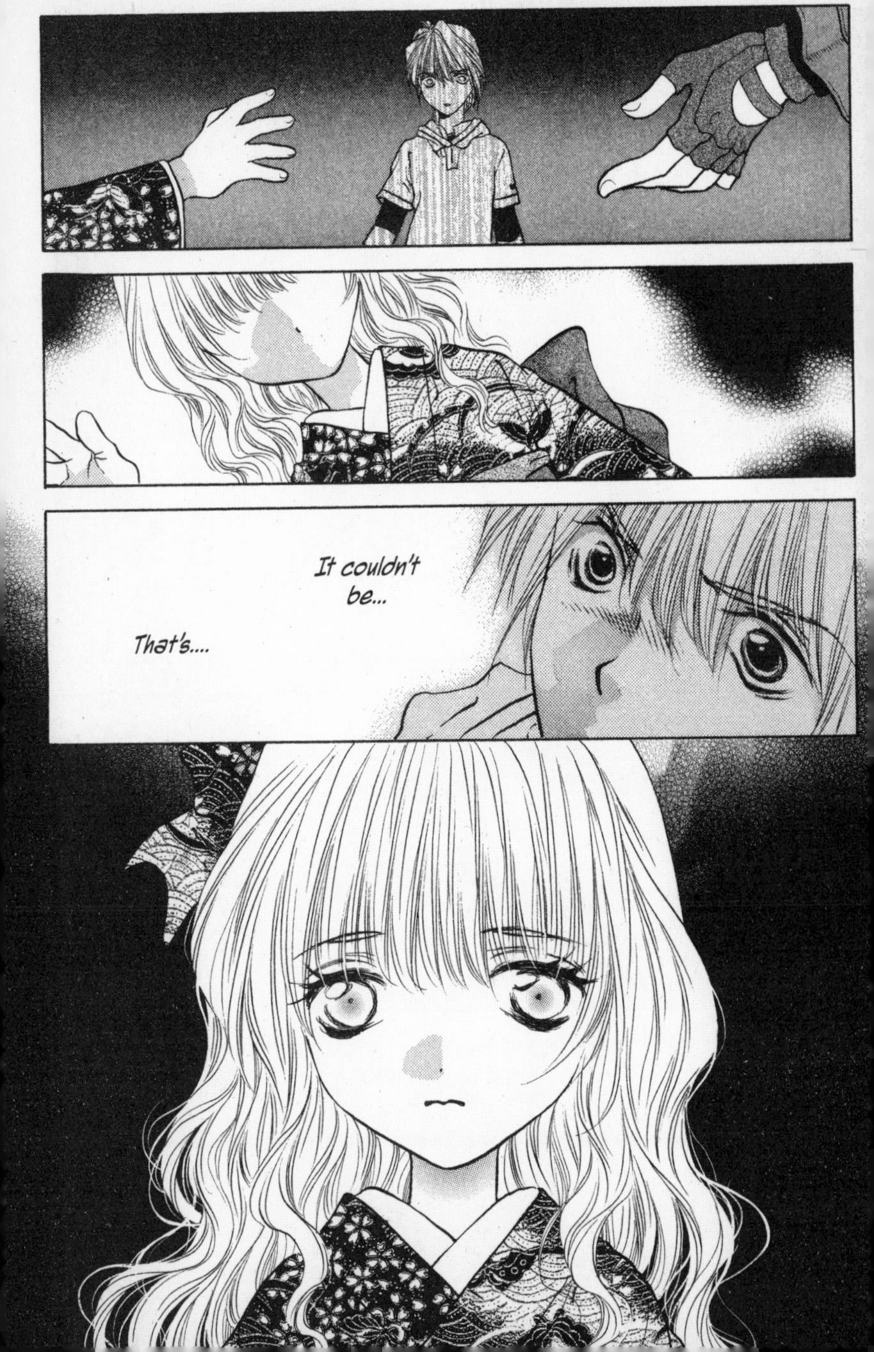
It couldn't be...
That's....

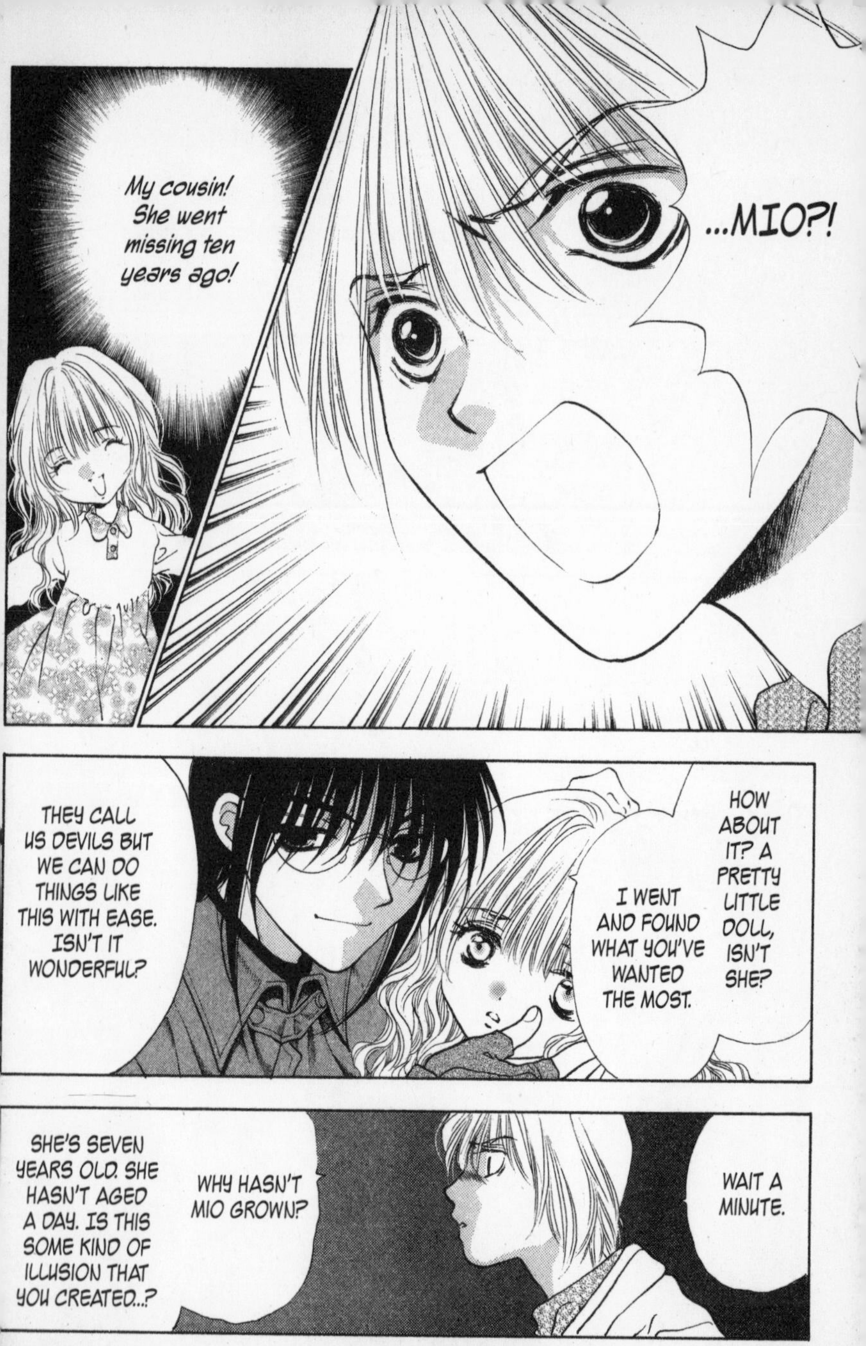
...MIO?!
My cousin! She went missing ten years ago!
HOW ABOUT IT? A PRETTY LITTLE DOLL, ISN'T SHE?
I WENT AND FOUND WHAT YOU'VE WANTED THE MOST.
THEY CALL US DEVILS BUT WE CAN DO THINGS LIKE THIS WITH EASE. ISN'T IT WONDERFUL?
WAIT A MINUTE.
WHY HASN'T MIO GROWN?
SHE'S SEVEN YEARS OLD. SHE HASN'T AGED A DAY. IS THIS SOME KIND OF ILLUSION THAT YOU CREATED...?

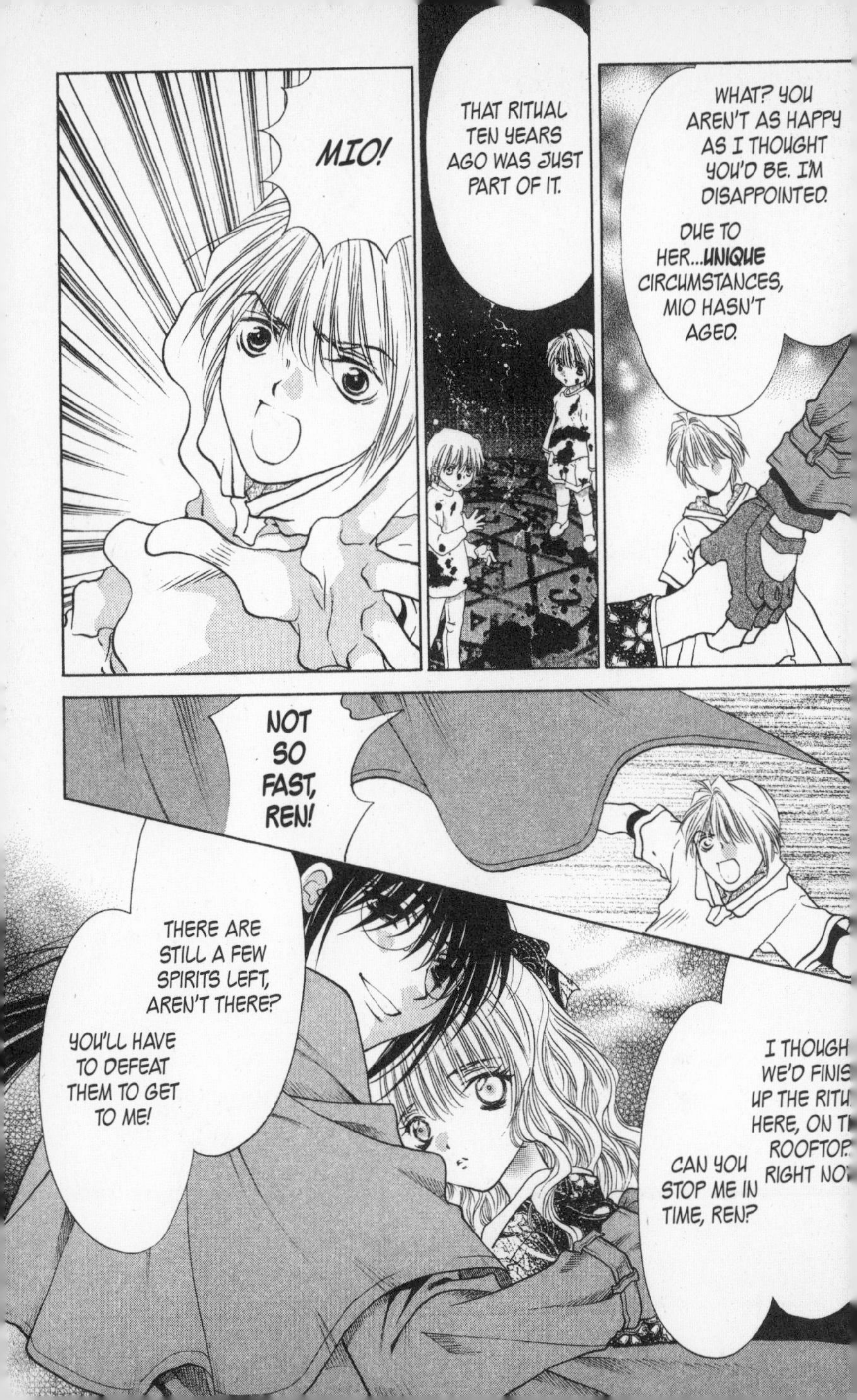
WHAT? YOU AREN'T AS HAPPY AS I THOUGHT YOU'D BE. I'M DISAPPOINTED.
DUE TO HER...**UNIQUE** CIRCUMSTANCES, MIO HASN'T AGED.
THAT RITUAL TEN YEARS AGO WAS JUST PART OF IT.
MIO!
NOT SO FAST, REN!
THERE ARE STILL A FEW SPIRITS LEFT, AREN'T THERE?
YOU'LL HAVE TO DEFEAT THEM TO GET TO ME!
I THOUGH WE'D FINIS UP THE RITU HERE, ON T ROOFTOP RIGHT NO
CAN YOU STOP ME IN TIME, REN?

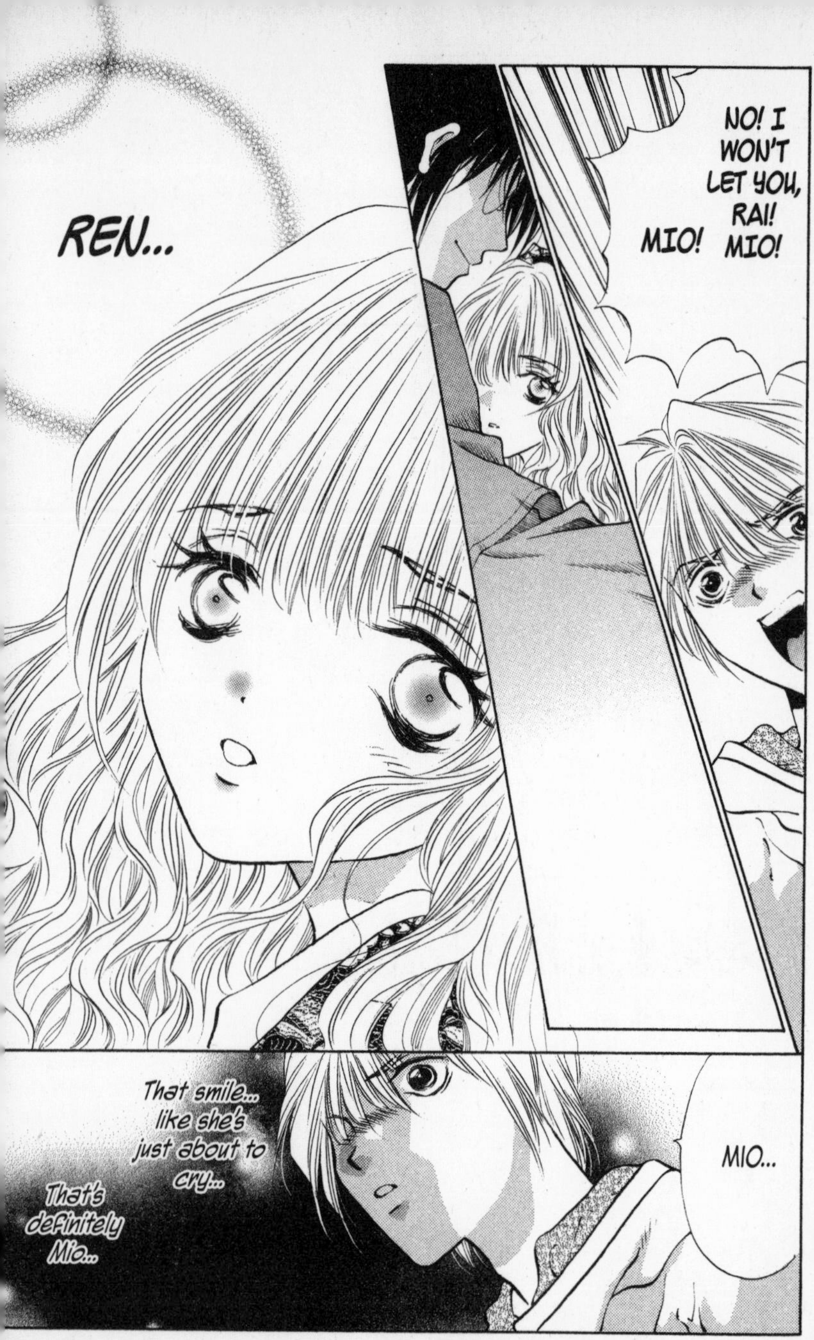
NO! I WON'T LET YOU, RAI! MIO!
MIO!
REN...
MIO...
That smile... like she's just about to cry...
That's definitely Mio...

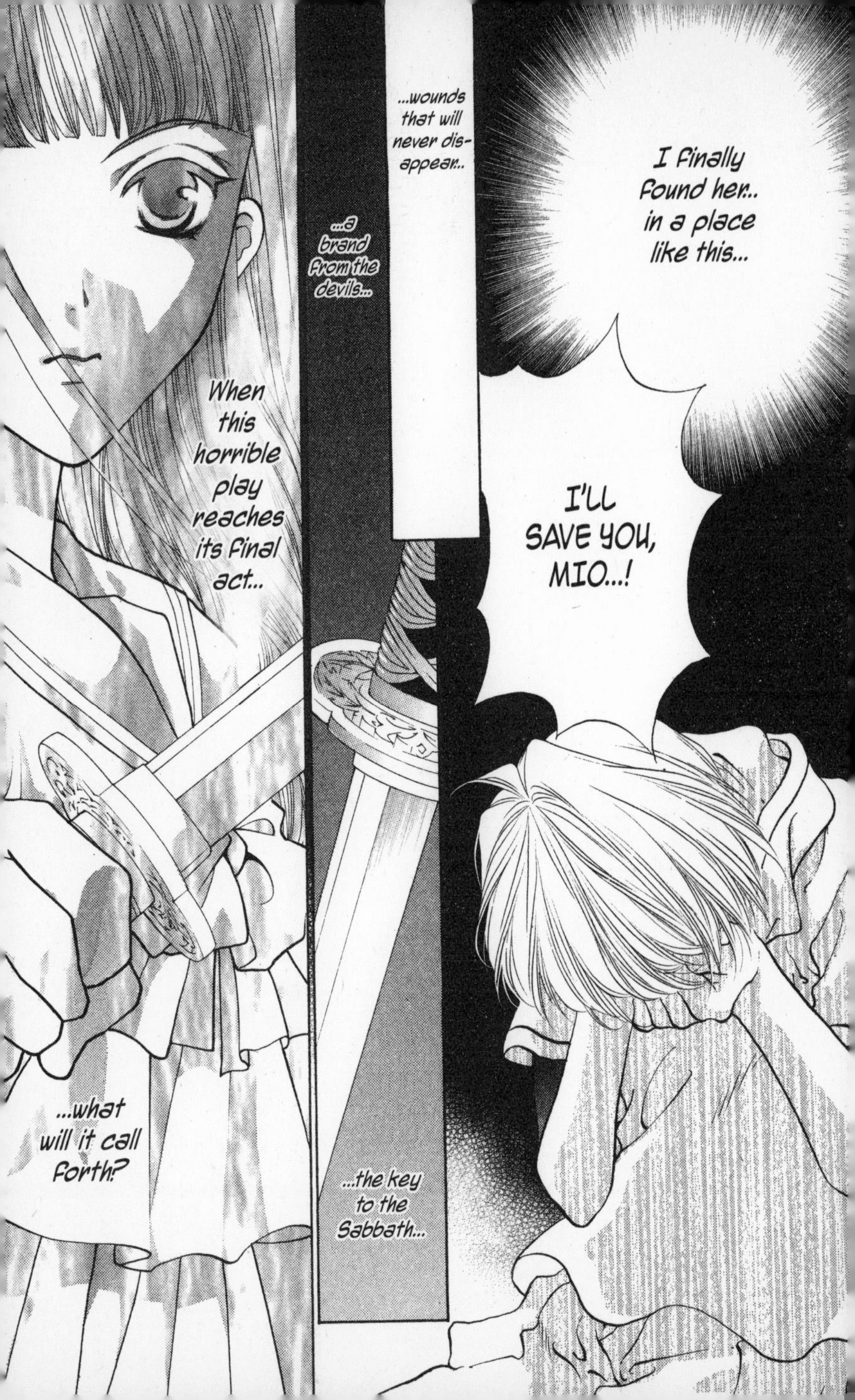
I finally found her.. in a place like this...
I'LL SAVE YOU, MIO...!
...wounds that will never dis-appear..
...a brand from the devils...
...the key to the Sabbath...
When this horrible play reaches its final act...
...what will it call forth?

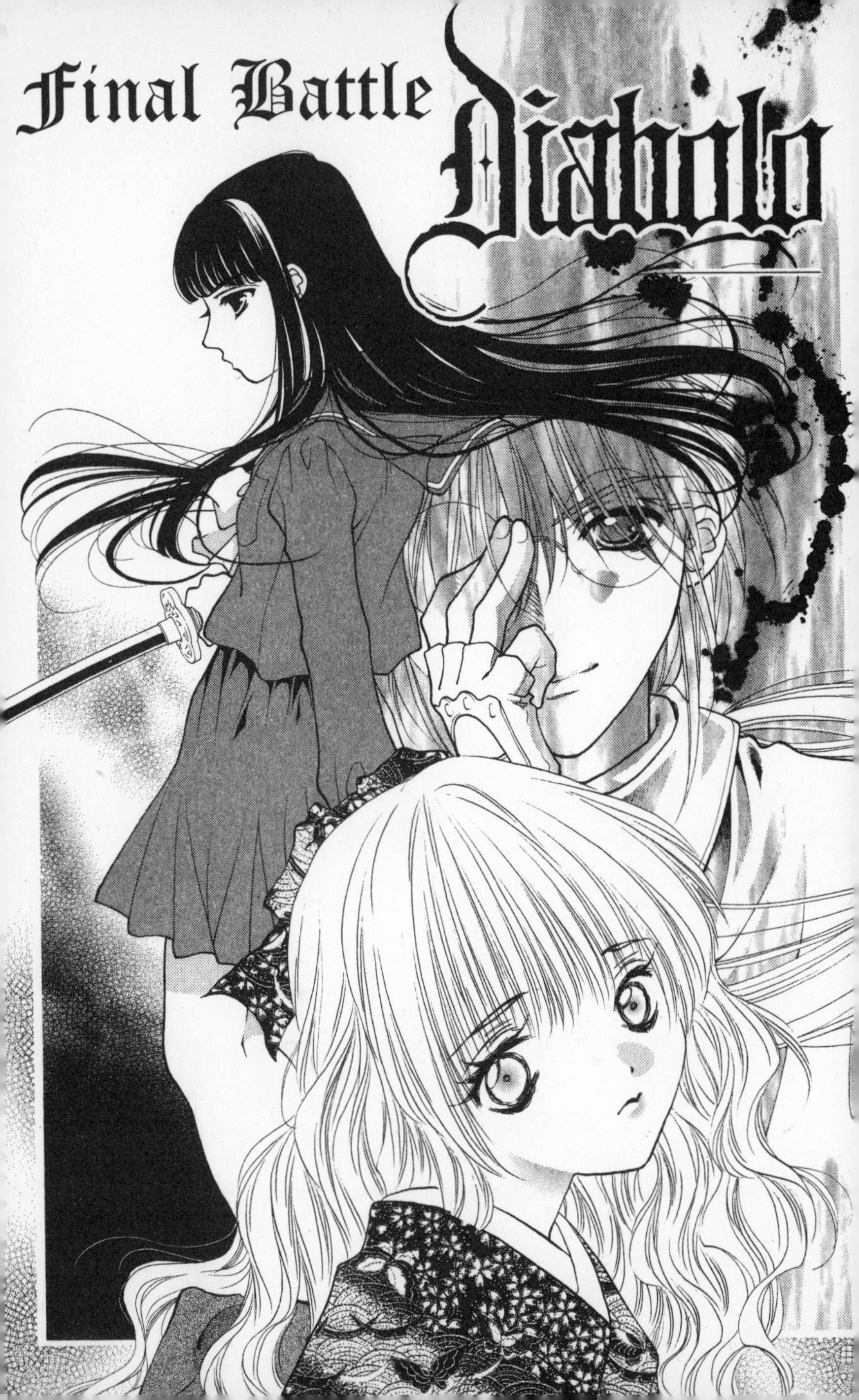
Final Battle
Diabolo

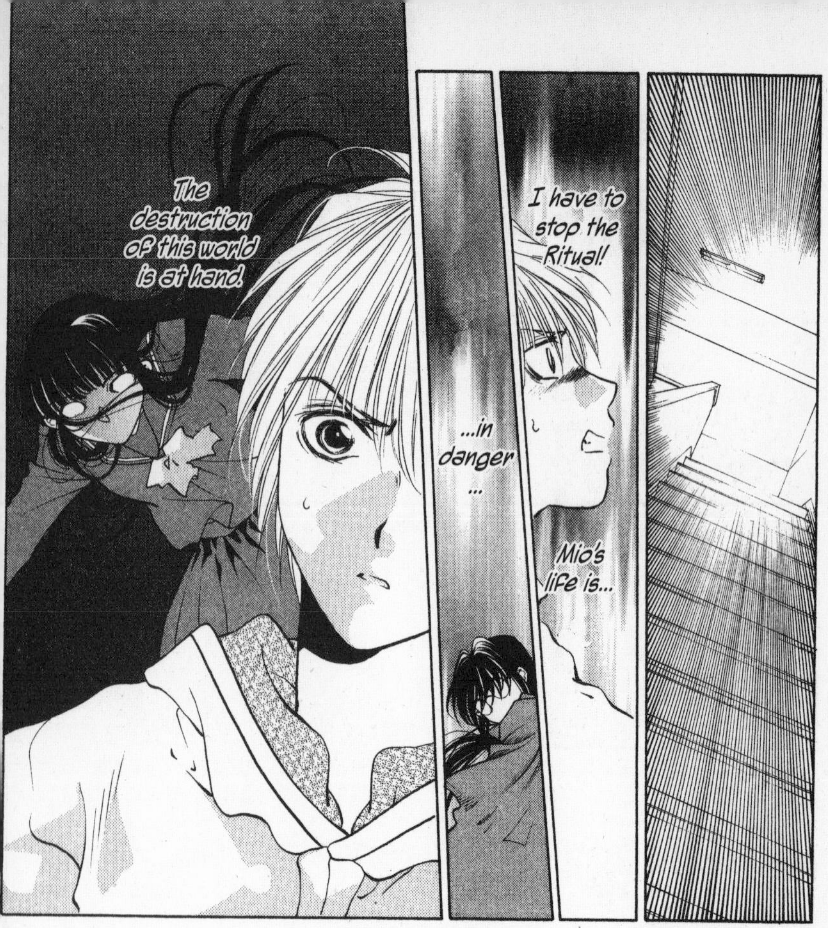
I have to stop the Ritual!
Mio's life is...
...in danger ...
The destruction of this world is at hand.

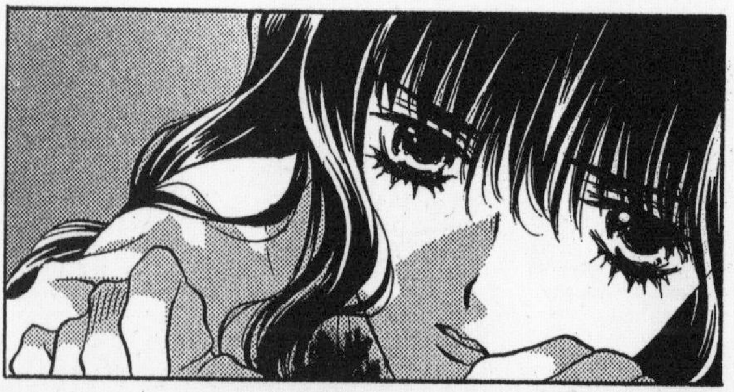

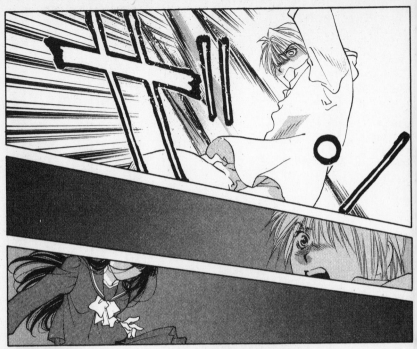

TSUKIKO?

NO,
YOU'RE...

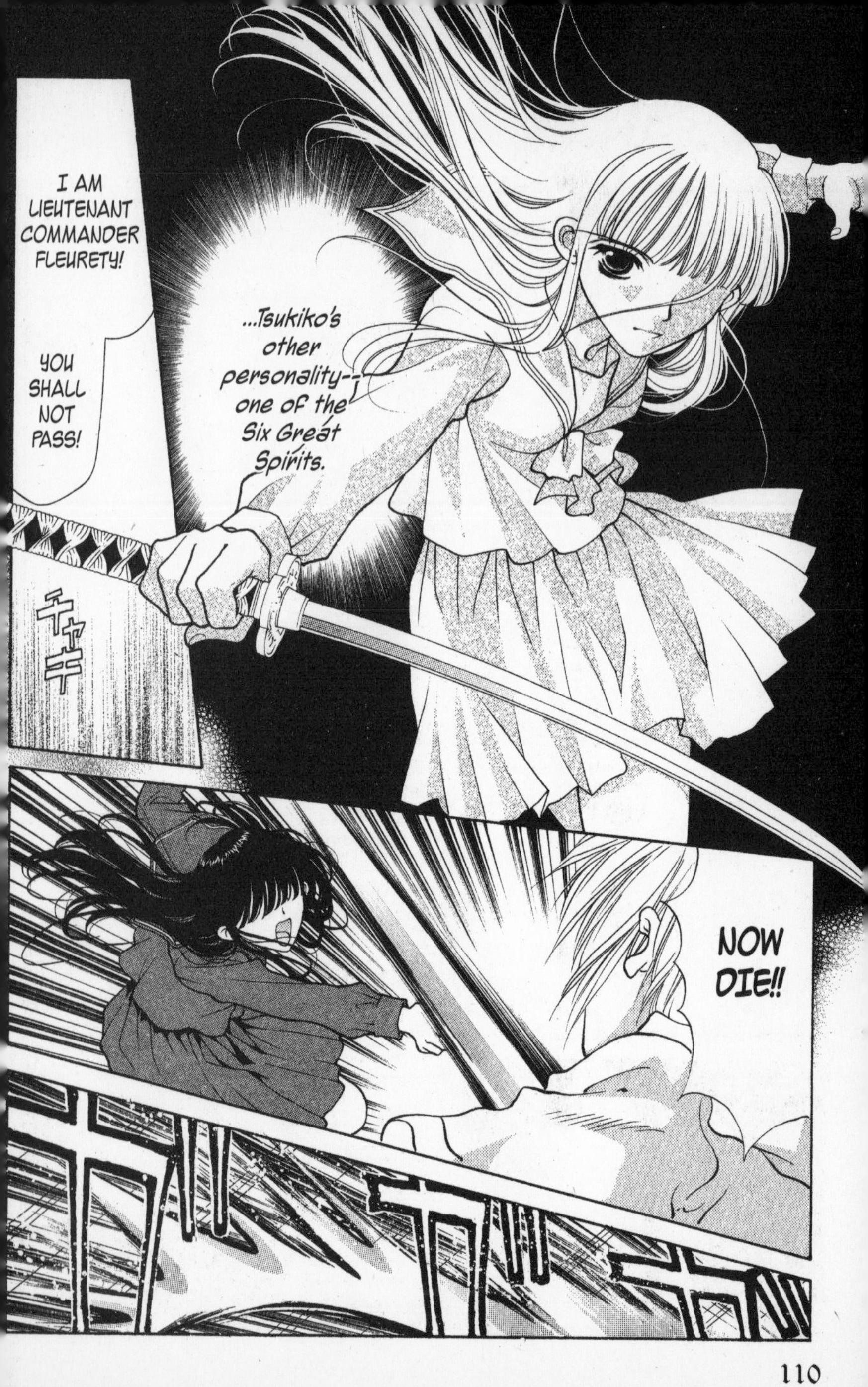
...Tsukiko's other personality--one of the Six Great Spirits.
I AM LIEUTENANT COMMANDER FLEURETY!
YOU SHALL NOT PASS!
チャキ
NOW DIE!!

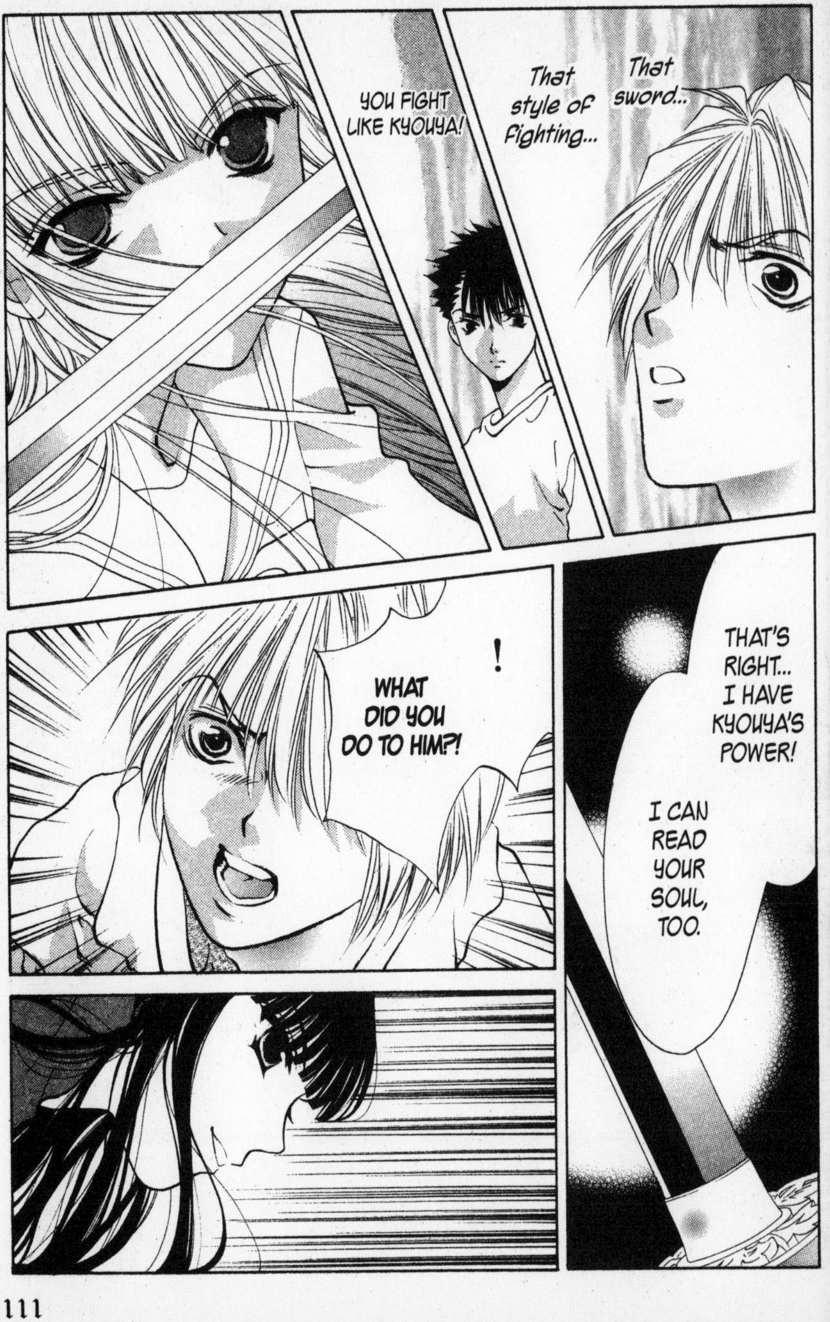
That sword...
That style of fighting...
YOU FIGHT LIKE KYOUYA!
THAT'S RIGHT... I HAVE KYOUYA'S POWER!
I CAN READ YOUR SOUL, TOO.
!
WHAT DID YOU DO TO HIM?!

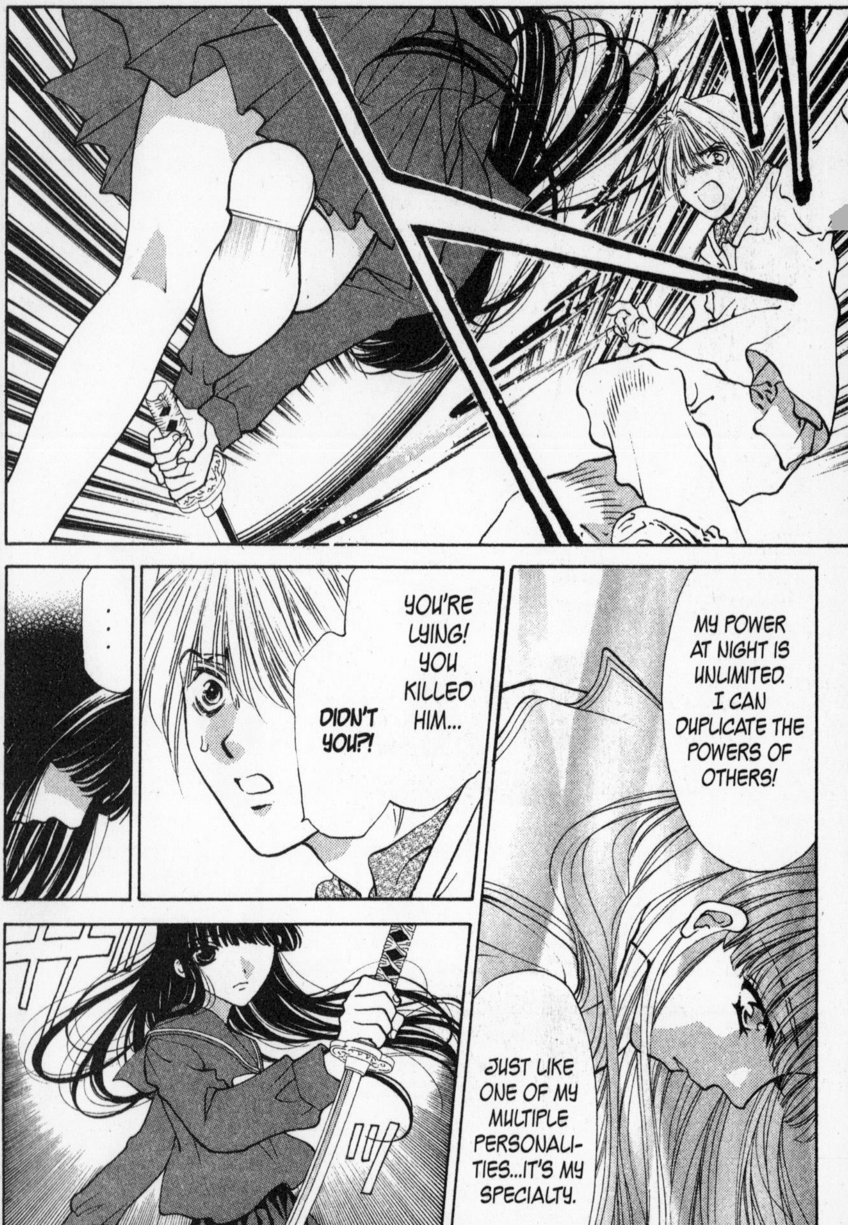
MY POWER AT NIGHT IS UNLIMITED. I CAN DUPLICATE THE POWERS OF OTHERS!
JUST LIKE ONE OF MY MULTIPLE PERSONALI-TIES...IT'S MY SPECIALTY.
YOU'RE LYING! YOU KILLED HIM...
DIDN'T YOU?!
...

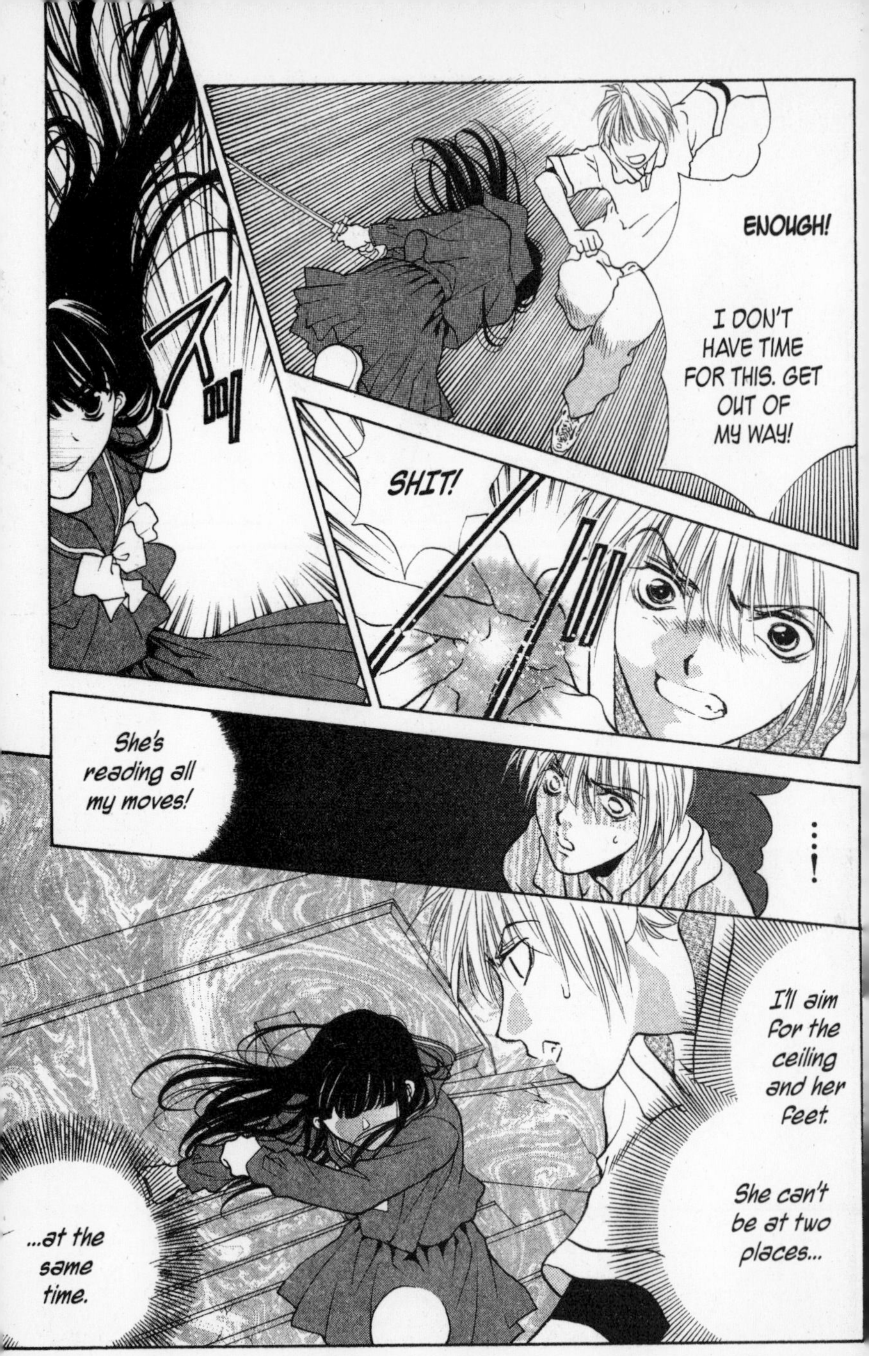
ENOUGH!
I DON'T HAVE TIME FOR THIS. GET OUT OF MY WAY!
SHIT!
...!
She's reading all my moves!
I'll aim for the ceiling and her feet.
She can't be at two places...
...at the same time.

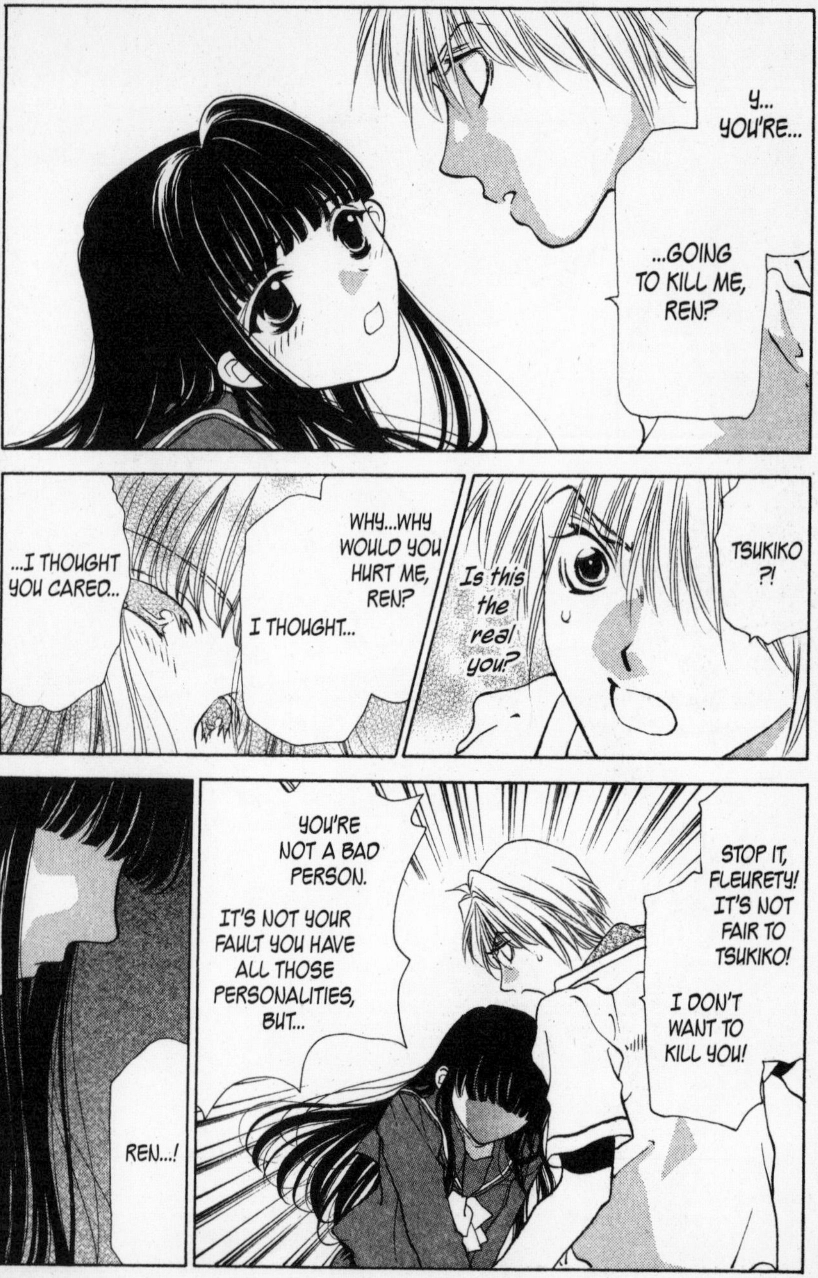
Y... YOU'RE...
...GOING TO KILL ME, REN?
TSUKIKO?!
Is this the real you?
WHY...WHY WOULD YOU HURT ME, REN?
I THOUGHT...
...I THOUGHT YOU CARED...
STOP IT, FLEURETY! IT'S NOT FAIR TO TSUKIKO!
I DON'T WANT TO KILL YOU!
YOU'RE NOT A BAD PERSON.
IT'S NOT YOUR FAULT YOU HAVE ALL THOSE PERSONALITIES, BUT...
REN...!

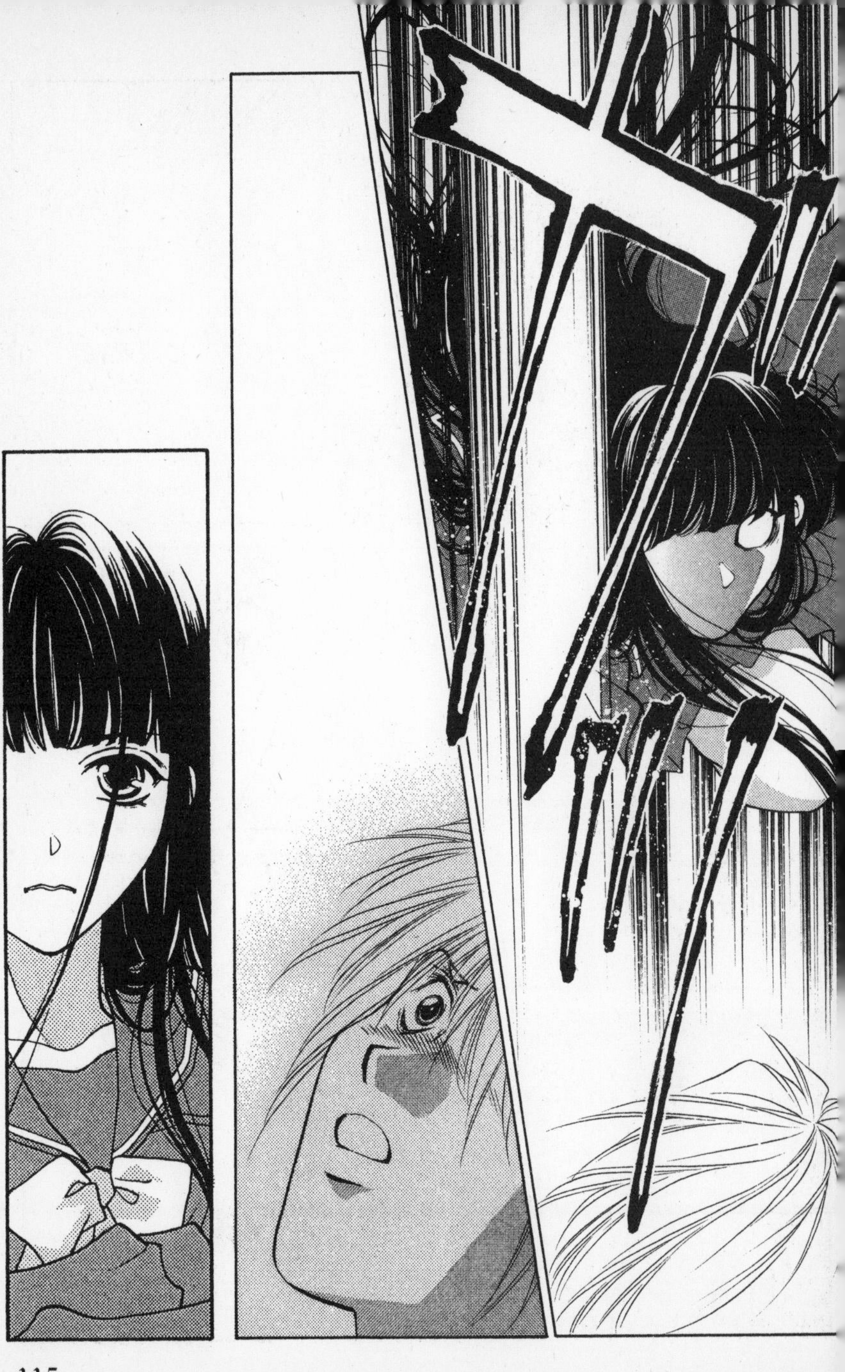

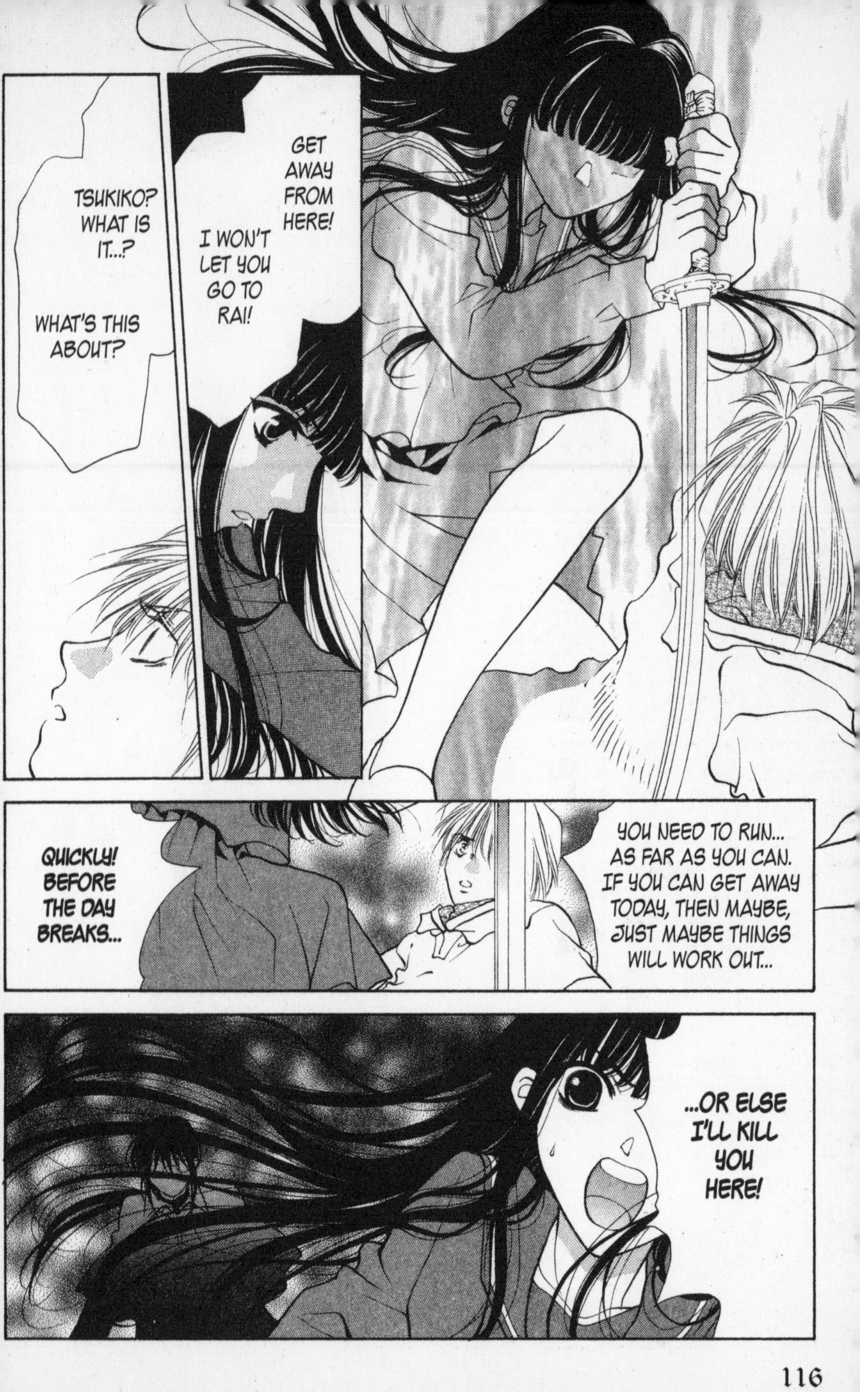
GET AWAY FROM HERE!
I WON'T LET YOU GO TO RAI!
TSUKIKO? WHAT IS IT...?
WHAT'S THIS ABOUT?
YOU NEED TO RUN... AS FAR AS YOU CAN. IF YOU CAN GET AWAY TODAY, THEN MAYBE, JUST MAYBE THINGS WILL WORK OUT...
QUICKLY! BEFORE THE DAY BREAKS...
...OR ELSE I'LL KILL YOU HERE!

RAI...!

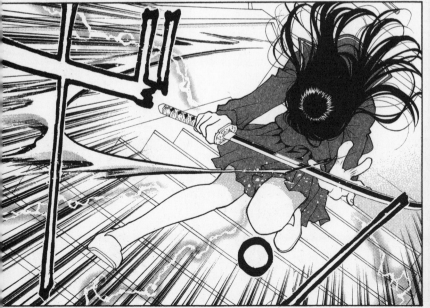

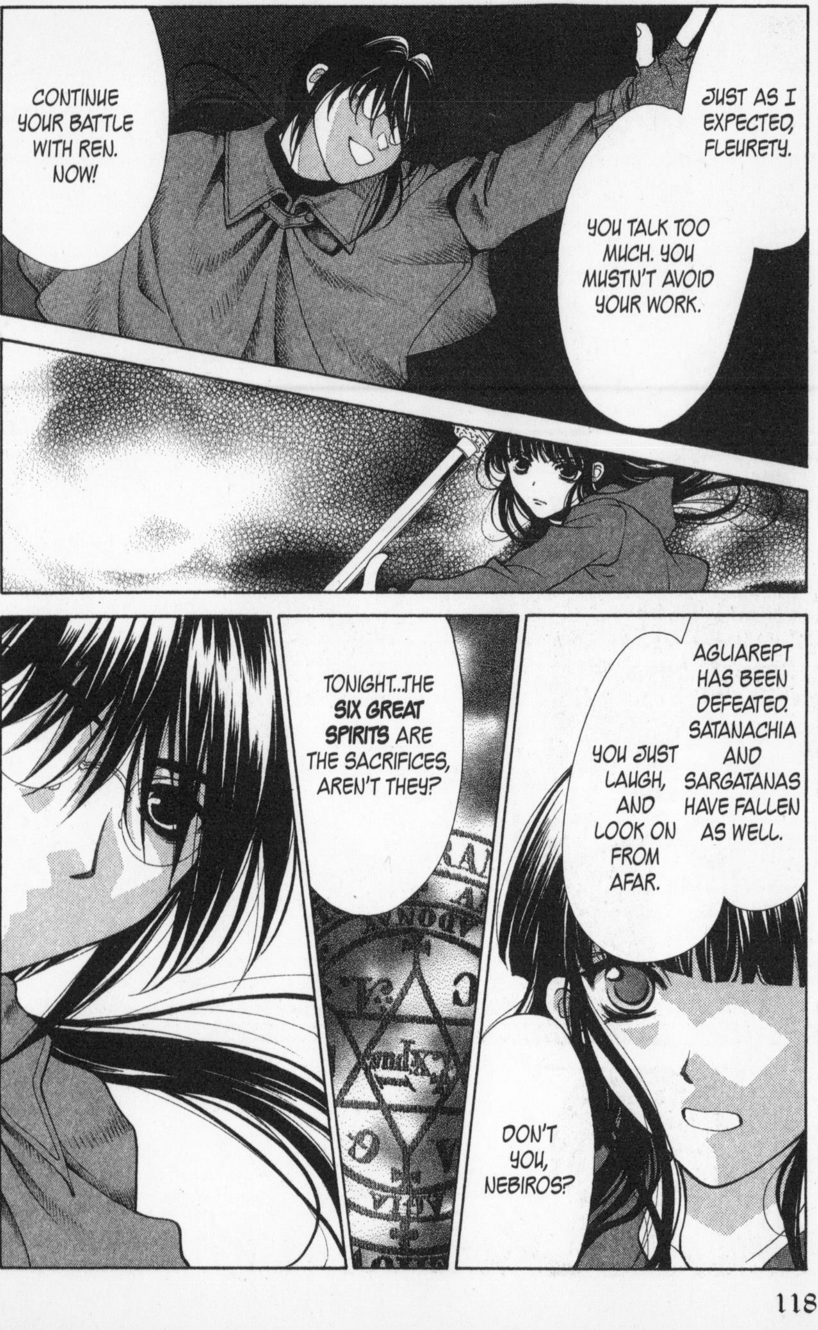
JUST AS I EXPECTED, FLEURETY.
YOU TALK TOO MUCH. YOU MUSTN'T AVOID YOUR WORK.
CONTINUE YOUR BATTLE WITH REN. NOW!
AGLIAREPT HAS BEEN DEFEATED. SATANACHIA AND SARGATANAS HAVE FALLEN AS WELL.
YOU JUST LAUGH, AND LOOK ON FROM AFAR.
DON'T YOU, NEBIROS?
TONIGHT...THE **SIX GREAT SPIRITS** ARE THE SACRIFICES, AREN'T THEY?

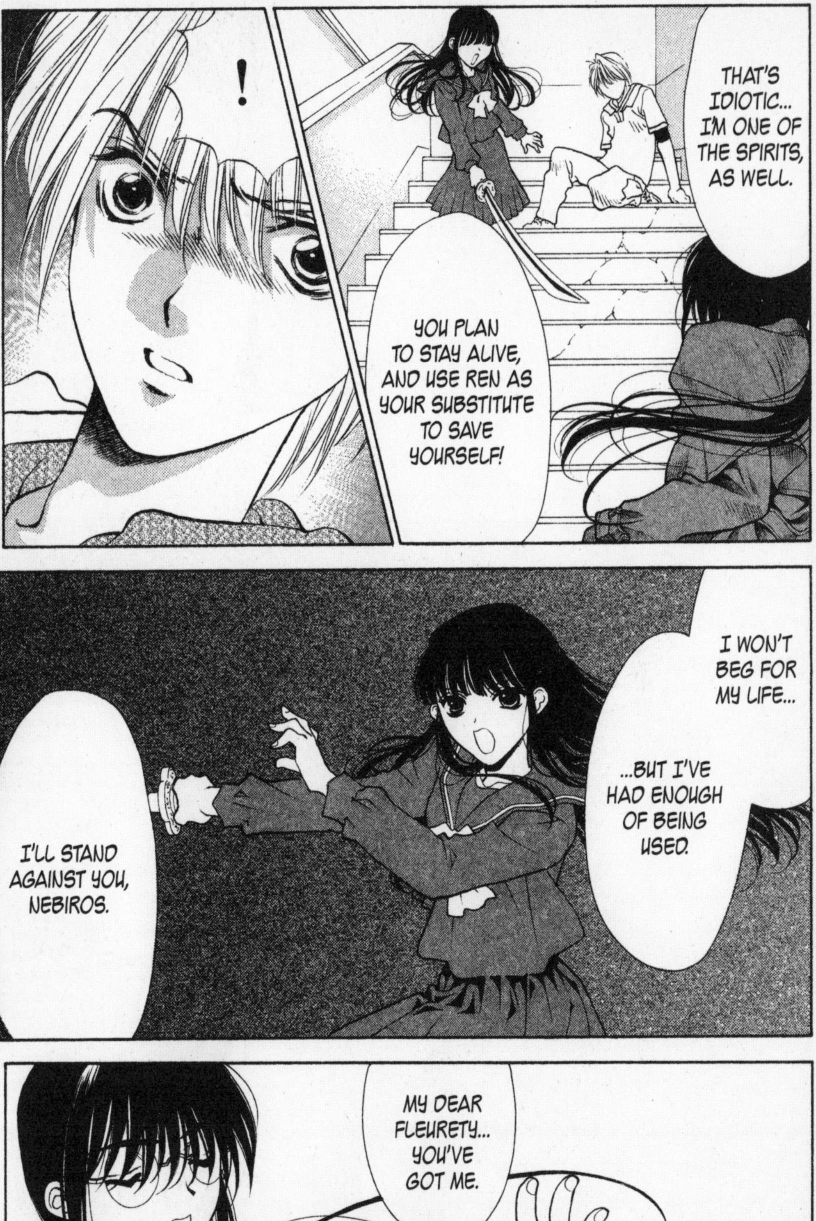
THAT'S IDIOTIC... I'M ONE OF THE SPIRITS, AS WELL.
YOU PLAN TO STAY ALIVE, AND USE REN AS YOUR SUBSTITUTE TO SAVE YOURSELF!
!
I WON'T BEG FOR MY LIFE...
...BUT I'VE HAD ENOUGH OF BEING USED.
I'LL STAND AGAINST YOU, NEBIROS.
MY DEAR FLEURETY... YOU'VE GOT ME.

STOP IT,
RAI!

I SHOULD
HAVE DONE
YOU BEFORE
I DID NANA.

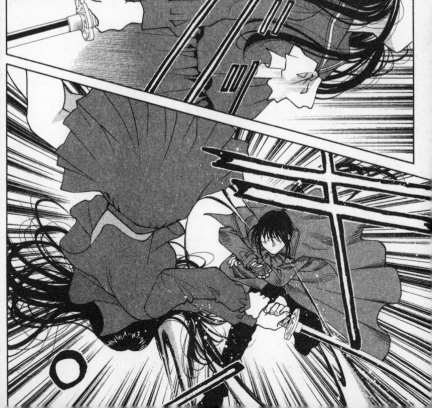

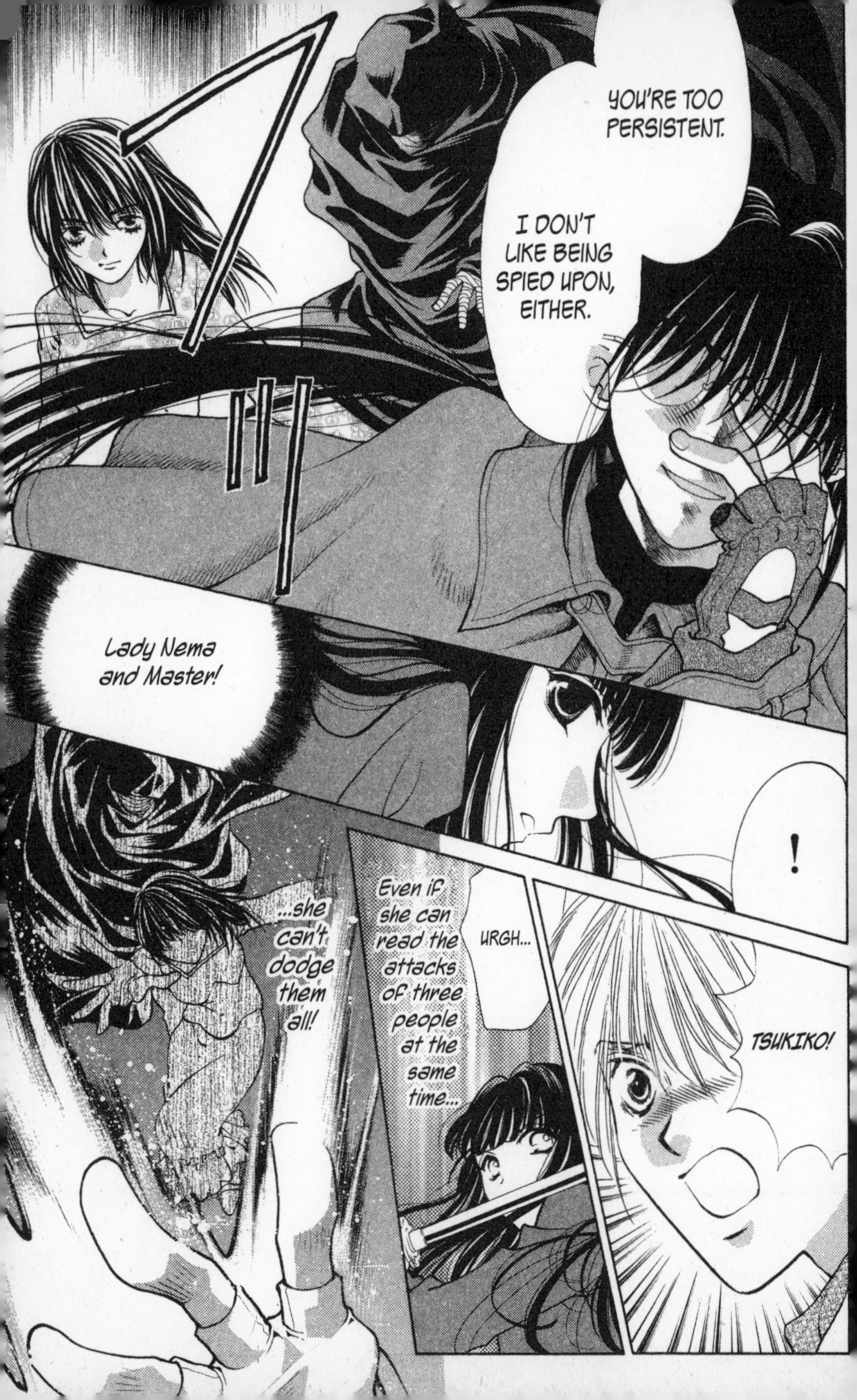
YOU'RE TOO PERSISTENT.
I DON'T LIKE BEING SPIED UPON, EITHER.
Lady Nema and Master!
!
URGH...
TSUKIKO!
Even if she can read the attacks of three people at the same time...
...she can't dodge them all!

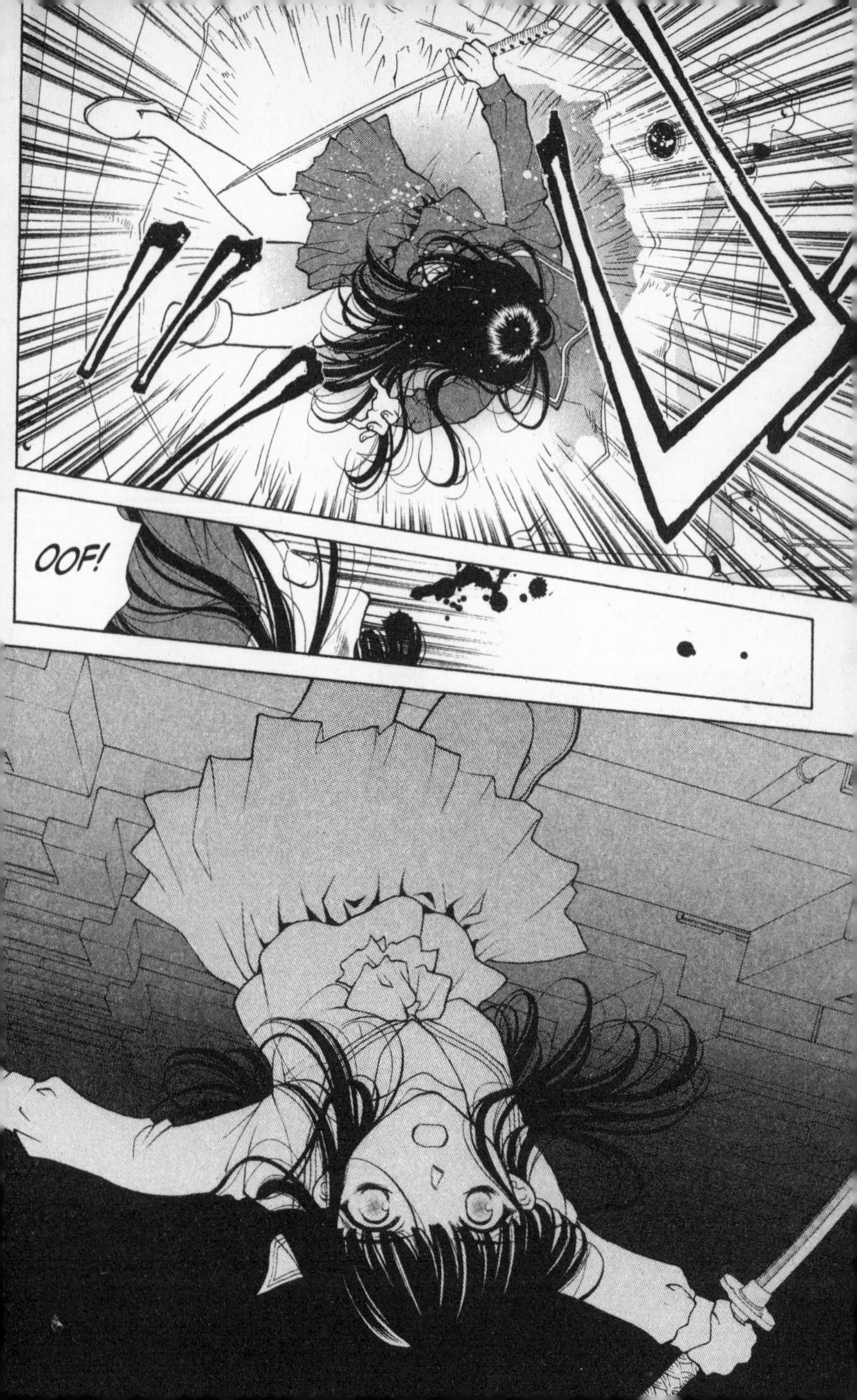
OOF!

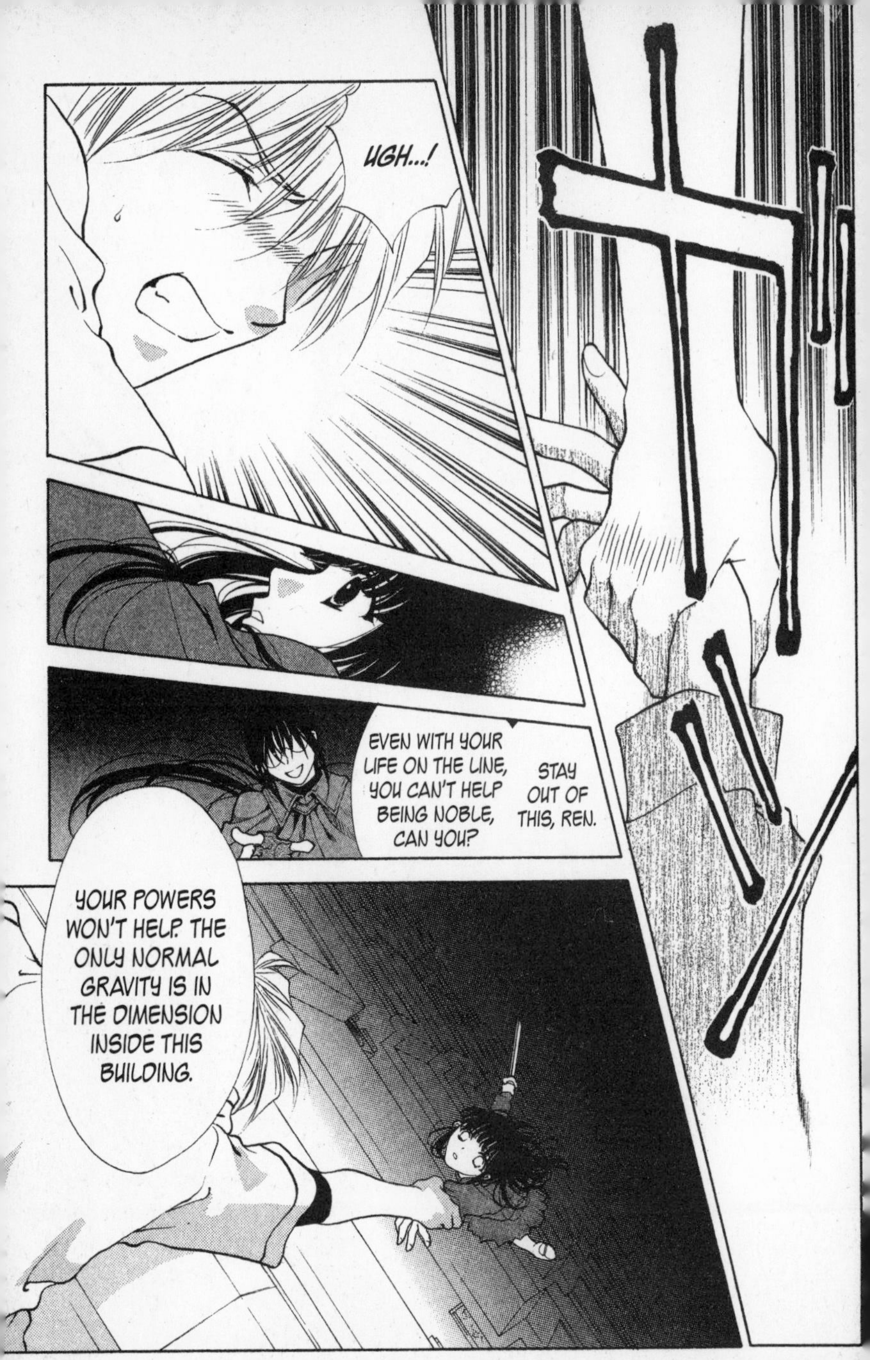
UGH...!
STAY OUT OF THIS, REN.
EVEN WITH YOUR LIFE ON THE LINE, YOU CAN'T HELP BEING NOBLE, CAN YOU?
YOUR POWERS WON'T HELP. THE ONLY NORMAL GRAVITY IS IN THE DIMENSION INSIDE THIS BUILDING.

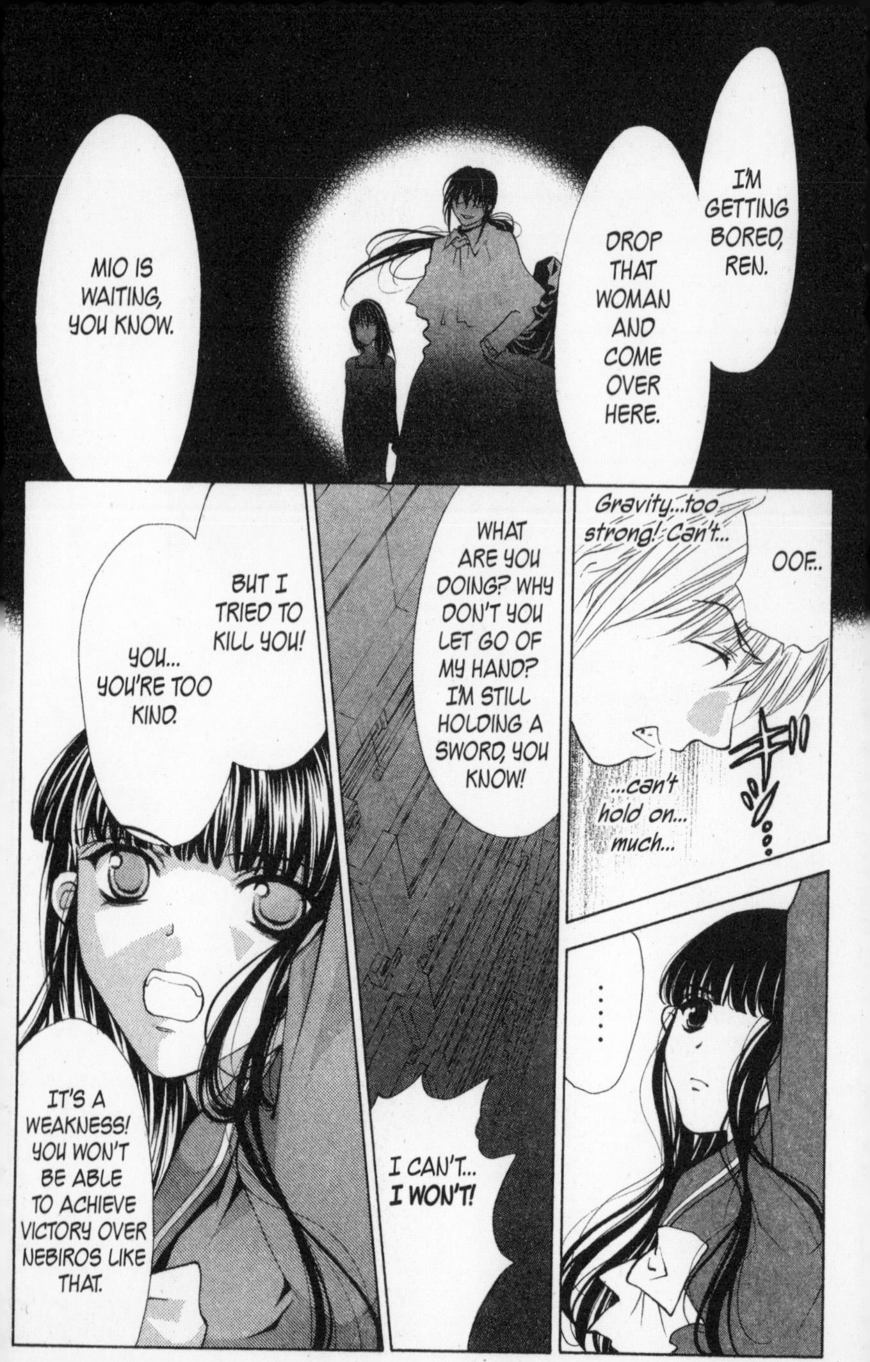
I'M GETTING BORED, REN.
DROP THAT WOMAN AND COME OVER HERE.
MIO IS WAITING, YOU KNOW.
Gravity...too strong! Can't...
OOF...
...can't hold on... much...
......
WHAT ARE YOU DOING? WHY DON'T YOU LET GO OF MY HAND? I'M STILL HOLDING A SWORD, YOU KNOW!
I CAN'T... **I WON'T!**
BUT I TRIED TO KILL YOU!
YOU... YOU'RE TOO KIND.
IT'S A WEAKNESS! YOU WON'T BE ABLE TO ACHIEVE VICTORY OVER NEBIROS LIKE THAT.

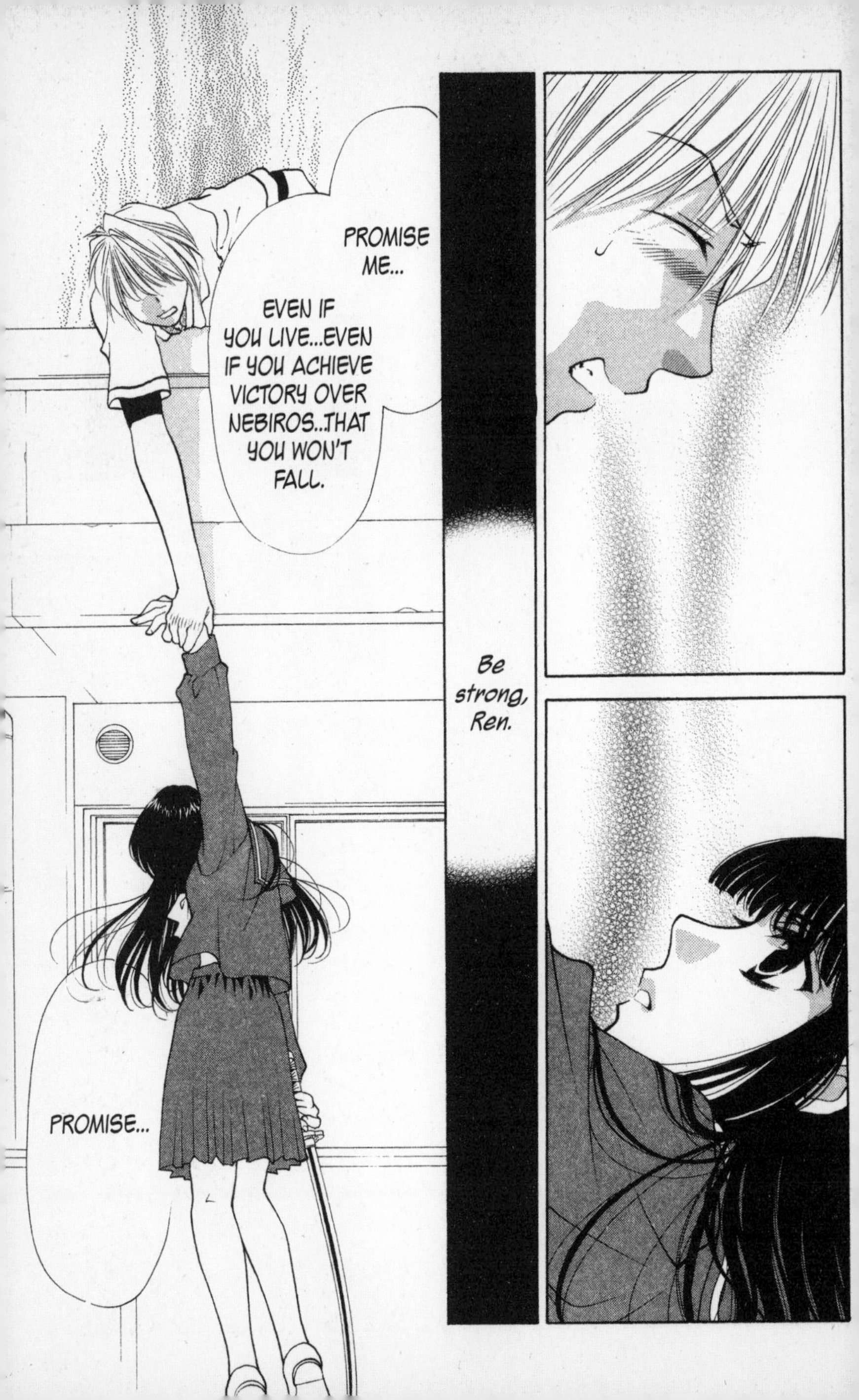

Be strong, Ren.
PROMISE ME...
EVEN IF YOU LIVE...EVEN IF YOU ACHIEVE VICTORY OVER NEBIROS...THAT YOU WON'T FALL.
PROMISE...

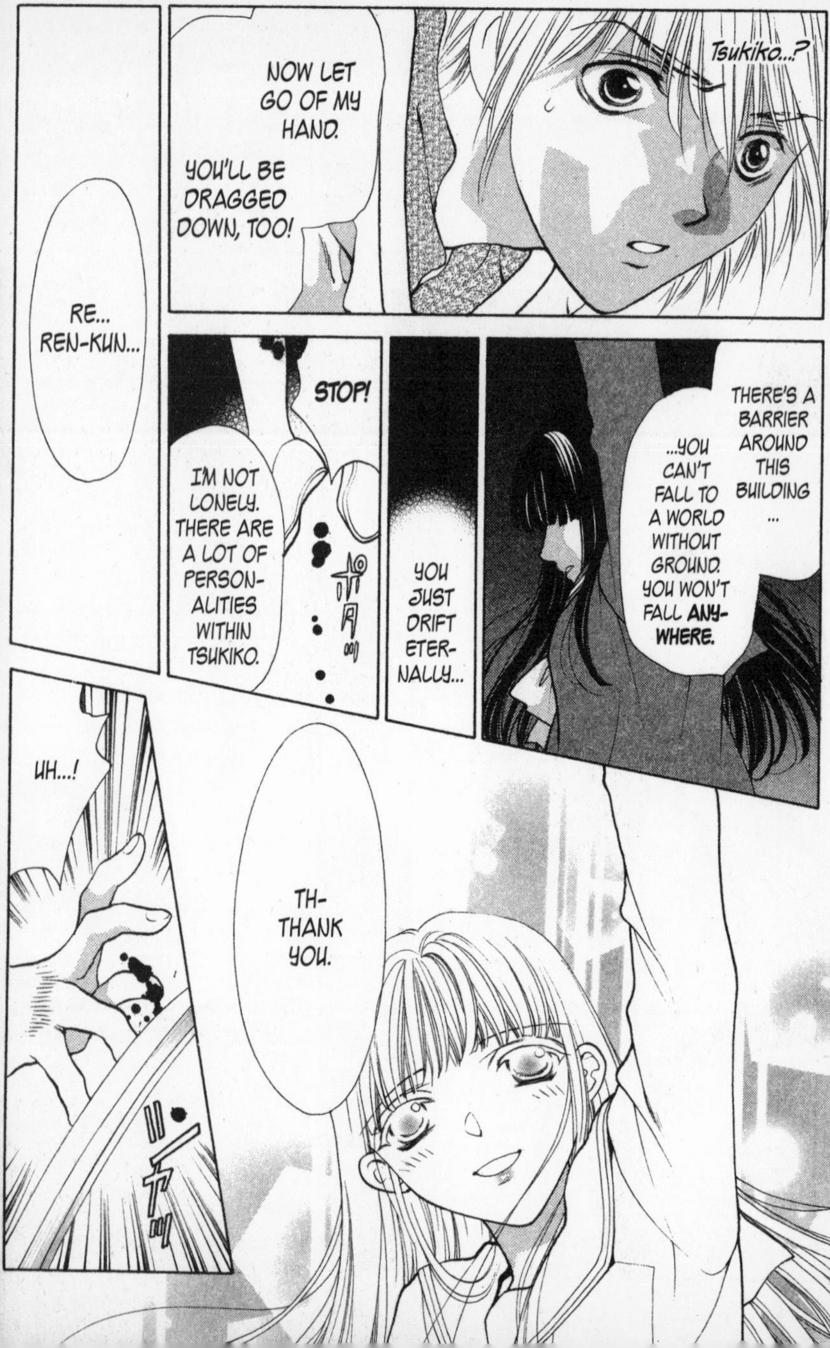
Tsukiko...?
NOW LET GO OF MY HAND.
YOU'LL BE DRAGGED DOWN, TOO!
THERE'S A BARRIER AROUND THIS BUILDING...
...YOU CAN'T FALL TO A WORLD WITHOUT GROUND. YOU WON'T FALL **ANYWHERE.**
YOU JUST DRIFT ETERNALLY...
STOP!
I'M NOT LONELY. THERE ARE A LOT OF PERSONALITIES WITHIN TSUKIKO.
RE... REN-KUN...
TH-THANK YOU.
UH...!

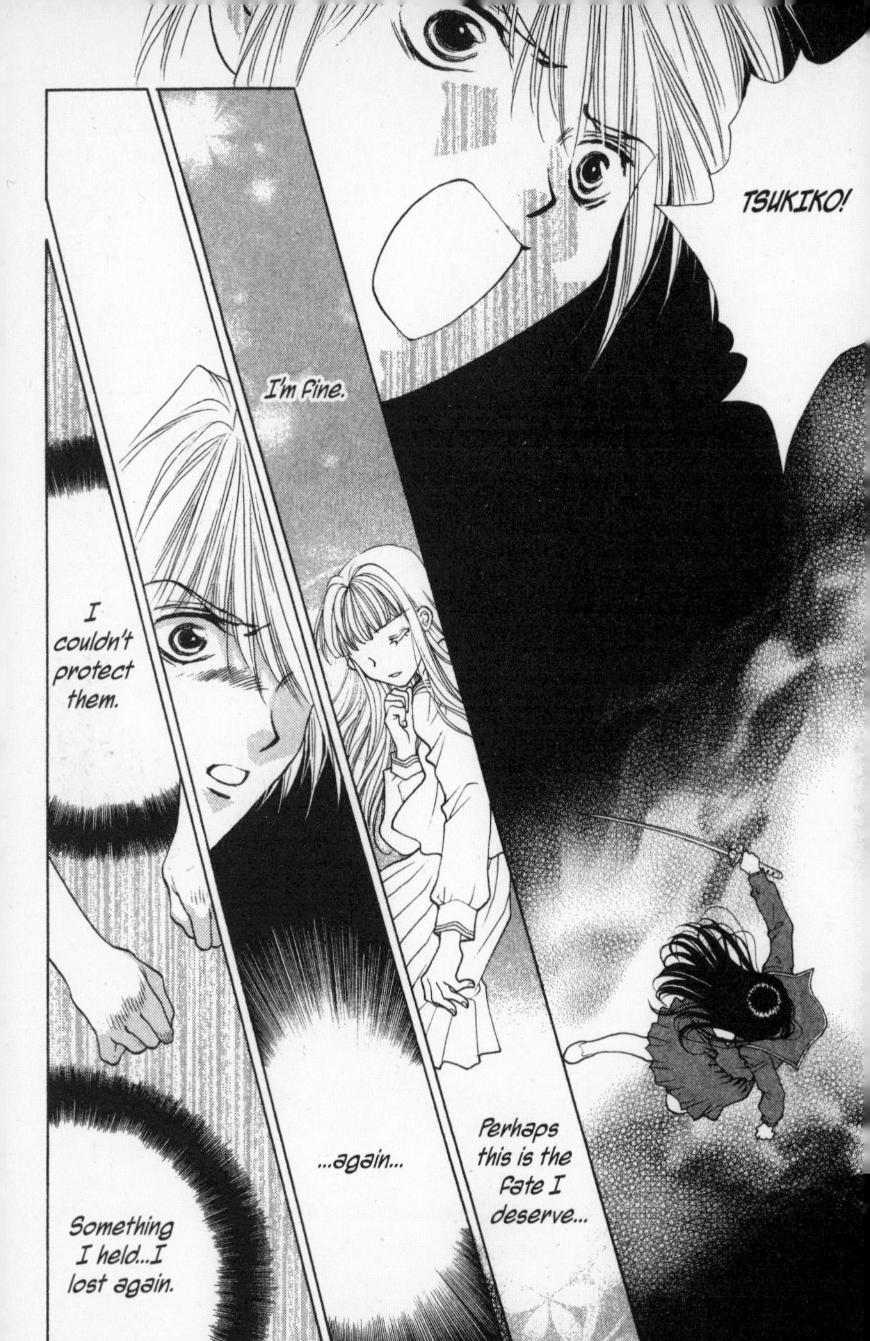
TSUKIKO!
Perhaps this is the fate I deserve...
I'm fine.
...again...
I couldn't protect them.
Something I held...I lost again.

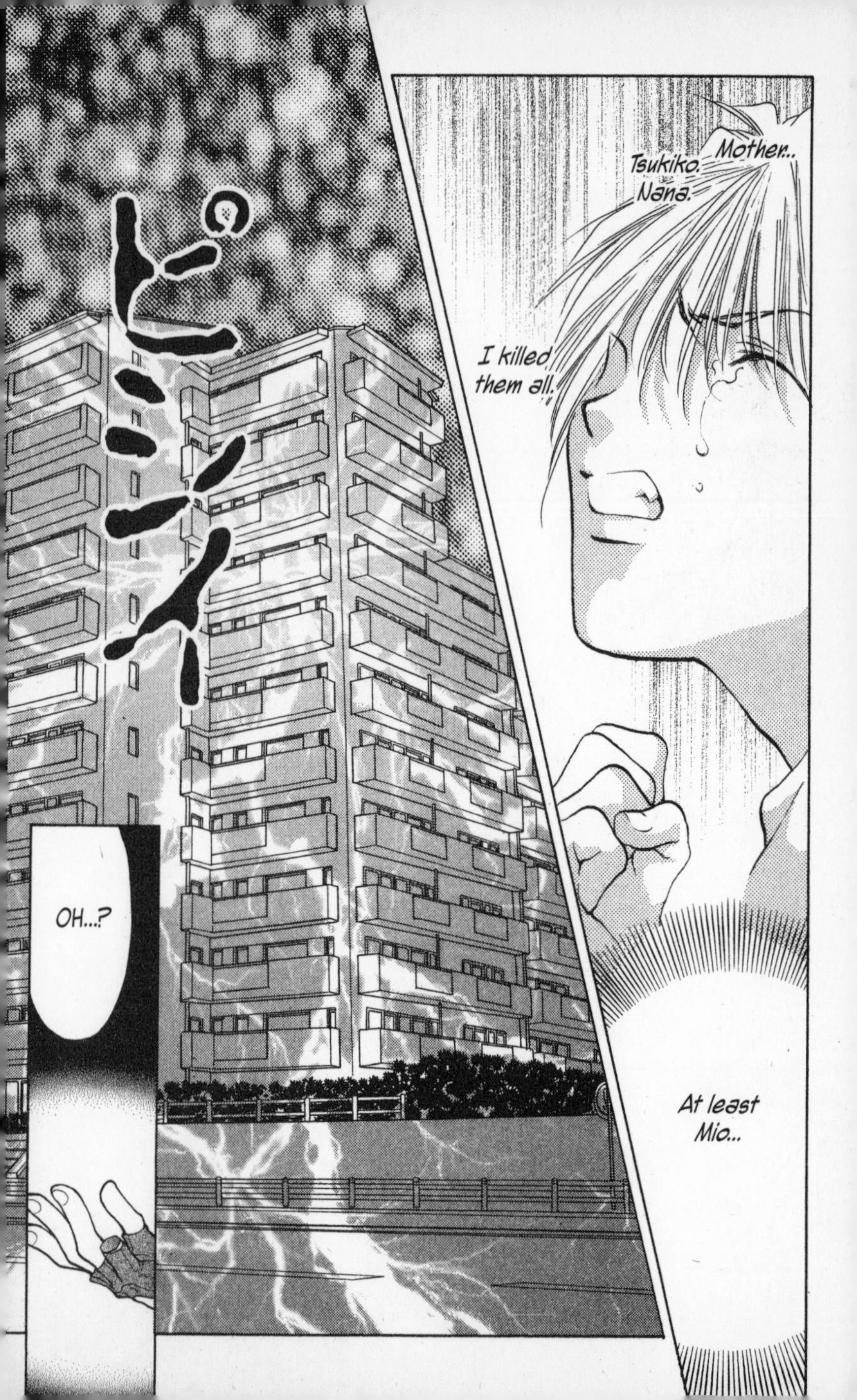
Mother..
Tsukiko.
Nana.
I killed them all.
At least Mio...
OH...?

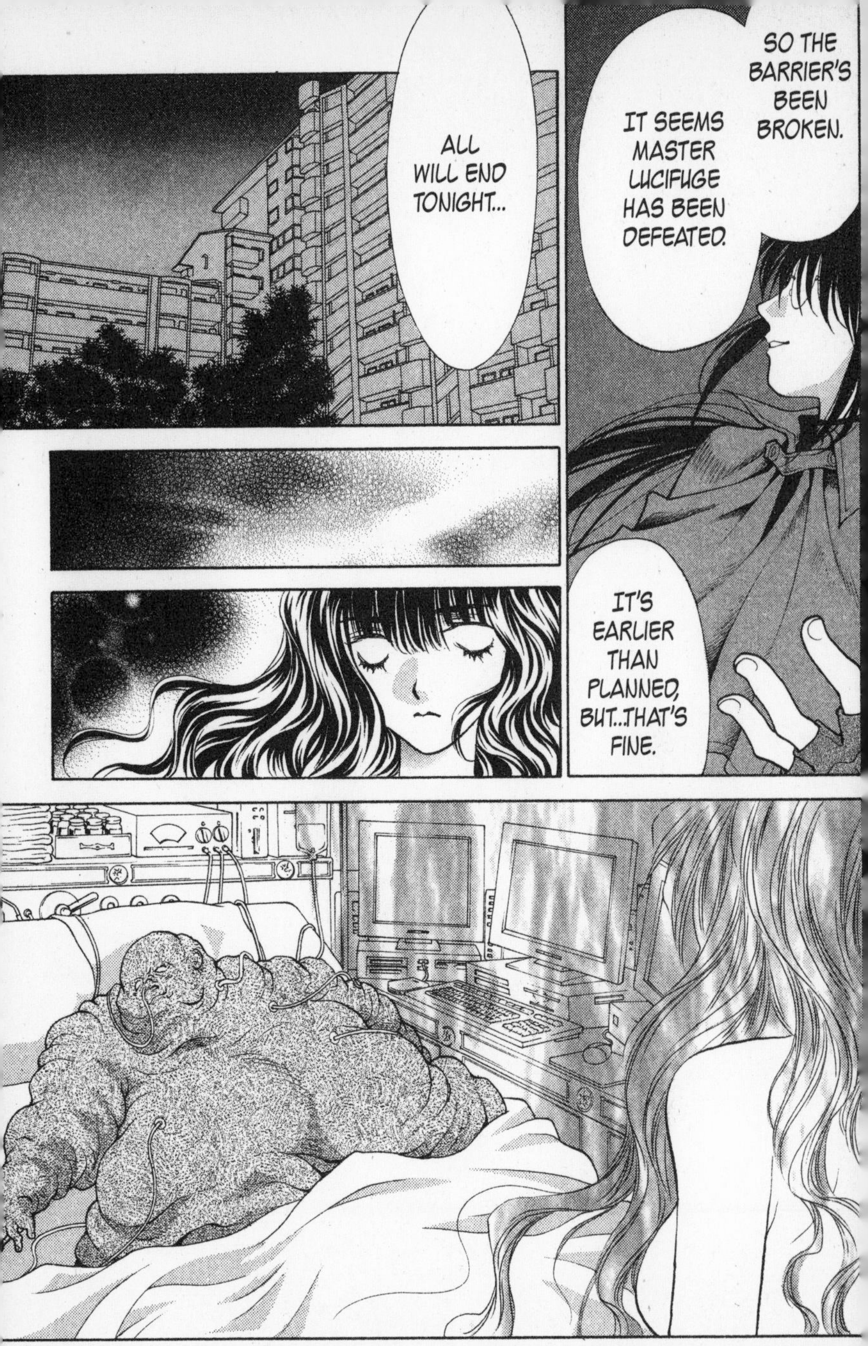
SO THE BARRIER'S BEEN BROKEN.
IT SEEMS MASTER LUCIFUGE HAS BEEN DEFEATED.
IT'S EARLIER THAN PLANNED, BUT...THAT'S FINE.
ALL WILL END TONIGHT...

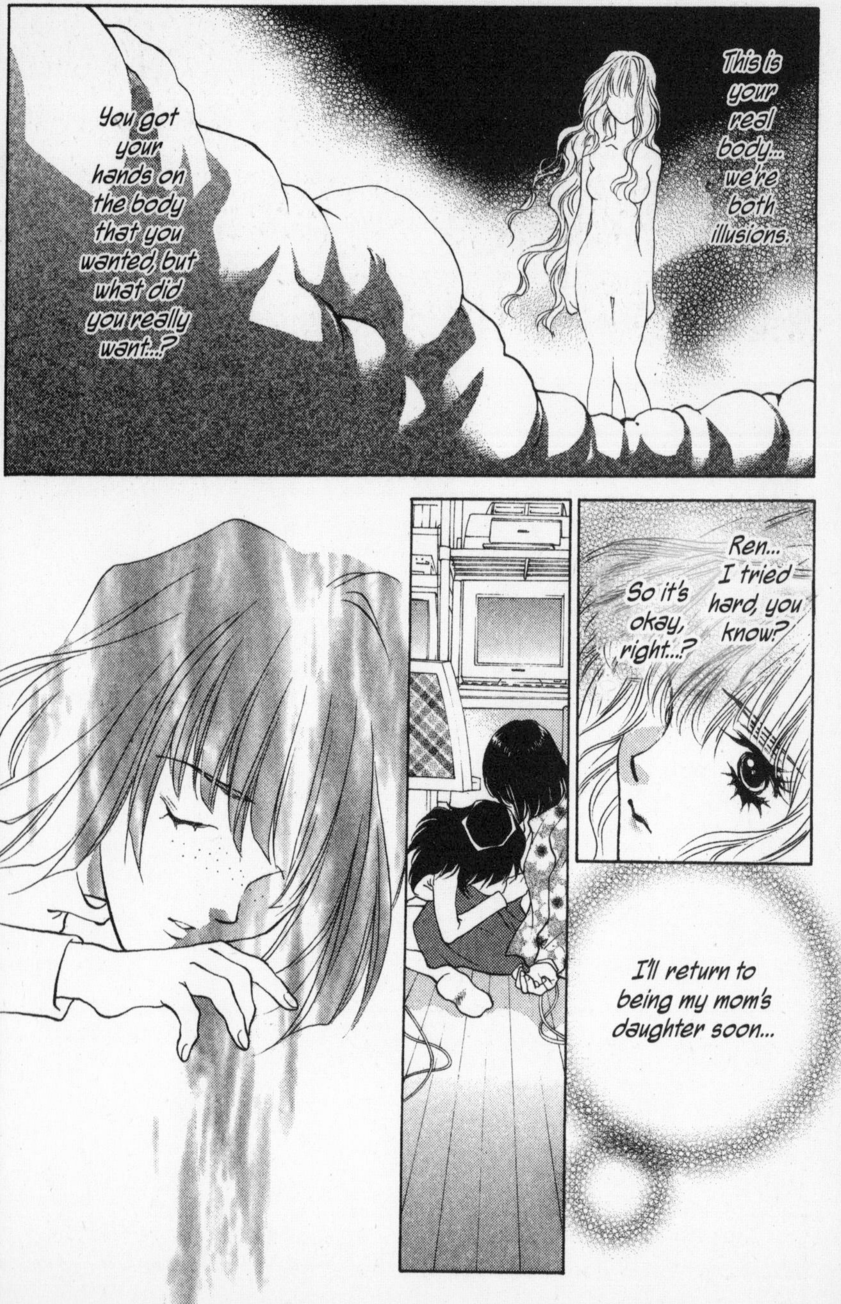
This is your real body... we're both illusions.
You got your hands on the body that you wanted, but what did you really want...?
Ren... I tried hard, you know?
So it's okay, right...?
I'll return to being my mom's daughter soon...

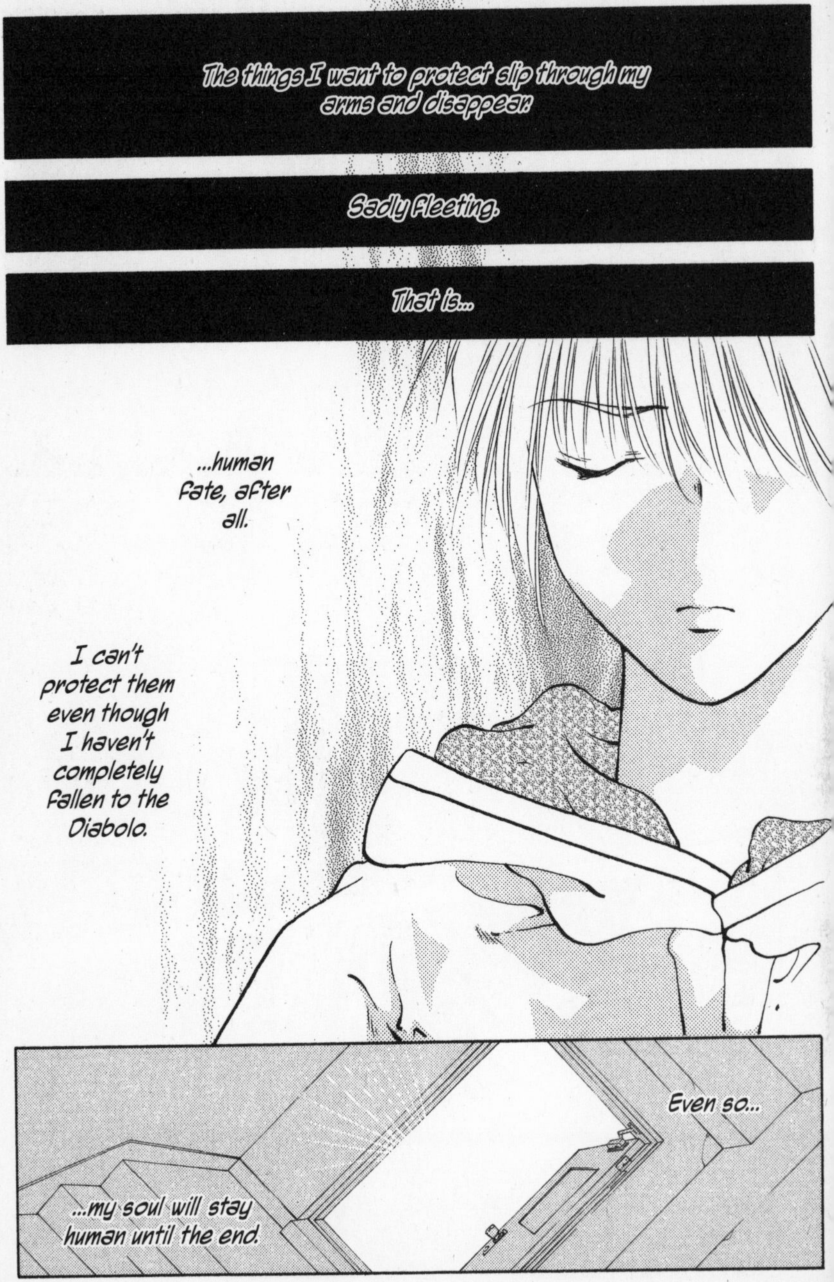
The things I want to protect slip through my arms and disappear.
Sadly fleeting.
That is...
...human fate, after all.
I can't protect them even though I haven't completely fallen to the Diabolo.
Even so...
...my soul will stay human until the end.

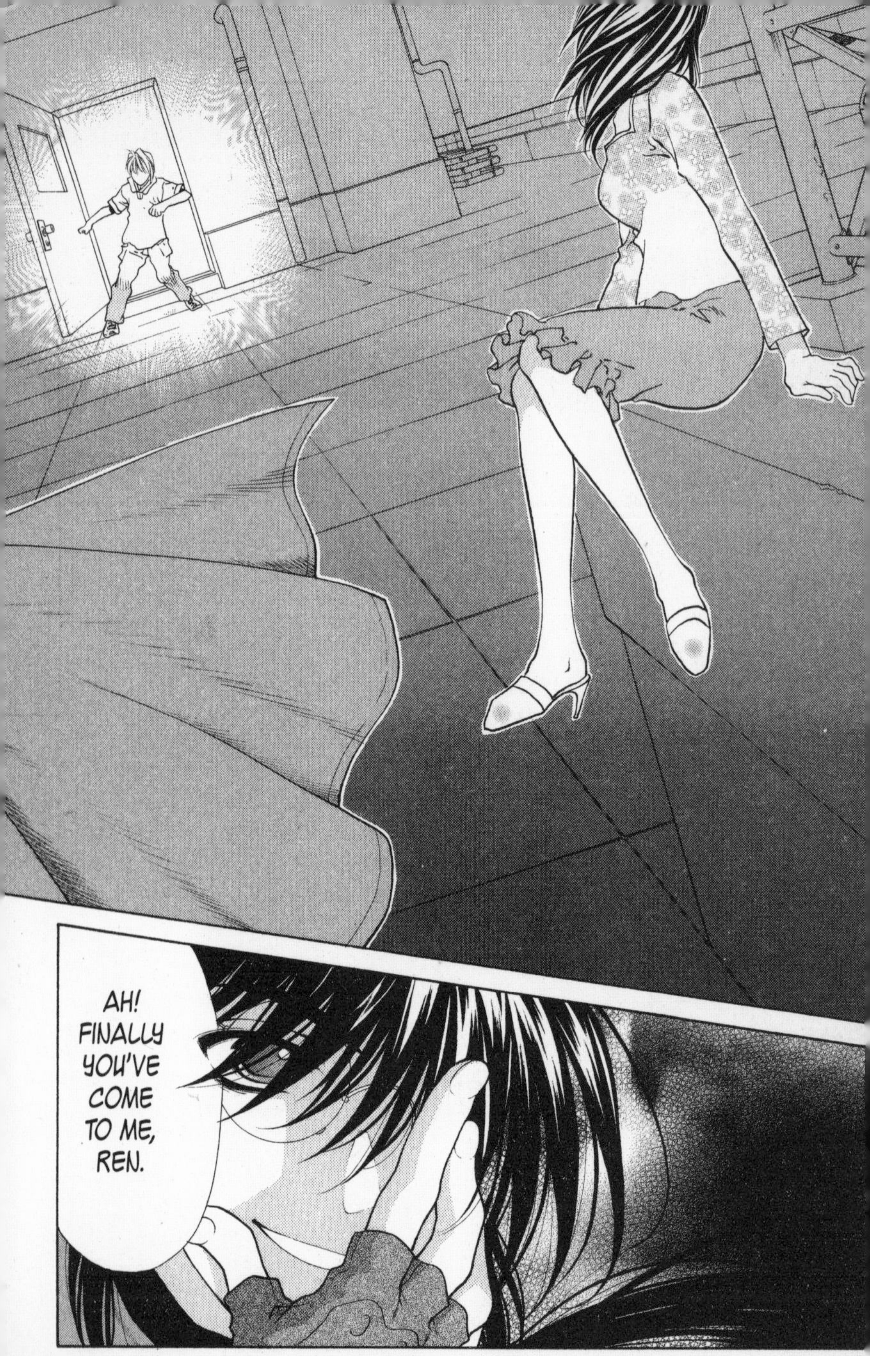
AH! FINALLY YOU'VE COME TO ME, REN.

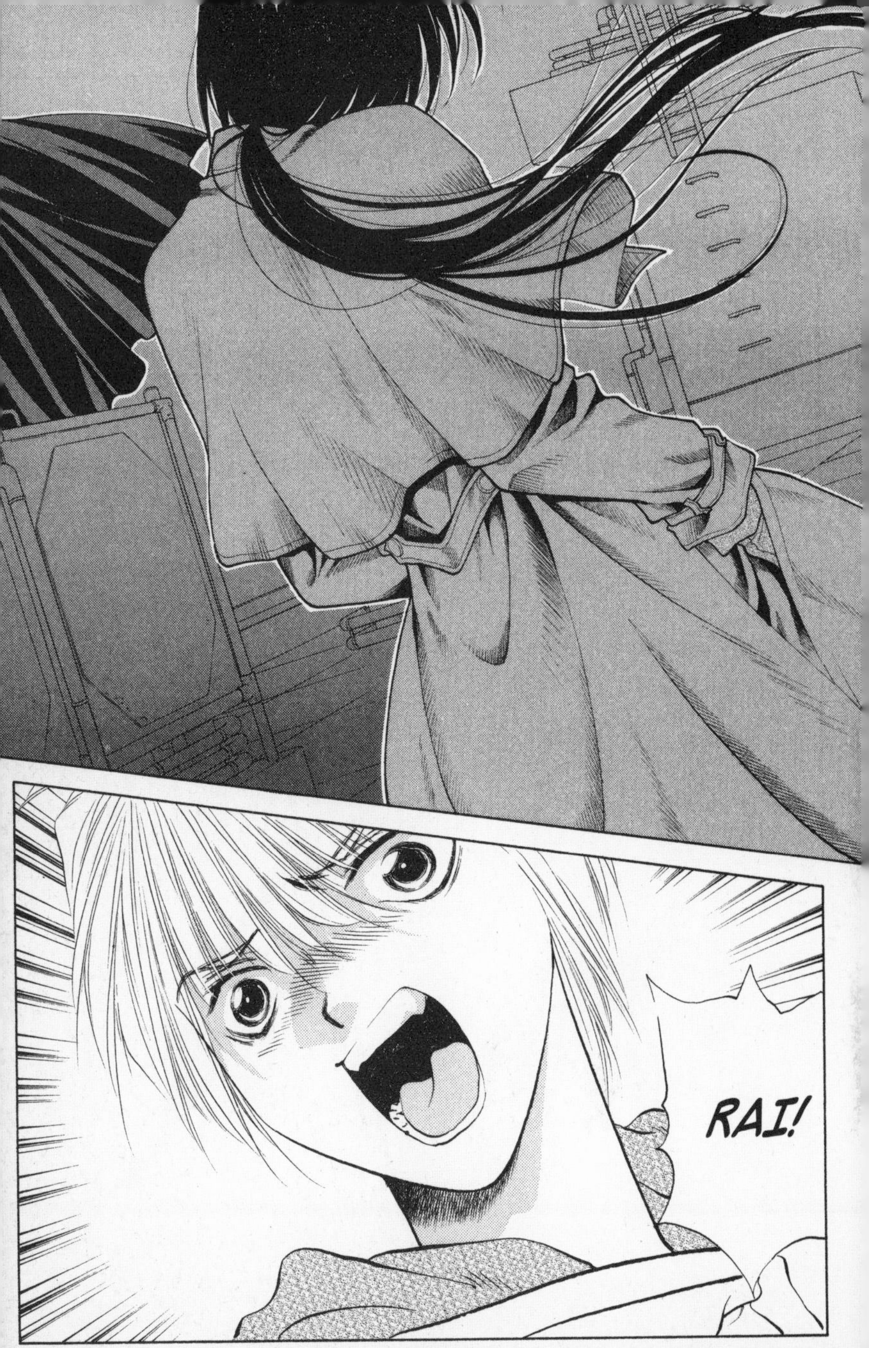
RAI!

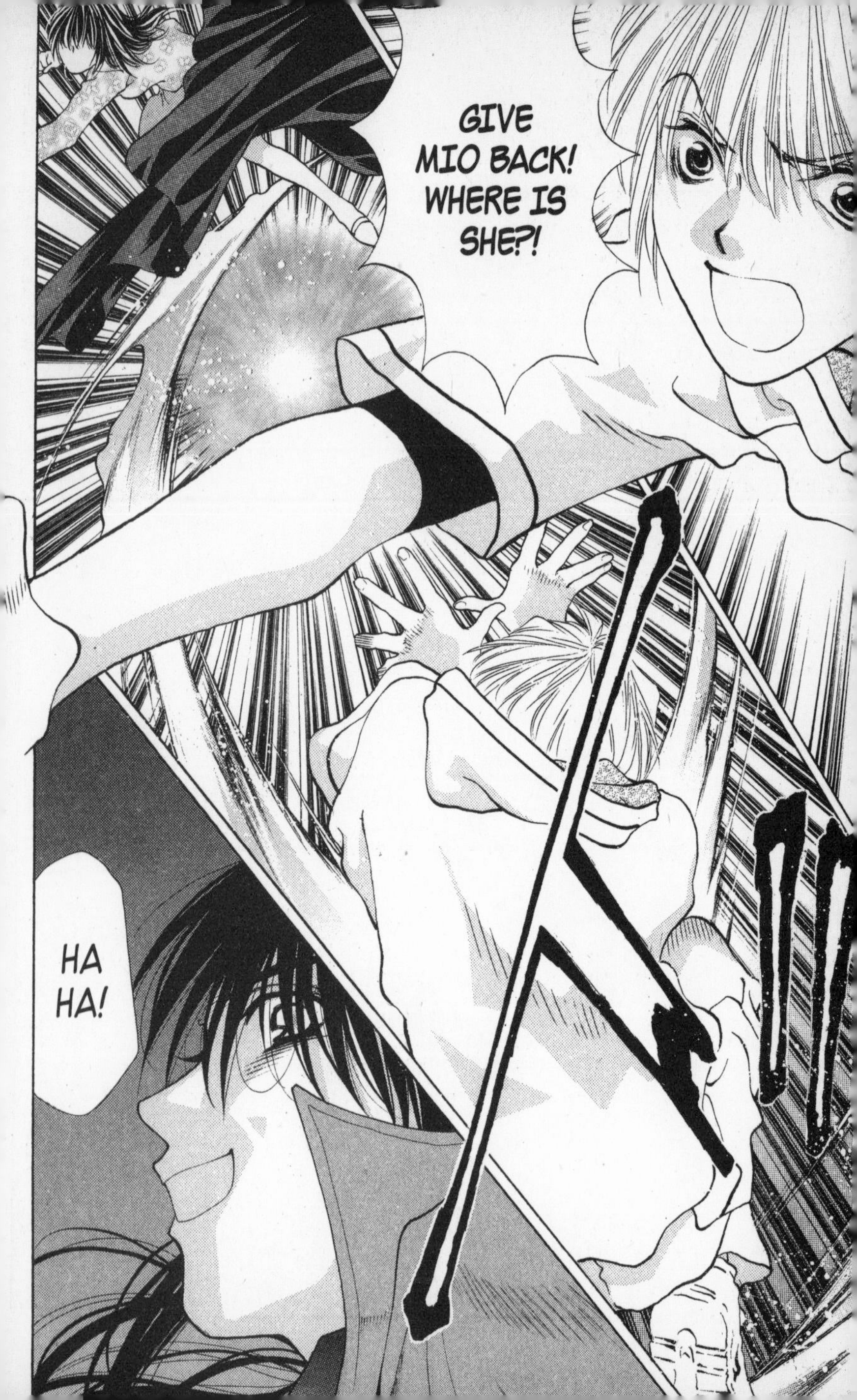
GIVE MIO BACK! WHERE IS SHE?!
HA HA!

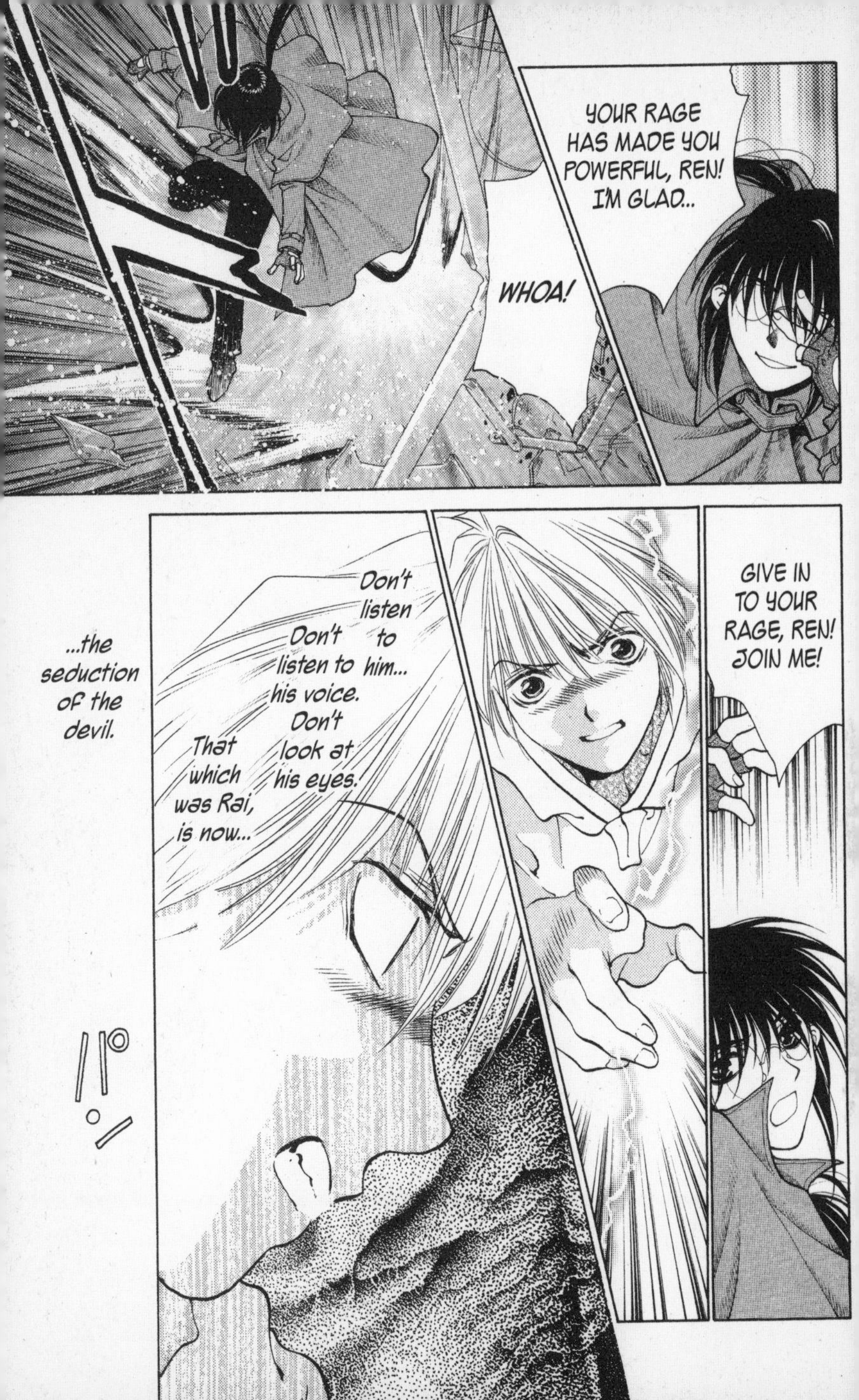
YOUR RAGE HAS MADE YOU POWERFUL, REN! I'M GLAD...
WHOA!
GIVE IN TO YOUR RAGE, REN! JOIN ME!
Don't listen to him...
Don't listen to his voice. Don't look at his eyes.
That which was Rai, is now...
...the seduction of the devil.

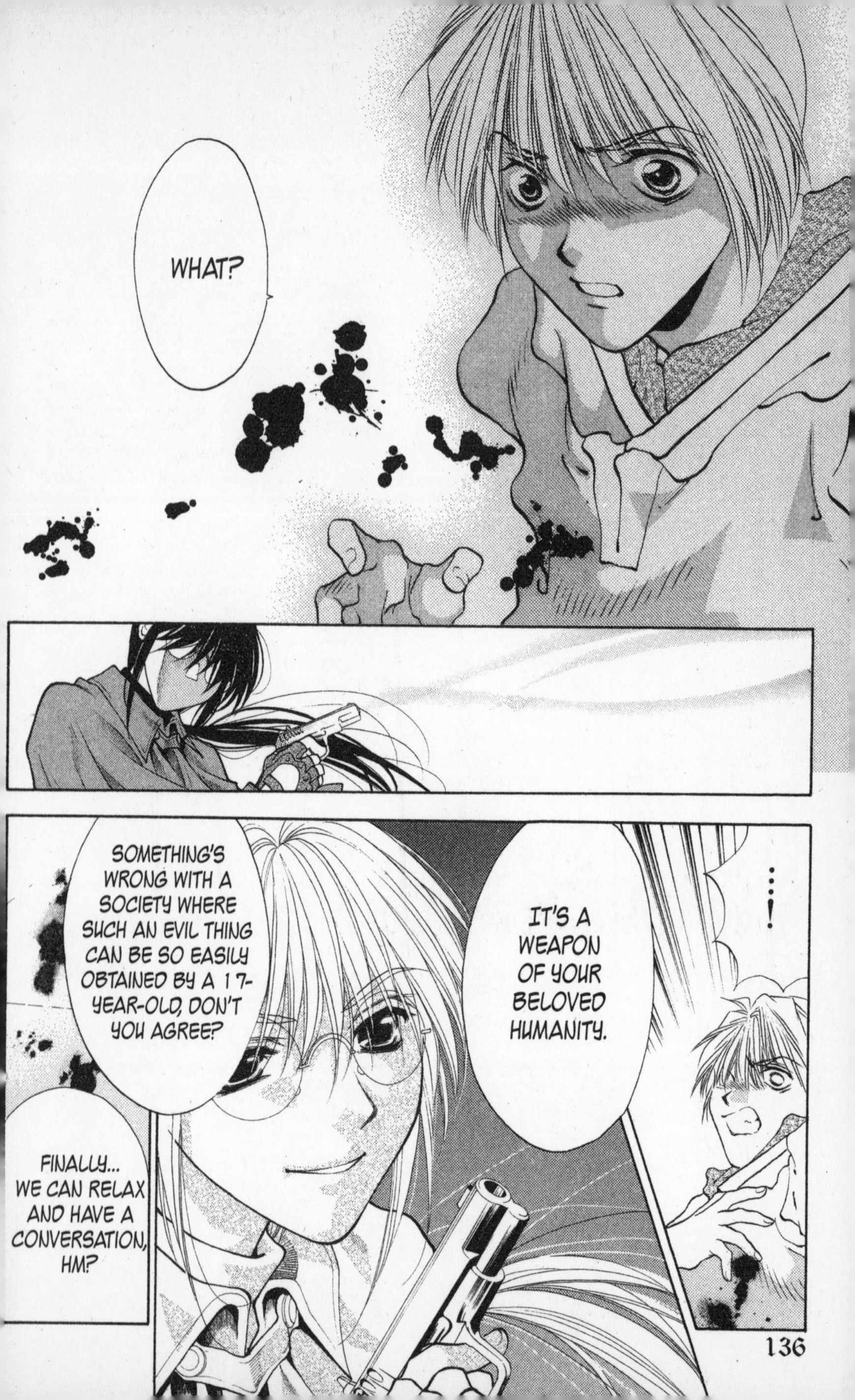
WHAT?
...!
IT'S A WEAPON OF YOUR BELOVED HUMANITY.
SOMETHING'S WRONG WITH A SOCIETY WHERE SUCH AN EVIL THING CAN BE SO EASILY OBTAINED BY A 17-YEAR-OLD, DON'T YOU AGREE?
FINALLY... WE CAN RELAX AND HAVE A CONVERSATION, HM?

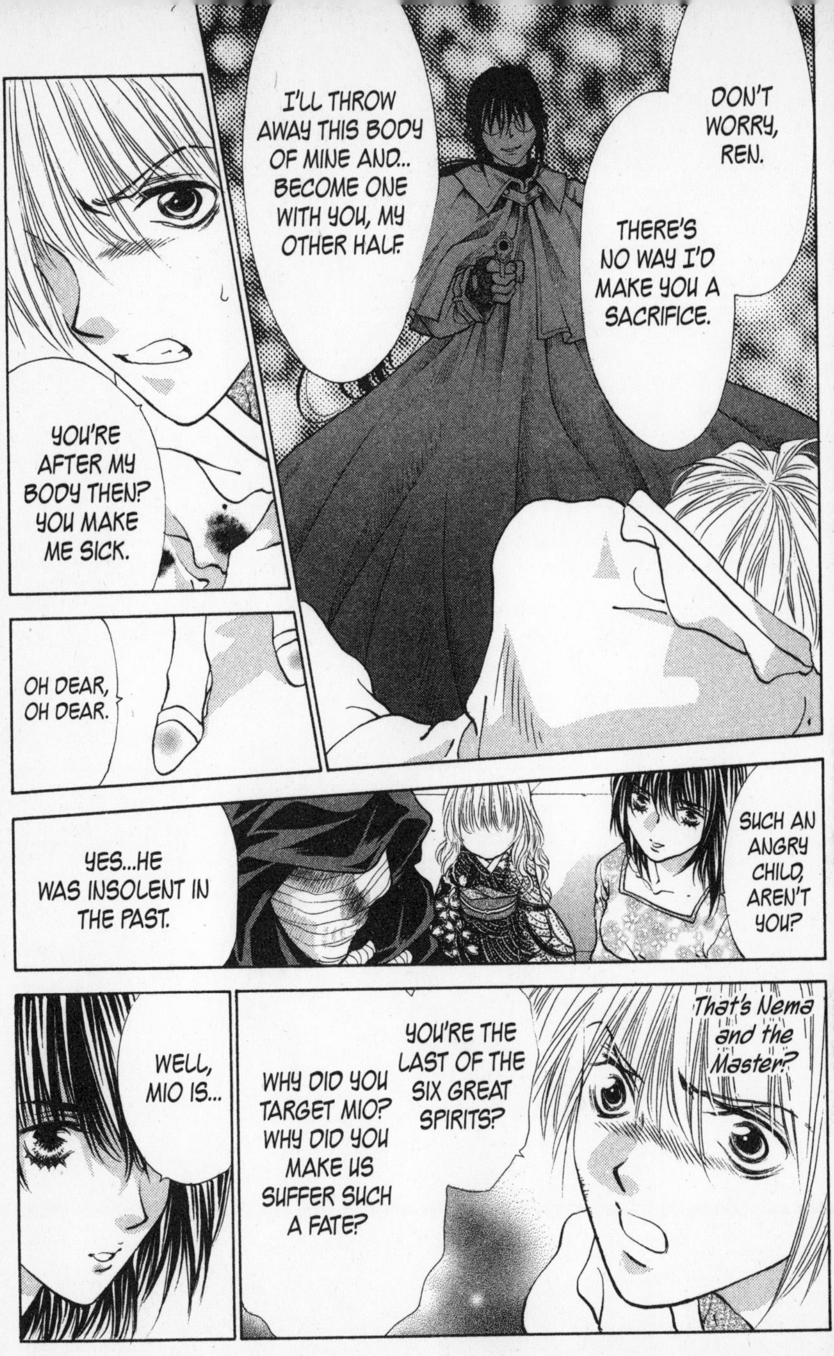
DON'T WORRY, REN.
THERE'S NO WAY I'D MAKE YOU A SACRIFICE.
I'LL THROW AWAY THIS BODY OF MINE AND... BECOME ONE WITH YOU, MY OTHER HALF.
YOU'RE AFTER MY BODY THEN? YOU MAKE ME SICK.
OH DEAR, OH DEAR.
SUCH AN ANGRY CHILD, AREN'T YOU?
YES...HE WAS INSOLENT IN THE PAST.
That's Nema and the Master?
YOU'RE THE LAST OF THE SIX GREAT SPIRITS?
WHY DID YOU TARGET MIO? WHY DID YOU MAKE US SUFFER SUCH A FATE?
WELL, MIO IS...

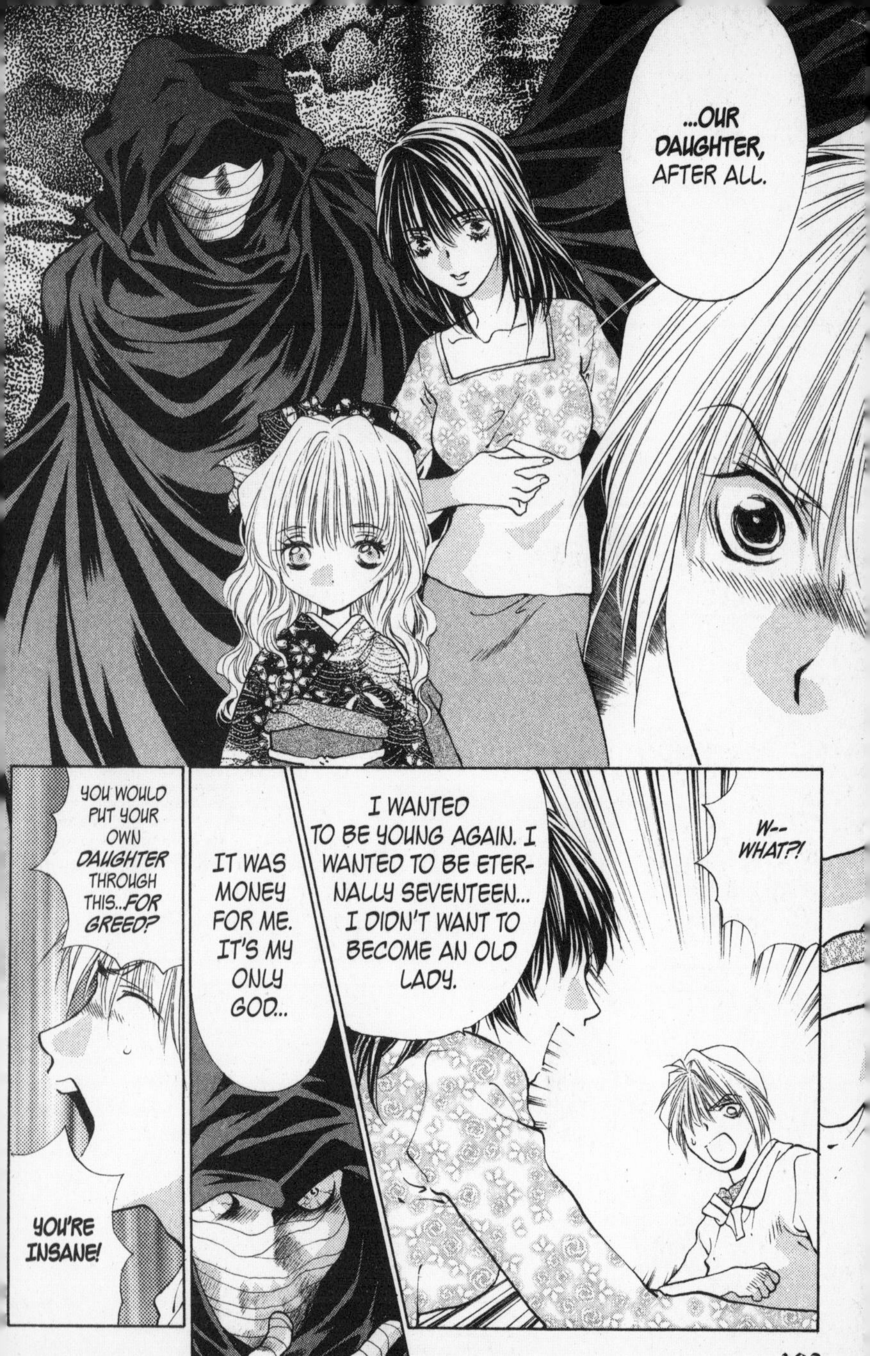
...OUR DAUGHTER, AFTER ALL.
W-- WHAT?!
I WANTED TO BE YOUNG AGAIN. I WANTED TO BE ETER-NALLY SEVENTEEN... I DIDN'T WANT TO BECOME AN OLD LADY.
IT WAS MONEY FOR ME. IT'S MY ONLY GOD...
YOU WOULD PUT YOUR OWN DAUGHTER THROUGH THIS...FOR GREED?
YOU'RE INSANE!

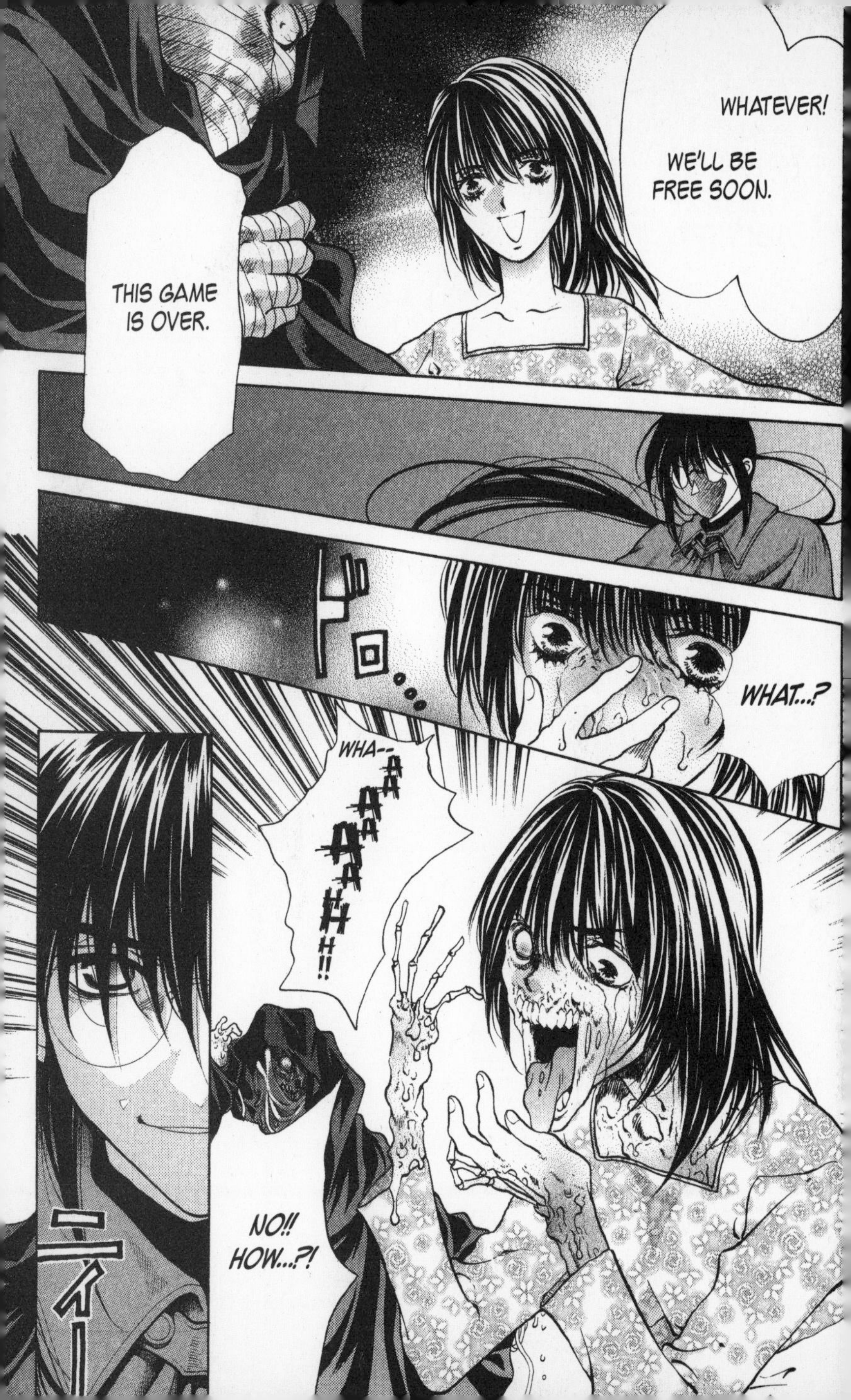
WHATEVER!
WE'LL BE FREE SOON.
THIS GAME IS OVER.
ドロ…
WHAT...?
WHA--AAAAAAAHH!!
NO!! HOW...?!
ニイー

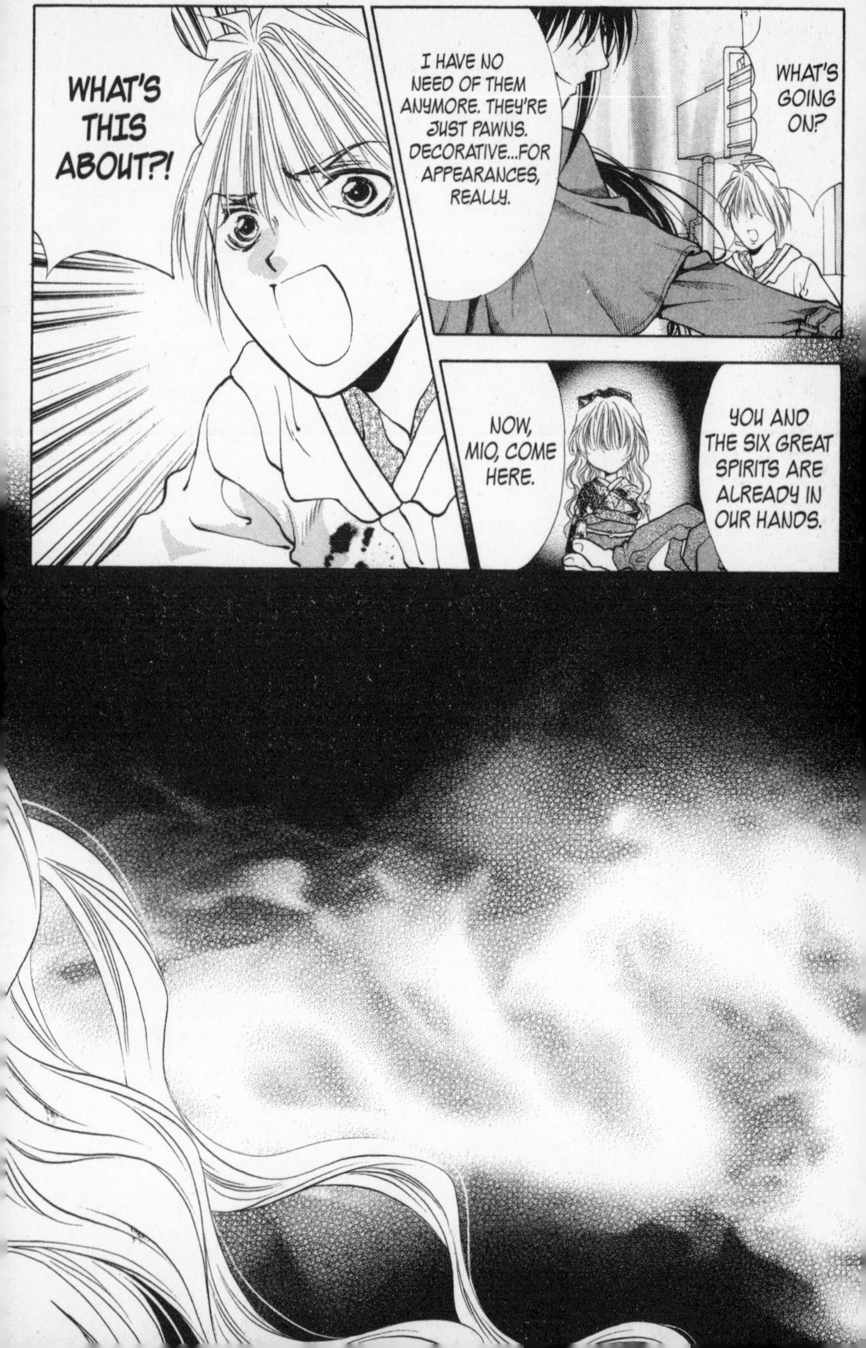
WHAT'S GOING ON?
I HAVE NO NEED OF THEM ANYMORE. THEY'RE JUST PAWNS. DECORATIVE...FOR APPEARANCES, REALLY.
YOU AND THE SIX GREAT SPIRITS ARE ALREADY IN OUR HANDS.
NOW, MIO, COME HERE.
WHAT'S THIS ABOUT?!

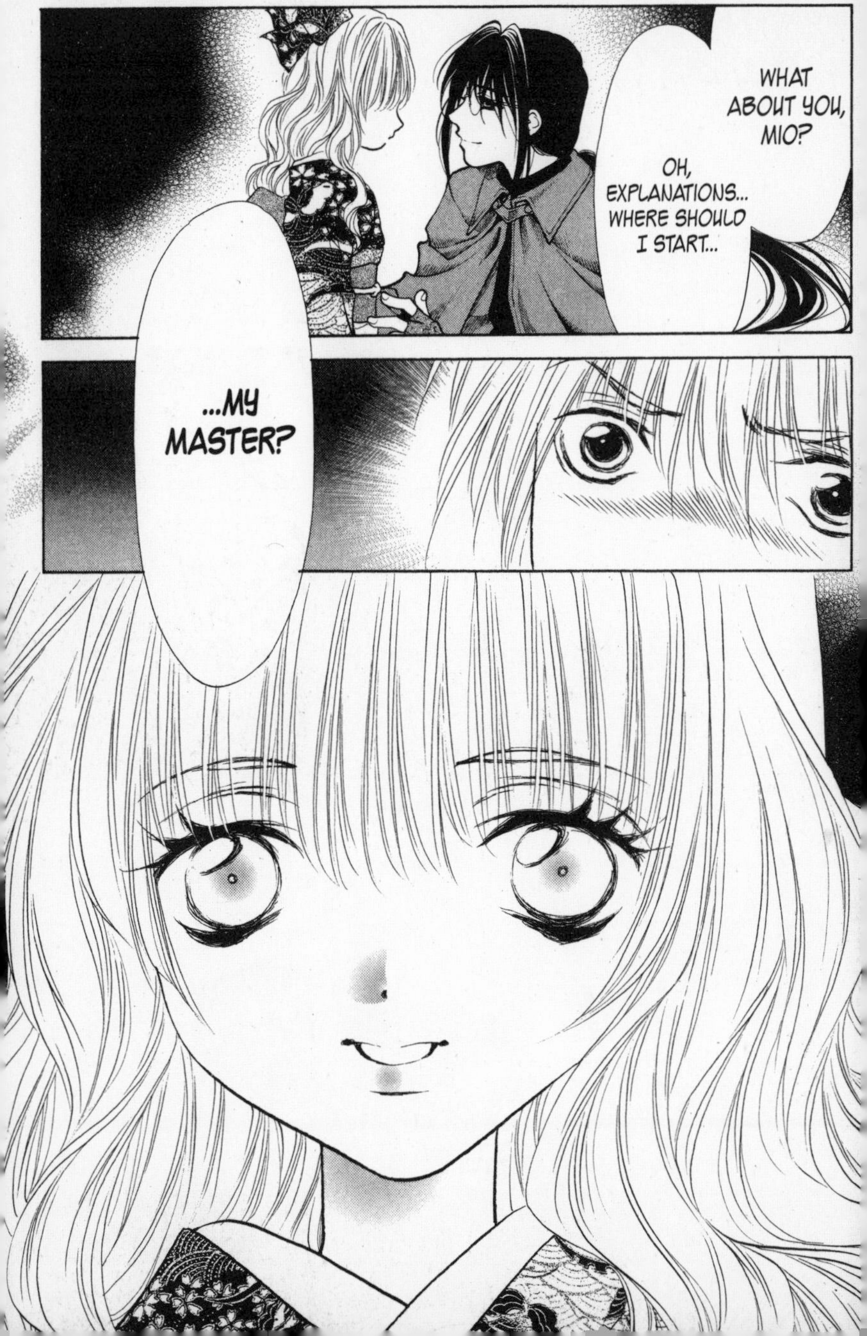
WHAT ABOUT YOU, MIO?
OH, EXPLANATIONS... WHERE SHOULD I START...
...MY MASTER?

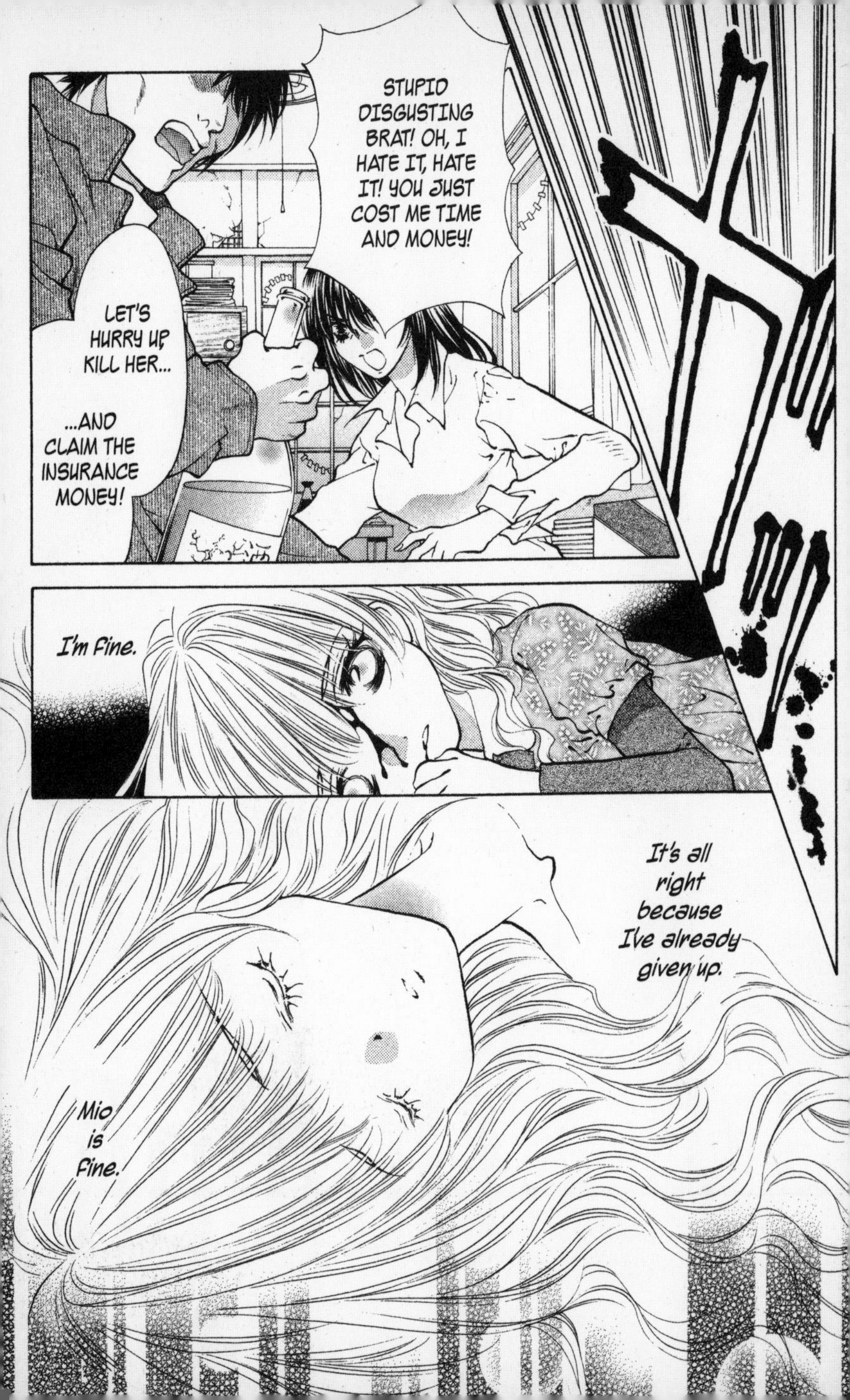
STUPID DISGUSTING BRAT! OH, I HATE IT, HATE IT! YOU JUST COST ME TIME AND MONEY!
LET'S HURRY UP, KILL HER...
...AND CLAIM THE INSURANCE MONEY!
I'm fine.
It's all right because I've already given up.
Mio is fine.

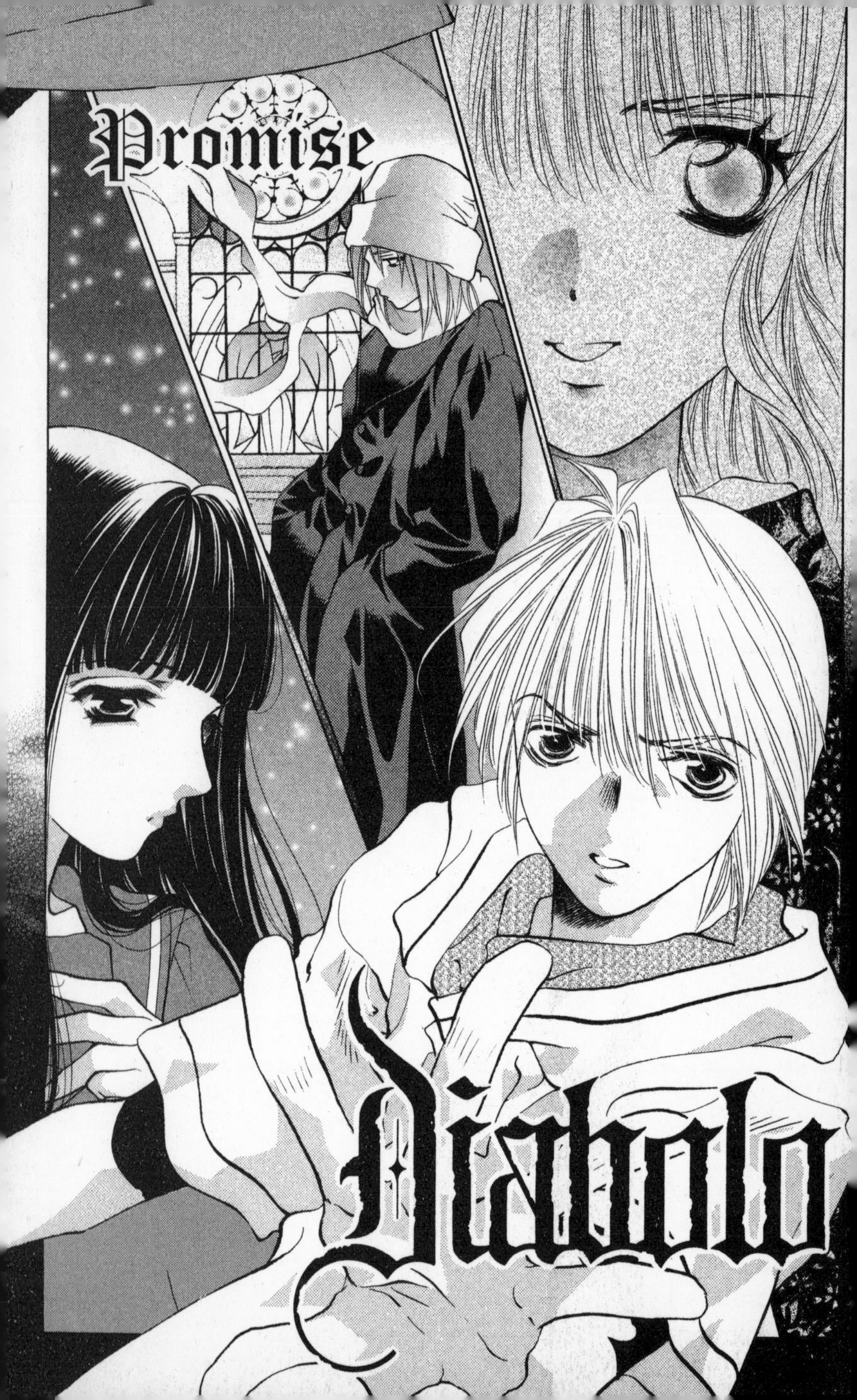
Promise
Diabolo

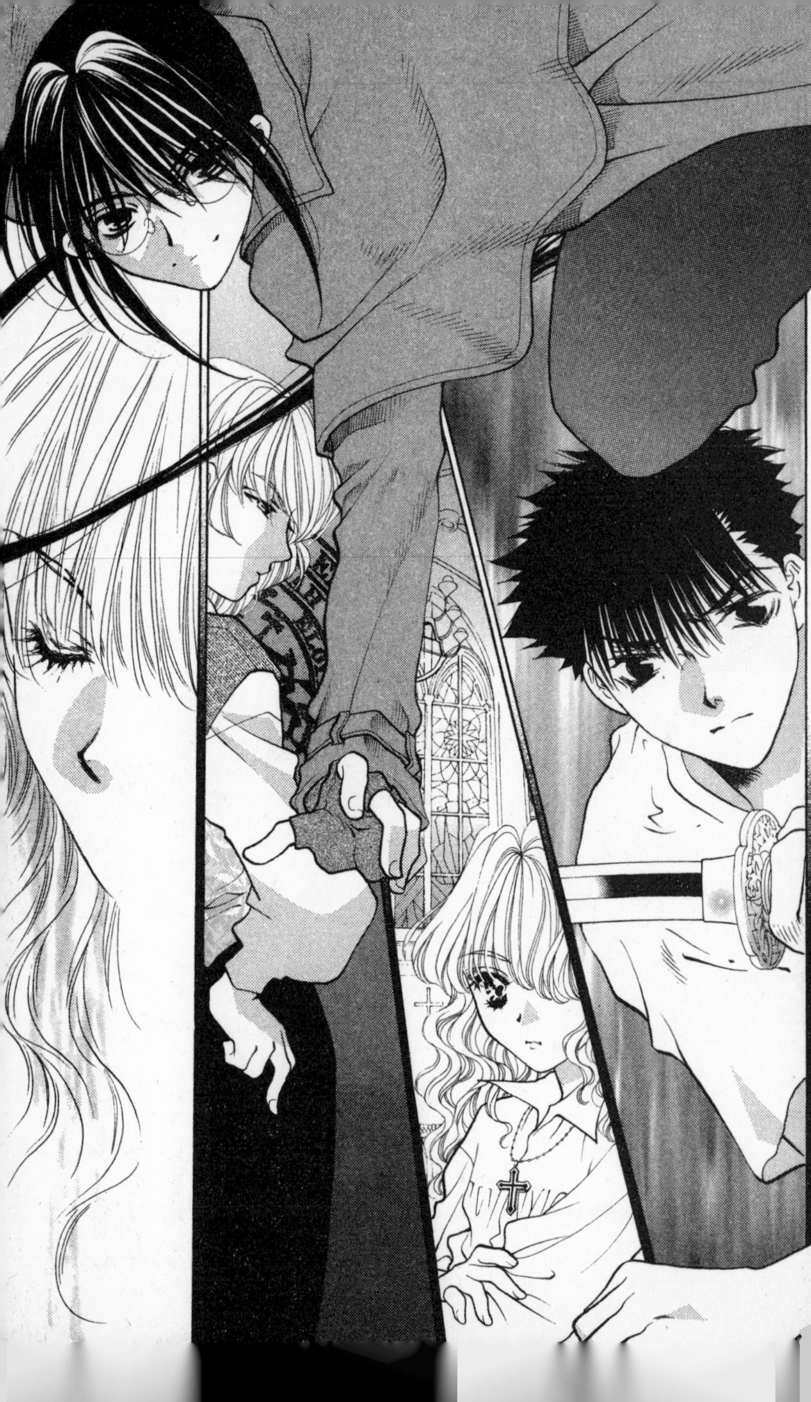

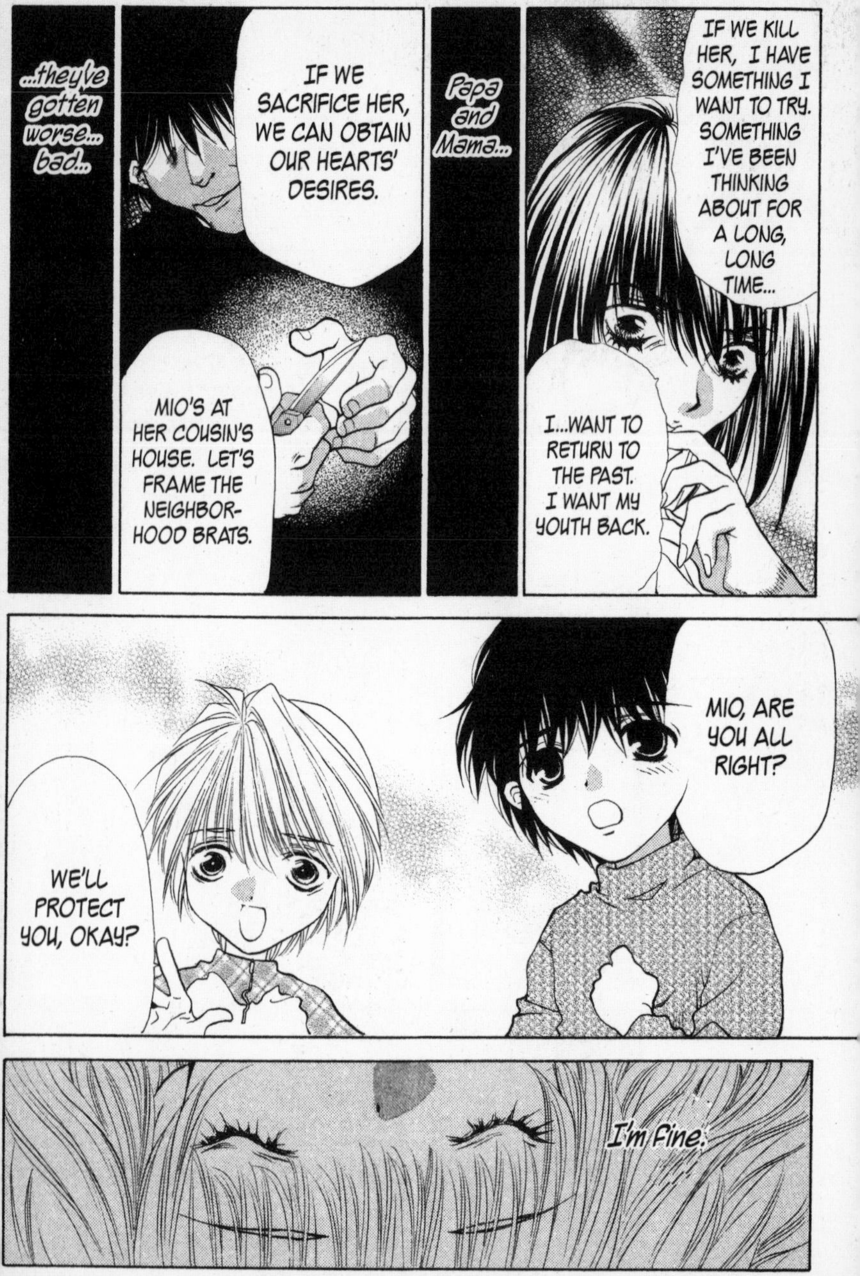
IF WE KILL HER, I HAVE SOMETHING I WANT TO TRY. SOMETHING I'VE BEEN THINKING ABOUT FOR A LONG, LONG TIME...
I...WANT TO RETURN TO THE PAST. I WANT MY YOUTH BACK.
Papa and Mama...
IF WE SACRIFICE HER, WE CAN OBTAIN OUR HEARTS' DESIRES.
MIO'S AT HER COUSIN'S HOUSE. LET'S FRAME THE NEIGHBOR-HOOD BRATS.
...they've gotten worse... bad...
MIO, ARE YOU ALL RIGHT?
WE'LL PROTECT YOU, OKAY?
I'm fine.

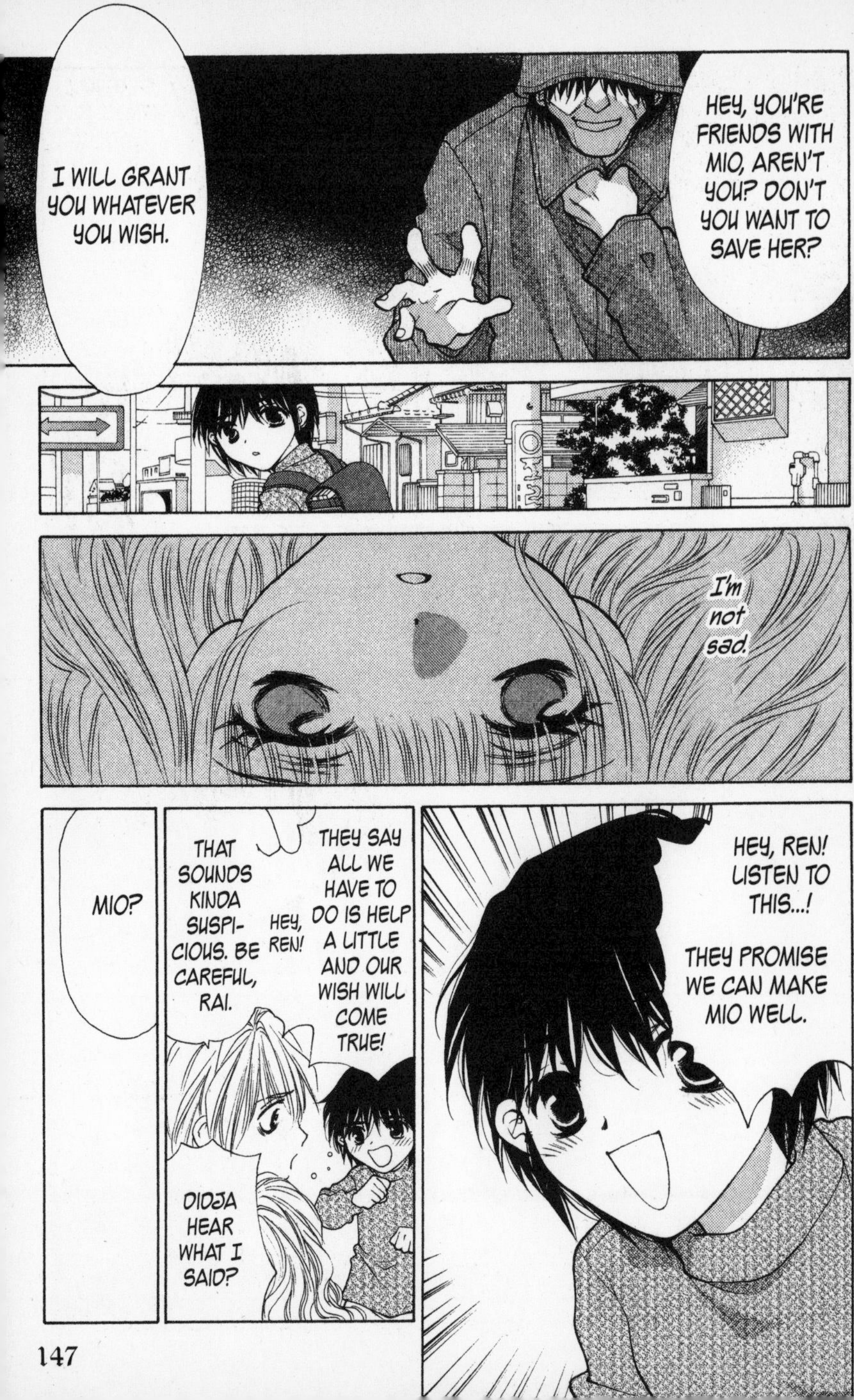
HEY, YOU'RE FRIENDS WITH MIO, AREN'T YOU? DON'T YOU WANT TO SAVE HER?
I WILL GRANT YOU WHATEVER YOU WISH.
I'm not sad.
HEY, REN! LISTEN TO THIS...!
THEY PROMISE WE CAN MAKE MIO WELL.
THEY SAY ALL WE HAVE TO DO IS HELP A LITTLE AND OUR WISH WILL COME TRUE!
HEY, REN!
THAT SOUNDS KINDA SUSPICIOUS. BE CAREFUL, RAI.
DIDJA HEAR WHAT I SAID?
MIO?

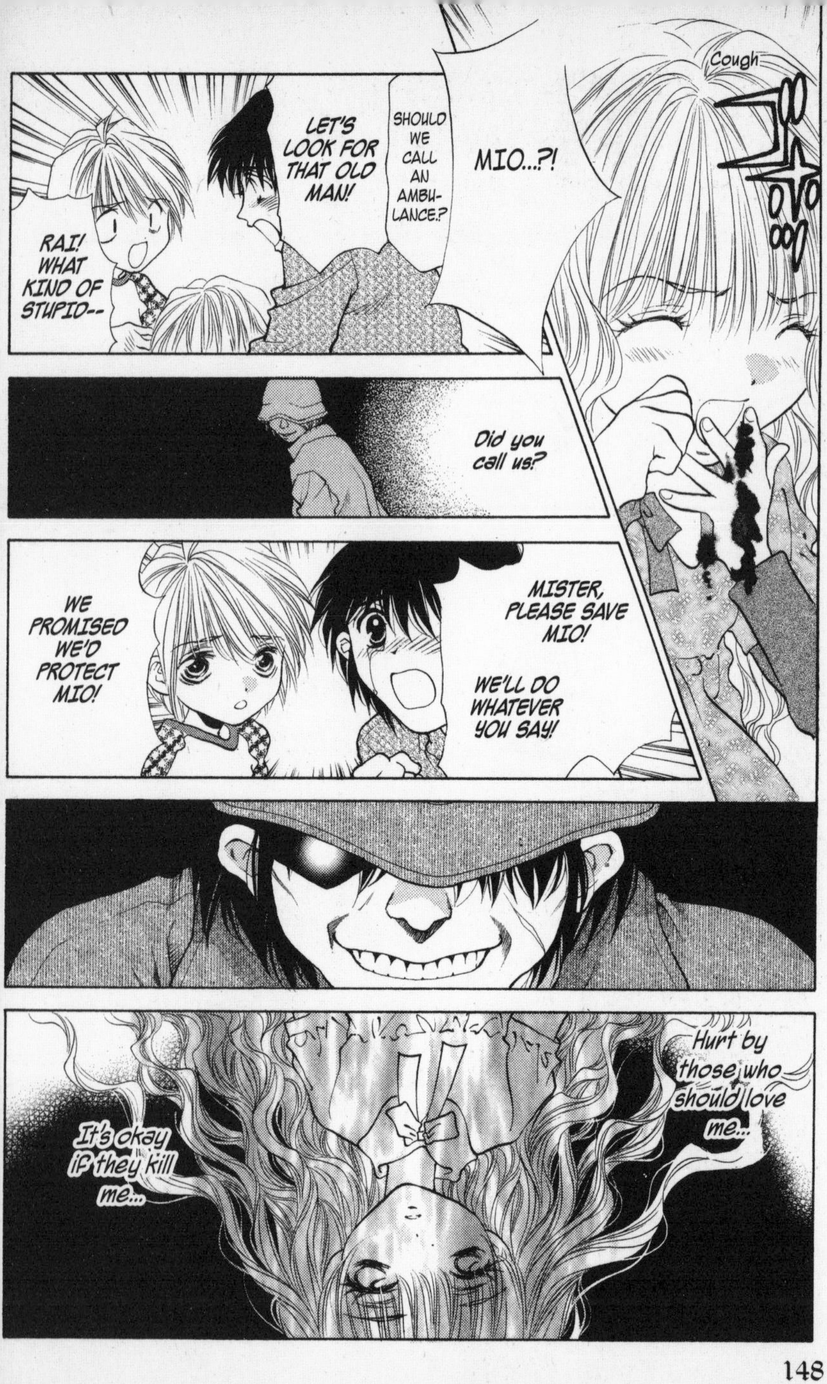
Cough
MIO...?!
SHOULD WE CALL AN AMBULANCE?
LET'S LOOK FOR THAT OLD MAN!
RAI! WHAT KIND OF STUPID--
Did you call us?
MISTER, PLEASE SAVE MIO!
WE'LL DO WHATEVER YOU SAY!
WE PROMISED WE'D PROTECT MIO!
Hurt by those who should love me...
It's okay if they kill me...

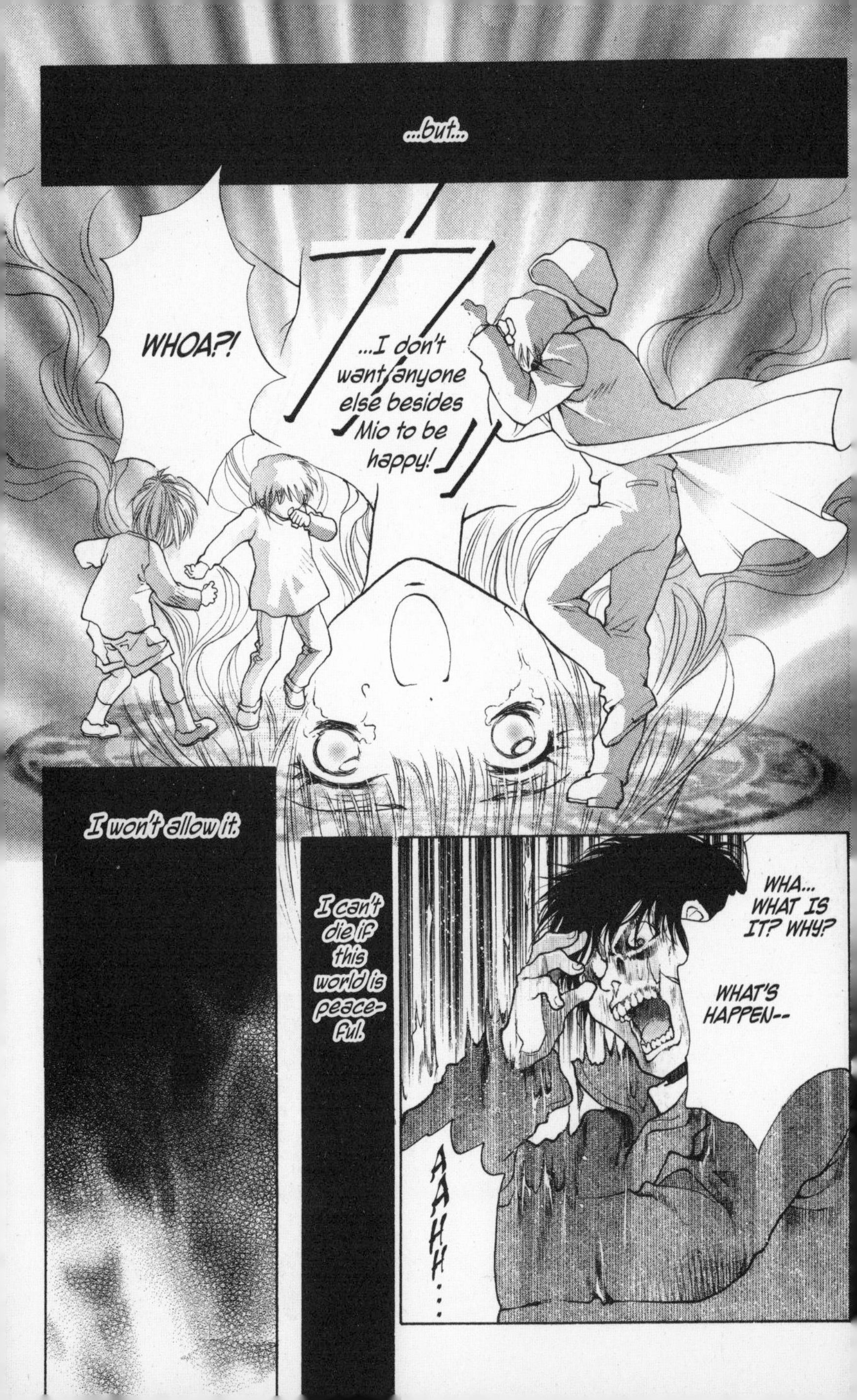
...but...
...I don't want anyone else besides Mio to be happy!
WHOA?!
WHA... WHAT IS IT? WHY?
WHAT'S HAPPEN--
AAHHH...
I can't die if this world is peace-ful.
I won't allow it.

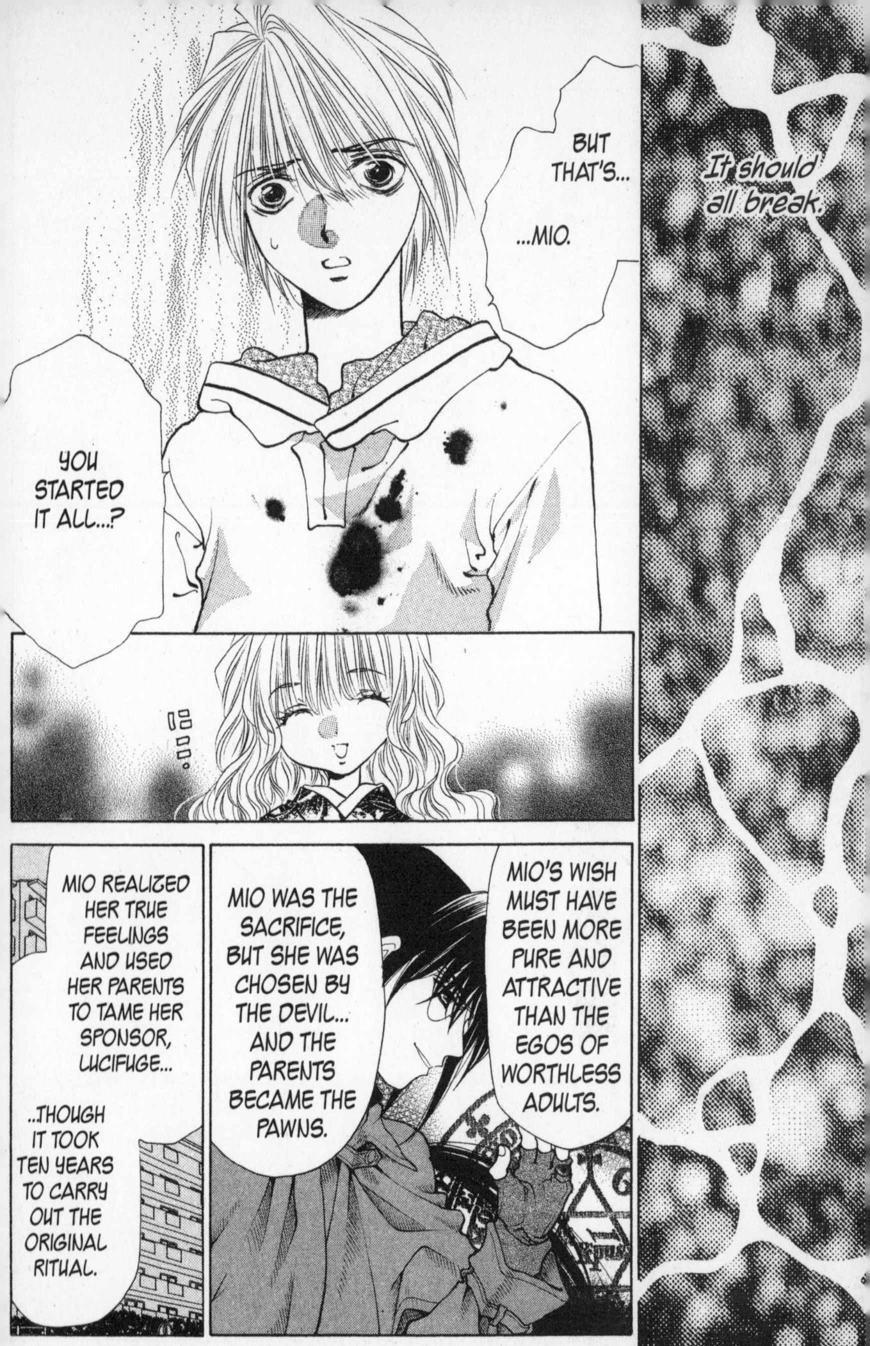
It should all break.
BUT THAT'S...
...MIO.
YOU STARTED IT ALL...?
MIO'S WISH MUST HAVE BEEN MORE PURE AND ATTRACTIVE THAN THE EGOS OF WORTHLESS ADULTS.
MIO WAS THE SACRIFICE, BUT SHE WAS CHOSEN BY THE DEVIL... AND THE PARENTS BECAME THE PAWNS.
MIO REALIZED HER TRUE FEELINGS AND USED HER PARENTS TO TAME HER SPONSOR, LUCIFUGE...
...THOUGH IT TOOK TEN YEARS TO CARRY OUT THE ORIGINAL RITUAL.

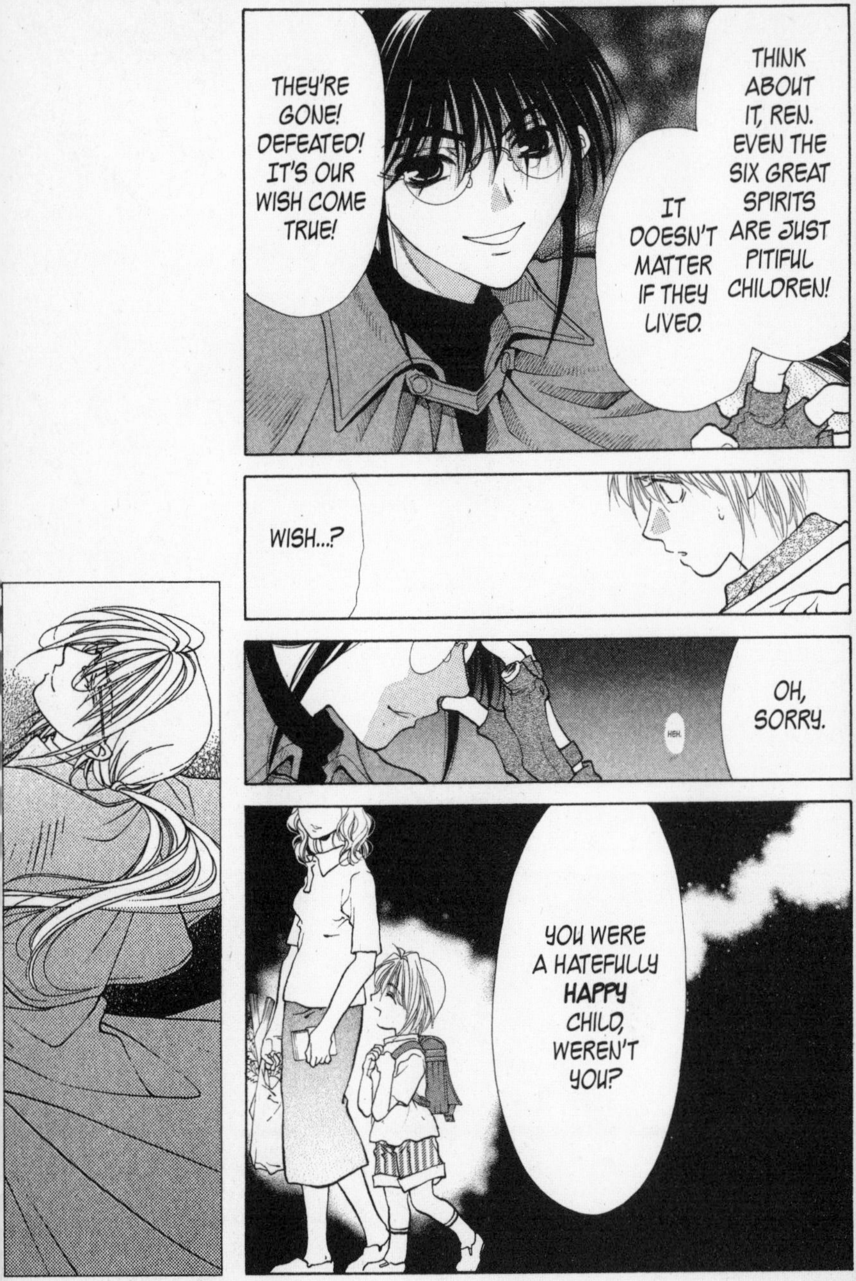
THINK ABOUT IT, REN. EVEN THE SIX GREAT SPIRITS ARE JUST PITIFUL CHILDREN!
IT DOESN'T MATTER IF THEY LIVED.
THEY'RE GONE! DEFEATED! IT'S OUR WISH COME TRUE!
WISH...?
OH, SORRY.
HEH.
YOU WERE A HATEFULLY **HAPPY** CHILD, WEREN'T YOU?

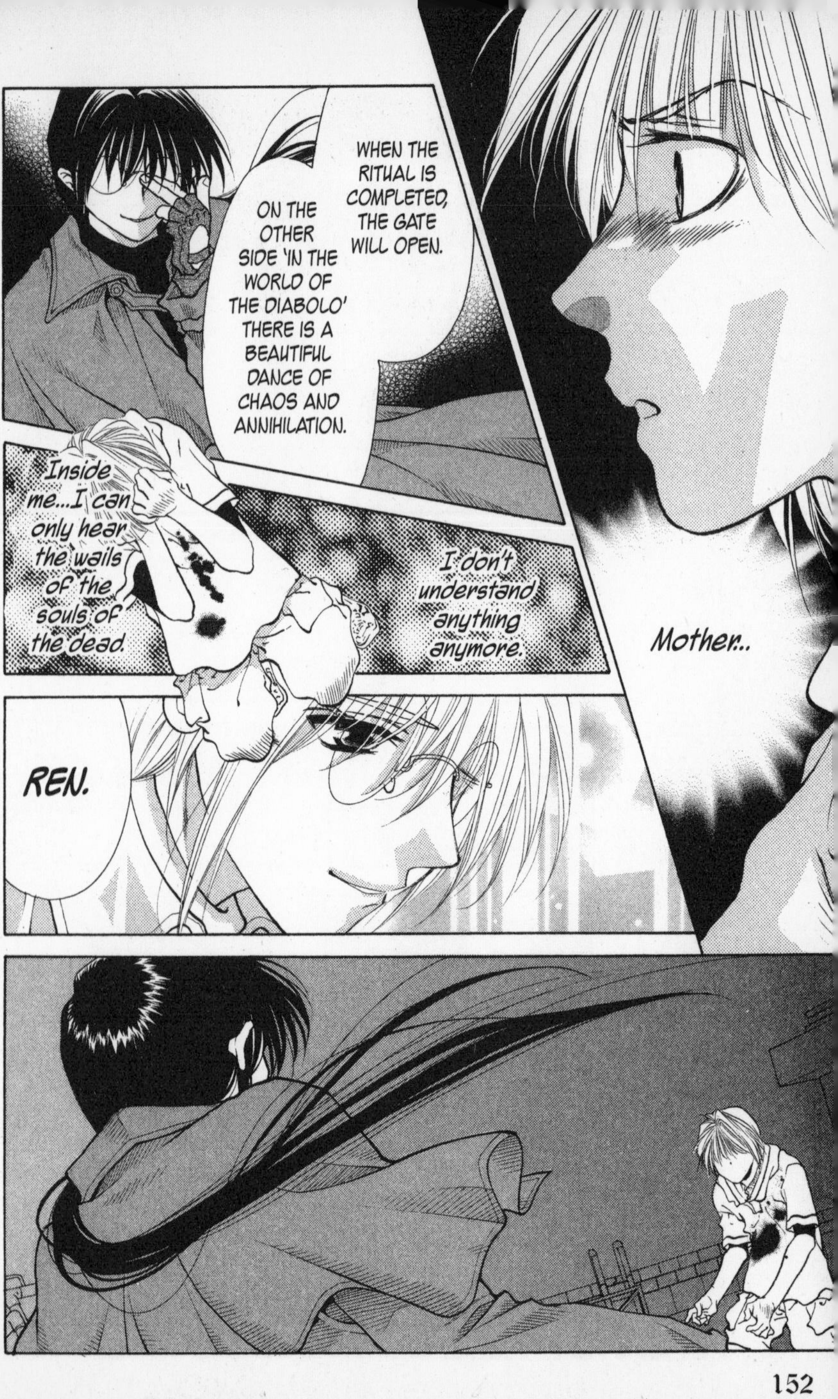
Mother...
WHEN THE RITUAL IS COMPLETED, THE GATE WILL OPEN.
ON THE OTHER SIDE 'IN THE WORLD OF THE DIABOLO' THERE IS A BEAUTIFUL DANCE OF CHAOS AND ANNIHILATION.
I don't understand anything anymore.
Inside me...I can only hear the wails of the souls of the dead.
REN.

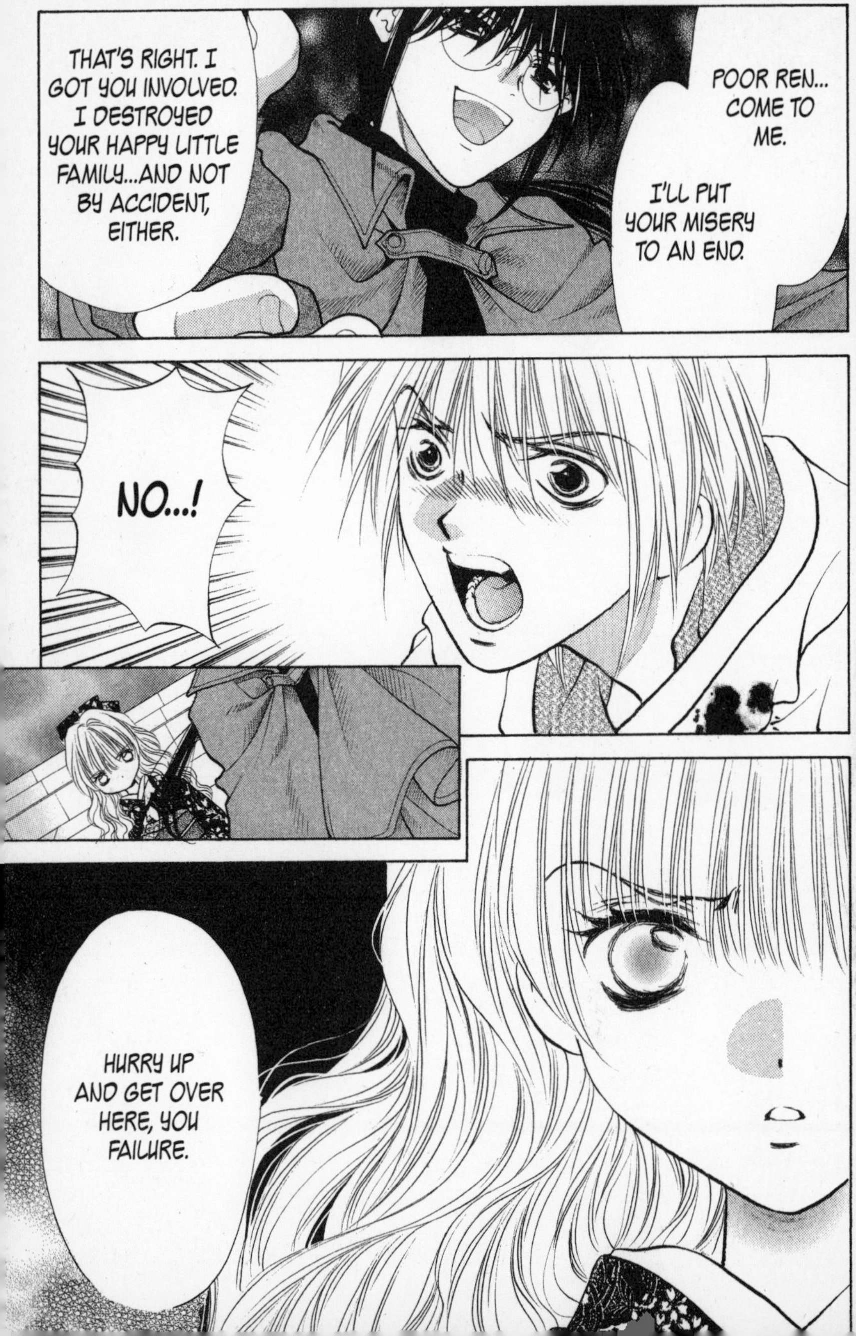
POOR REN... COME TO ME.
I'LL PUT YOUR MISERY TO AN END.
THAT'S RIGHT. I GOT YOU INVOLVED. I DESTROYED YOUR HAPPY LITTLE FAMILY...AND NOT BY ACCIDENT, EITHER.
NO...!
HURRY UP AND GET OVER HERE, YOU FAILURE.

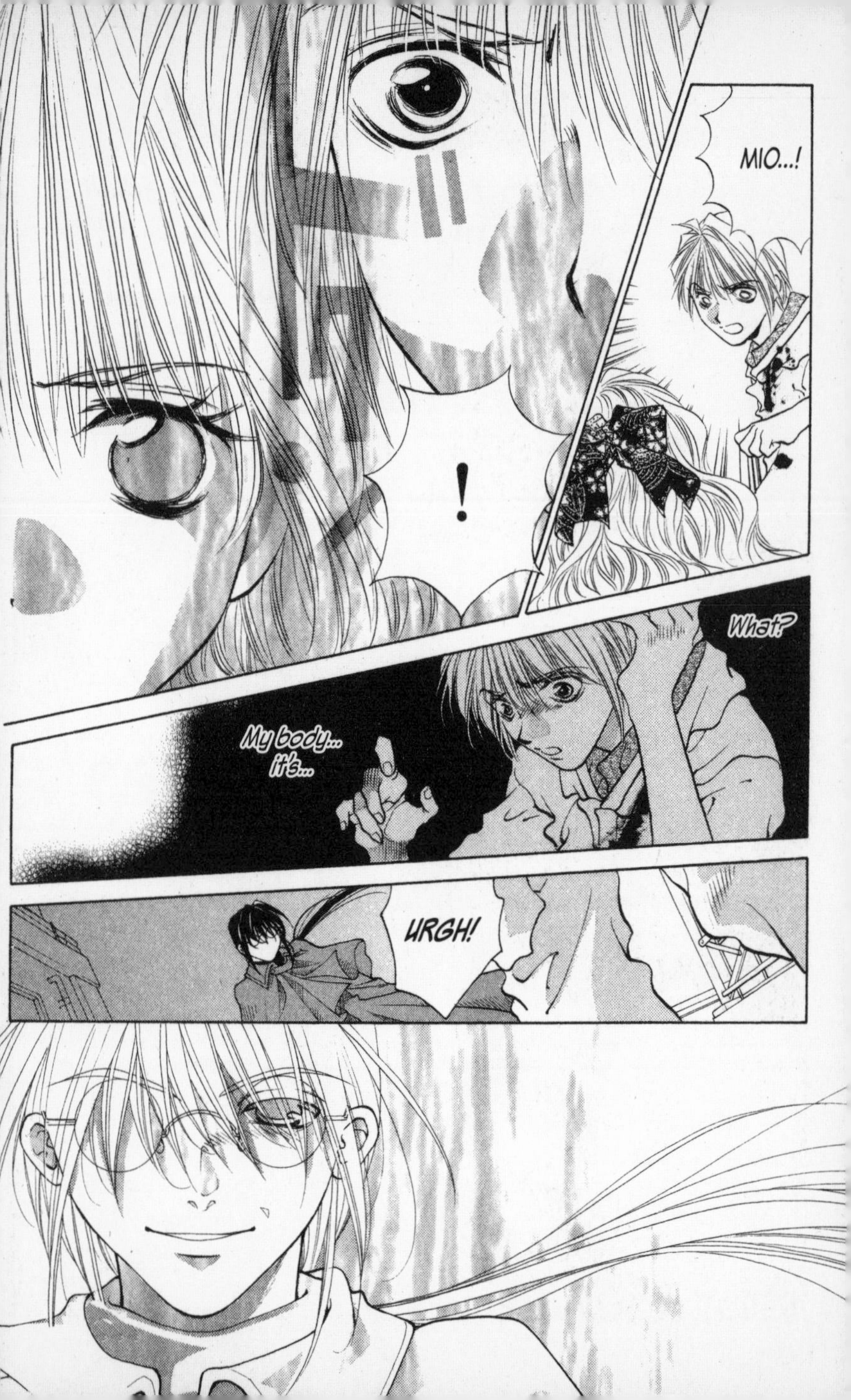
MIO...!
!
What?
My body... it's...
URGH!

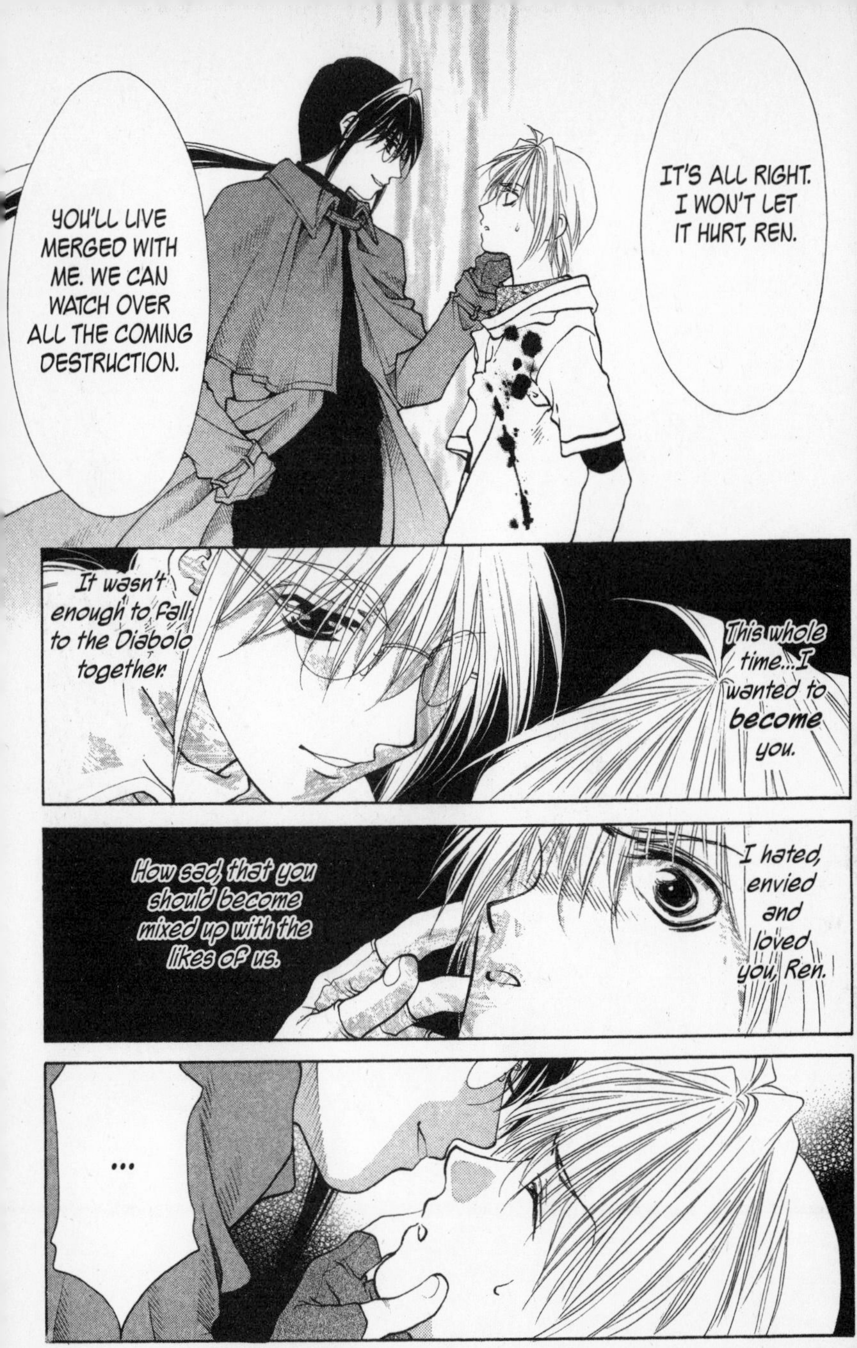
IT'S ALL RIGHT. I WON'T LET IT HURT, REN.
YOU'LL LIVE MERGED WITH ME. WE CAN WATCH OVER ALL THE COMING DESTRUCTION.
This whole time...I wanted to become you.
It wasn't enough to fall to the Diabolo together.
I hated, envied and loved you, Ren.
How sad, that you should become mixed up with the likes of us.
...

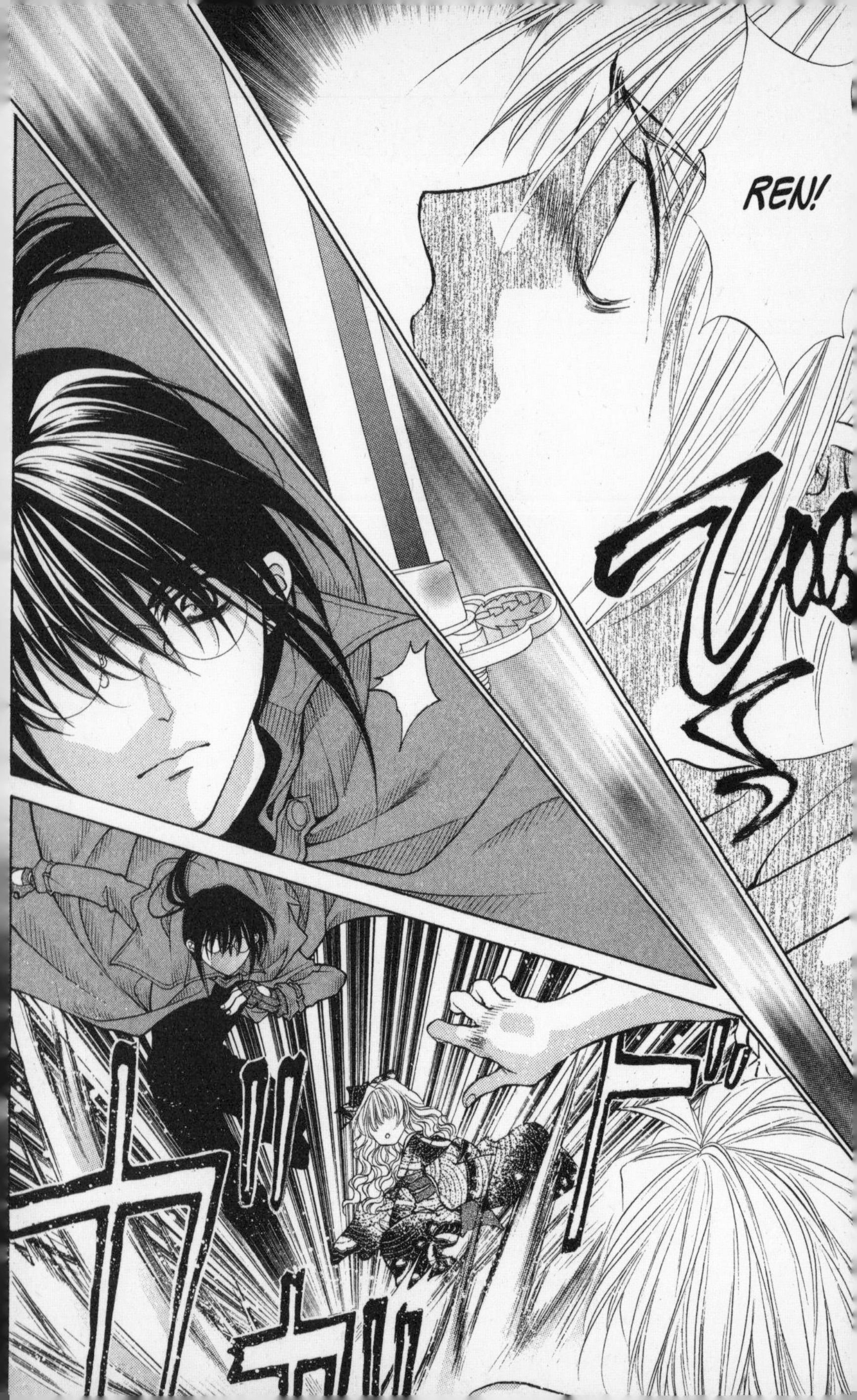
REN!

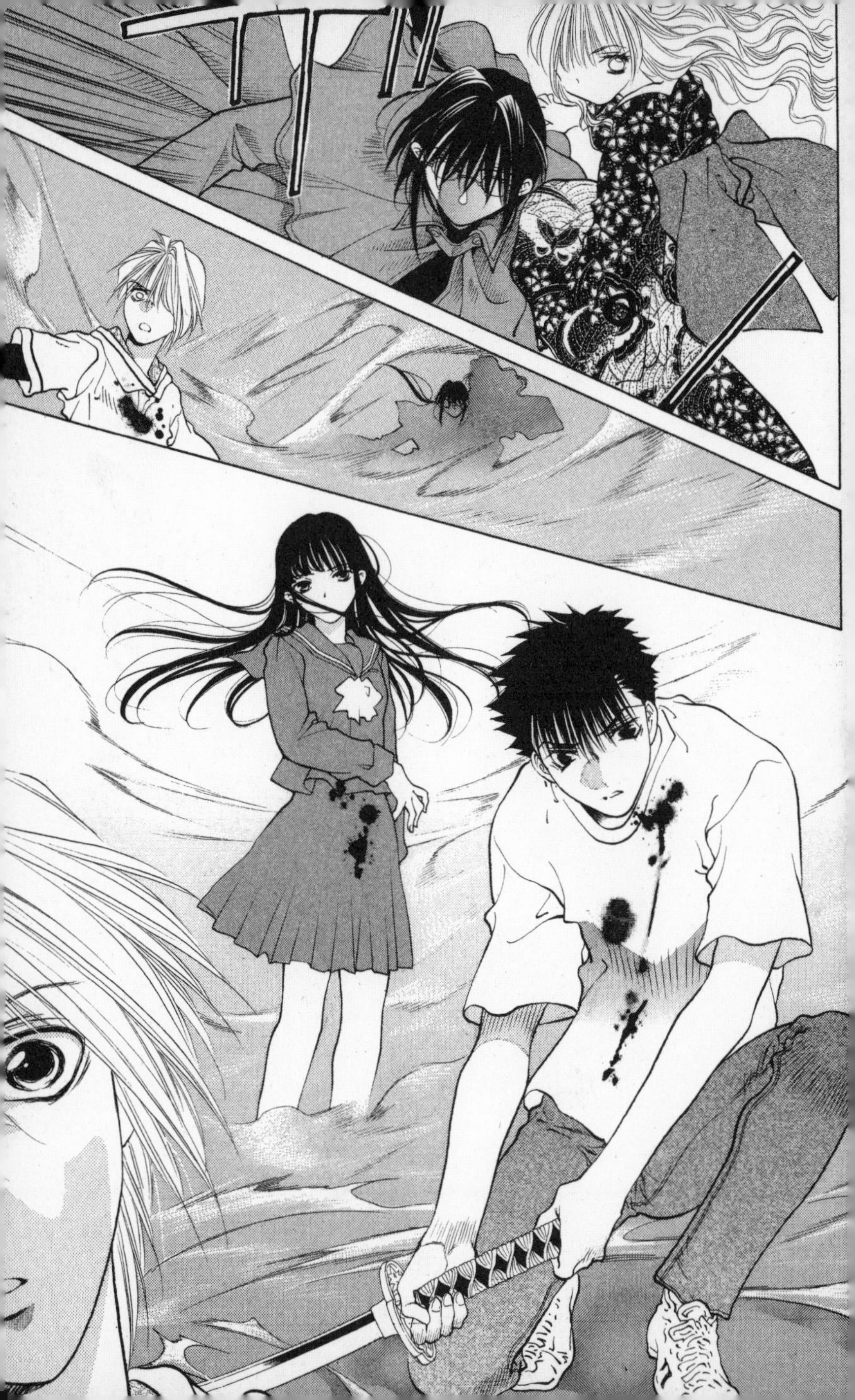

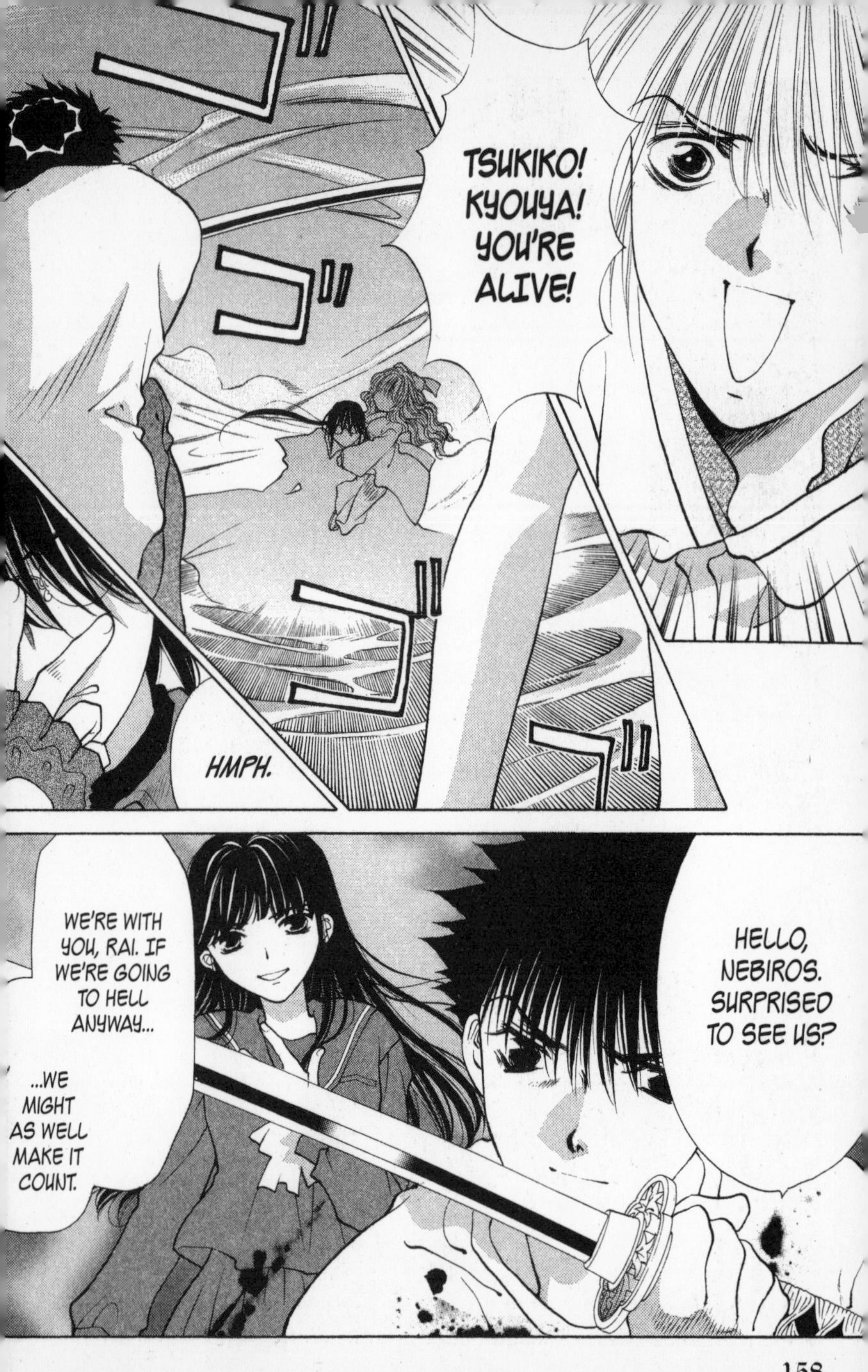
ゴゴゴゴ
TSUKIKO! KYOUYA! YOU'RE ALIVE!
HMPH.
HELLO, NEBIROS. SURPRISED TO SEE US?
WE'RE WITH YOU, RAI. IF WE'RE GOING TO HELL ANYWAY...
...WE MIGHT AS WELL MAKE IT COUNT.

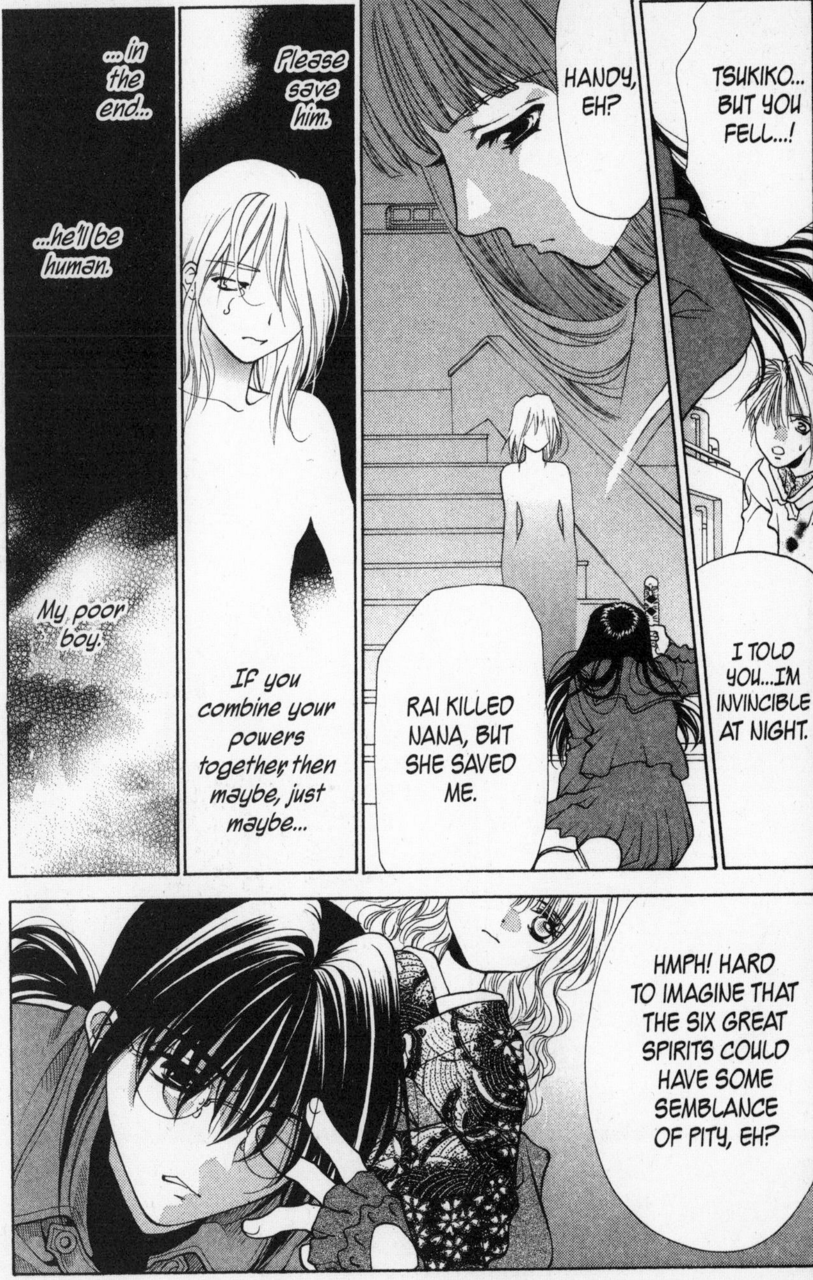
TSUKIKO... BUT YOU FELL...!
I TOLD YOU...I'M INVINCIBLE AT NIGHT.
HANDY, EH?
RAI KILLED NANA, BUT SHE SAVED ME.
Please save him.
If you combine your powers together, then maybe, just maybe...
...in the end...
...he'll be human.
My poor boy.
HMPH! HARD TO IMAGINE THAT THE SIX GREAT SPIRITS COULD HAVE SOME SEMBLANCE OF PITY, EH?

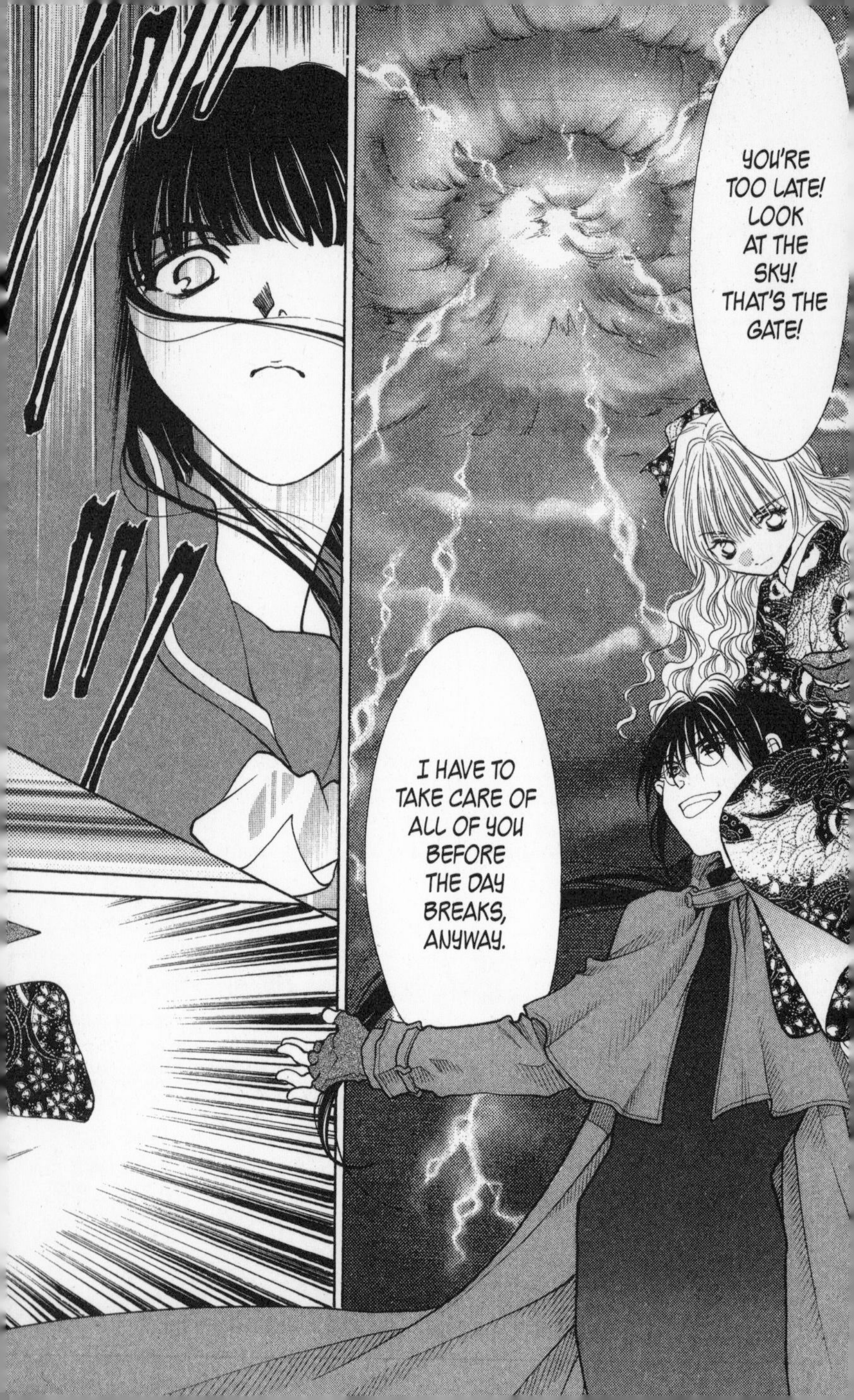
YOU'RE TOO LATE! LOOK AT THE SKY! THAT'S THE GATE!
I HAVE TO TAKE CARE OF ALL OF YOU BEFORE THE DAY BREAKS, ANYWAY.

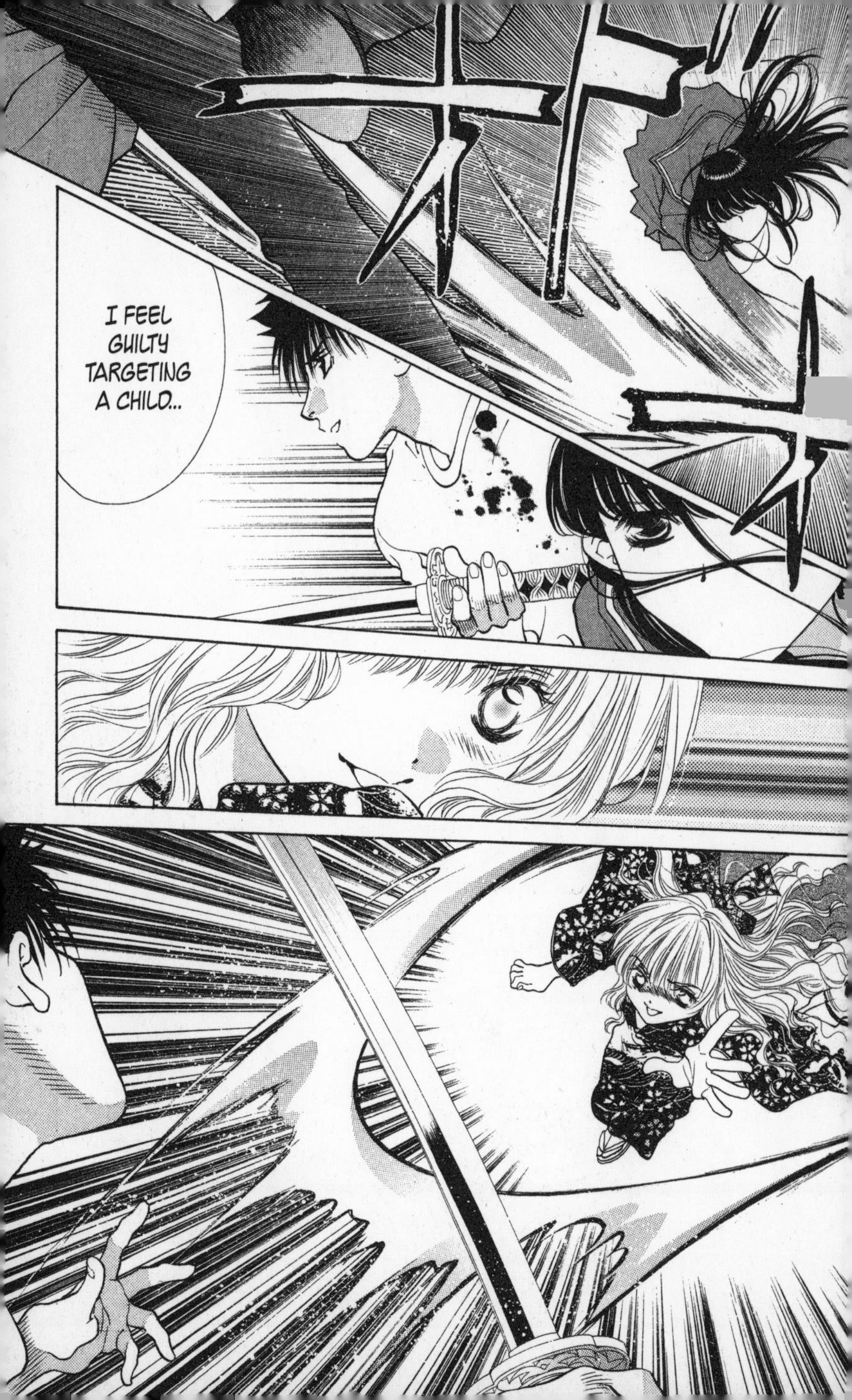
I FEEL GUILTY TARGETING A CHILD...

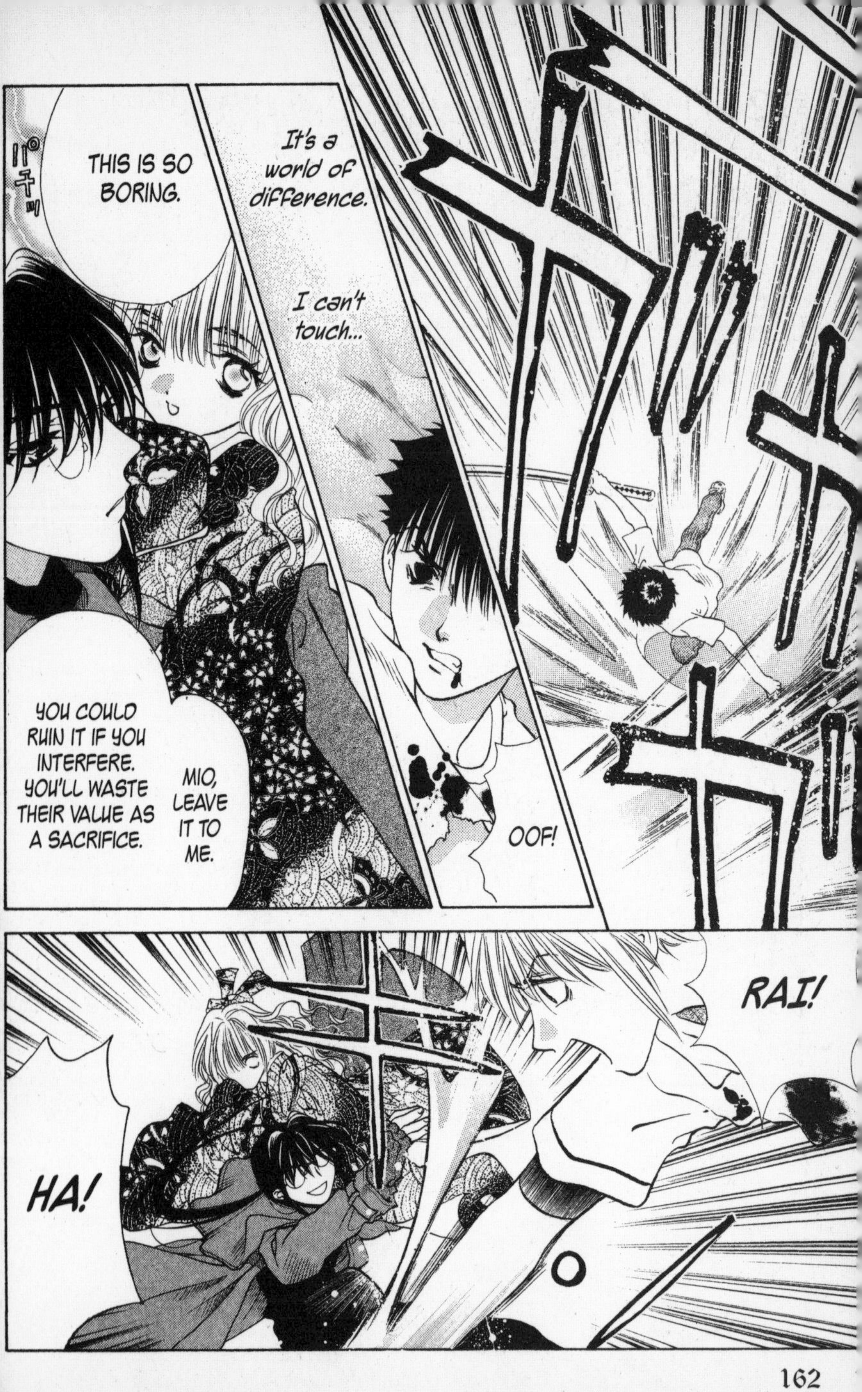

It's a world of difference.
I can't touch...
OOF!
THIS IS SO BORING.
MIO, LEAVE IT TO ME.
YOU COULD RUIN IT IF YOU INTERFERE. YOU'LL WASTE THEIR VALUE AS A SACRIFICE.
RAI!
HA!

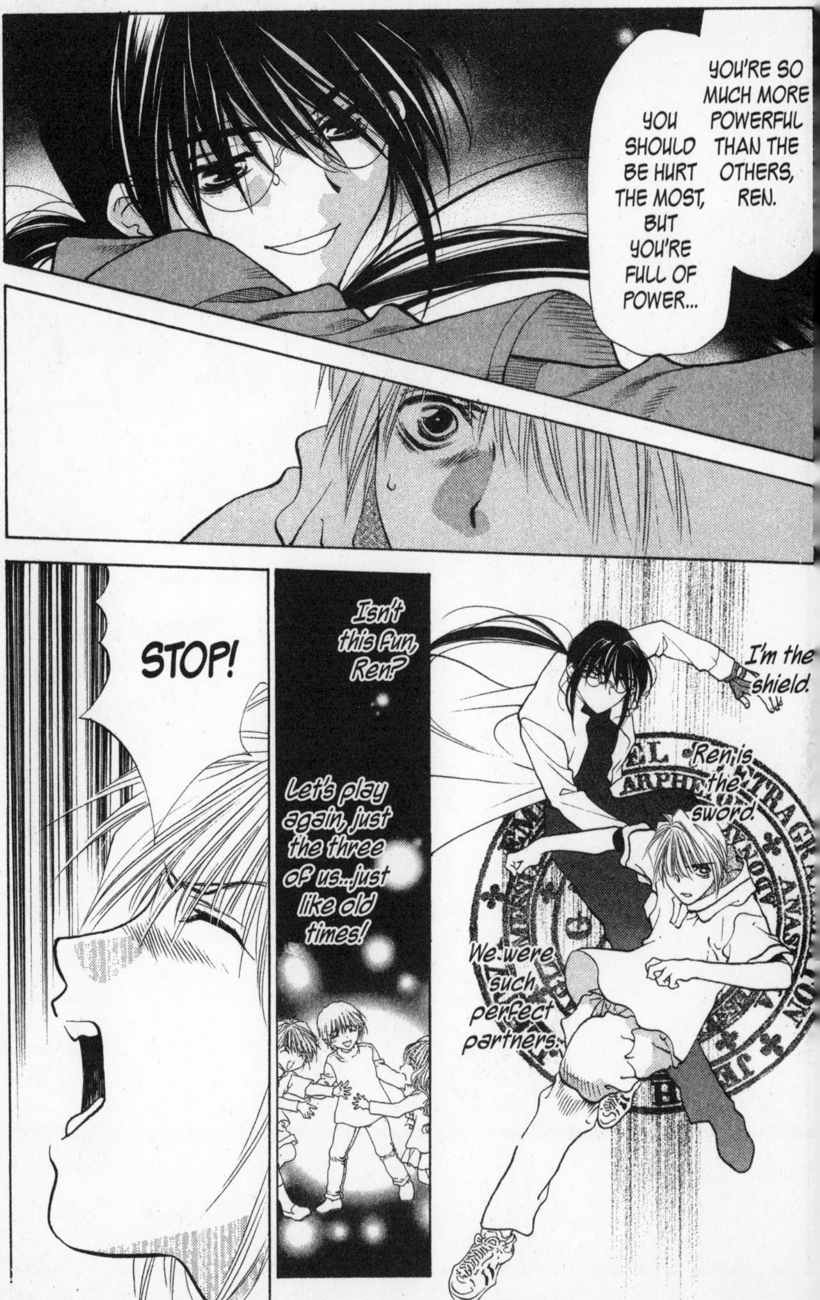
YOU'RE SO MUCH MORE POWERFUL THAN THE OTHERS, REN.
YOU SHOULD BE HURT THE MOST, BUT YOU'RE FULL OF POWER...
I'm the shield.
Ren is the sword.
We were such perfect partners.
Isn't this fun, Ren?
Let's play again, just the three of us...just like old times!
STOP!

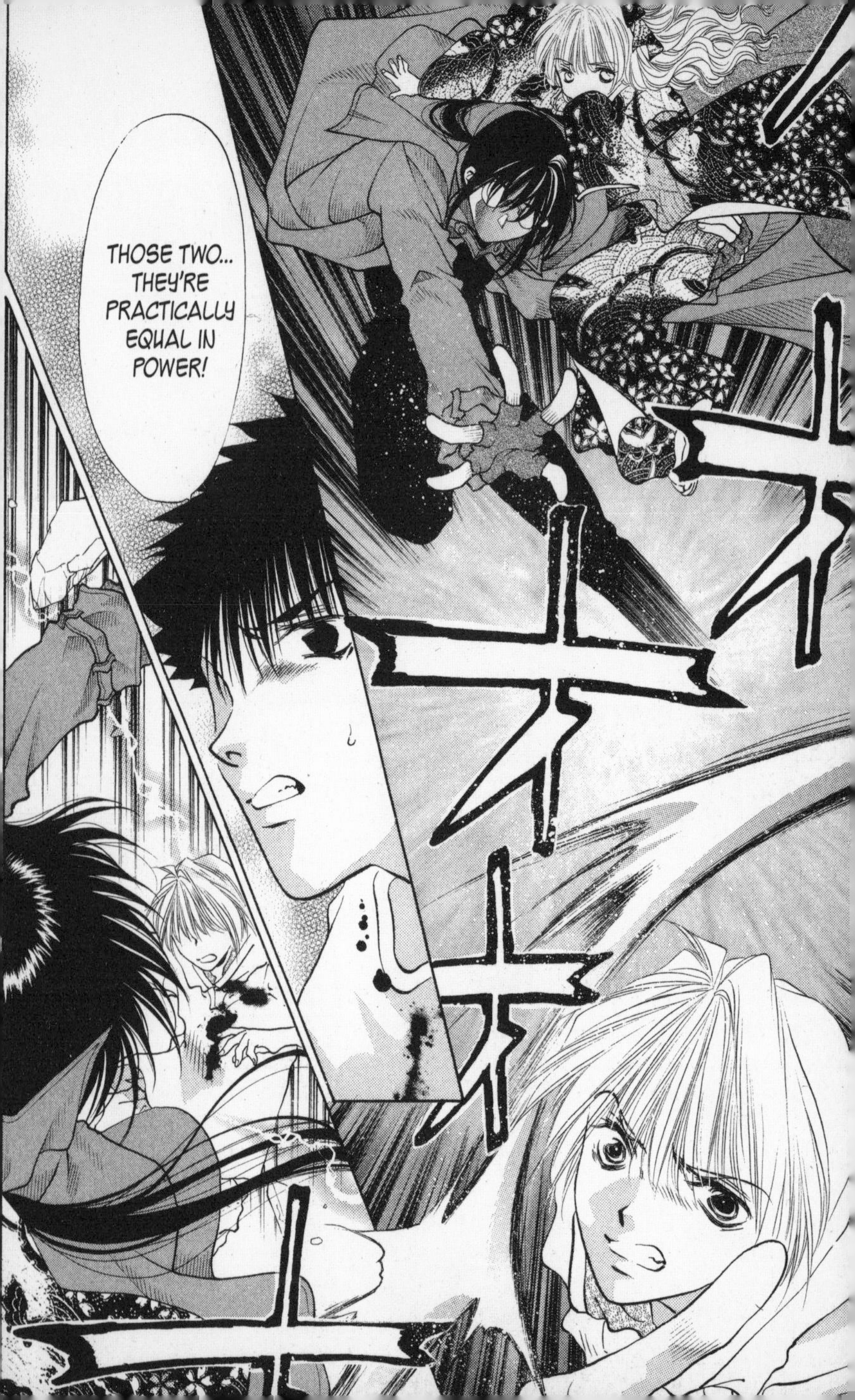
THOSE TWO... THEY'RE PRACTICALLY EQUAL IN POWER!

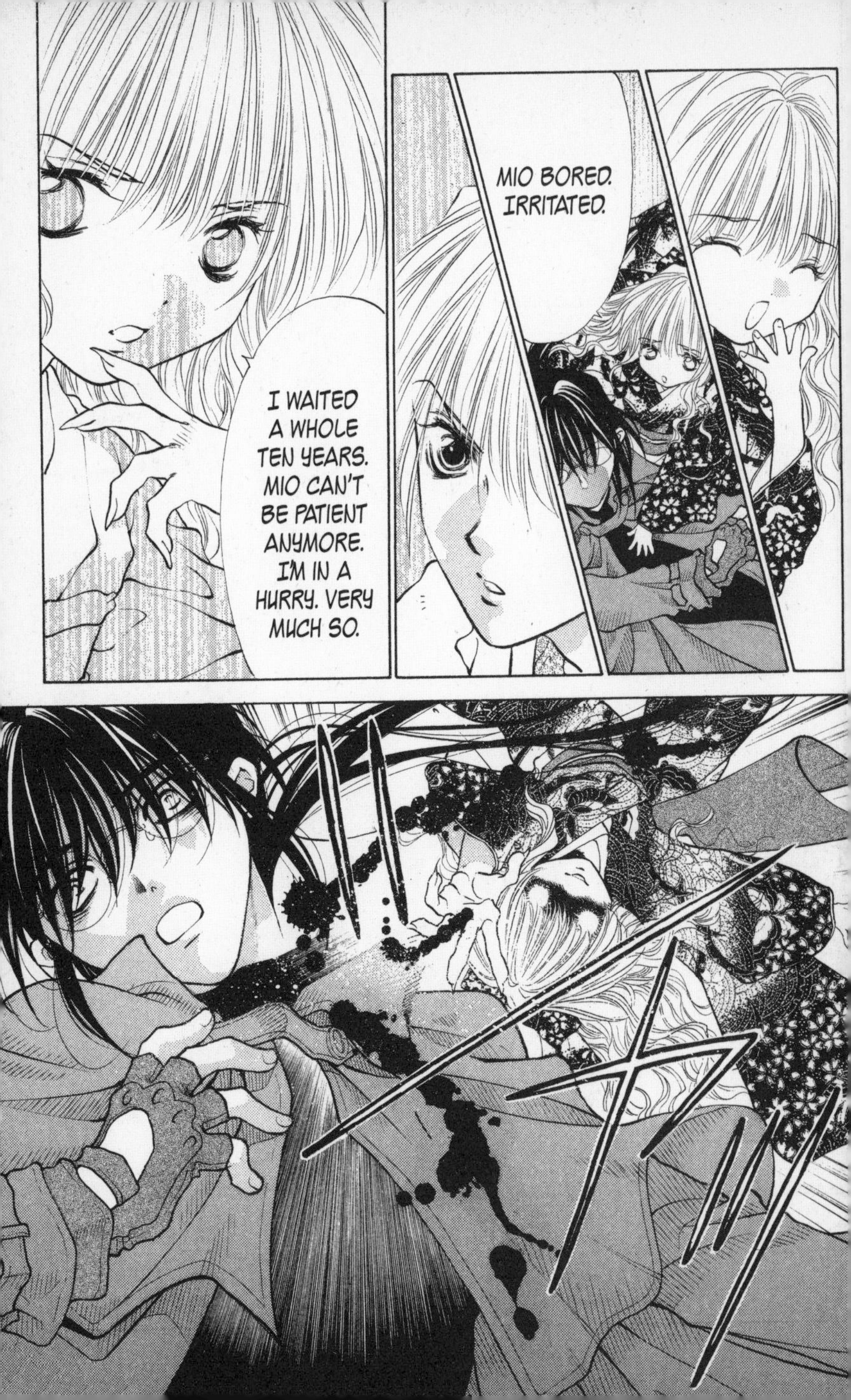
MIO BORED. IRRITATED.
I WAITED A WHOLE TEN YEARS. MIO CAN'T BE PATIENT ANYMORE. I'M IN A HURRY. VERY MUCH SO.

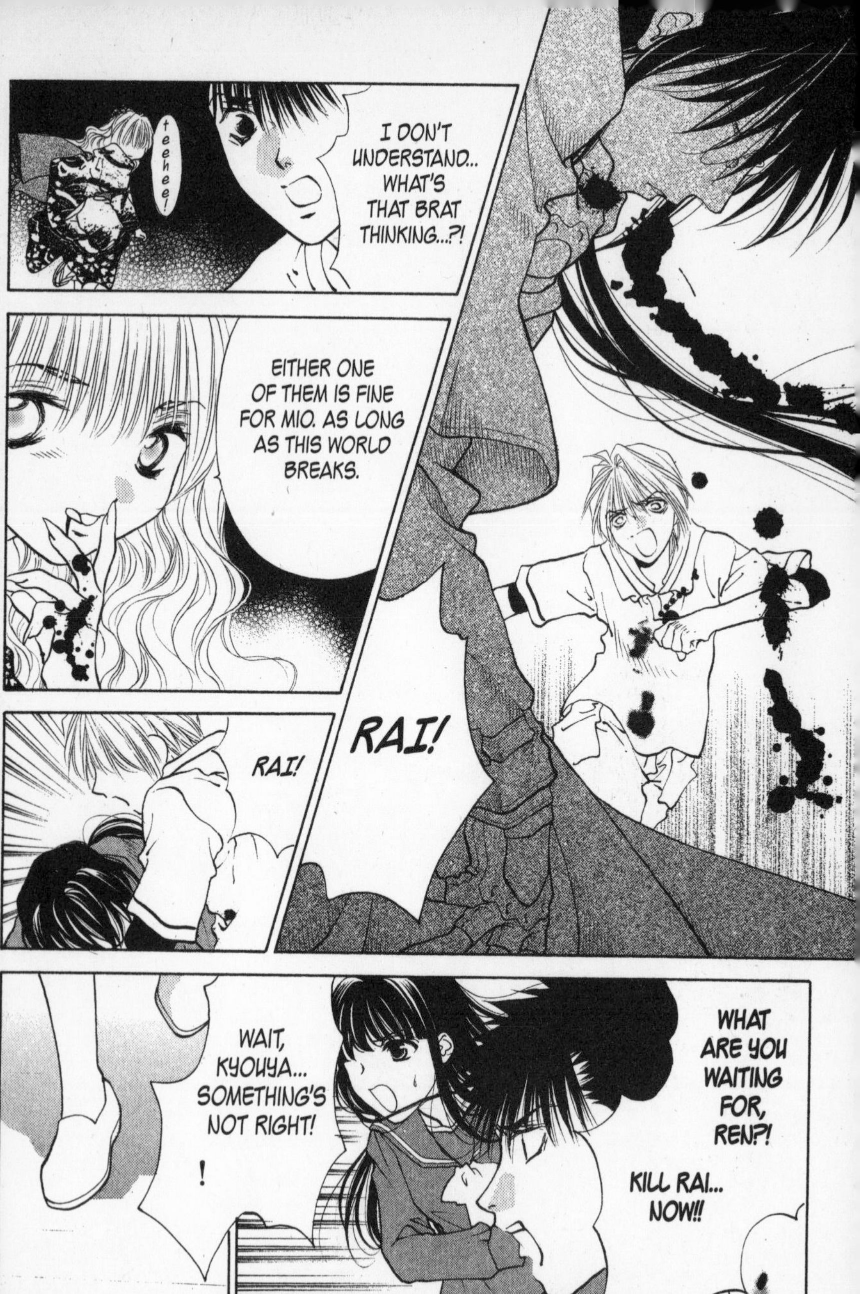
teehee!
I DON'T UNDERSTAND... WHAT'S THAT BRAT THINKING...?!
EITHER ONE OF THEM IS FINE FOR MIO. AS LONG AS THIS WORLD BREAKS.
RAI!
RAI!
WHAT ARE YOU WAITING FOR, REN?!
KILL RAI... NOW!!
WAIT, KYOUYA... SOMETHING'S NOT RIGHT!
!

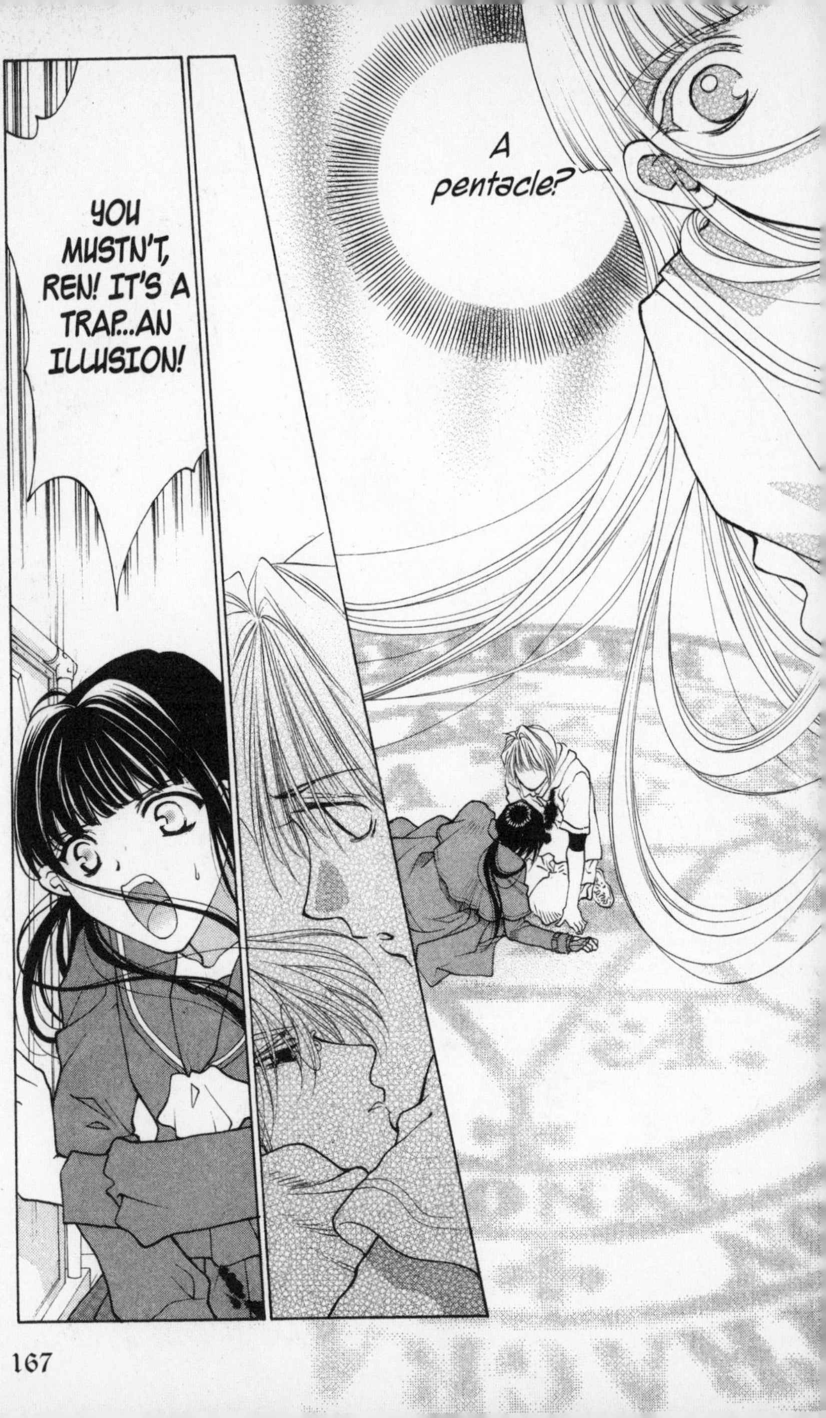
A pentacle?
YOU MUSTN'T, REN! IT'S A TRAP...AN ILLUSION!

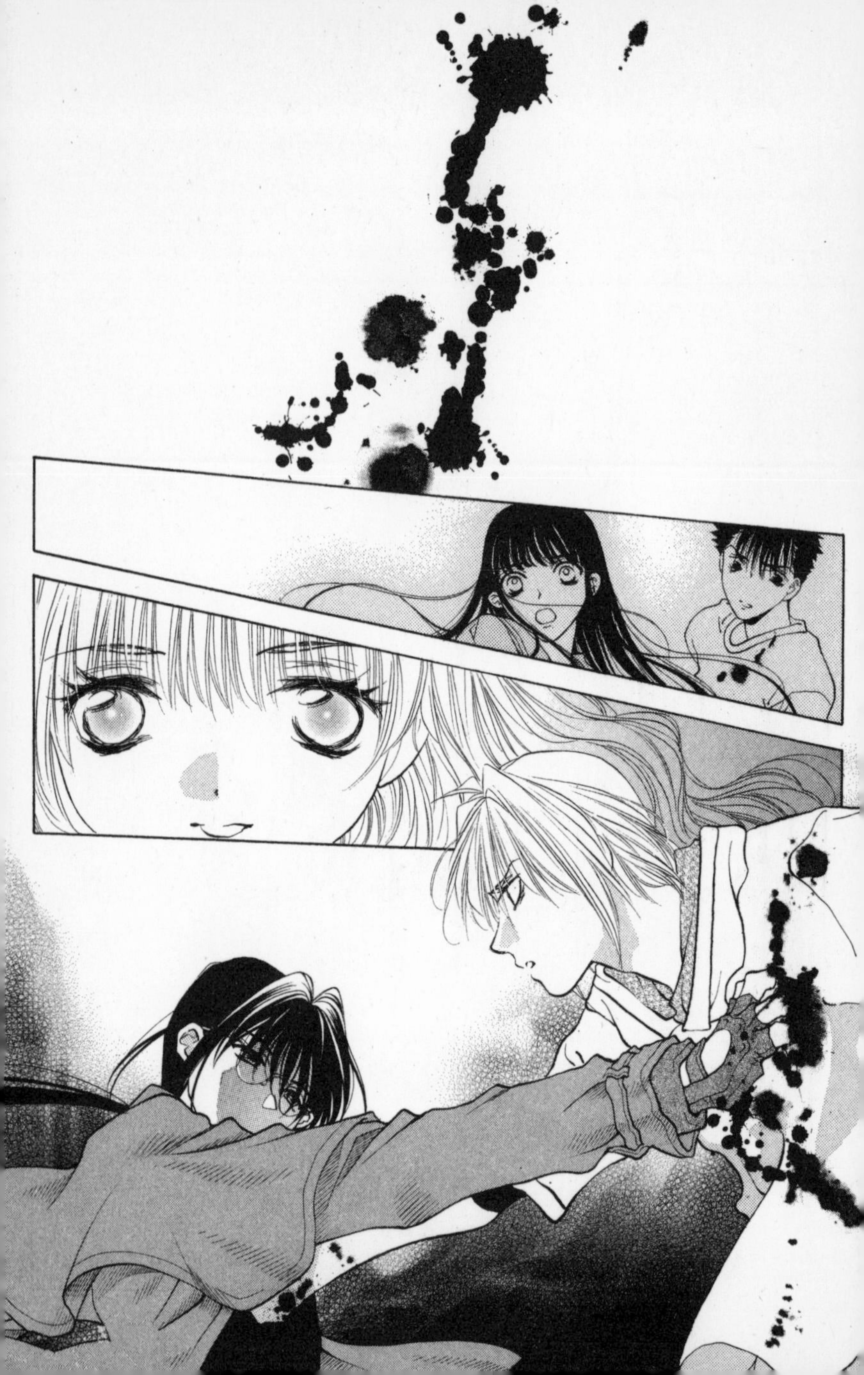

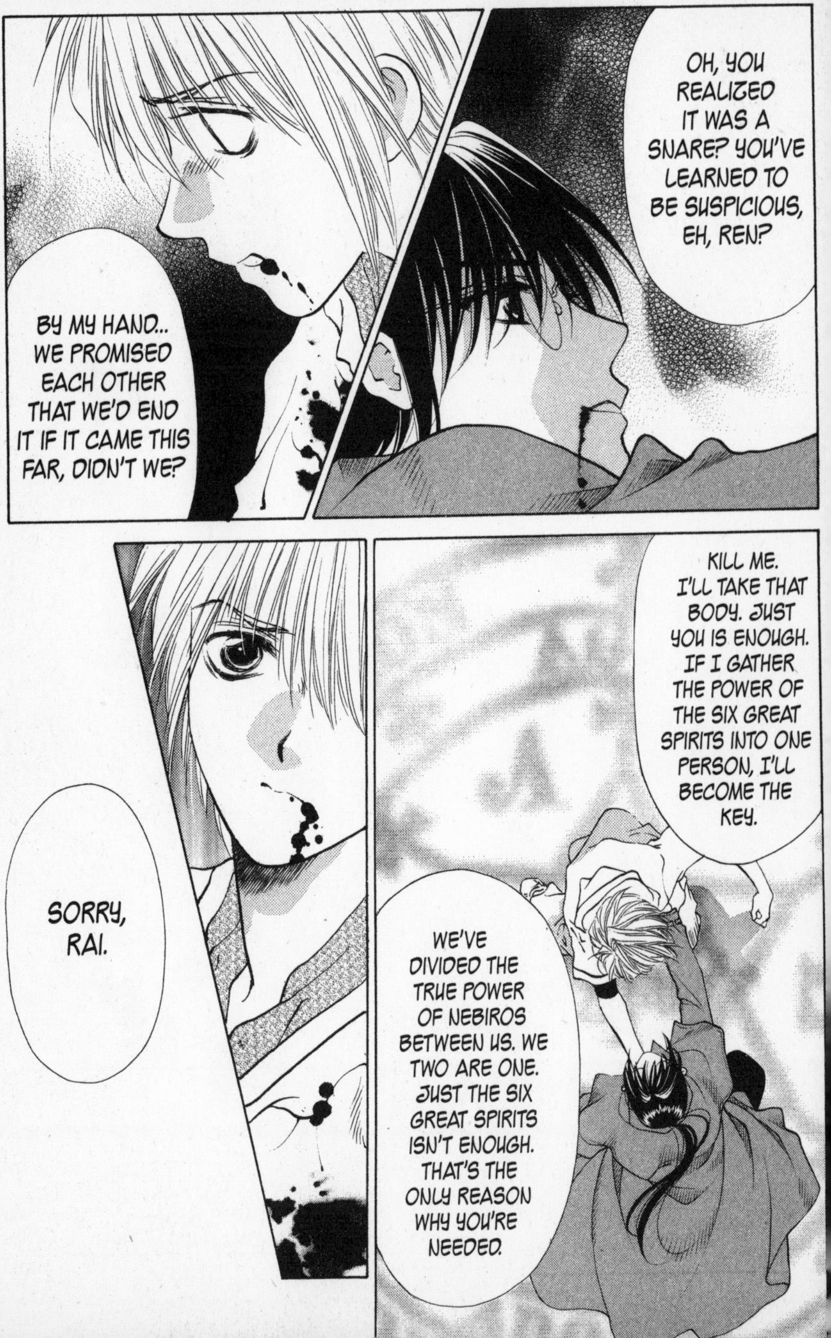
OH, YOU REALIZED IT WAS A SNARE? YOU'VE LEARNED TO BE SUSPICIOUS, EH, REN?
BY MY HAND... WE PROMISED EACH OTHER THAT WE'D END IT IF IT CAME THIS FAR, DIDN'T WE?
KILL ME. I'LL TAKE THAT BODY. JUST YOU IS ENOUGH. IF I GATHER THE POWER OF THE SIX GREAT SPIRITS INTO ONE PERSON, I'LL BECOME THE KEY.
WE'VE DIVIDED THE TRUE POWER OF NEBIROS BETWEEN US. WE TWO ARE ONE. JUST THE SIX GREAT SPIRITS ISN'T ENOUGH. THAT'S THE ONLY REASON WHY YOU'RE NEEDED.
SORRY, RAI.

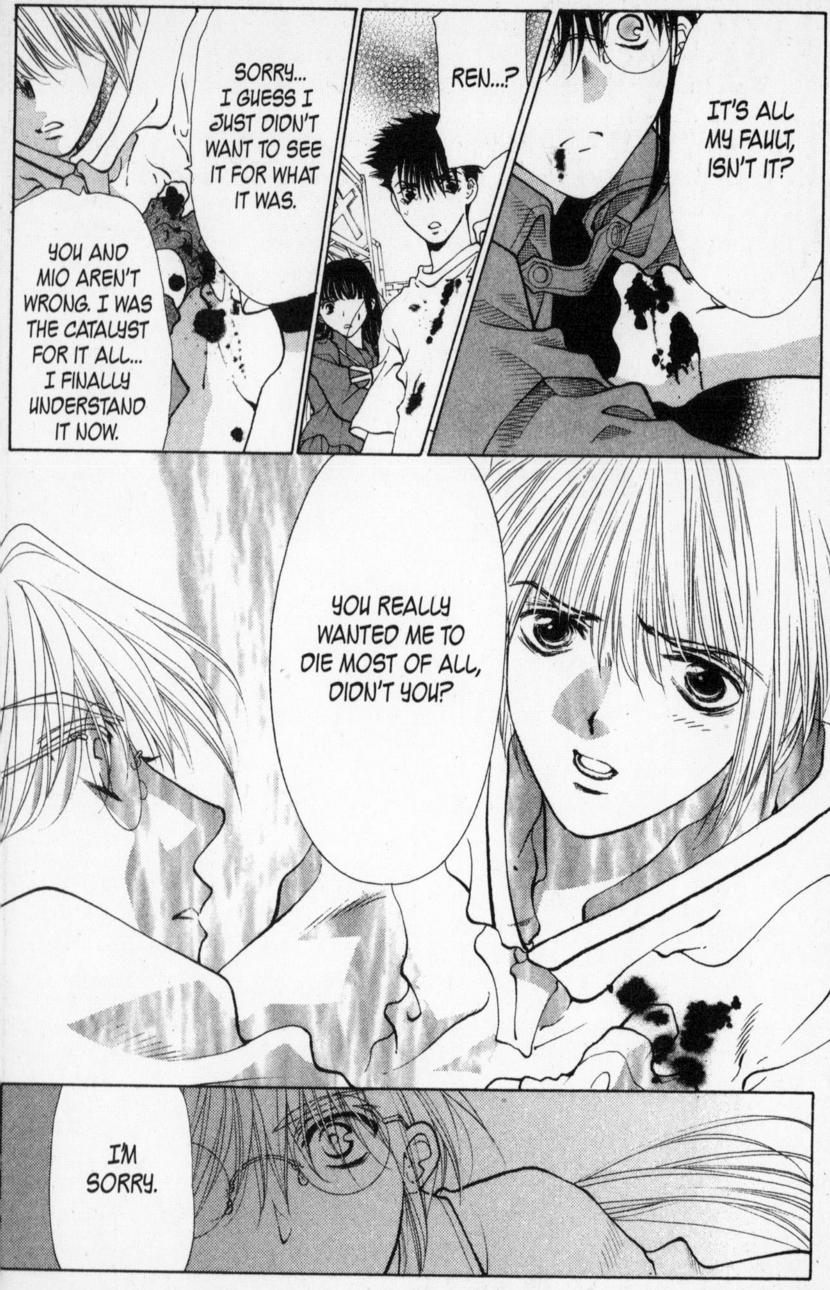
IT'S ALL MY FAULT, ISN'T IT?
REN...?
SORRY... I GUESS I JUST DIDN'T WANT TO SEE IT FOR WHAT IT WAS.
YOU AND MIO AREN'T WRONG. I WAS THE CATALYST FOR IT ALL... I FINALLY UNDERSTAND IT NOW.
YOU REALLY WANTED ME TO DIE MOST OF ALL, DIDN'T YOU?
I'M SORRY.

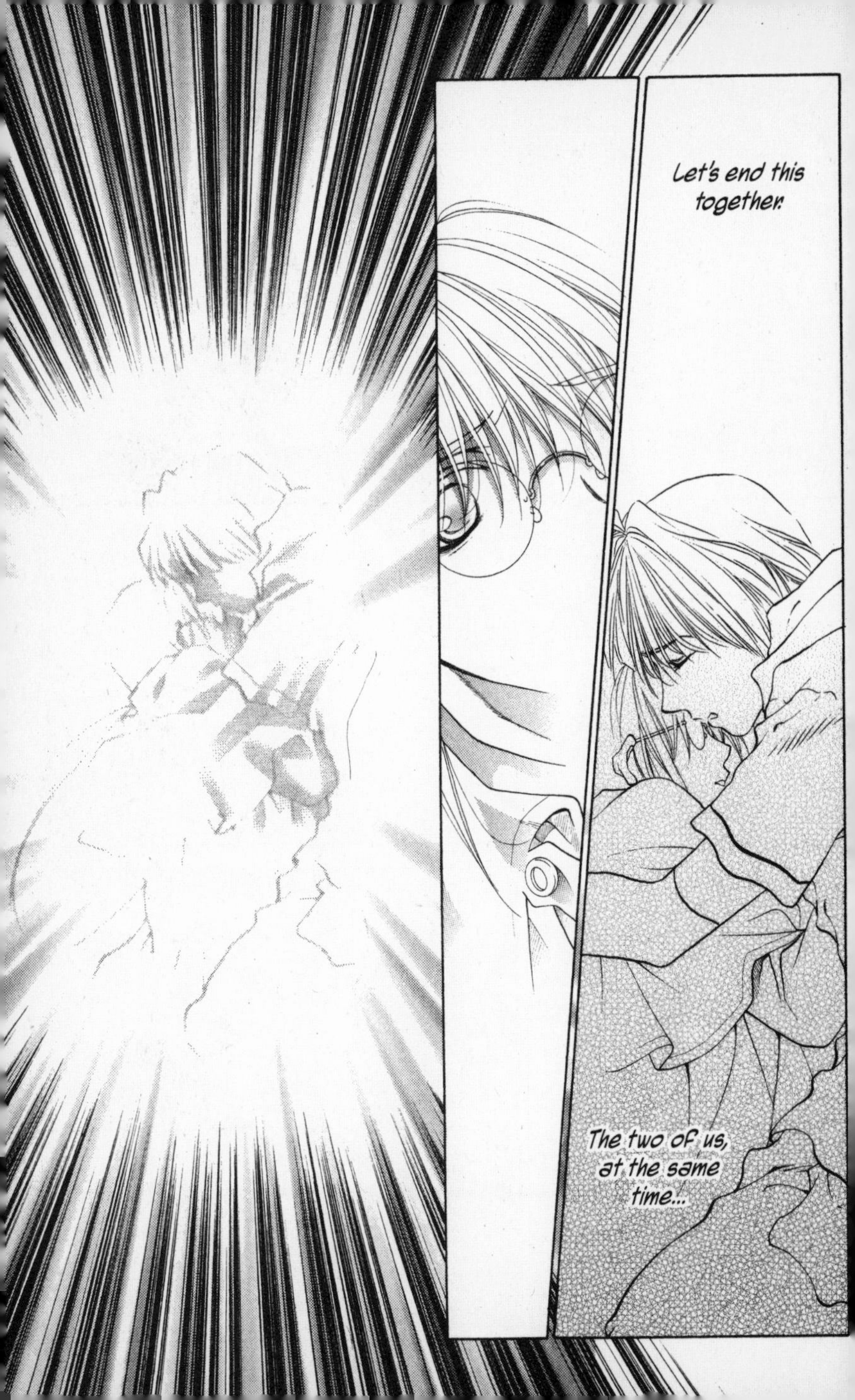
Let's end this together.
The two of us, at the same time...

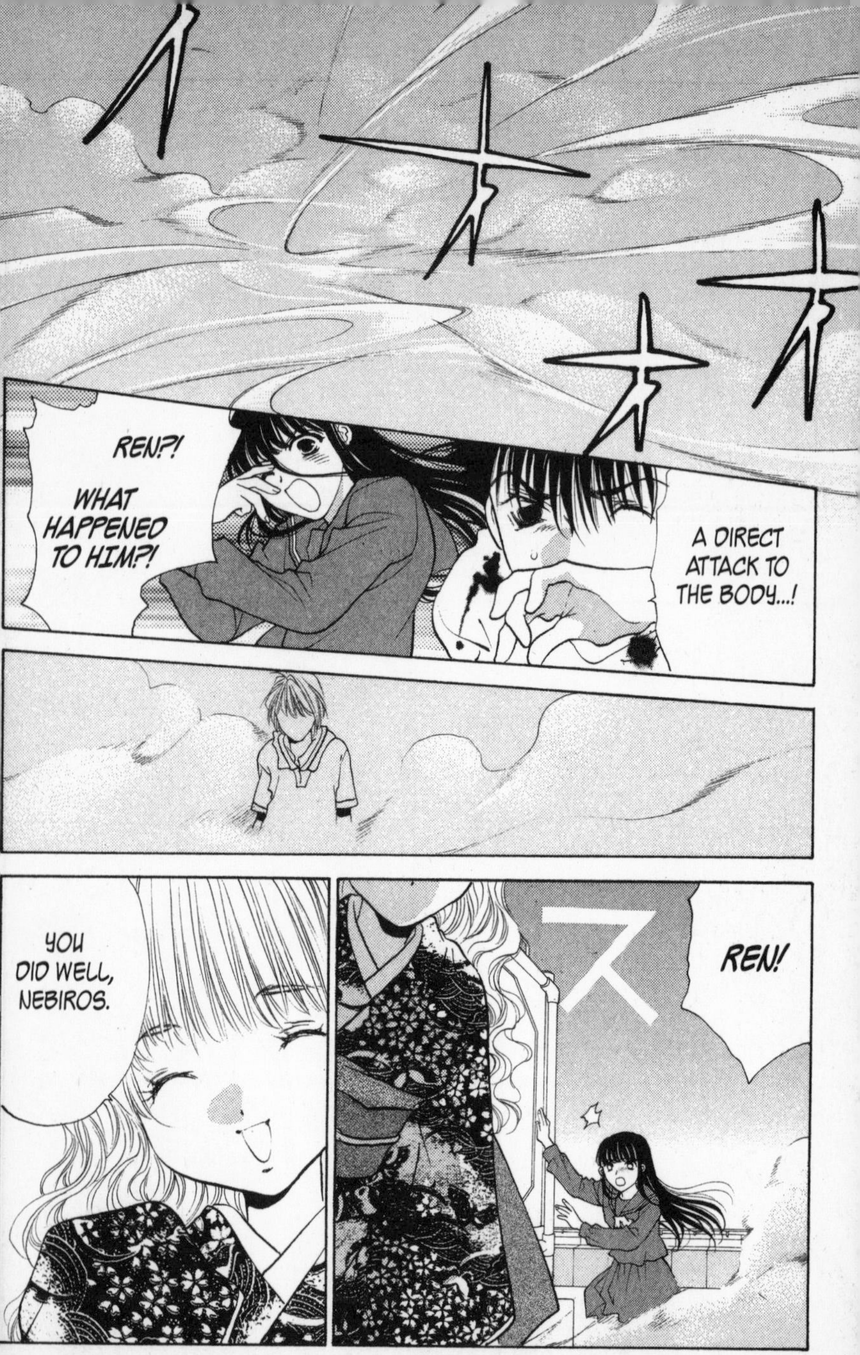
A DIRECT ATTACK TO THE BODY...!
REN?!
WHAT HAPPENED TO HIM?!
ス
REN!
YOU DID WELL, NEBIROS.

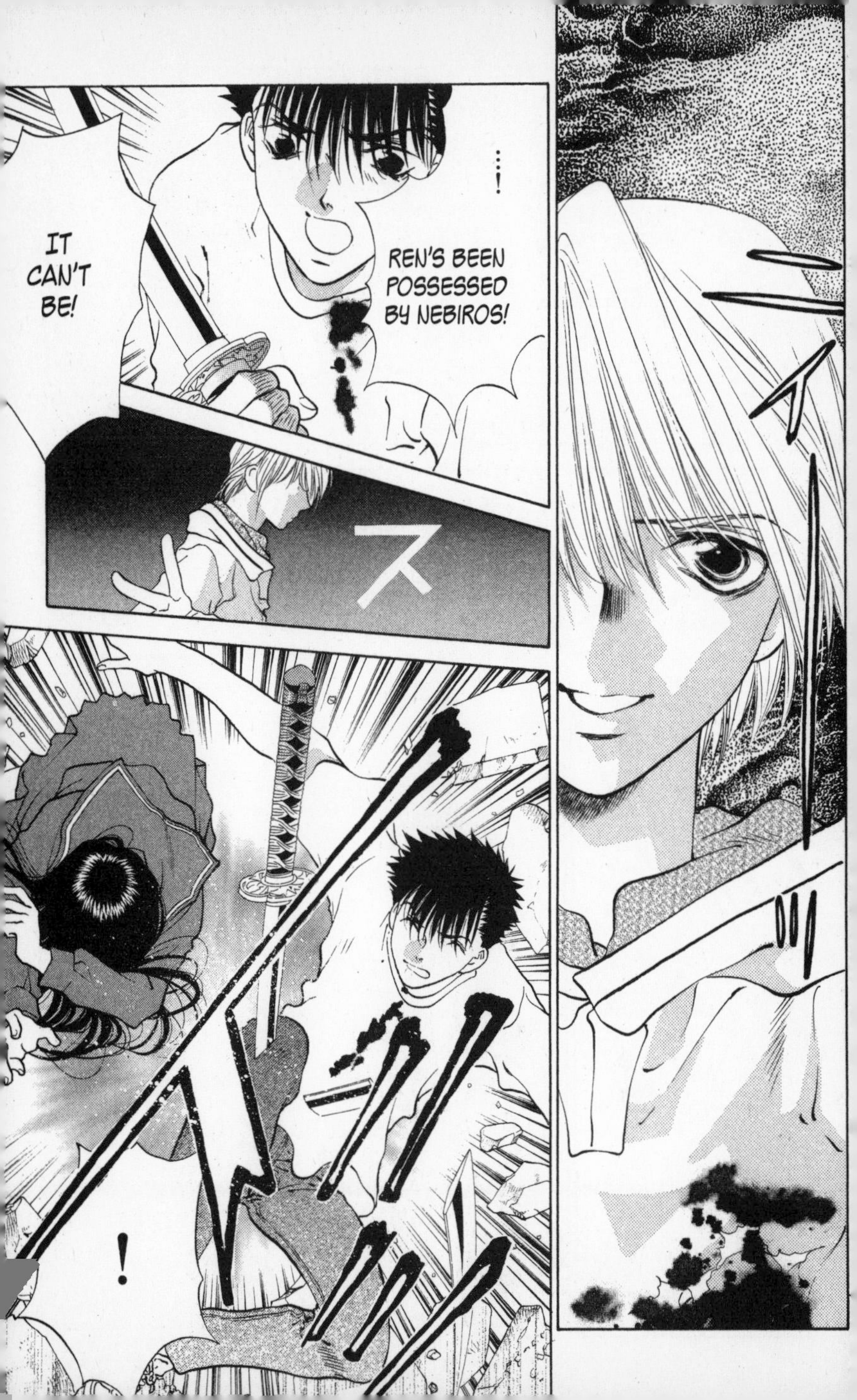
...!
REN'S BEEN POSSESSED BY NEBIROS!
IT CAN'T BE!
ス
!

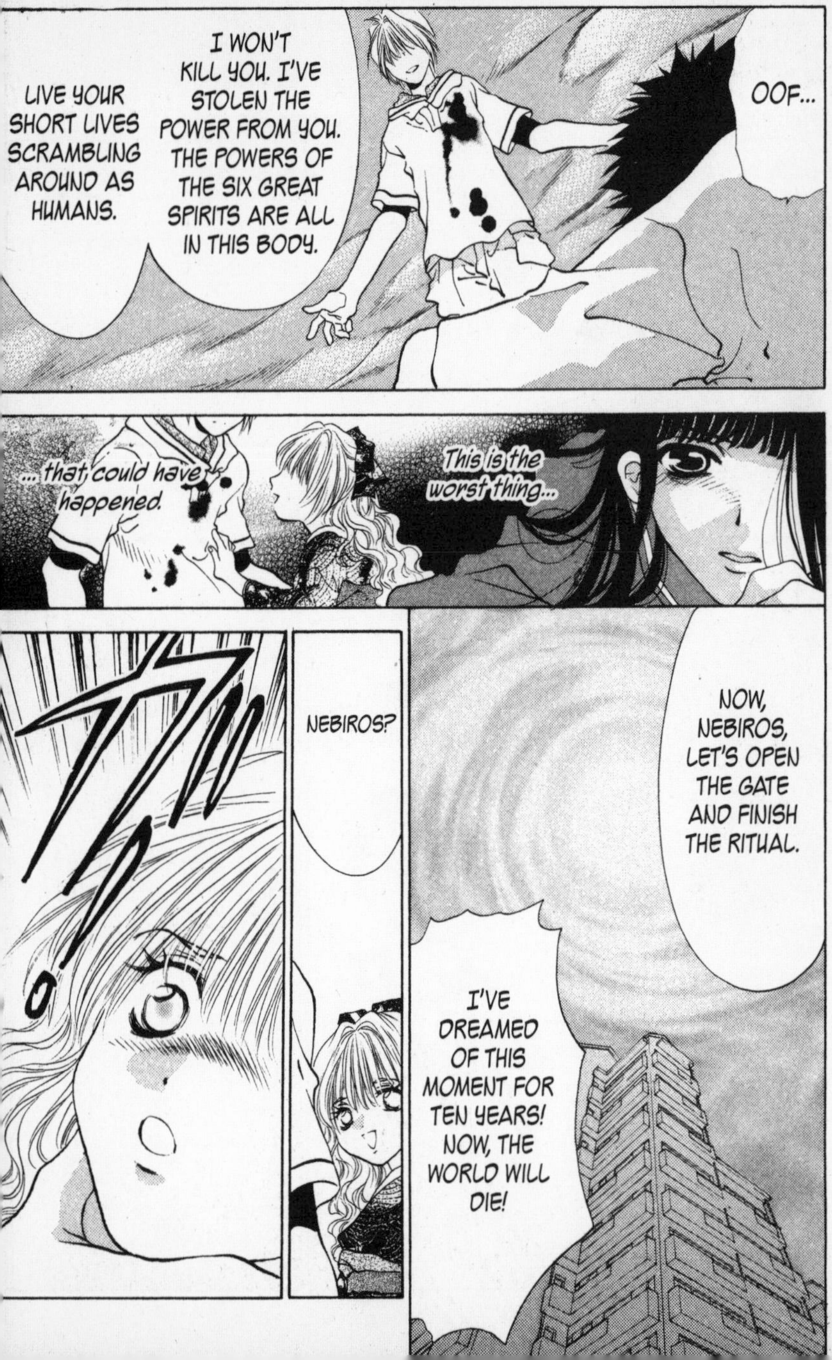
OOF...
I WON'T KILL YOU. I'VE STOLEN THE POWER FROM YOU. THE POWERS OF THE SIX GREAT SPIRITS ARE ALL IN THIS BODY.
LIVE YOUR SHORT LIVES SCRAMBLING AROUND AS HUMANS.
This is the worst thing...
...that could have happened.
NOW, NEBIROS, LET'S OPEN THE GATE AND FINISH THE RITUAL.
I'VE DREAMED OF THIS MOMENT FOR TEN YEARS! NOW, THE WORLD WILL DIE!
NEBIROS?

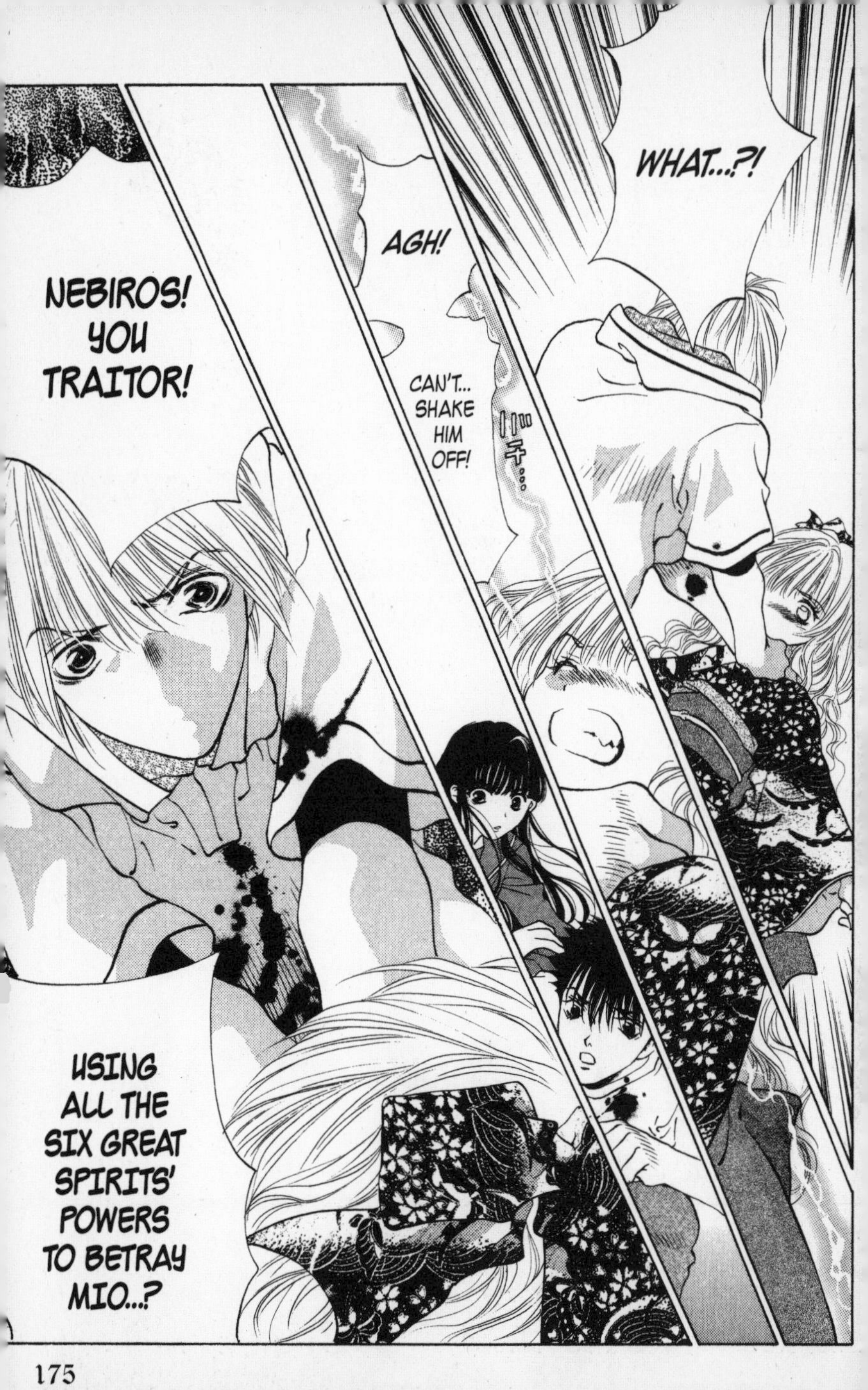
WHAT...?!
AGH!
CAN'T... SHAKE HIM OFF!
NEBIROS! YOU TRAITOR!
USING ALL THE SIX GREAT SPIRITS' POWERS TO BETRAY MIO...?

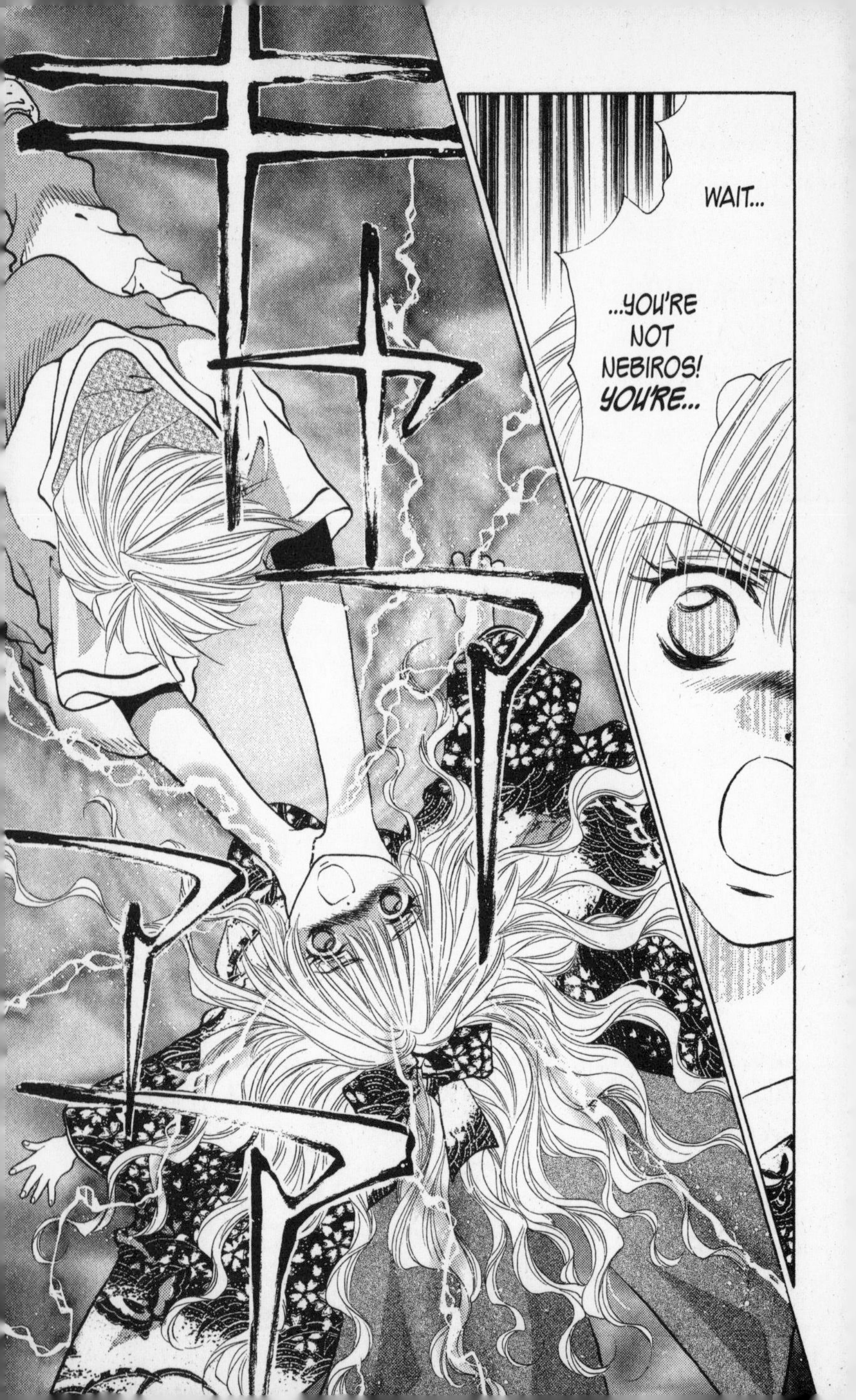
WAIT...
...YOU'RE NOT NEBIROS! YOU'RE...

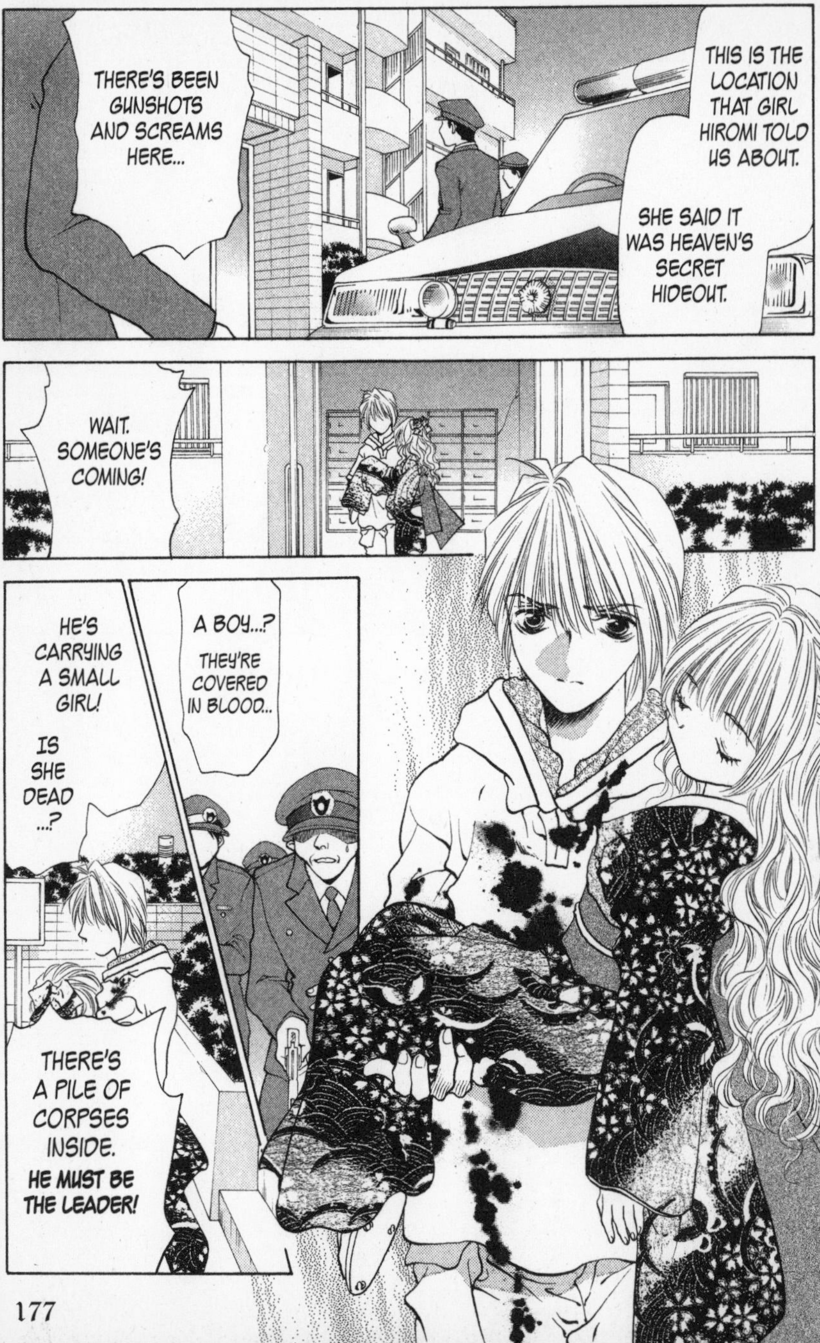
THIS IS THE LOCATION THAT GIRL HIROMI TOLD US ABOUT.
SHE SAID IT WAS HEAVEN'S SECRET HIDEOUT.
THERE'S BEEN GUNSHOTS AND SCREAMS HERE...
WAIT. SOMEONE'S COMING!
A BOY...?
THEY'RE COVERED IN BLOOD...
HE'S CARRYING A SMALL GIRL!
IS SHE DEAD ...?
THERE'S A PILE OF CORPSES INSIDE.
HE MUST BE THE LEADER!

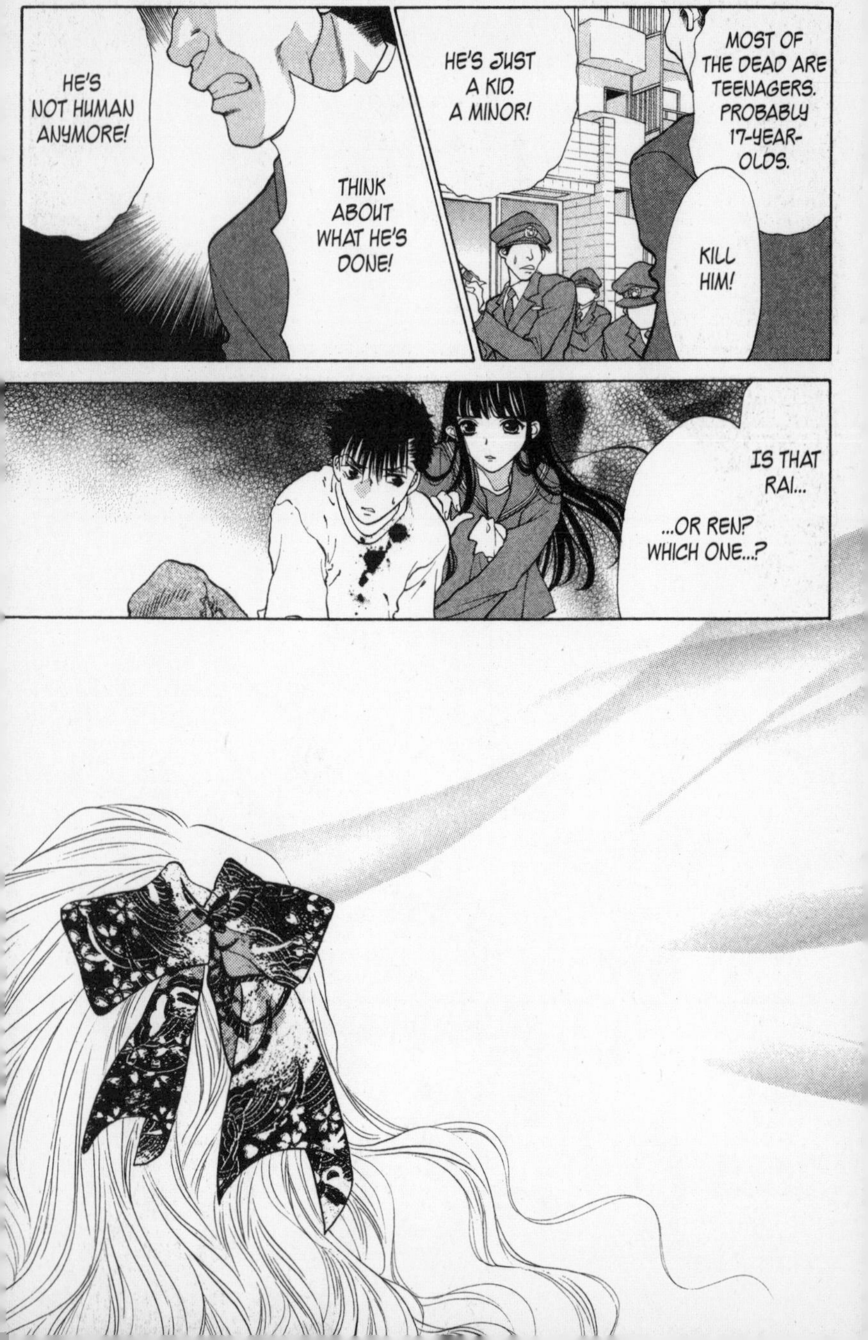
MOST OF THE DEAD ARE TEENAGERS. PROBABLY 17-YEAR-OLDS.
HE'S JUST A KID. A MINOR!
KILL HIM!
THINK ABOUT WHAT HE'S DONE!
HE'S NOT HUMAN ANYMORE!
IS THAT RAI...
...OR REN? WHICH ONE...?

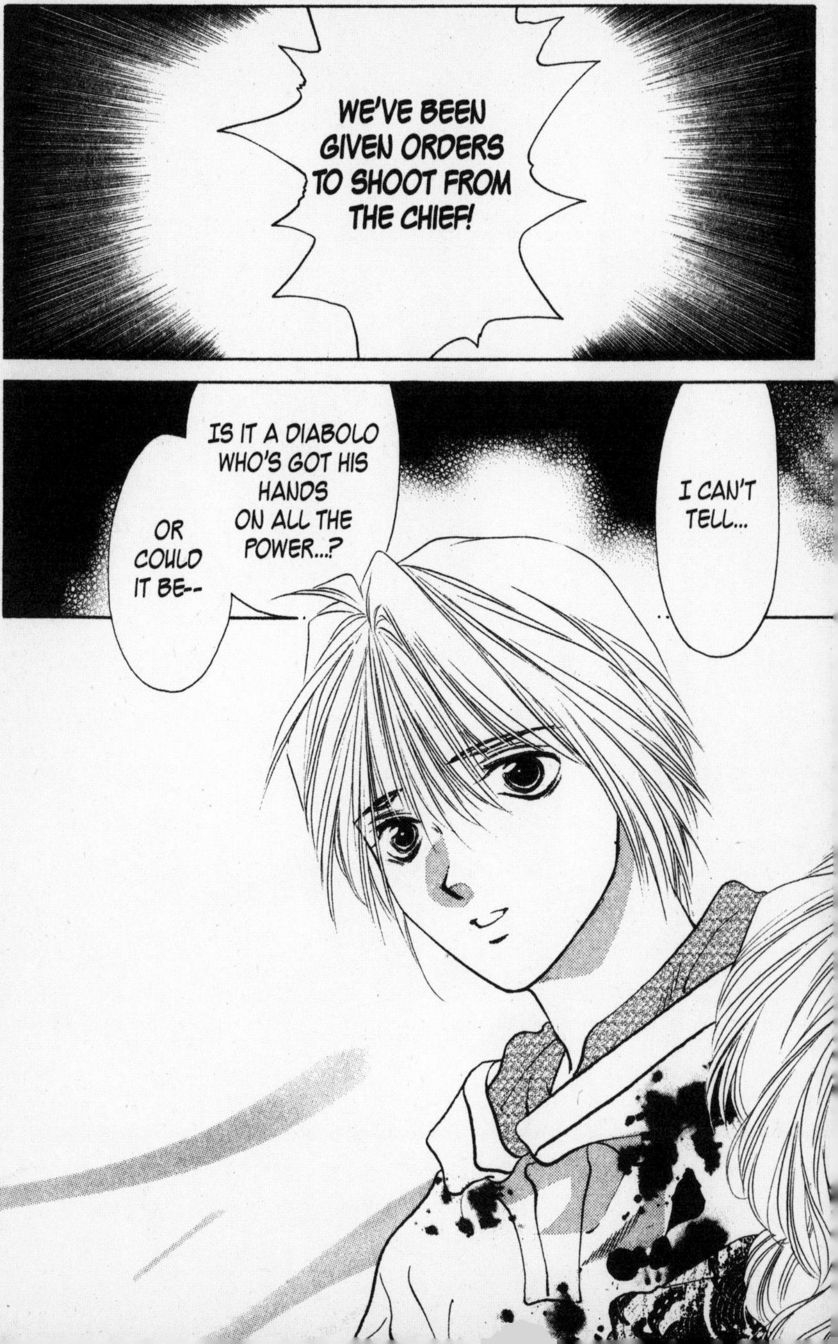
WE'VE BEEN GIVEN ORDERS TO SHOOT FROM THE CHIEF!
I CAN'T TELL...
IS IT A DIABOLO WHO'S GOT HIS HANDS ON ALL THE POWER...?
OR COULD IT BE--

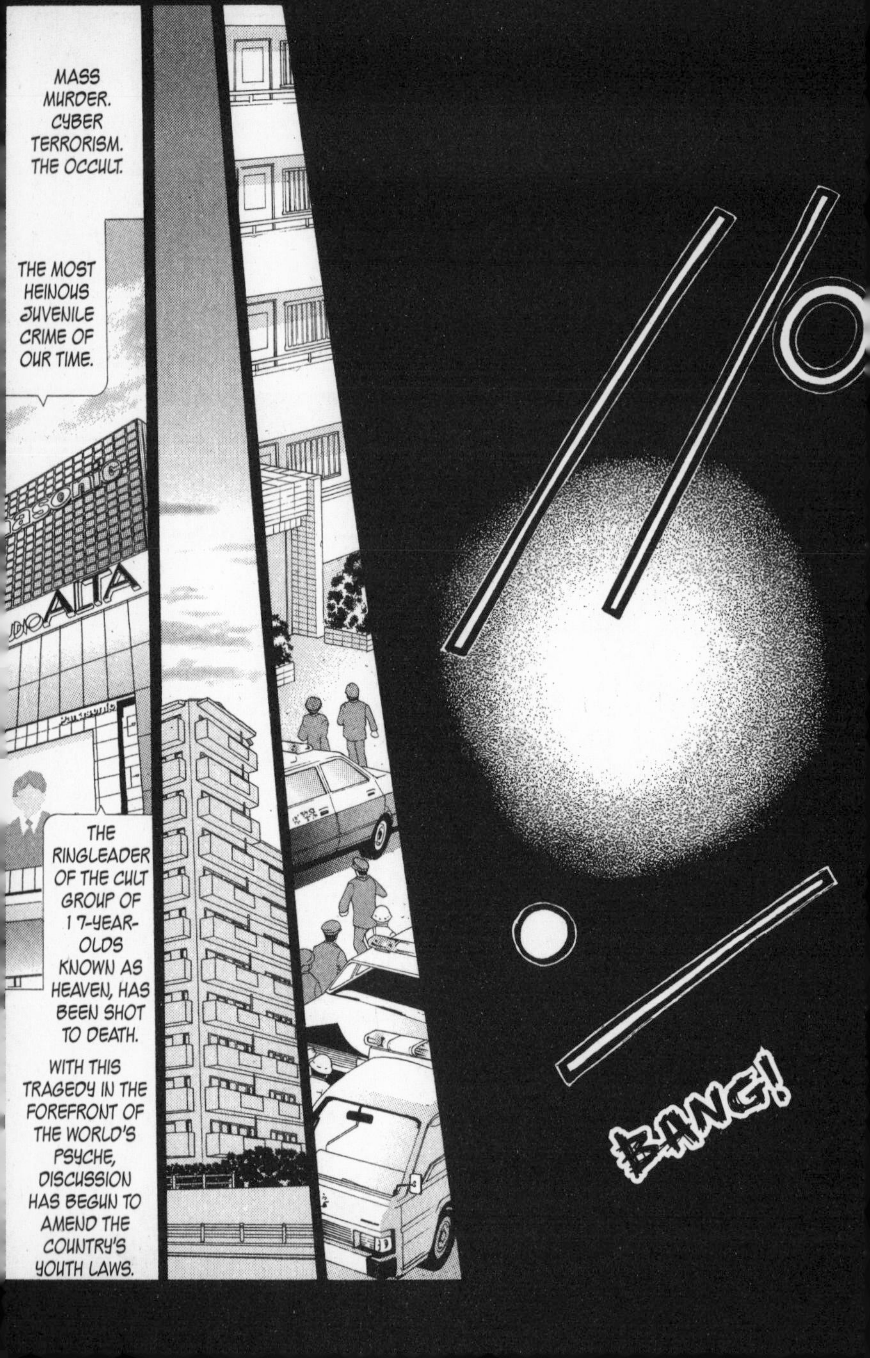
BANG!
MASS MURDER. CYBER TERRORISM. THE OCCULT.
THE MOST HEINOUS JUVENILE CRIME OF OUR TIME.
THE RINGLEADER OF THE CULT GROUP OF 17-YEAR-OLDS KNOWN AS HEAVEN, HAS BEEN SHOT TO DEATH.
WITH THIS TRAGEDY IN THE FOREFRONT OF THE WORLD'S PSYCHE, DISCUSSION HAS BEGUN TO AMEND THE COUNTRY'S YOUTH LAWS.
ALTA

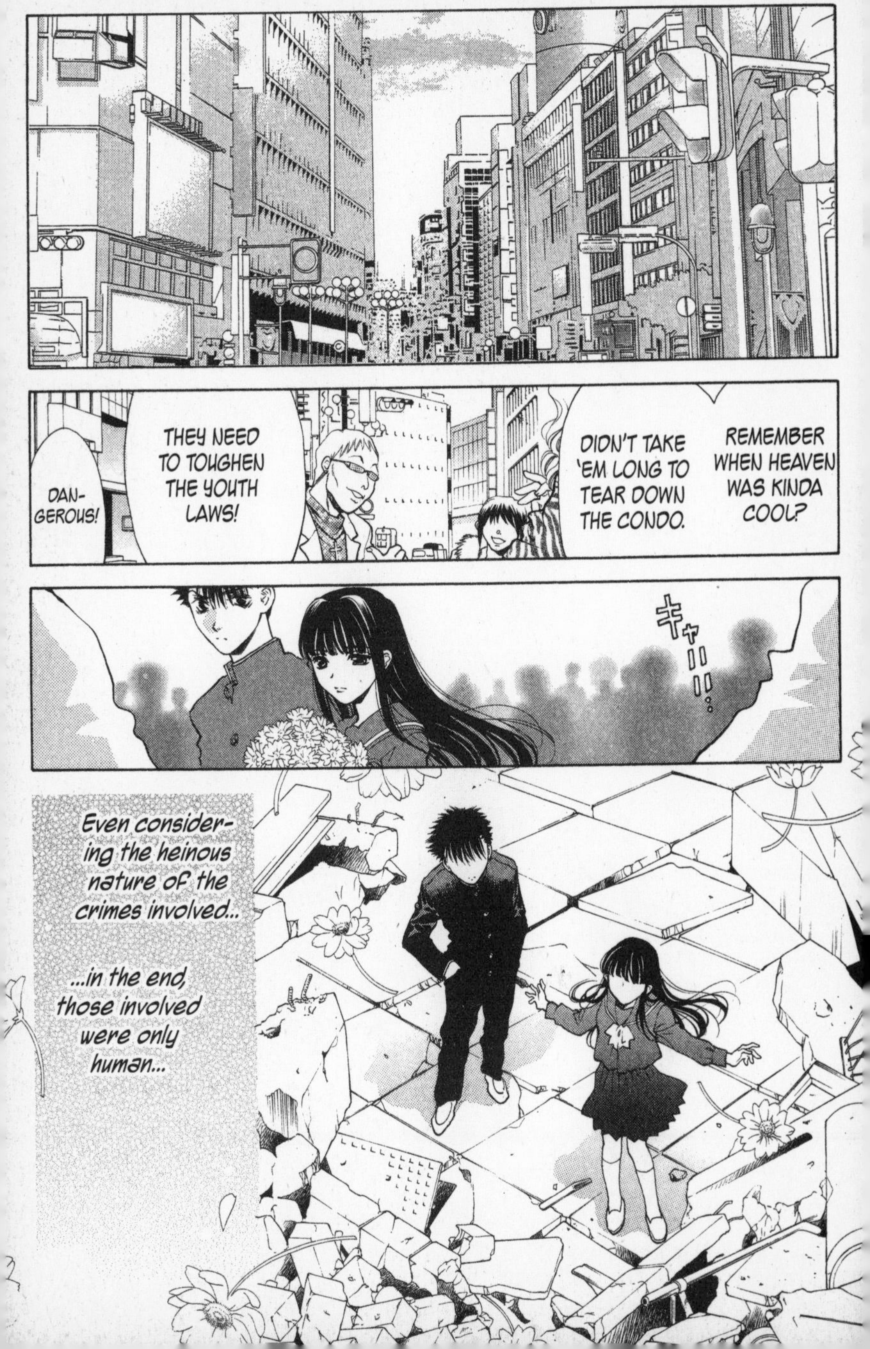
REMEMBER WHEN HEAVEN WAS KINDA COOL?
DIDN'T TAKE 'EM LONG TO TEAR DOWN THE CONDO.
THEY NEED TO TOUGHEN THE YOUTH LAWS!
DAN-GEROUS!
キャ
Even consider-ing the heinous nature of the crimes involved...
...in the end, those involved were only human...

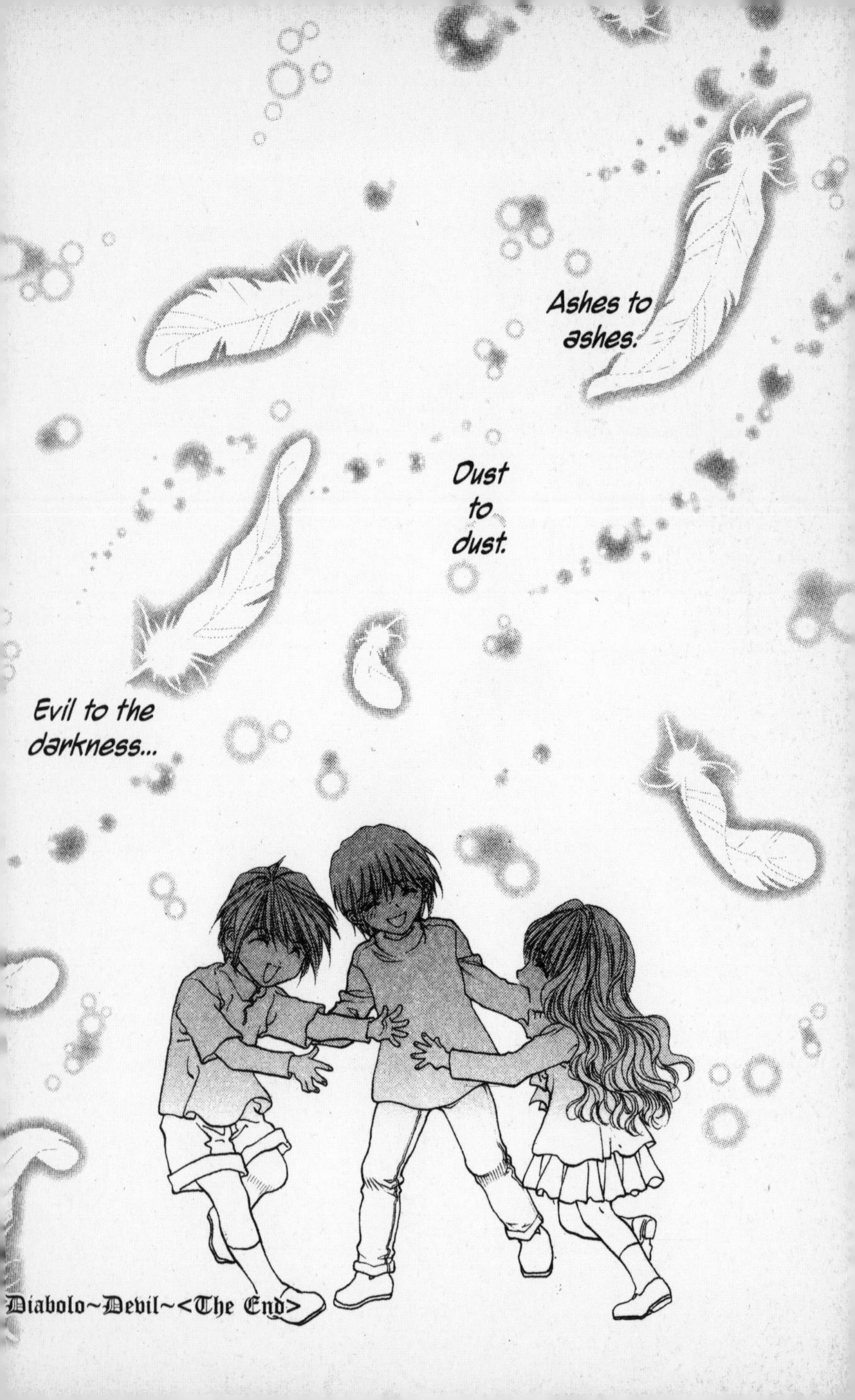
Ashes to ashes.
Dust to dust.
Evil to the darkness...
Diabolo~Devil~<The End>

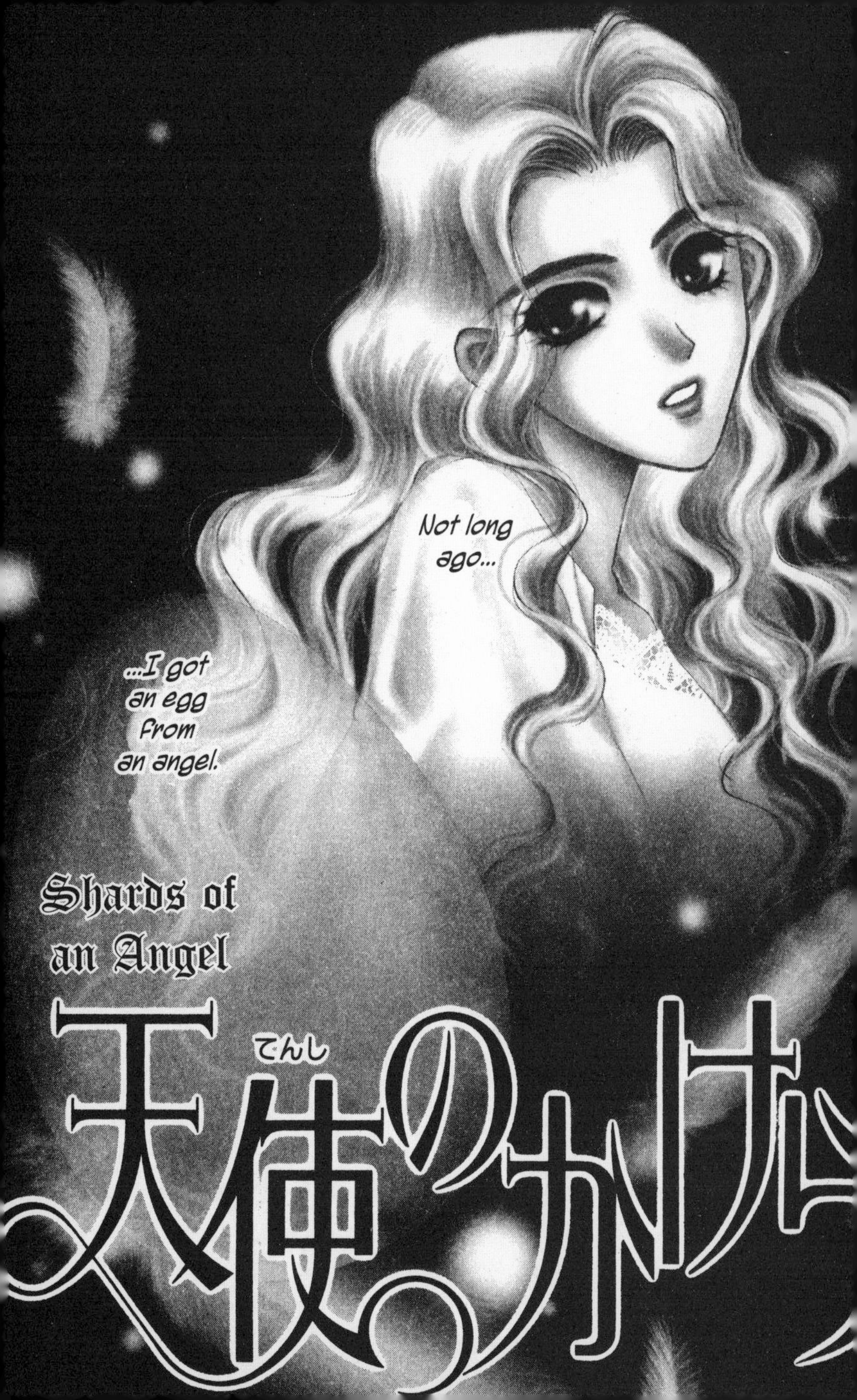
Not long ago...
...I got an egg from an angel.
Shards of an Angel
てんし
天使のカケ

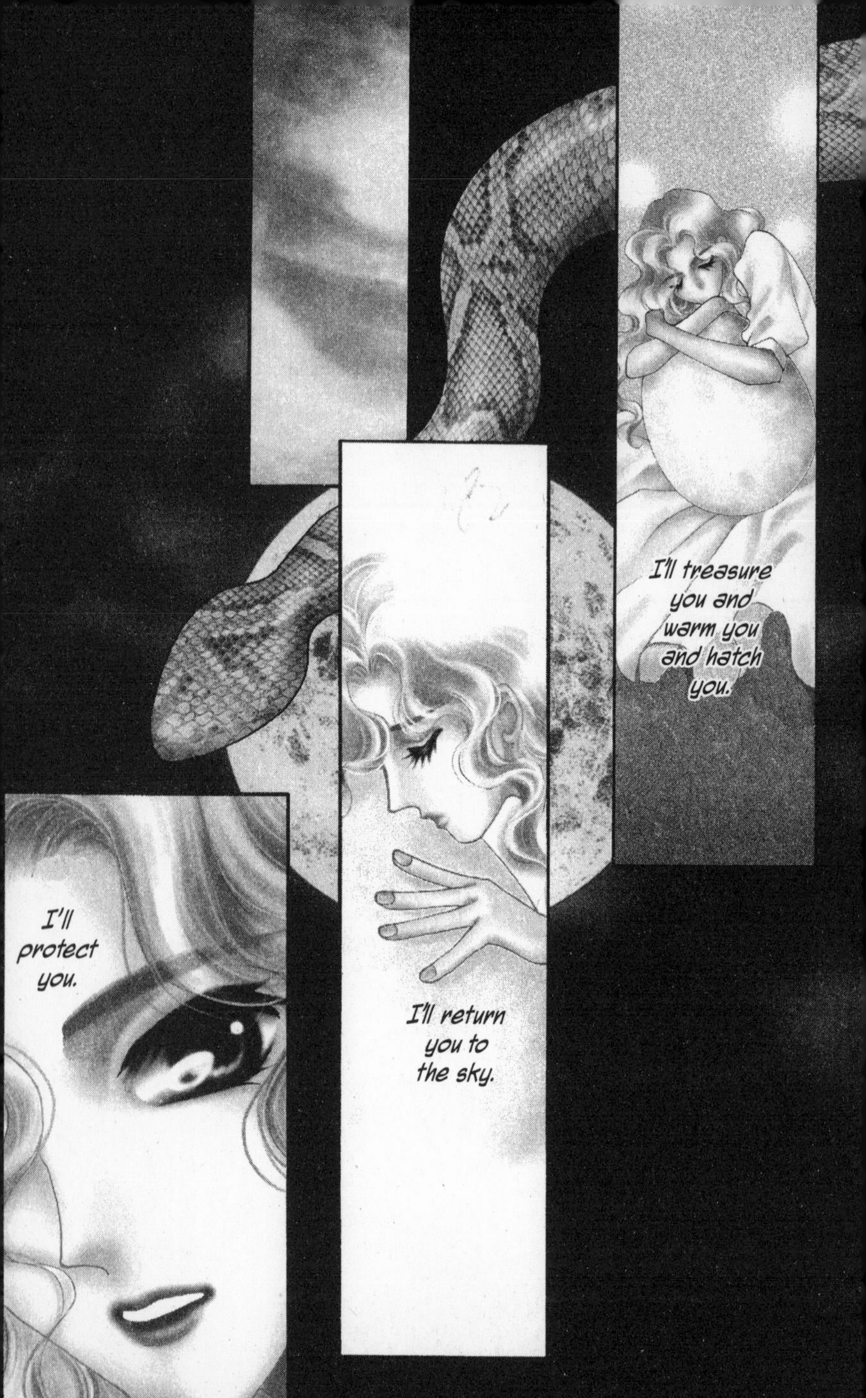
I'll treasure you and warm you and hatch you.
I'll return you to the sky.
I'll protect you.

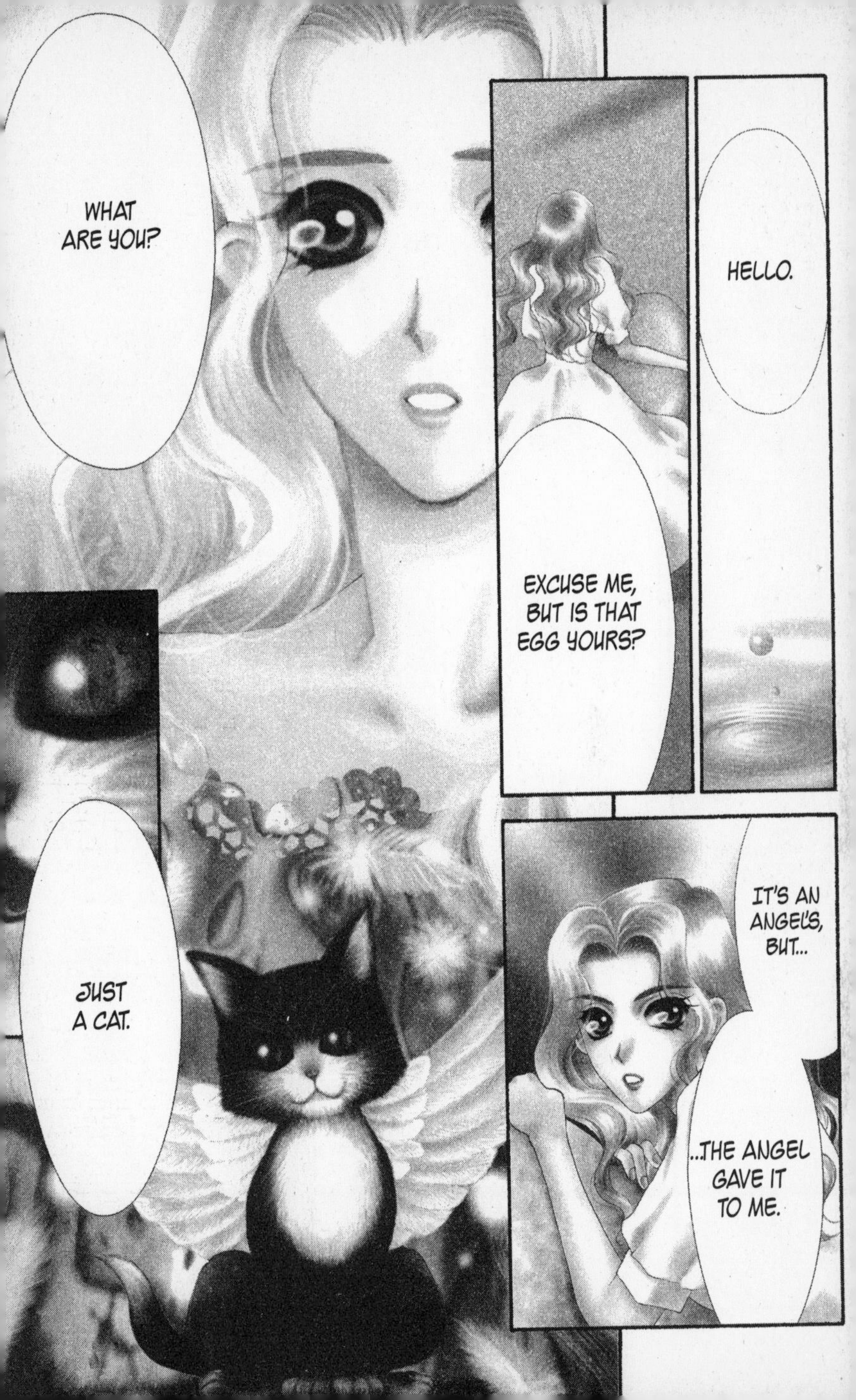
HELLO.
EXCUSE ME, BUT IS THAT EGG YOURS?
IT'S AN ANGEL'S, BUT...
...THE ANGEL GAVE IT TO ME.
WHAT ARE YOU?
JUST A CAT.

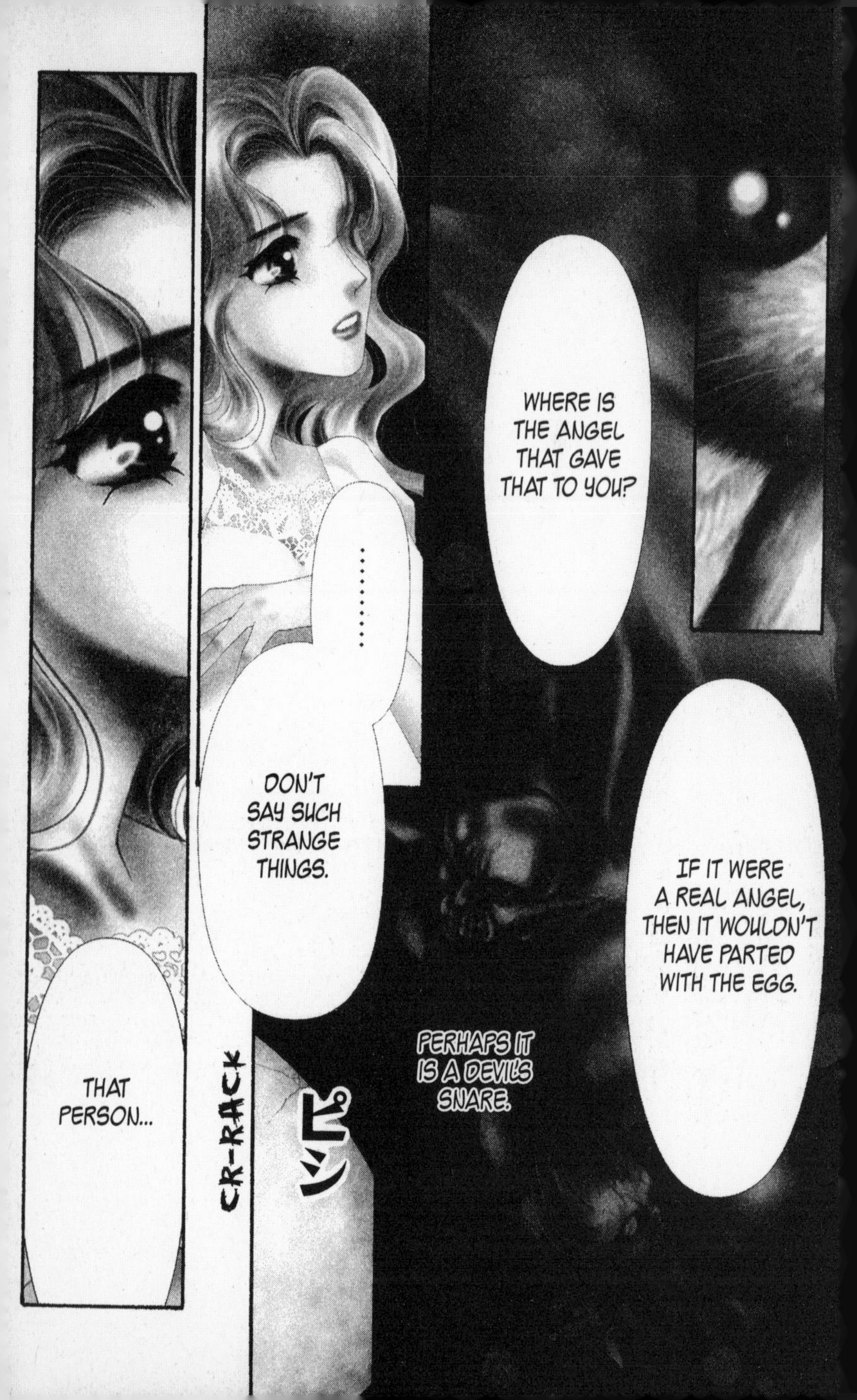
WHERE IS THE ANGEL THAT GAVE THAT TO YOU?
IF IT WERE A REAL ANGEL, THEN IT WOULDN'T HAVE PARTED WITH THE EGG.
PERHAPS IT IS A DEVIL'S SNARE.
......
DON'T SAY SUCH STRANGE THINGS.
CR-RACK
THAT PERSON...

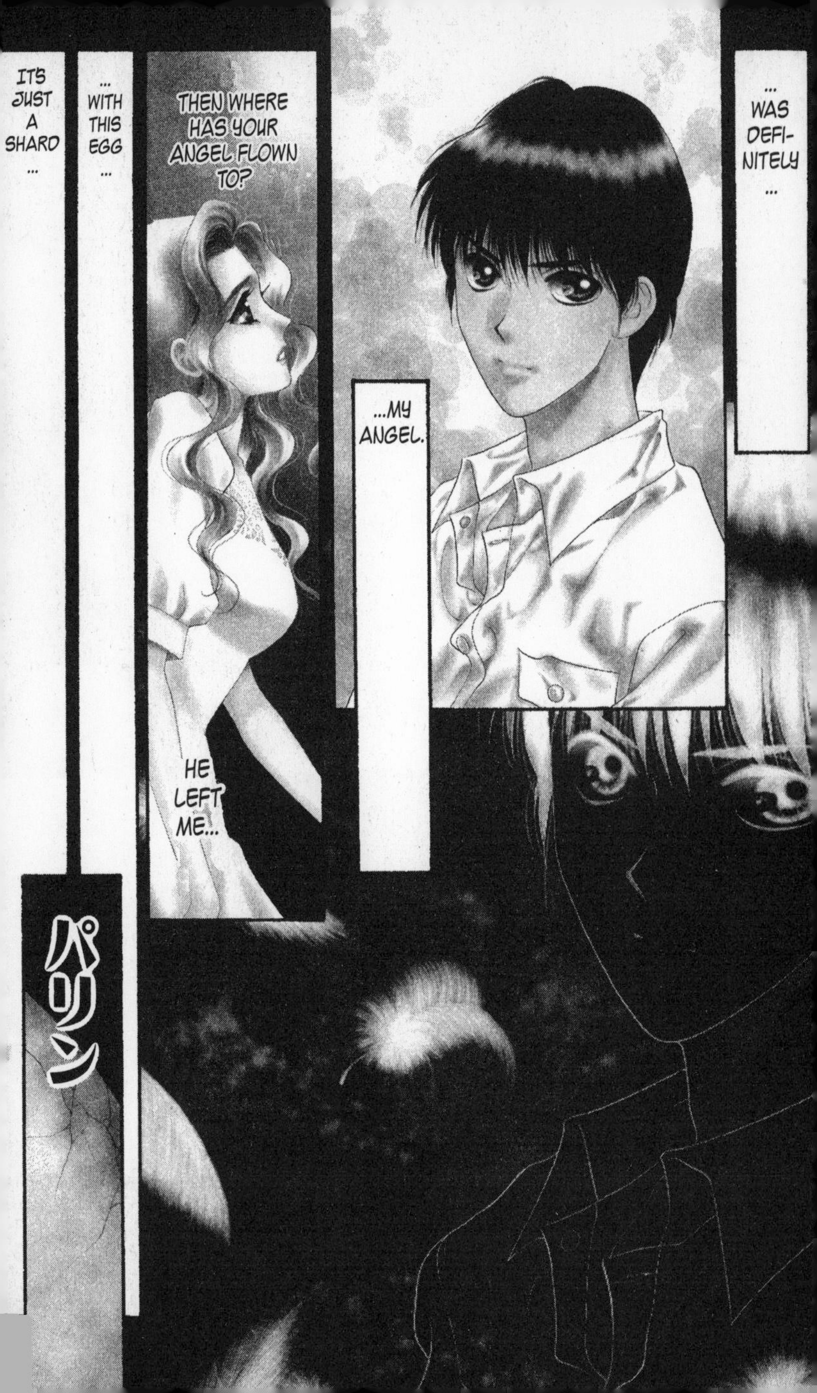
... WAS DEFI- NITELY ...
...MY ANGEL.
THEN WHERE HAS YOUR ANGEL FLOWN TO?
HE LEFT ME...
... WITH THIS EGG ...
IT'S JUST A SHARD ...
パリン

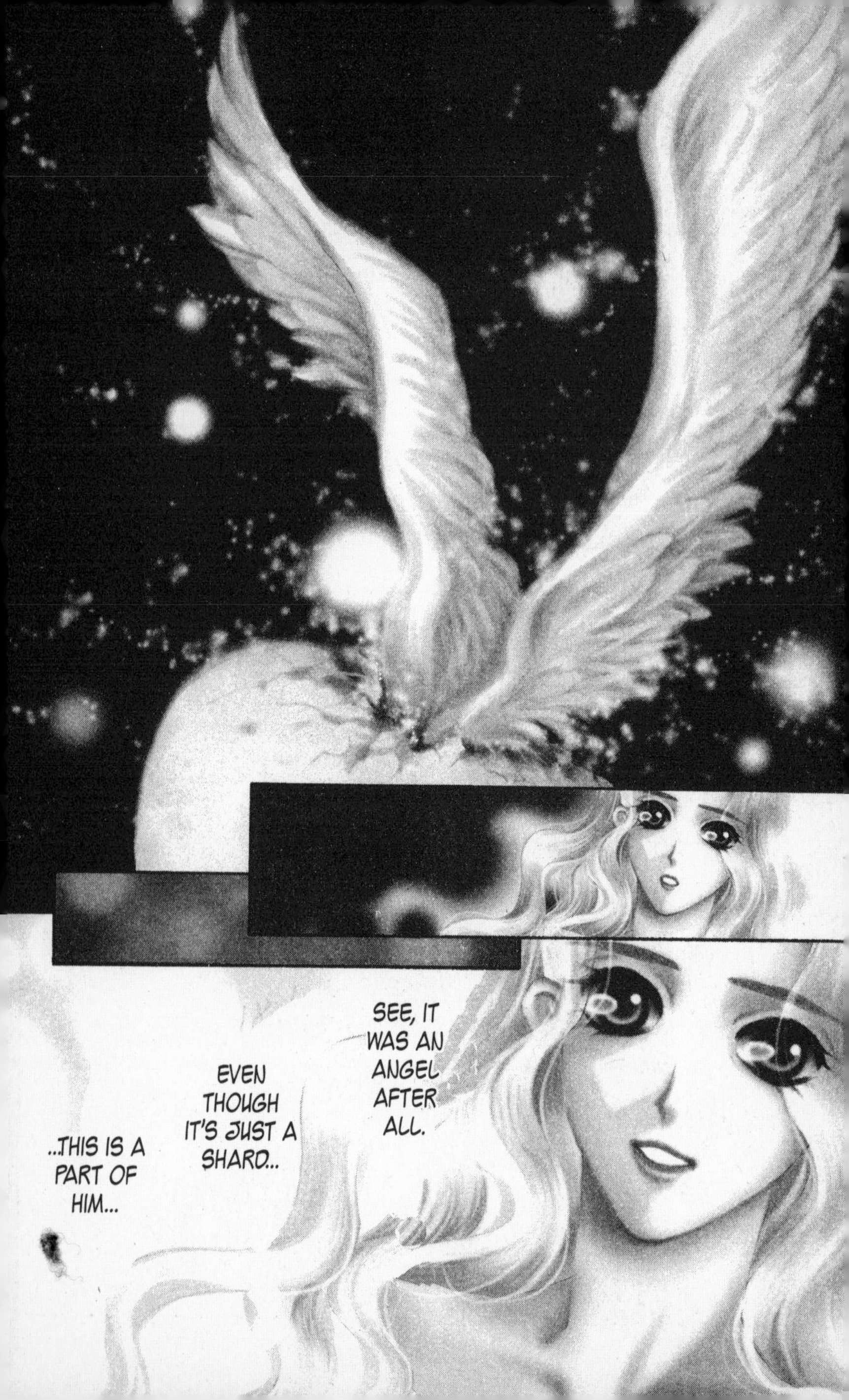
SEE, IT WAS AN ANGEL AFTER ALL.
EVEN THOUGH IT'S JUST A SHARD...
...THIS IS A PART OF HIM...

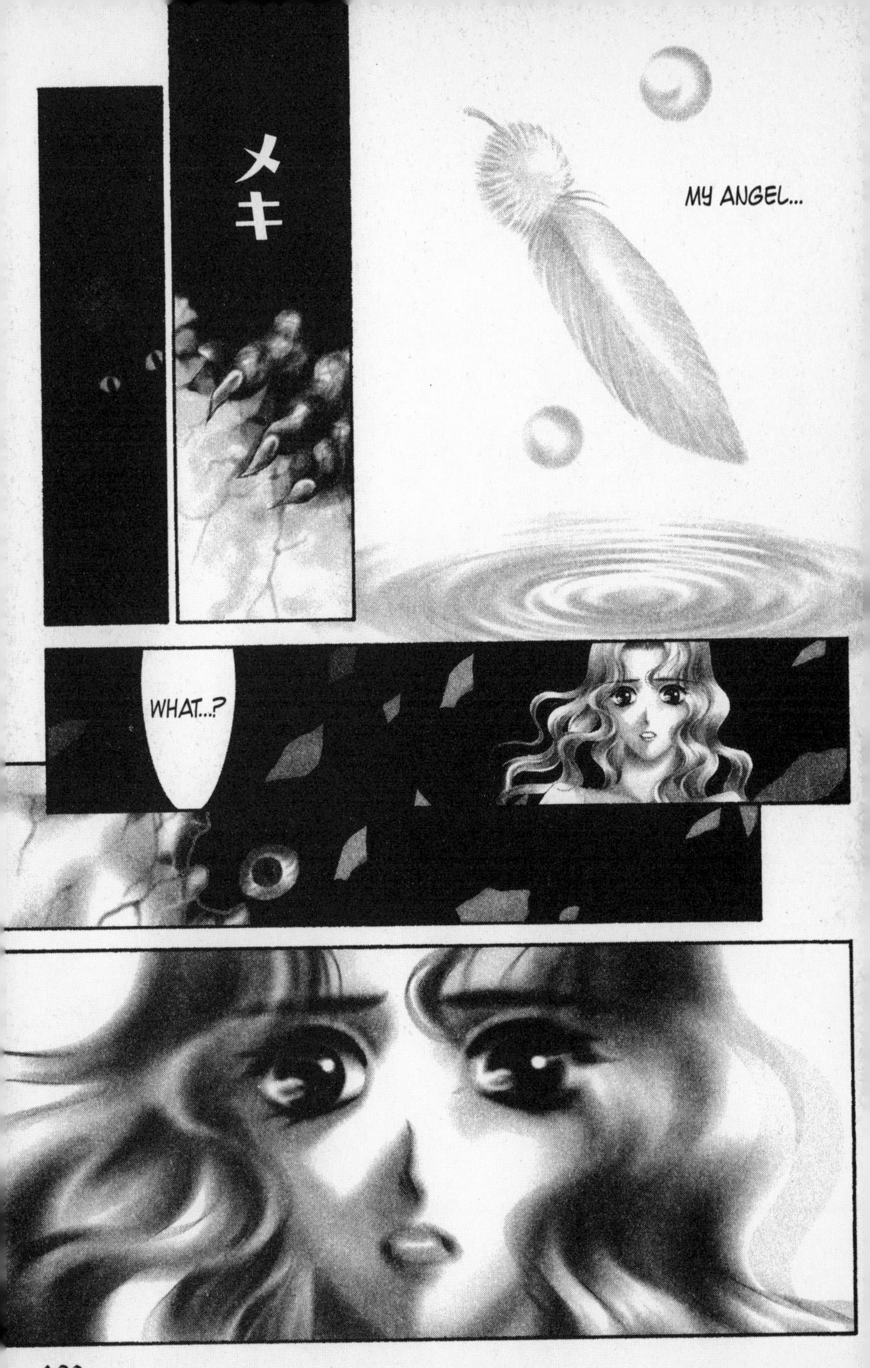
メキ
MY ANGEL...
WHAT...?

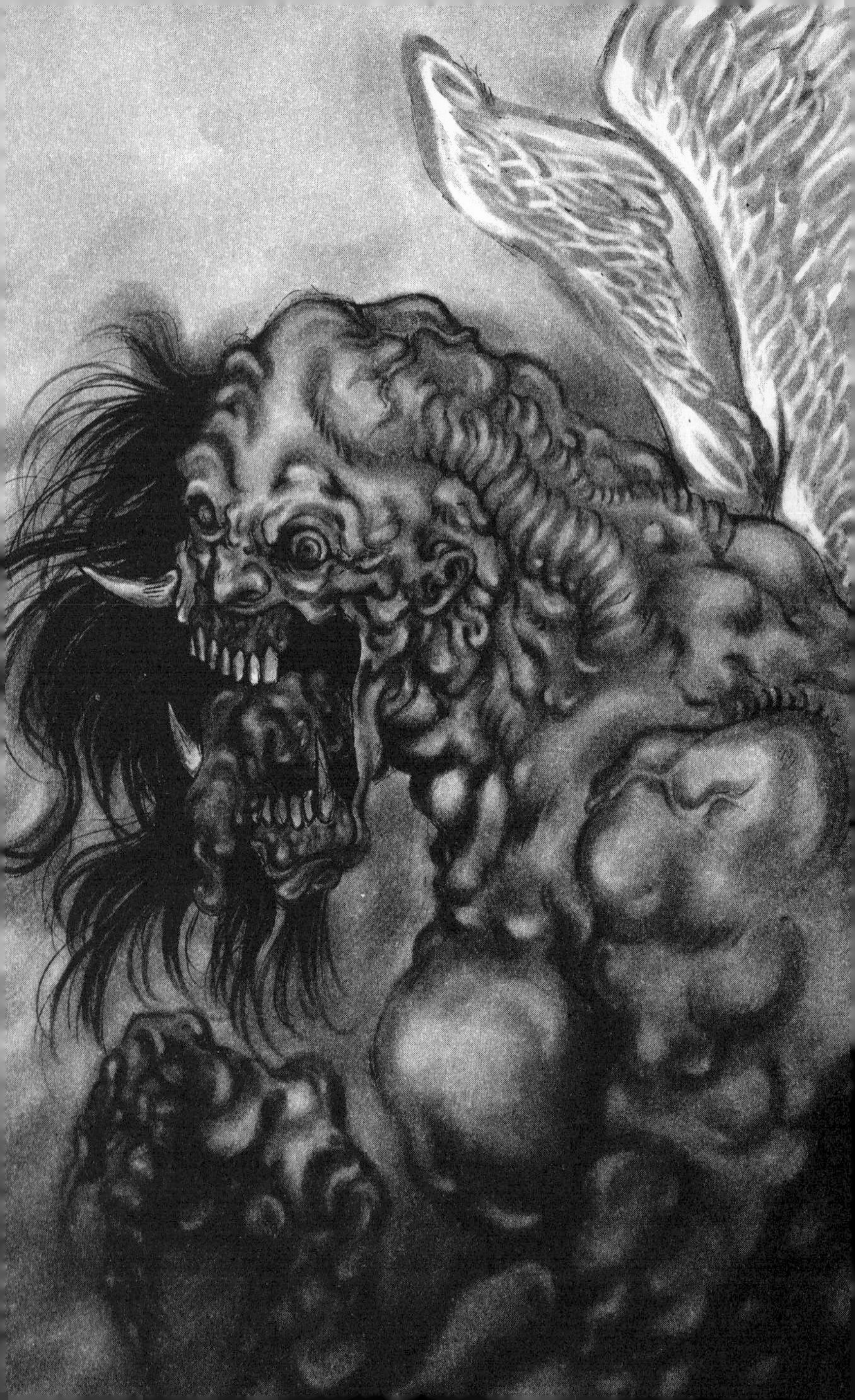

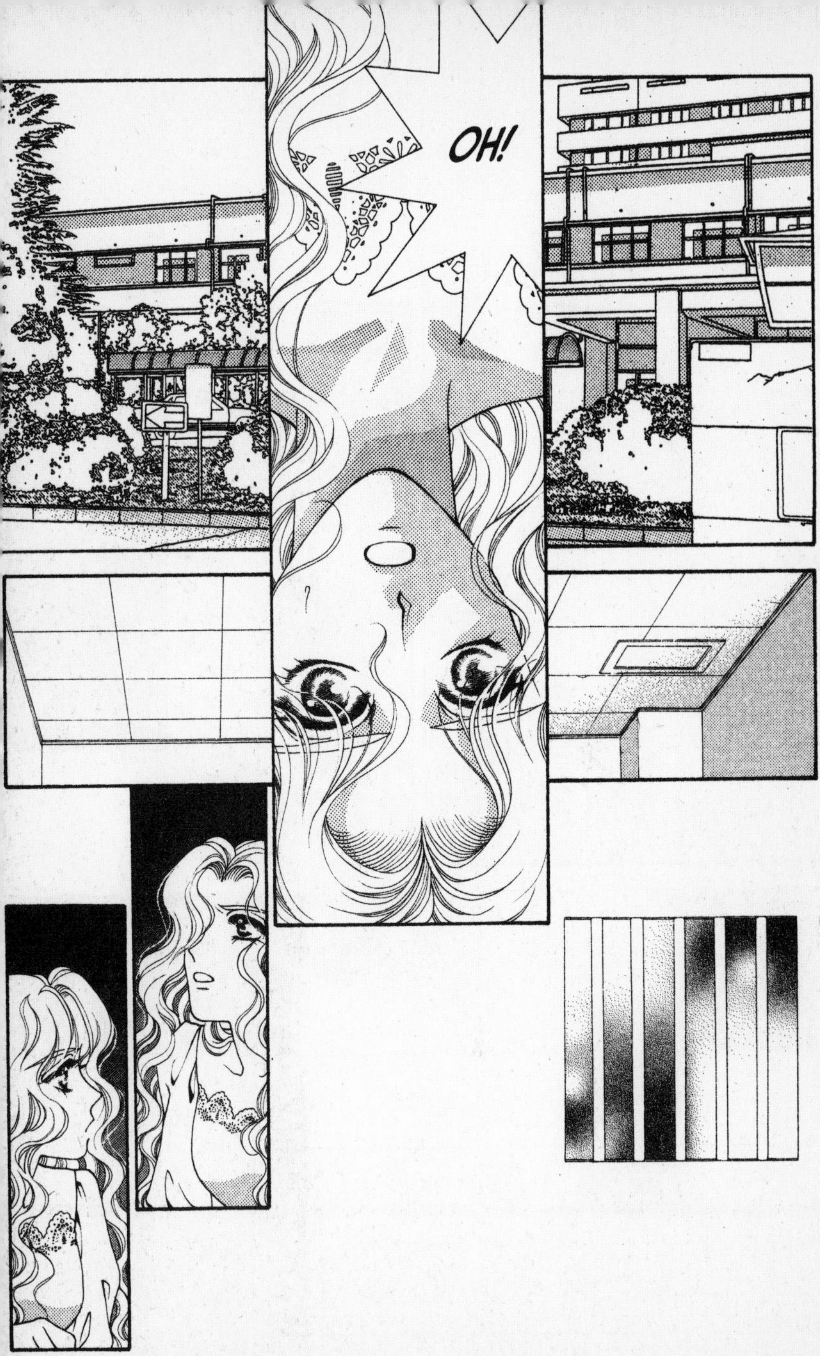
OH!

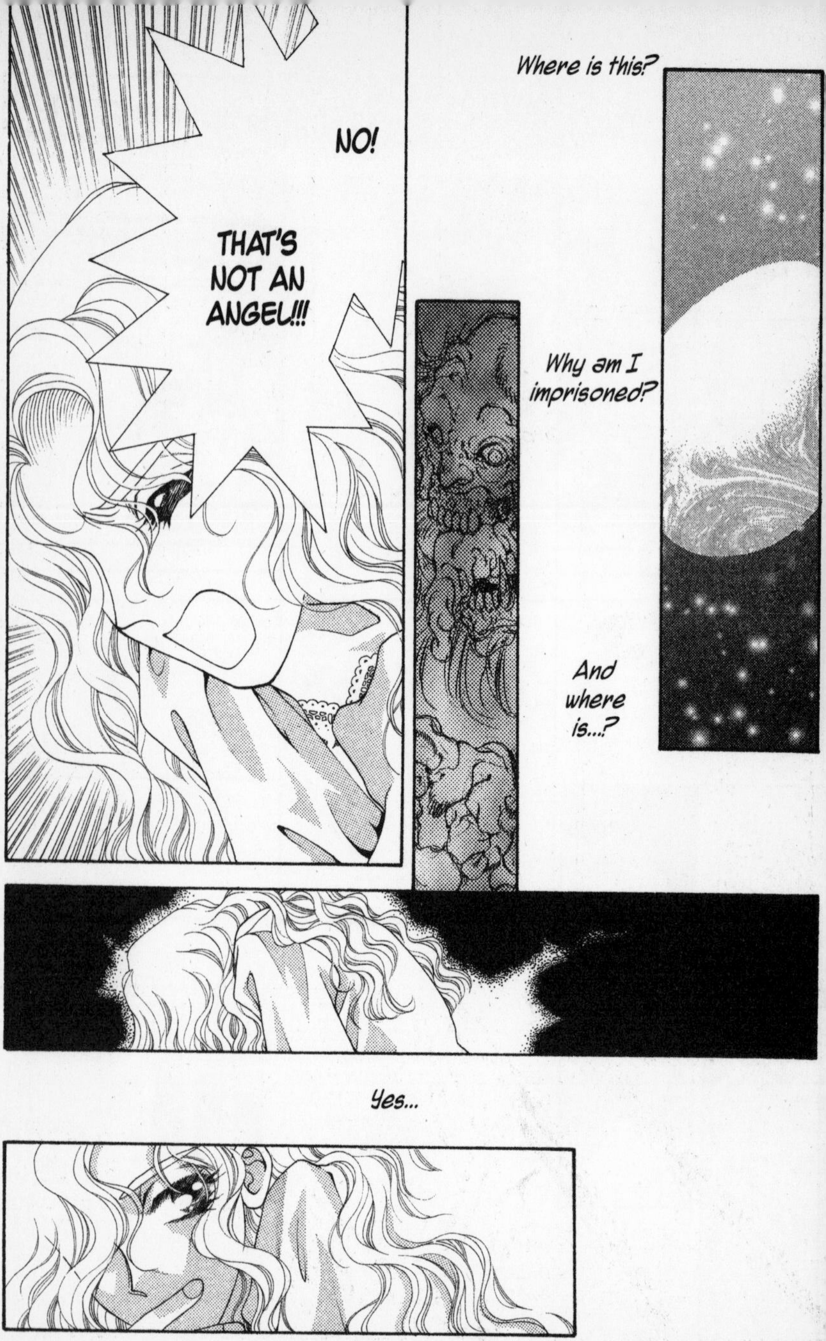
Where is this?
Why am I imprisoned?
And where is...?
NO!
THAT'S NOT AN ANGEL!!!
Yes...

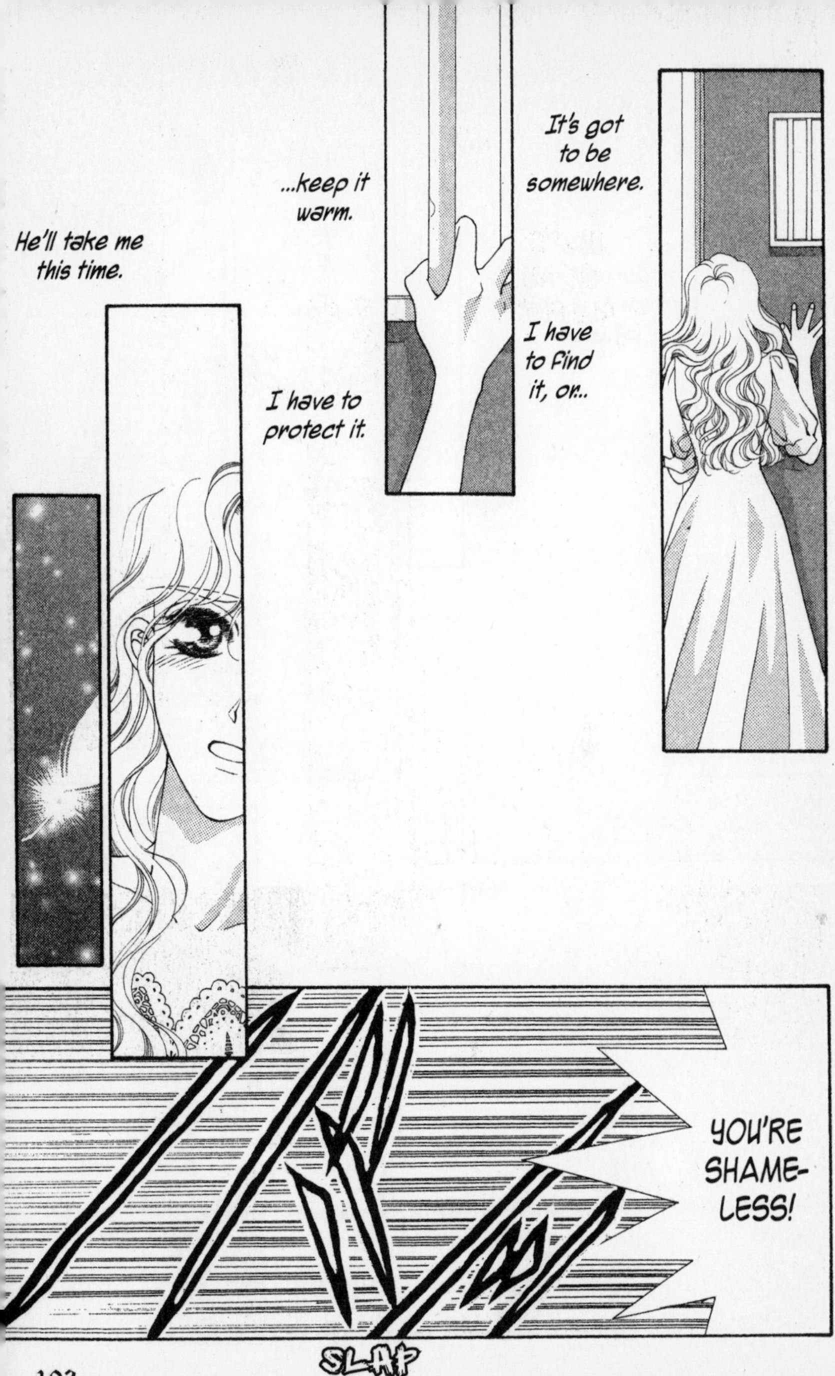
It's got to be somewhere.
I have to find it, or...
...keep it warm.
I have to protect it.
He'll take me this time.
YOU'RE SHAME-LESS!
SLAP

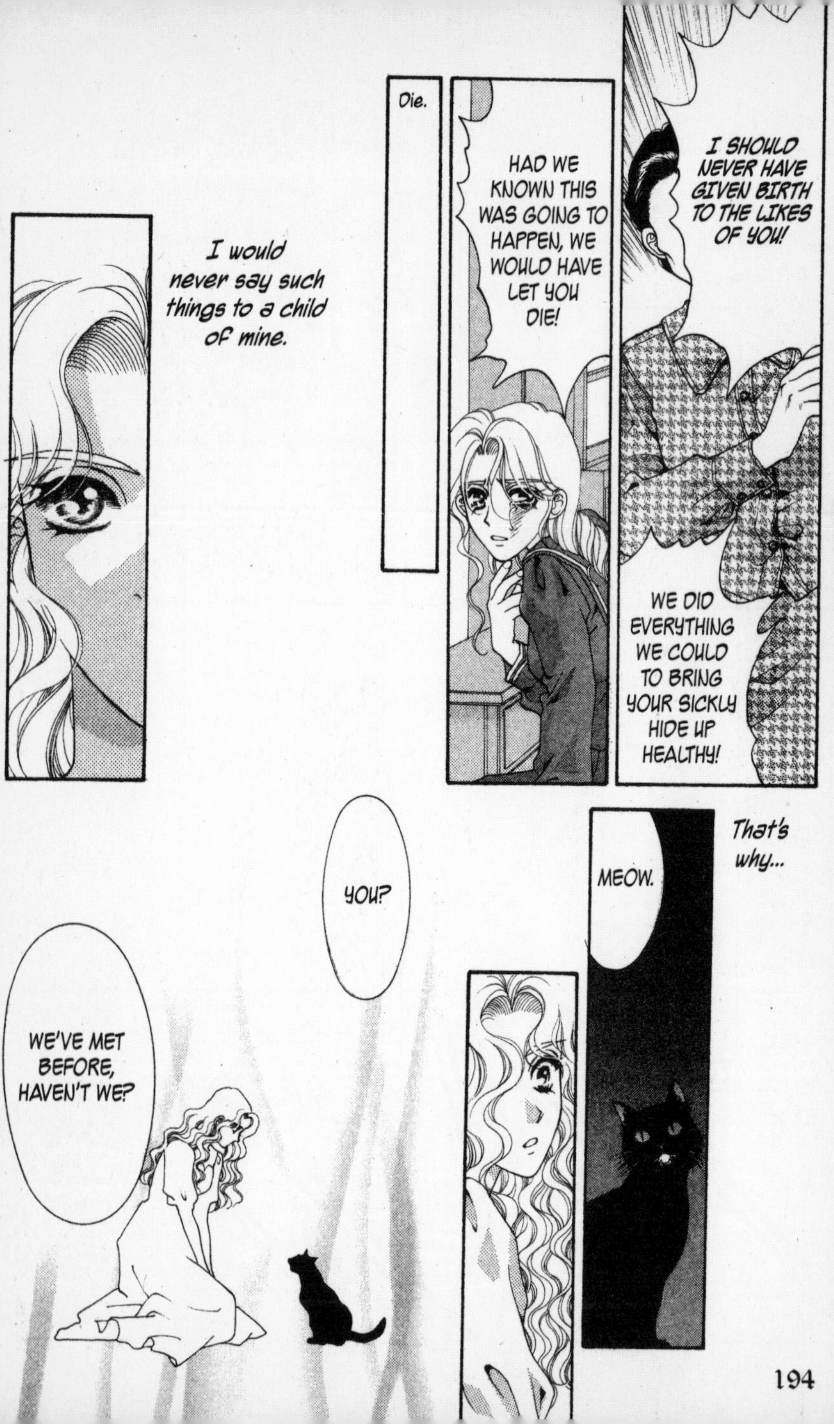
I SHOULD NEVER HAVE GIVEN BIRTH TO THE LIKES OF YOU!
WE DID EVERYTHING WE COULD TO BRING YOUR SICKLY HIDE UP HEALTHY!
HAD WE KNOWN THIS WAS GOING TO HAPPEN, WE WOULD HAVE LET YOU DIE!
Die.
I would never say such things to a child of mine.
That's why...
MEOW.
YOU?
WE'VE MET BEFORE, HAVEN'T WE?

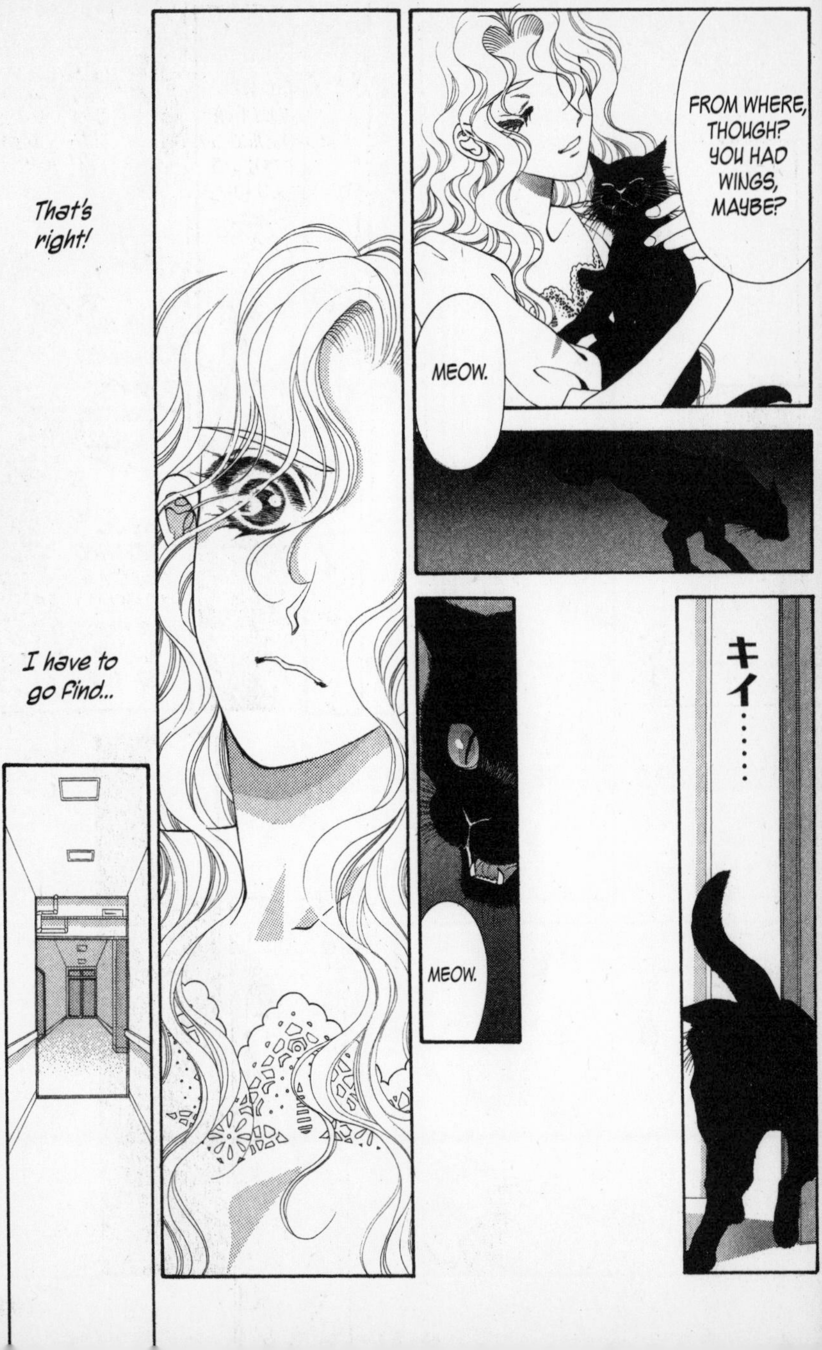
FROM WHERE, THOUGH? YOU HAD WINGS, MAYBE?
MEOW.
キイ……
MEOW.
That's right!
I have to go find...

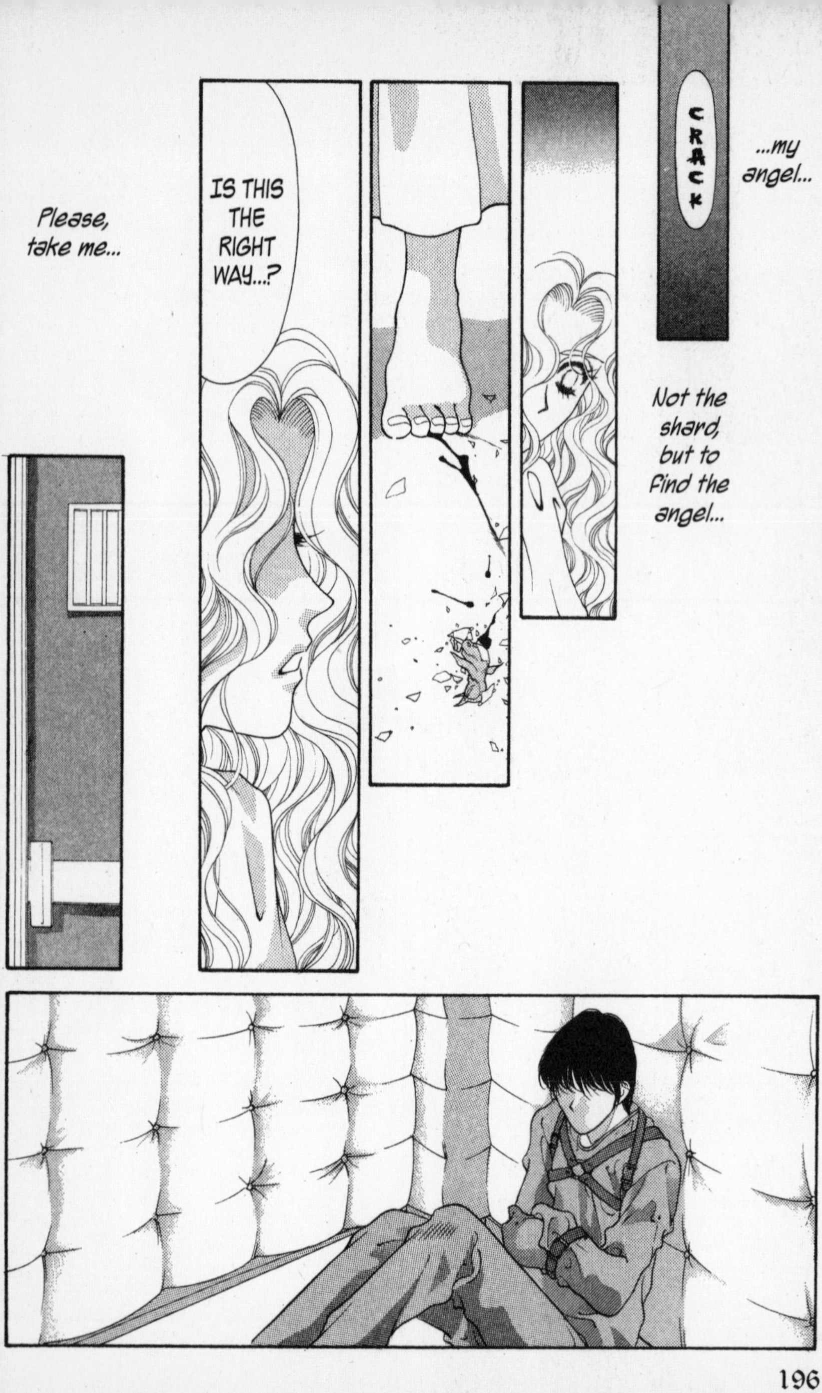
CRACK
...my angel...
Not the shard, but to find the angel...
IS THIS THE RIGHT WAY...?
Please, take me...

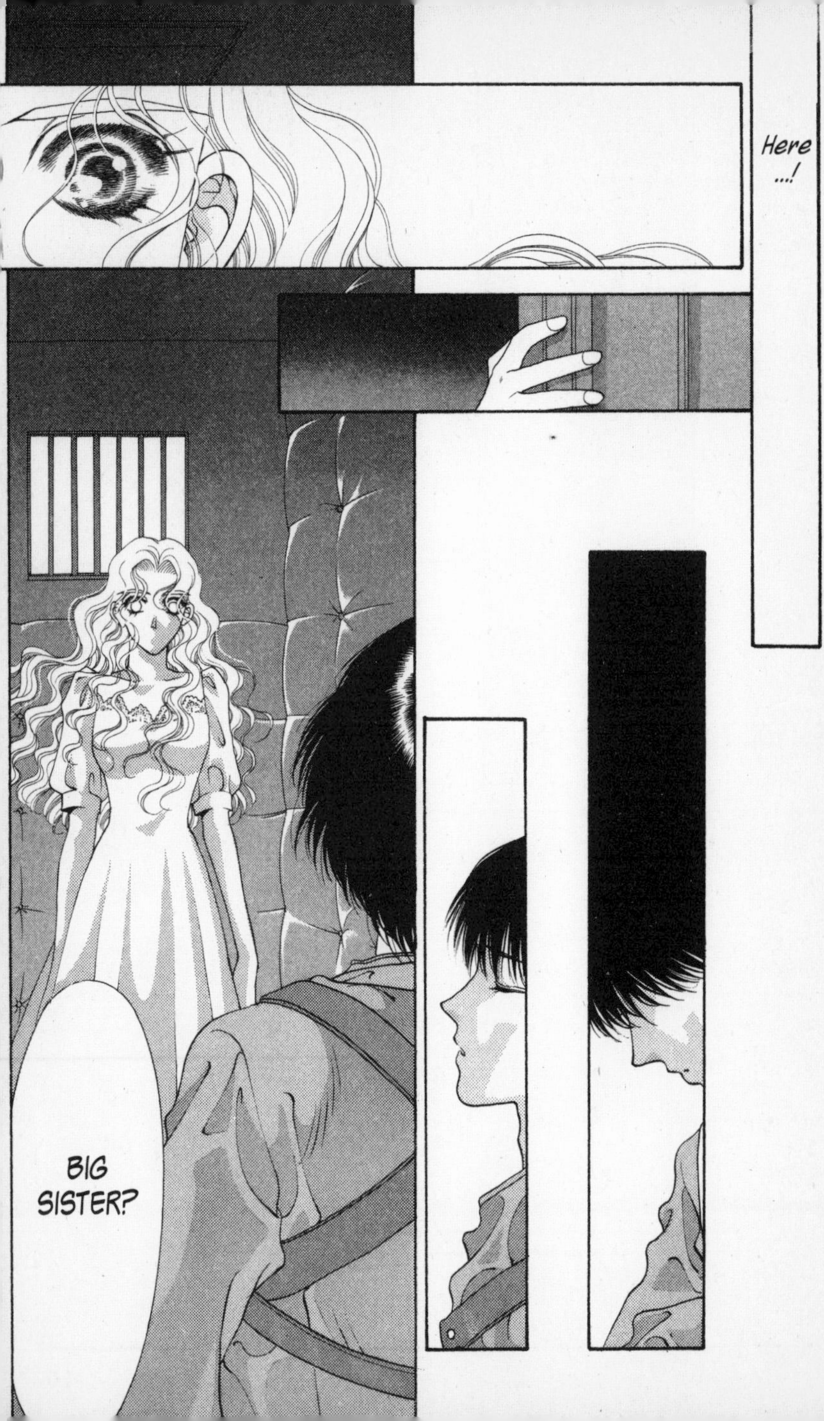
Here ...!
BIG SISTER?

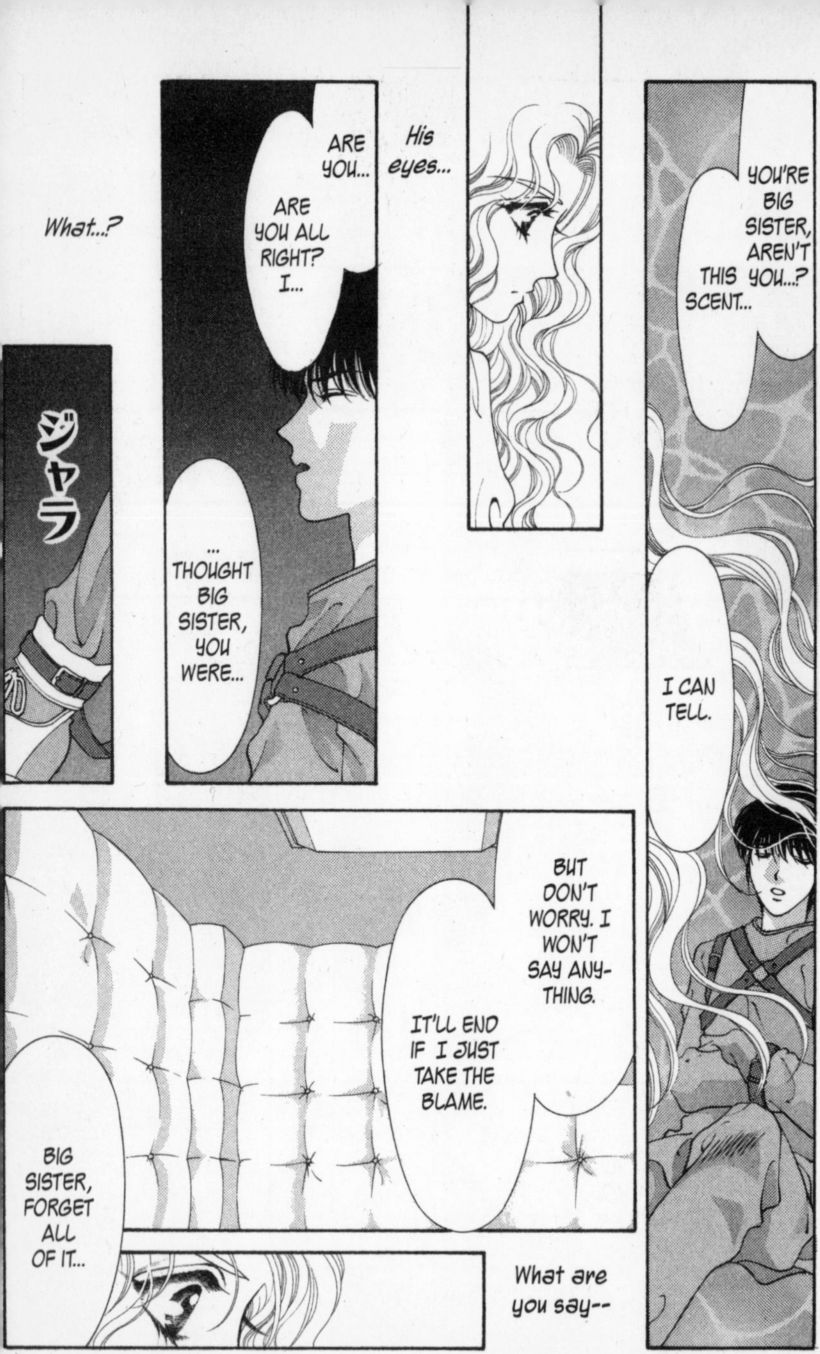
YOU'RE BIG SISTER, AREN'T YOU...?
THIS SCENT...
I CAN TELL.
His eyes...
ARE YOU...
ARE YOU ALL RIGHT? I...
...THOUGHT BIG SISTER, YOU WERE...
What...?
ジャラ
BUT DON'T WORRY. I WON'T SAY ANY-THING.
IT'LL END IF I JUST TAKE THE BLAME.
BIG SISTER, FORGET ALL OF IT...
What are you say--

IF WE KEEP QUIET, THE POLICE WILL GIVE UP.

IT'S OKAY IF I STAY "HERE" LIKE THIS.

I'LL FORGET ALREADY. BIG SISTER, PLEASE FORGET, TOO.

SOMETHING SO HORRIBLE, I...DON'T KNOW.

MEOW.

You're going to leave...

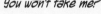

...me...

I...

You won't take me?

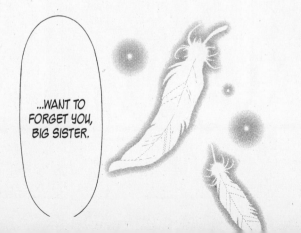

...WANT TO FORGET YOU, BIG SISTER.

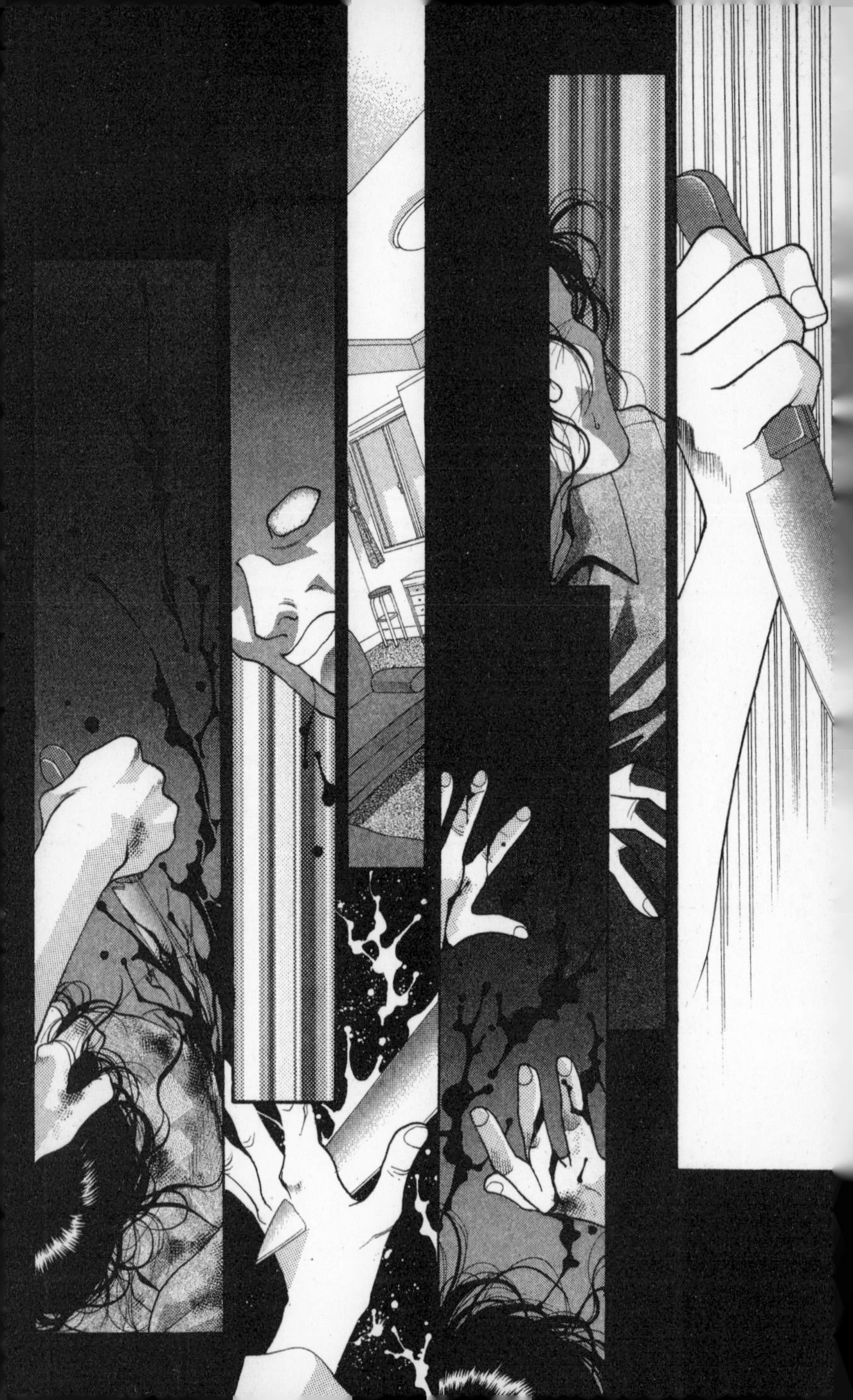

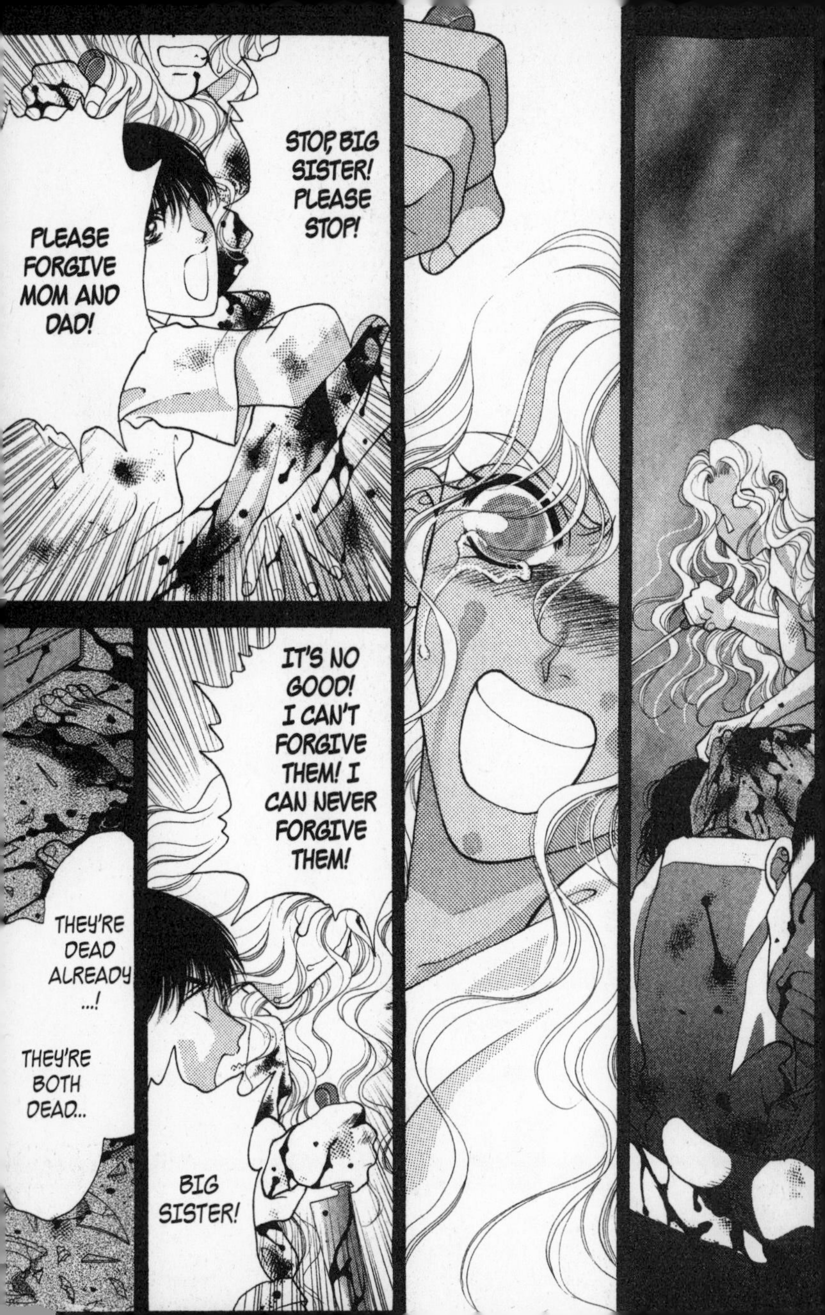
STOP, BIG SISTER! PLEASE STOP!
PLEASE FORGIVE MOM AND DAD!
IT'S NO GOOD! I CAN'T FORGIVE THEM! I CAN NEVER FORGIVE THEM!
BIG SISTER!
THEY'RE DEAD ALREADY ...!
THEY'RE BOTH DEAD...

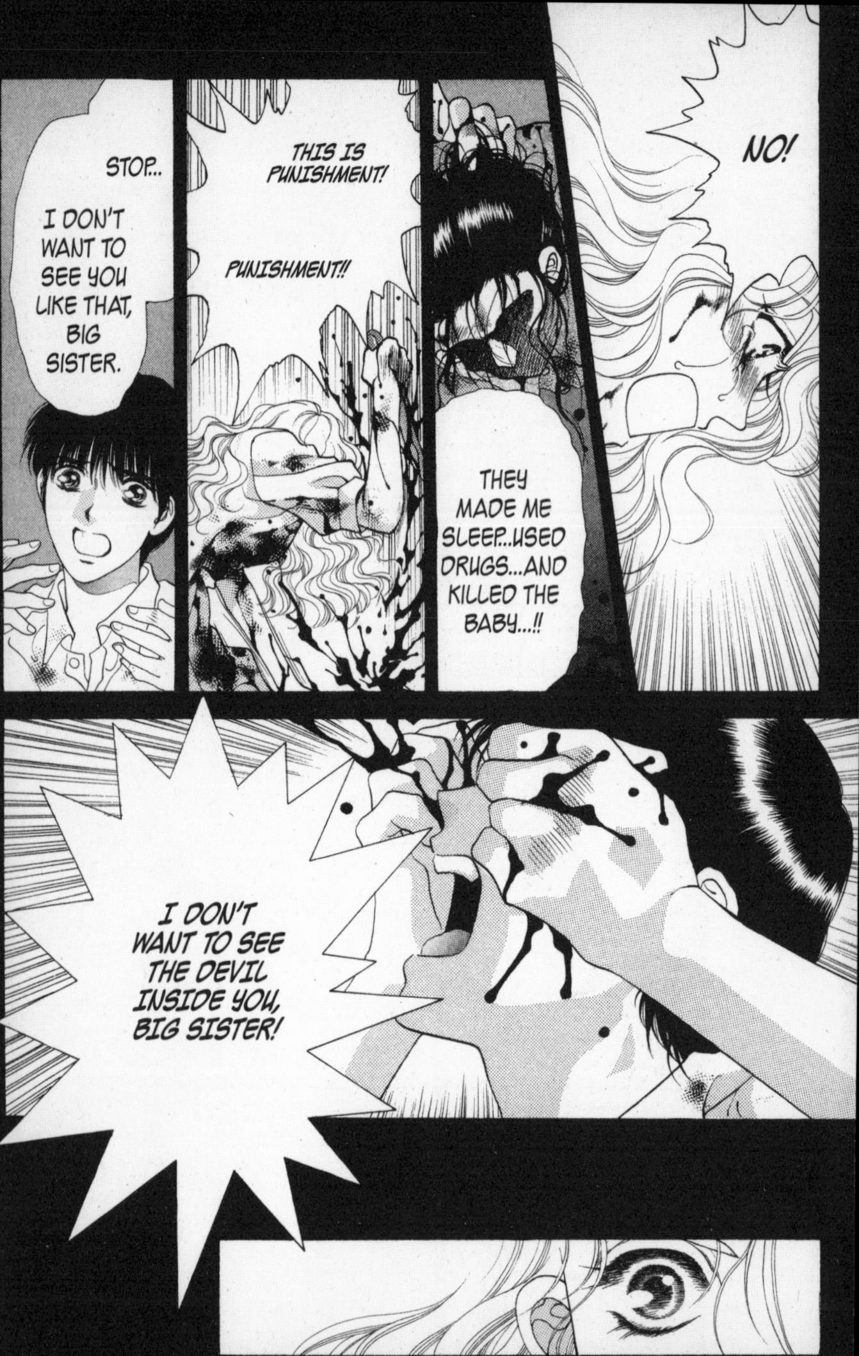
NO!
THEY MADE ME SLEEP...USED DRUGS...AND KILLED THE BABY...!!
THIS IS PUNISHMENT!
PUNISHMENT!!
STOP...
I DON'T WANT TO SEE YOU LIKE THAT, BIG SISTER.
I DON'T WANT TO SEE THE DEVIL INSIDE YOU, BIG SISTER!

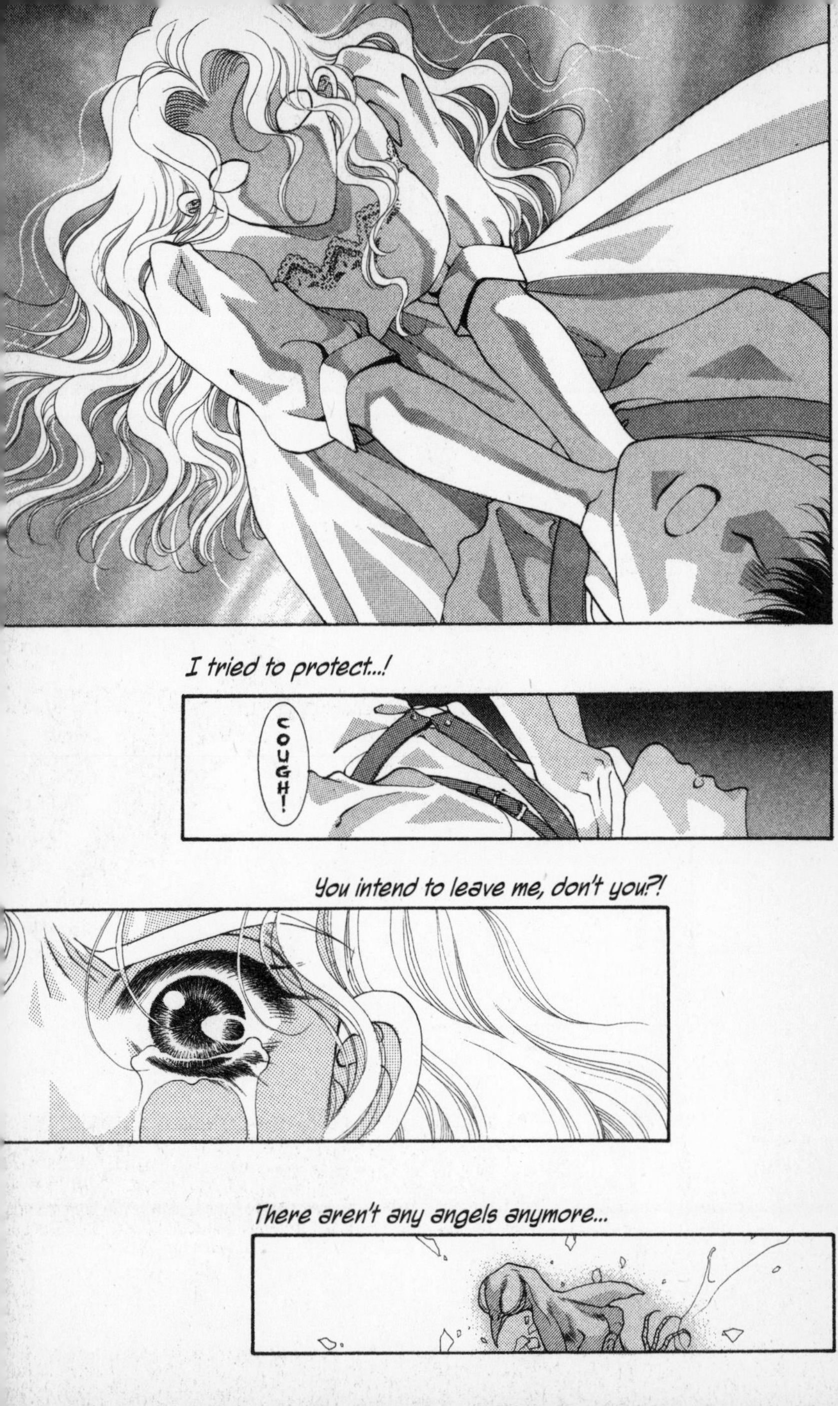
I tried to protect...!
COUGH!
You intend to leave me, don't you?!
There aren't any angels anymore...

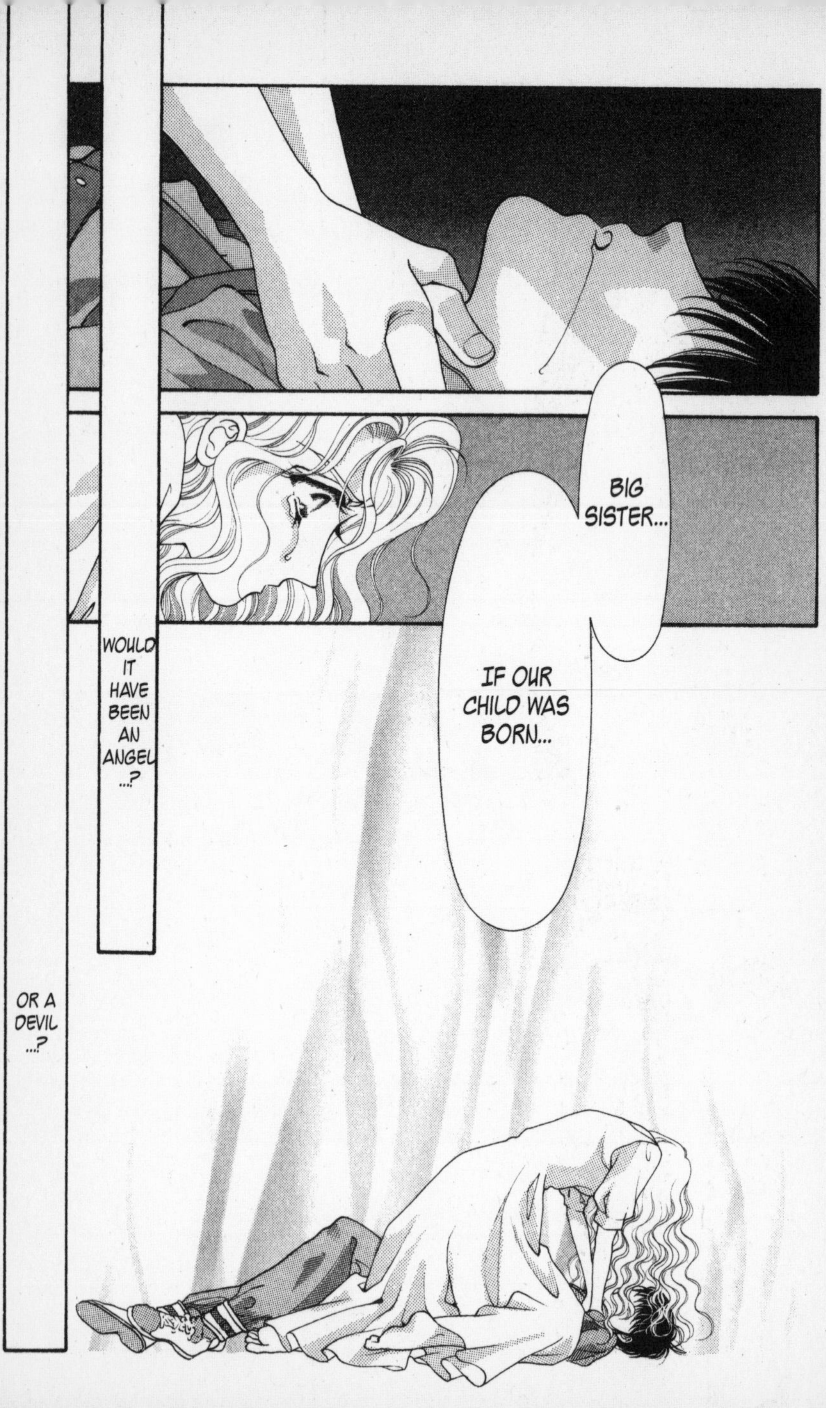
BIG SISTER...
IF OUR CHILD WAS BORN...
WOULD IT HAVE BEEN AN ANGEL ...?
OR A DEVIL ...?

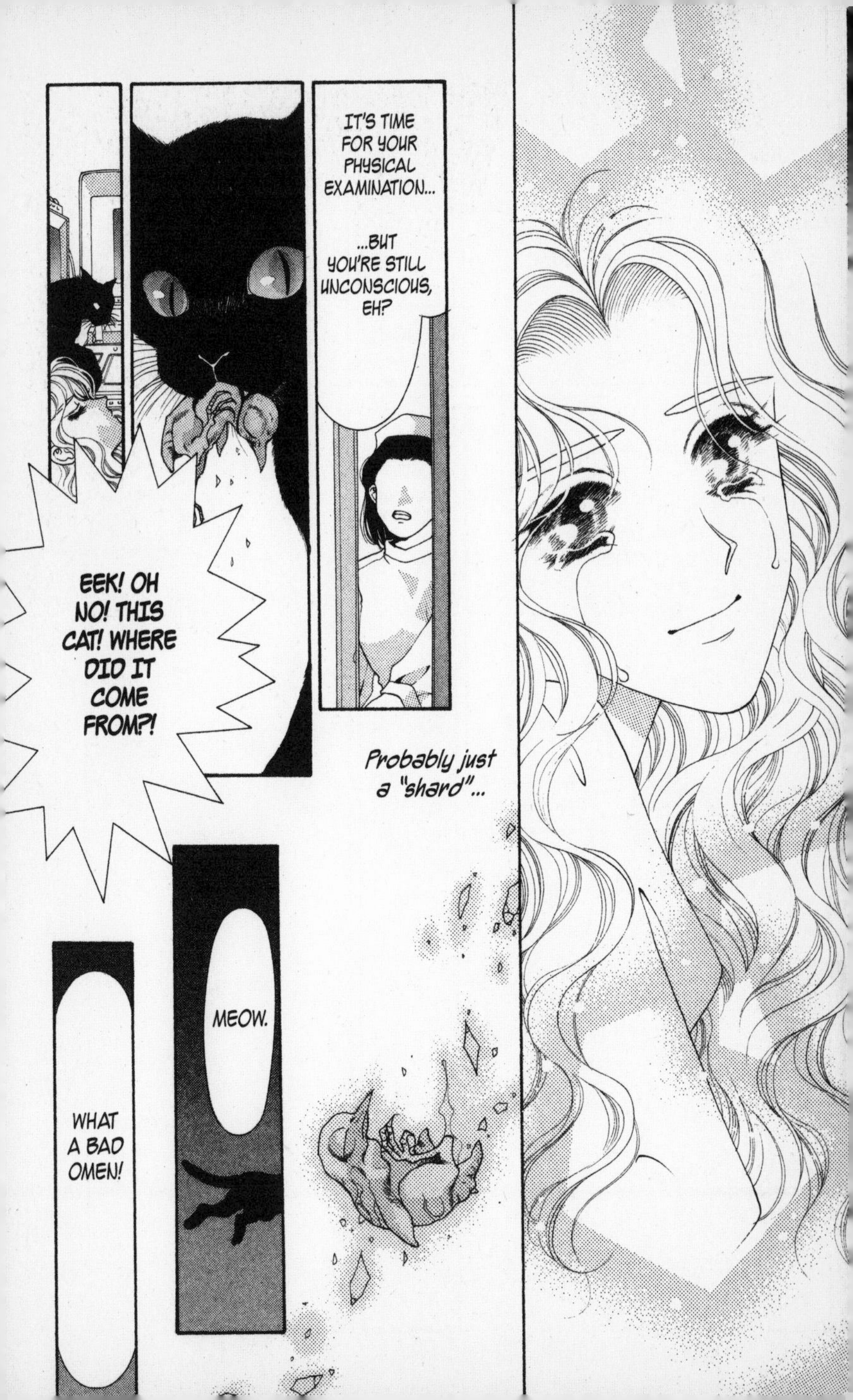
IT'S TIME FOR YOUR PHYSICAL EXAMINATION...
...BUT YOU'RE STILL UNCONSCIOUS, EH?
EEK! OH NO! THIS CAT! WHERE DID IT COME FROM?!
Probably just a "shard"...
MEOW.
WHAT A BAD OMEN!

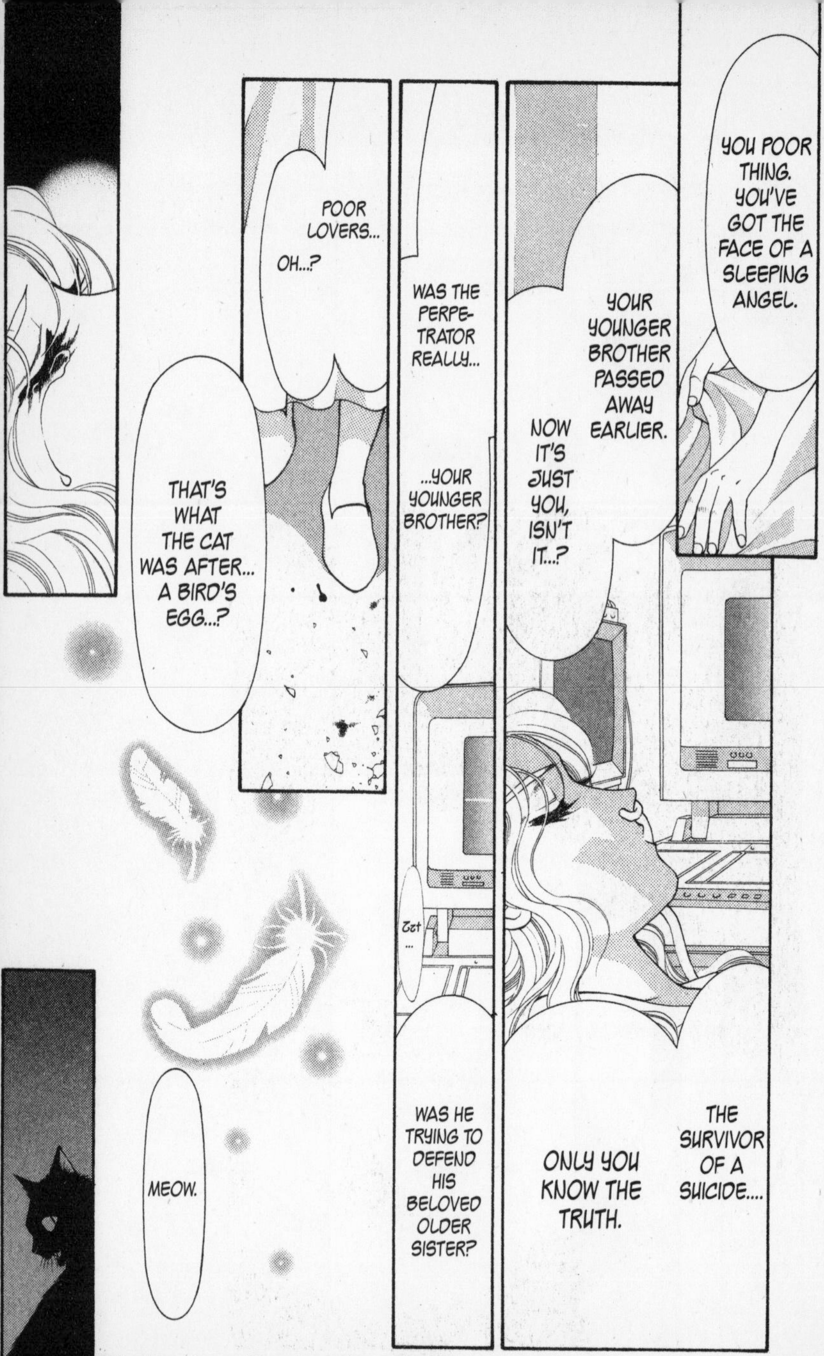
YOU POOR THING. YOU'VE GOT THE FACE OF A SLEEPING ANGEL.
YOUR YOUNGER BROTHER PASSED AWAY EARLIER.
NOW IT'S JUST YOU, ISN'T IT...?
THE SURVIVOR OF A SUICIDE....
ONLY YOU KNOW THE TRUTH.
WAS THE PERPE-TRATOR REALLY...
...YOUR YOUNGER BROTHER?
WAS HE TRYING TO DEFEND HIS BELOVED OLDER SISTER?
POOR LOVERS...
OH...?
THAT'S WHAT THE CAT WAS AFTER... A BIRD'S EGG...?
MEOW.

Shards of an Angel <The End>

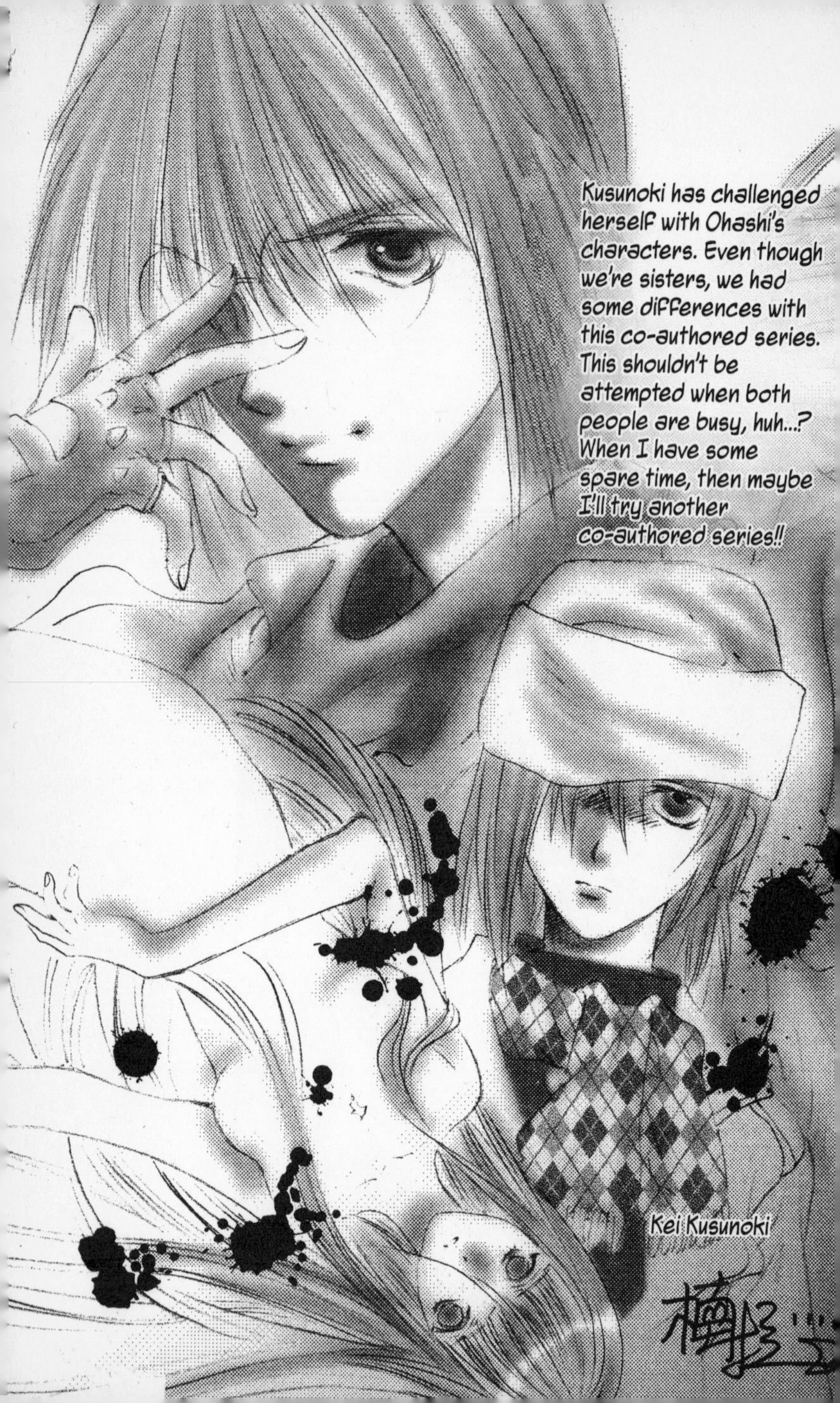
Kusunoki has challenged herself with Ohashi's characters. Even though we're sisters, we had some differences with this co-authored series. This shouldn't be attempted when both people are busy, huh...? When I have some spare time, then maybe I'll try another co-authored series!!
Kei Kusunoki

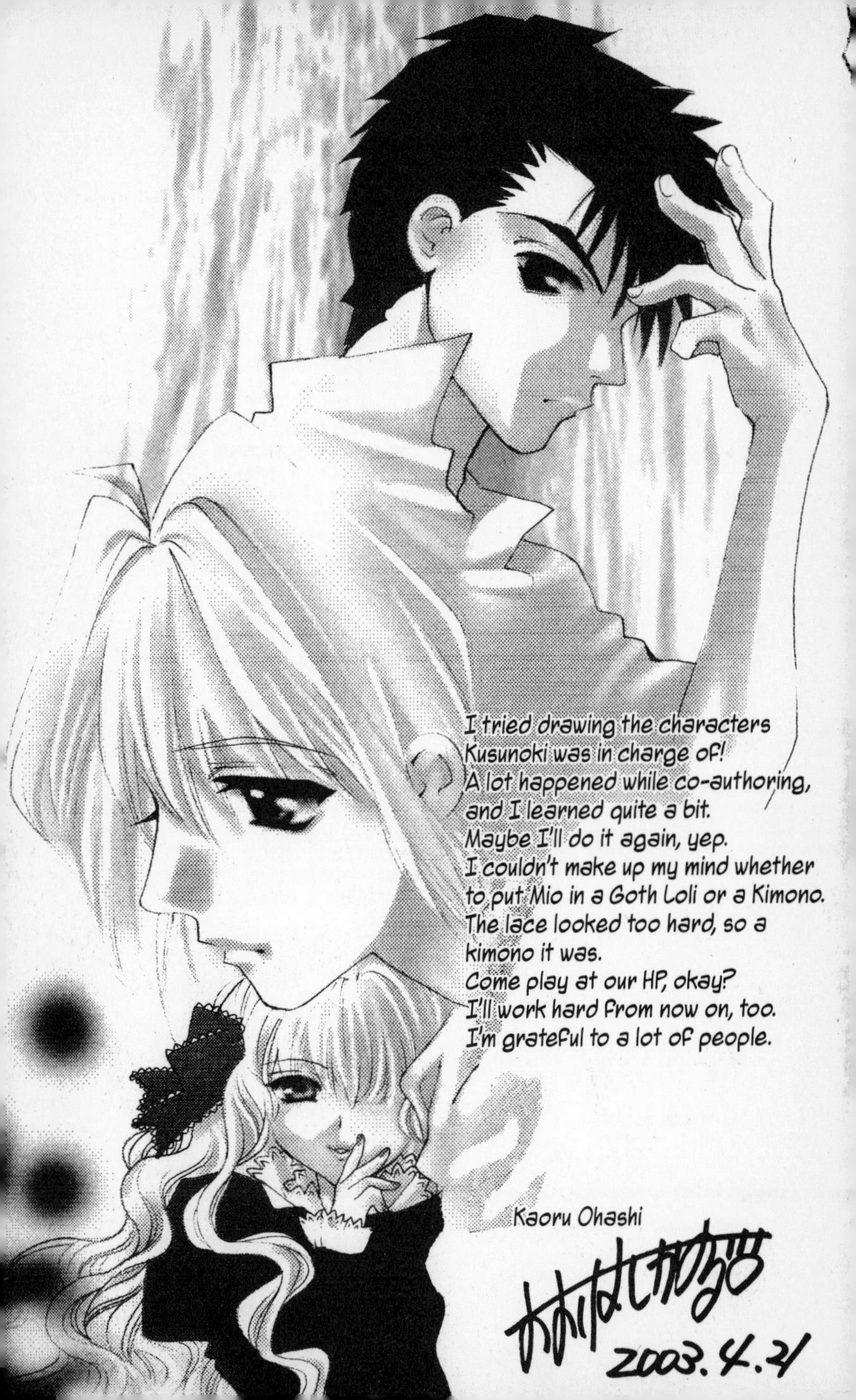
I tried drawing the characters
Kusunoki was in charge of!
A lot happened while co-authoring,
and I learned quite a bit.
Maybe I'll do it again, yep.
I couldn't make up my mind whether
to put Mio in a Goth Loli or a Kimono.
The lace looked too hard, so a
kimono it was.
Come play at our HP, okay?
I'll work hard from now on, too.
I'm grateful to a lot of people.
Kaoru Ohashi
おおはしかおる
2003.4.21

ALSO AVAILABLE FROM TOKYOPOP®

MANGA

.HACK//LEGEND OF THE TWILIGHT
@LARGE
ABENOBASHI: MAGICAL SHOPPING ARCADE
A.I. LOVE YOU
AI YORI AOSHI
ALICHINO
ANGELIC LAYER
ARM OF KANNON
BABY BIRTH
BATTLE ROYALE
BATTLE VIXENS
BOYS BE...
BRAIN POWERED
BRIGADOON
B'TX
CANDIDATE FOR GODDESS, THE
CARDCAPTOR SAKURA
CARDCAPTOR SAKURA - MASTER OF THE CLOW
CHOBITS
CHRONICLES OF THE CURSED SWORD
CLAMP SCHOOL DETECTIVES
CLOVER
COMIC PARTY
CONFIDENTIAL CONFESSIONS
CORRECTOR YUI
COWBOY BEBOP
COWBOY BEBOP: SHOOTING STAR
CRAZY LOVE STORY
CRESCENT MOON
CROSS
CULDCEPT
CYBORG 009
D•N•ANGEL
DEARS
DEMON DIARY
DEMON ORORON, THE
DEUS VITAE
DIABOLO
DIGIMON
DIGIMON TAMERS
DIGIMON ZERO TWO
DOLL
DRAGON HUNTER
DRAGON KNIGHTS
DRAGON VOICE
DREAM SAGA
DUKLYON: CLAMP SCHOOL DEFENDERS
EERIE QUEERIE!
ERICA SAKURAZAWA: COLLECTED WORKS
ET CETERA
ETERNITY
EVIL'S RETURN
FAERIES' LANDING
FAKE
FLCL
FLOWER OF THE DEEP SLEEP
FORBIDDEN DANCE
FRUITS BASKET
G GUNDAM
GATEKEEPERS
GETBACKERS

GIRL GOT GAME
GRAVITATION
GTO
GUNDAM SEED ASTRAY
GUNDAM SEED ASTRAY R
GUNDAM WING
GUNDAM WING: BATTLEFIELD OF PACIFISTS
GUNDAM WING: ENDLESS WALTZ
GUNDAM WING: THE LAST OUTPOST (G-UNIT)
HANDS OFF!
HAPPY MANIA
HARLEM BEAT
HYPER POLICE
HYPER RUNE
I.N.V.U.
IMMORTAL RAIN
INITIAL D
INSTANT TEEN: JUST ADD NUTS
ISLAND
JING: KING OF BANDITS
JING: KING OF BANDITS - TWILIGHT TALES
JULINE
KARE KANO
KILL ME, KISS ME
KINDAICHI CASE FILES, THE
KING OF HELL
KODOCHA: SANA'S STAGE
LAGOON ENGINE
LAMENT OF THE LAMB
LEGAL DRUG
LEGEND OF CHUN HYANG, THE
LES BIJOUX
LILING-PO
LOVE HINA
LOVE OR MONEY
LUPIN III
LUPIN III: WORLD'S MOST WANTED
MAGIC KNIGHT RAYEARTH I
MAGIC KNIGHT RAYEARTH II
MAHOROMATIC: AUTOMATIC MAIDEN
MAN OF MANY FACES
MARMALADE BOY
MARS
MARS: HORSE WITH NO NAME
MINK
MIRACLE GIRLS
MIYUKI-CHAN IN WONDERLAND
MODEL
MOURYOU KIDEN: LEGEND OF THE NYMPH
NECK AND NECK
ONE
ONE I LOVE, THE
PARADISE KISS
PARASYTE
PASSION FRUIT
PEACH FUZZ
PEACH GIRL
PEACH GIRL: CHANGE OF HEART
PET SHOP OF HORRORS
PHD: PHANTASY DEGREE
PITA-TEN
PLANET BLOOD
PLANET LADDER

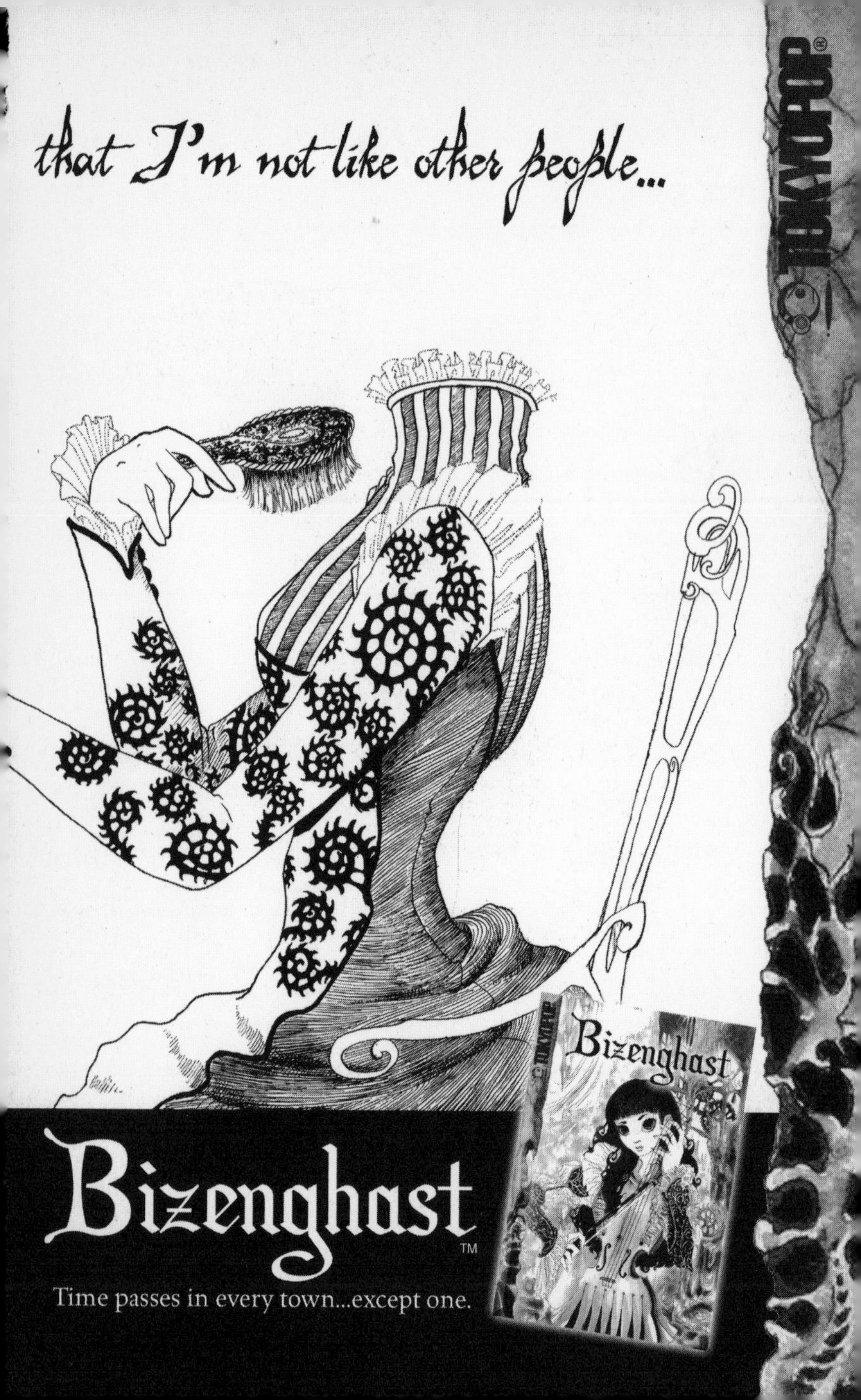
that I'm not like other people...
TOKYOPOP
Bizenghast
TOKYOPOP
Bizenghast™
Time passes in every town...except one.

Dear Diary,
I'm starting to feel

When a young girl moves to the forgotten town of
Bizenghast, she uncovers a terrifying collection of lost
souls that leads her to the brink of insanity. One thing
becomes painfully clear: The residents of Bizenghast are

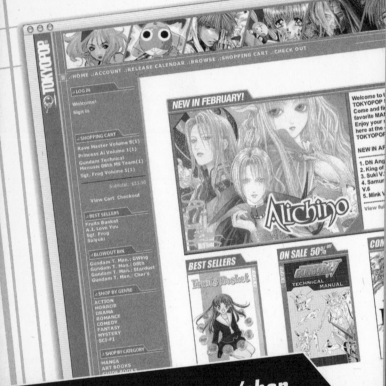

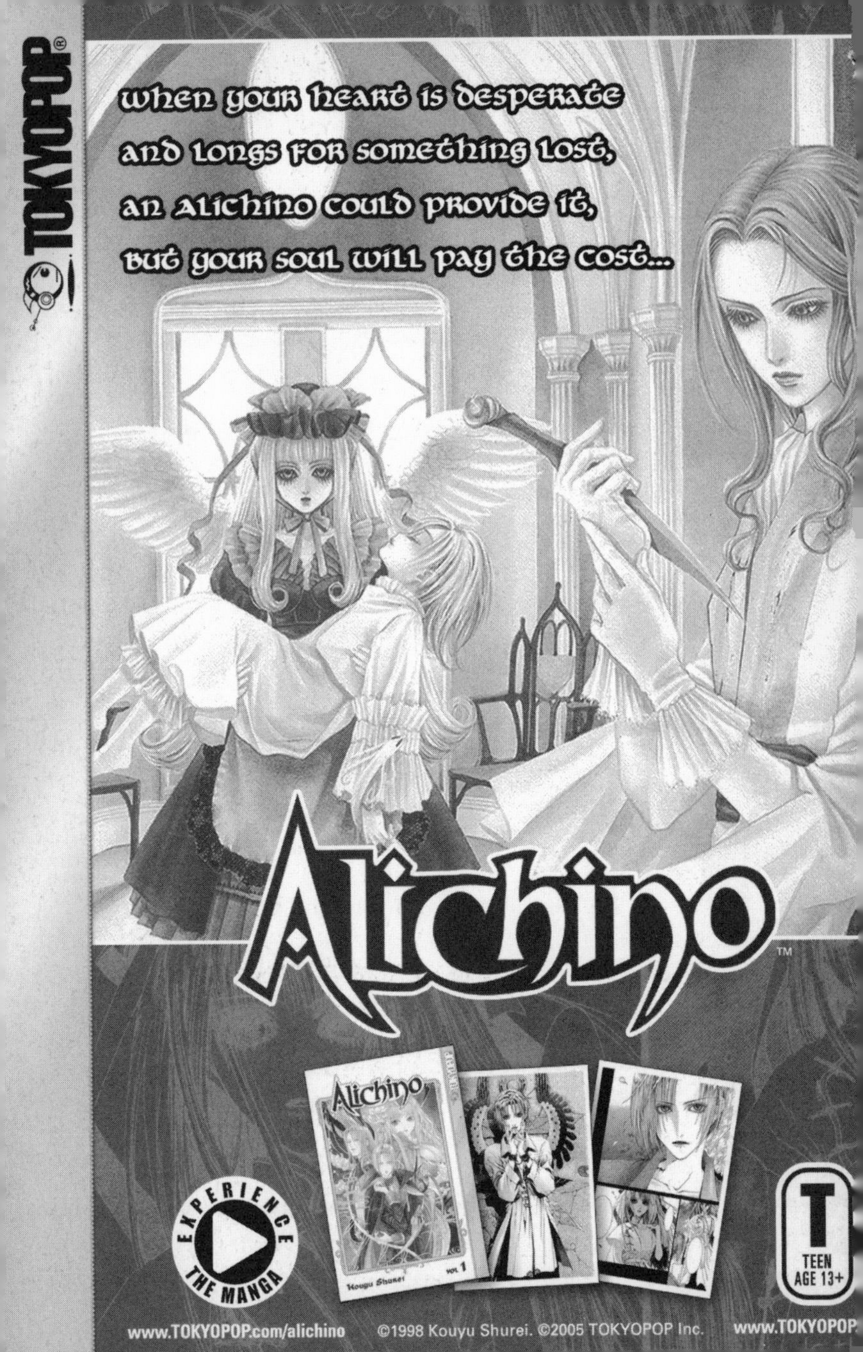
TOKYOPOP
When your heart is desperate
and longs for something lost,
an Alichino could provide it,
but your soul will pay the cost...
Alichino™
EXPERIENCE THE MANGA
T
TEEN
AGE 13+
www.TOKYOPOP.com/alichino
©1998 Kouyu Shurei. ©2005 TOKYOPOP Inc.
www.TOKYOPOP.

STOP!

This is the back of the book.
You wouldn't want to spoil a great ending!

This book is printed "manga-style," in the authentic Japanese right-to-left format. Since none of the artwork has been flipped or altered, readers get to experience the story just as the creator intended. You've been asking for it, so TOKYOPOP® delivered: authentic, hot-off-the-press, and far more fun!

DIRECTIONS

If this is your first time reading manga-style, here's a quick guide to help you understand how it works.

It's easy... just start in the top right panel and follow the numbers. Have fun, and look for more 100% authentic manga from TOKYOPOP®!